Date Due

Belmore			
Bayfield			
BC 2 '75			
Goderich			
BC282			
ᴊᴇɴFeL89			

114506

917.103 Kilbourn, William Morley, 1926–
Kil   Canada: a guide to the peaceable
         kingdom. Ed. and with an introd. by
         William Kilbourn. Toronto, Macmillan,
         1970.
            xviii, 345 p.

            Bibliography included.

RELATED   1. Canada – Civilization – Addresses,
BOOKS IN essays, lectures. I. Title.
CATALOG
UNDER   (78-125590)
                                         79996
                                              6

Canada
A Guide
to the
Peaceable
Kingdom

Canada

A Guide to the Peaceable Kingdom

Edited and with
an introduction by
**WILLIAM
KILBOURN**

St. Martin's Press
New York

Library of Congress Catalogue
Card No. 78-125590

Printed in England for
The Macmillan Company of
Canada Limited
70 Bond Street, Toronto

For
Philippa, Hilary,
Nicholas, Timothy
and Michael

Contents

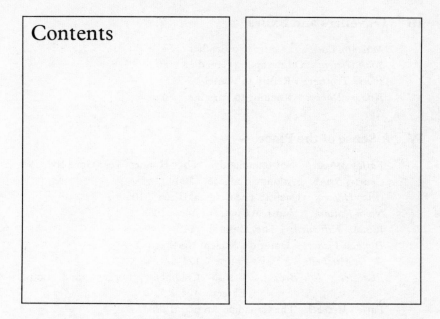

III   Travellers and Exiles

IV   A Sense of the Place

V   Peoples: First Canadians and New Canadians

VI   Patterns: Mores, Religion, and Life Styles

VII Policies: **Relating to the New Romans**

VIII Politics

(a) Three P.M.s and a Joker

(b) Choices for French Canada

(c) A Political Style for English Canada

IX The Past

A*

X   Place des Arts

Introduction

William Kilbourn

Seventy years ago our most inspired of prime ministers foretold that the dawning century would belong to Canada. In the time since, world wars and cold wars, depression and racial divisions, self-doubts and alien dominations, have turned Laurier's sanguine words to a mockery — the windy rhetoric of the hustings best forgotten. Such terrible things have made truer prophets of those who mourned for our nation's death. And yet, as we approach the eleventh hour of our age, I cannot help feeling, along with many of the writers represented in this book, that Canada, merely by existing, does offer a way and a hope, an alternative to insanity, in so far as there is a way and a hope for any of us in an insane world.

The title of this book was chosen to suggest that it would serve as a travel companion for explorers of the Canadian spiritual landscape. But the title also hints at something else: the astonishing notion that this two-cultured, multi-ghettoed, plural community, this non-nation, nay-saying no-place of an un-Eden, this faceless unidentifiable blank on the map, 'this wind that lacks a flag', this Canada of ours, might be a guide to other peoples who seek a path to the peaceable kingdom. We are no longer merely 'a something possible, a chance, a dance that is not danced'. The 'child of nations, giant-limbed', as Sir Charles G. D. Roberts called it back in Laurier's day, may even have grown up, no longer ungainly, no longer immature, ready at last to be a father to a few of the world's lost and abandoned children and a brother to all mankind.

In the 1970s there is a new urgency to Canadian nationalism that it did not possess before. Things have changed so fast, so recently. In the past to be a patriot in Canada has often been a bit pointless – as dispiriting as our running-pink flag, as official as a Centennial Commissioner, as silly as that 100-per-cent CBC listener whose favourite program was the Dominion Observatory Official Time Signal. The new sense of conviction and purpose to Canadian nationalism derives in part, of course, from strong feelings about the direction of American society. These feelings certainly add substance to the new radical attack on United States economic domination, and to Jane Jacobs's plea for us to preserve Toronto and Montreal from the fate of the American metropolis. They add an extra poignancy to Joyce Wieland's pastoral vision of Canada in her film *Rat Life and Diet in North America*.

This book began putting itself together because friends of mine at York University – newly arrived Americans and repatriated Canadians – kept asking to borrow articles about Canada and I never got them back. But what they and I really wanted was a book about the Canadian identity of a kind that did not then exist.

A Guide to the Peaceable Kingdom does not pretend to be an anthology of our best contemporary writing. For one thing, there are no poems or short stories here. Some writers are represented only indirectly, by articles about their work. Others, notably the younger generation of French Canadians, are hardly represented at all. What the book does try to do is to make a single pattern of found prose, most of it taken in bits and pieces from longer works about Canada. What appears here was dictated more by the structure and purpose of the book as a whole than by considerations of whether particular authors ought to be represented.

There is one book, published in 1954, to which *A Guide to the Peaceable Kingdom* may serve as a companion piece. *Our Sense of Identity* ('our sense of our density', as Marshall McLuhan described it to me), edited by Malcolm Ross, is a valuable anthology of Canadian prose ranging from the early nineteenth century up to the early 1950s. But what I was most looking for was a Canadian sense of where we have been in the past decade and where we are now.

This book points in four directions: past, present, future, and south.

The past is mostly an immediate one, but no less fixed and final for that. It reflects the Canada of the long-lost sixties – that era of Quiet Revolution, Comfortable Pew, Seven Days, and Expo 67; the Flag Debate, Gerda Munsinger, the several falls of the unsinkable John Diefenbaker, and the whirlwind rise to power of a new kind of Canadian hero whose name wasn't even listed among the ten thousand worthies of our *Who's Who* on the day he became prime minister. And for Canada, as for all the world, the sixties saw the dawn of the age of Aquarius, *Hair,* Marshall McLuhan, and men on the moon, and the public drama and death of the only four universal heroes of our time: John XXIII, Martin Luther King, and John and Robert Kennedy.

Almost all the pieces in this book were written in that decade; the majority of them were published after centennial year or during it. So inevitably they reflect a Canadian identity, whether of the sixties or of the fifties, or of a century before, which is already a thing of the past. But they are also about a Canada of the present, the here and now of the 1970s. And since one of the writer's roles is that of prophet and visionary, the book points to the future as well. If these pieces are true to the past and present of the Canadian experience, they will also tell us something about our identity in the years to come.

This *Guide*'s fourth compass point is south. The basic experience of Canadian history has been that of sharing the northern part of the continent with the other, larger America. We can best explore our identity by comparing it with that of the United States.

Everywhere in the twentieth century man is becoming American, or, to put it another way, is moving in some way towards a condition of high industrial-ization, affluence and leisure, instant communication, an urban man-made environment, and a mingling of cultures and traditions in a mobile, classless, global society. There is no country in the world, except the United States, which has gone further in this direction than Canada; none that has done so in such an American way; and none that is so experienced in the art of living with, emulating, and differing from the United States. If Canadians (and perhaps others) wish to explore the real freedoms open to them in such a society and to escape the blandness and boredom, the sameness and despair latent in such a brave new world, they could usefully examine the subtle but profound ways in which Canada differs from the United States. For what emerges clearly to me from reflecting on the pieces in this book is that Canada is a different kind of American society, an American alternative to what has happened in the United States.

When William Van Horne gave up his American citizenship after completing the C.P.R., he is said to have remarked, 'Building that railroad would have made a Canadian out of the German Emperor.' The inexorable land, like the Canadian climate, has always commanded the respect of those who have tried to master it. It is simply overwhelming. The voyager from Europe is not suddenly confronted by the rational outlines of a colossal liberty goddess; he is slowly swallowed, Jonah-like, by a twenty-two-hundred-mile-long river gulf and lake system. Coming in by air, he finds himself, scarcely past Ireland, flying above the shining blue-set islands of Bonavista-Twillingate, hours before he touches down in Toronto or Montreal. Farther inland, islands come by the Thousand — or the Thirty Thousand; there are more lakes than people, and more forests than lakes. Except in small pastoral slices of southern Ontario and Quebec, the original wilderness of bush or prairie presses close to the suburban edge of every Canadian town. Even Toronto surprised one British visitor who called it 'a million people living in a forest'. In summer the boreal lights, a shaking skyful of LSD visions, can remind the most urban of Canadians that they are a northern people, that winter will bring again its hundred-degree drop in the weather, and that their wilderness stretches straight to the permafrost, the ice pack, and the pole.

Nature dreadful and infinite has inhibited the growth of the higher amenities in Canada. The living has never been easy. The need to wrestle a livelihood from a cruel land has put a premium on some of the sterner virtues – frugality and caution, discipline and endurance. Geography even more than religion has made us puritans, although ours is a puritanism tempered by orgy. Outnumbered by the trees and unable to lick them, a lot of Canadians look as though they had joined them – having gone all faceless or a bit pulp-and-papery, and mournful as the evening jackpine round the edges of the voice, as if (in Priestley's phrase) something long lost and dear were being endlessly regretted. Or there are those who run – by car, train or plane (flying more air miles per capita than any other people), lickety-split as if the spirit of the northern woods, the Wendigo himself, were on their trails. Nature has not always been an enemy, but she has rarely been something to be tamed either. At best we have exploited her quickly and moved on. No wonder the atmosphere of our towns still often suggests that of the mining camp or the logging drive, the trading post or the sleeping compound. If transportation has been crucial for Canada, and our main-street towns attest the worship of train and motor car, then communications (more telephone calls than anybody else), particularly radio and television (the world's longest networks), have been vital. It is no surprise when some of old Rawhide's Canadian characters become so addicted to the telegraph key that they can only talk in the dah-dah-dits of Morse code.

Survival itself is a virtue and a triumph. Images of survival abound in our popular mythologies: whooping cranes and Hutterites, dwarf ponies on the Sable Island sand dunes, the Eskimo in their howling prison of ice and snow. Ask the Nova Scotian or the French Canadian what he has done in this country of his these two or three centuries and more. 'I survived,' is the answer – though neither of them is satisfied with mere survival any longer.

But Canadians have also learned to live with nature and derive strength from her. It is not just the Group of Seven who came to terms with her terrible grandeur. From the first military surveyors and the C.P.R. artists down to the abstract expressionists of post-modern Toronto, our painters have been profoundly influenced by the Canadian landscape. 'Everything that is central in Canadian writing,' says Northrop Frye, 'seems to be marked by the immanence of the natural world.' The American critic Edmund Wilson sees the most distinguishing feature of Hugh MacLennan's work as the unique way he places his characters in 'their geographical and even their meteorological setting'. Our historians do not argue about the amount but the kind of influence geography has had on our history – whether it has been the north-south pull of North American regionalism or the east-west thrust of the St. Lawrence and Saskatchewan river systems and the Laurentian Shield. The fur trade of the Precambrian forest was not only crucial to Canada's economic life for two centuries, but by 1867 it had literally determined the basic outlines of our political boundaries.

Precisely because life has been so bleak and minimal for so long in so much of Canada, the frontiers, far more than in the United States, have been dependent on the metropolitan centres of Toronto and Montreal and Europe. A visitor to pioneer Saskatchewan in 1907 remarked at the strange sight of a sod hut with a big Canadian Bank of Commerce sign on it, open for business. The essence of the Canadian west is in that image. Organized society usually arrived with the settlers or ahead of them — not only the branch bank manager, but the mounted policeman and the railway agent, the missionary and the Hudson's Bay factor. Dawson City at the height of the gold rush had its sins and shortcomings, but even here lawlessness was not one of them. Violence and terror do not yet stalk the subways or the streets of darkest Toronto. The posse and the desperado belong to the American wild west, the citizen vigilante to the American metropolis.

Among peoples as different as the Métis and the Doukhobors, the community and its custom was the dominating force in western settlement. Even the most self-reliant Protestant pioneer in Canada West or Alberta was never quite a Davy Crockett or a Daniel Boone. From the founding of the Hudson's Bay Company in 1670 to that of the C.P.R. and the dozens of modern Crown corporations, the large, centrally planned enterprise, dominating its field and supported by government regulation, has been typical of Canadian development. As the historian William Morton says, Canada, in contrast to the United States, is founded on the principle of allegiance rather than social contract, on the organic growth of tradition rather than on an explicit act of reason or assertion of the revolutionary will. The B.N.A. Act sets up the objectives of peace, order, and good government, rather than those of life, liberty, and the pursuit of happiness. The fact and principle of authority is established prior to the fact and principle of freedom. In the British tradition of monarchy, parliament, and law, specific liberties are carved out within the ordered structure of society.

There is in Canadian political, business, and social life a certain formality and conservatism that reflect this fact. This conservatism has its regrettable side, of course. The walking dead are out in numbers — the mediocrats, the anti-hothead vote. We are 'the elected squares' to one writer and 'the white baboos' to another; for our inefficiencies there is no excuse. A little talent will get you a long way in an uncompetitive society, protected by tariffs and government rewards. A Canadian has been defined as somebody who does not play for keeps. Even his anti-trust laws fail to enforce business competition as ruthlessly as the American ones.

The Canadian, unlike the Frenchman, the Britisher, or the American, has had no single dominant metropolis. The English-speaking Canadian has had New York and London as well as Toronto and Montreal, and for the French Canadian there has been Paris as well. This condition breeds a divided vision, sometimes paralysing, sometimes detached and ironic, always multiple, and useful for living in the electronic age's global village. It has meant that Canadians have been better interpreters and critics of culture than creators of it – better as performing musicians and actors, for example, than as composers or playwrights. In politics and diplomacy this has led to an extreme pragmatism. Our two major parties are even less the preserve of one class or doctrine than the American parties. Certainly there has been nothing like the Republicans' monopoly of the rich and of the free-enterprise creed. There are no strong ideological overtones about the Canadian approach to other peoples and world affairs.

When a distinguished American advocate of socialism, pacifism, and free love was turned back by Canadian immigration authorities in 1965, the liberal governor of Minnesota deplored this unexpected evidence of McCarthyism in Canada. It was of course nothing of the kind. In a sense, it was just the opposite – an almost touchingly stupid application of the letter of the law, born of respect for regulations. There was little real concern about doctrines. In Canada ideas abound and rebound with Hindu proliferation, and except among some French Canadians are not taken very seriously anyway.

There is a lingering aura of the European established church in Canada which is very different from the American separation of church and state and its consequence, the political religion of America that has prevailed so long in the U.S. The Canadian churches' influence and status can be a strain on some people's liberties, but they are also a bastion against the more absolute dogma of an all-embracing spiritual patriotism. Canada is a land of no one ideology, no single vision; it is a cultural freeport, a way station for travellers (who often move on soon to the other America), a no-man's-land even, or at least no abiding city, a place not easily confused with paradise or the promised land. This 'indigestible Canada', this Marx Brothers' Freedonia, this Austro-Hungary of the new world, with its two official peoples and its multitudes of permitted ones, its ethnic islands and cultural archipelagos, its ghettos of the unpasteurized and unhomogenized, this harbour of old Adams unable or unwilling to be reborn or to burn just yet their old European clothes, but growing attached, many of them, as deeply as the Indian or the pioneer to the landscape of farm and city – this Canada has, alas, not even carried diversity and toleration nearly as far as it might (perhaps lest they become principles), since in practice it has been extremely difficult for Asians and West Indians to immigrate to Canada. (The first use of the newly acquired Canadian navy in 1914 was to escort an unwanted shipload of Sikhs out of Vancouver harbour.) By contrast, one conjures up a hopeful vision of the year 2070 in which the majority of Canadians will be of Chinese origin – though the ones that speak English, who will be called 'Anglo-Saxons' in Quebec, will undoubtedly have their quarrels with those who speak French, some of whom will be unable to get their children taught in French in British Columbia.

Canadians often apologize for or feel guilty about the lack of revolution or civil war in their history to stir up their phlegmatic souls. The poet James Reaney recalls someone at a cocktail party sneering at one of the Riel rebellions because so few people were killed. 'What on earth would he be satisfied with? Tamburlaine's pyramid of human skulls?' Many new nations, from the United States to Indonesia, have found it necessary to make war almost immediately on other people in order to prove their virility. Canadians have gone to war chiefly because other people in distant parts of the earth have been invaded. They have not even held any imperial possessions, like those of Australia and New Zealand. Just a bit more easily than Englishmen or Americans, Canadians can imagine what it was like to be an Indian in Gandhi's day, a Chinese at the time of the Boxer Rebellion, or a Dominican rebel in 1965. We have been invaded by the forces of manifest destiny four times, and we have been a nation of defeated peoples, a refuge of exiles, from the beginning. Most of us first came here merely to get away from something worse – tsarist pogroms or Soviet tanks, black slavery or Vietnam draft boards, Irish potato famine or Highland eviction, unemployment, scandal, revolutionary zeal, or the dead hand of the past. Or else, hardest of all, we were a conquered people in our own land, and only now, after two hundred years of something less than first-class citizenship, have begun to be *maîtres chez nous*.

Canadian history has been a passion rather than an action. It has been, as one writer put it, 'a stolid and phlegmatic struggle against heavy odds. Canadians dealt as a rule with forces beyond their control, in many cases the byproducts of other lands. "Courage in Adversity", the motto of the old Nor'wester, remained a stark national necessity for the Canadian brigades that shot the rapids and toiled across the portages of their stormy history.'

The Canadian hero in the poetry of Ned Pratt is the anonymous representative of a beleaguered society. He has, as Northrop Frye says, confronted and survived both the 'grey shape of the paleolithic face' and the diabolic, shrill commands of the 'Great Panjandrum', Pratt's symbol for 'the mechanical power of the universe, who controls the stars, the movement of matter, the automatic instincts of living things, even of reason and consciousness', that Prince of Darkness who thinks he is God. The hero's real source of strength is his knowledge that the Panjandrum is not God, 'that for him there can be no God who has not also been a human being, suffered with the beleaguered society, yielded to the power of death and yet conquered it'. Indeed it is no idle fancy to see, as the archetypal Canadian hero, the figure of the child who was born in a humble shelter and brought up in a country town among an obscure colonial people, the figure of the man who responded to the power of evil not by attacking but by letting it have its way with him so that he might in the end become fully human.

To identify that which is most essentially Canadian in our literature, Frye recalls a painting, 'The Peaceable Kingdom', which depicts a treaty between Indians and Quakers, and a group of animals – lions, bears, oxen – illustrating the prophecy of Isaiah; it is a haunting and serene vision of the reconciliation of man with man and man with nature. Frye suggests the Canadian tradition as revealed in literature might well be called a quest for the peaceable kingdom.

In a world where independence often arrives with swift violence, it may be good to have one nation where it has matured slowly: in a world of fierce national prides, to have a state about which it is hard to be solemn and religious without being ridiculous, and impossible to be dogmatic. In a world with tendencies to political division and cultural homogeneity, Canada is a country that still stands for the alternative of political federation and cultural and regional variety. In a world that strives for absolute freedom and often gains only oppressive power, Canada presents a tradition that sees freedom in a subtle creative tension with authority; in a world of vast, anonymous power élites, Canada is a society whose leaders number no more than Aristotle's five thousand and can know each other personally without being stifled or hopelessly parochial. In a world haunted by the fear of overpopulation, one is grateful for a place with room for more. In a world of striving for moral victories, it is good to have a country where a sort of moral disarmament is possible. ('You and your goddam moral victories,' says an Arthur Miller character who might be a Canadian. 'We're killing one another with abstractions. Why can't we ever speak *below* the issues?') In a world of ideological battles, it is good to have a place where the quantity and quality of potential being in a person means more than what he believes: in a masculine world of the assertive will and the cutting edge of intellect, a certain Canadian tendency to the amorphous permissive feminine principle of openness and tolerance and acceptance offers the possibility of healing.

The Fathers of Confederation chose the title 'Dominion' for the country they had made. Typically it was a second choice, after their British rulers, afraid of offending the United States, rejected the title the Canadians wanted. It comes from the Hebrew scriptures, the seventy-second Psalm, a few other words from which may serve as a loose-fitting epigraph to what we have been saying here.

Let men flourish out of the city like grass upon the earth
Let there be an abundance of grain in the land
The mountains also shall bring peace, and the hills righteousness unto the people
He shall come down like rain upon the mown grass, even as the showers that water the earth
Let all nations call him happy, let his name continue as long as the sun
For he shall deliver the poor when he cries, the needy also and him that has no helper
Let his dominion also be from sea to sea, and from river unto the world's end
And blessed be the name of his majesty forever. Amen and Amen.

Canada
A Guide
to the
Peaceable
Kingdom

I
As We See Ourselves

Douglas LePan
Hugh MacLennan
Pierre Trudeau
Jean Le Moyne
Kildare Dobbs
James Reaney
Hugh Hood

Douglas LePan

In Frock Coat and Moccasins

Abridged by the editor from the original article which appeared as "The Dilemma of the Canadian Author" in *Atlantic Monthly*, November 1964.

No one can tell yet what mask to carve for Canada, which type to choose – a pulp savage or a bank teller, a civil servant or a broke hustler or a signalman helping to keep the peace in Cyprus or the Gaza Strip – whether the face should be serene and adventurous, or withdrawn and introspective. No one can tell for certain yet whether Canada is one nation or two. The country reveals itself only slowly even to those who love it most, and much of its character still remains ambiguous.

In the farthest distance – and not so far as all that, either – is the wilderness, 'up to the foot of the blue pole star. . . .' That is one silence, a silence of rigor, of the boreal forest, of tundra, of permafrost, which has influenced much of our earlier poetry and fiction and which, through such works as *Maria Chapdelaine* and the stories of Charles G. D. Roberts and the poetry of Robert Service, has given many readers in other countries their principal impression of Canadian literature and even of Canadian life. But what can be won from the wilderness nowadays? Perhaps little but resolution, because it remains remote, untamed, inhuman, inarticulate, something with a sympathy and resonance of its own, but in the end a resonance of silence, a tympanum of ice crystals, something before writing, before history, where a rifle crack rings back immemorially. Yet that is where our history starts. And with our history we are launched on a chasm of other silences and solitudes. The silence of the explorers. Or the solitude of the two races, French and English, which one of our best novelists, Hugh MacLennan, has examined so perceptively.

3

Occasionally in retracing the course of Canadian history the writer will have the sense of having come upon an image or a face that can help to orient him and make him know himself better. One such for me has always been LaSalle's. His appeal lies not so much in the magnitude of his endeavors, although there will always be something almost stupefying about those voyages that tore the heart out of a continent; or in the extremity of what he endured and the savagery of his death; or in the strange intermingling in his life of considerations of commerce and policy and sheer adventure. What returns an echo is, rather, the mystery about his motives and the fact that he himself admitted the mystery, acknowledging that he did not know what it was — it might have been weakness — that had driven him into the wilderness and made him so avid, avid almost to the point of madness, for something that could not be specified.

Here is consanguinity, an image of intimacy and value. But LaSalle was as alien and suspect to much of the Canadian society of his day as he would be now. And so the image is drowned in sobriety and respectability. We pass on to an age of merchants, and of good farmers, and good crops, and good husbands and fathers. But perhaps there is something that can be plucked and rescued from the encompassing dimness. An image, a conjoined image of bourgeois and voyageur: the Nor'wester who in youth travels the canoe routes westward and lives on Lake Athabasca or Great Slave Lake as a wintering partner, and who only when he is middle-aged returns to settle permanently in Montreal and to build himself a big house on the side of the mountain where he can look out and see the 'River of Canada' flowing by and remember when he was young and lived hard and was ready for anything that might come at the next portage or the next turn of the river. Bourgeois and voyageur: it is a phrase that can be coaxed into summing up much in Canadian history, making long stretches of it seem more evocative and attractive than they would be otherwise; and sometimes the two qualities can be miraculously combined in the one person. So it must have been with many of the fur traders. And even with Louis Riel, that baffling, rebellious spirit, of whom it is related that when he would receive official visitors at Fort Garry as the leader of the provisional government of the Northwest in 1869, he would be wearing leather moccasins and a frock coat. It will be a long time before either of those trappings will have altogether ceased to indicate something about the Canadian scene and the Canadian consciousness.

The frock coat suggests how buttoned-up and reserved and respectable — yes, and how stuffy — Canadian life can often be. And Canadian writing often suffers from the same faint whiff of mothballs. And sometimes it can be depressingly official and academic. Duncan Campbell Scott was a fine poet of an older generation, one of our best, with a sensitive lyric and romantic gift, but on the occasion of a royal visit in the thirties, he consented (what else could he do? he was a civil servant after all) to write a ceremonial ode. The great moment came: the company in the Prime Minister's study in Laurier House in Ottawa had been hushed, the royal personages were dutifully receptive, the spaniel was silent, the poet was asked to begin. But he had not read more than a stanza in appropriately scholarly tones when Mackenzie King, with the parliamentarian's itch for oratorial effect, could stand it no longer, snatched the paper from the hands of the helpless bard, took out his pince-nez, and boomed on to the end in his best House of Commons voice embellished with gestures. Encounters between the arts and officialdom can be ludicrous enough anywhere. But nowhere else have they been more ludicrous than in Canada. It is little wonder that the writers here who have taken a stand against what is official and academic in Canadian life have sometimes done so a little stridently. For example, it sometimes seems to me that Irving Layton's great power of imagination and purity of phrase are marred in some poems by a savagery that verges on the histrionic. And it can be objected that his strictures on the academic temper are perhaps overdrawn: 'The poet roams,' he writes,

> the professor ruminates. The one experiences; the other expatiates. The one is a vulgarian; the other must permit his training and associations to turn him into a gentleman.

Perhaps. Perhaps not. But however that may be, it is good to know that there are still some in Canada who want to roam, whose hearts are still savage and unappeasable, that there are still moccasins showing somewhere in the national life beneath the enveloping frock coat.

These are some of the images that may come to a writer in Canada as he thinks of his own country. A wilderness. (But what can be made of that nowadays?) Or the face of a voyageur, a *coureur de bois*. (But what place can there be for him in wastes of respectability and matriarchal good taste and good manners?) Or an image – is it a real possibility, or something as mythical as a hippogriff? – of bourgeois and voyageur joined. Someone sitting at last in authority in moccasins and a frock coat.

However much the writer in Canada is engrossed in his environment, he cannot be entirely oblivious to the fact that, with luck, he might command a larger audience abroad than he could ever expect at home. This is a kind of siren music that flickers almost constantly around the margins of his consciousness, the possibility of winning a larger public, particularly in the United States and Britain; and it is difficult for him to know how to deal with it skilfully. It can betray him into falsification of his own experience. But it also can spur him on to relish the keenest competition and to take the stiffest fences, and so to outsoar parochial limitations. In that case, though – and it is only one aspect of the problem – he will be confronted by difficult decisions about idiom. Although the English spoken by Canadians is, of course, essentially the same as the language spoken by Americans and Englishmen, it has its own peculiarities not only of accent and intonation but of diction and phrasing as well. One question for the writer in Canada is how far these should be smoothed out in the interests of gaining a wider reception and a wider audience.

Another problem that arises largely from the national environment is uncertainty about how deep to make the incision. When Alden Nowlan writes

My best poems
Don't get written,
Because I'm still scared

he is touching on the problem I have in mind. Always and in all countries the writer has felt some secret horror about telling the terrible truth. But there have been societies, or at least moments in some societies, when the writer has been encouraged to cut through appearances and tell what he sees, however bestial or frightening or terrible it may be. Canada is not such a society and never has been. Its sky is rigorous, and its climate. But there is something in the social atmosphere that has operated to blur sharp edges and to restrain the hand of the artist who might try to reproduce them faithfully. Canada is no more immune than any other country to the miseries and flaws of human-kind – which are inseparable from its glories. But this chiaroscuro has long been muffled in the folds of a conformity which has been insidiously but relentlessly propagated by the leaders of a society, small, unsure of itself, and not far from the comparative simplicities of pioneer agricultural life. Whatever the reasons for it may have been – whether they are to be found in the abruptness of the transition from a rural to an urban society or in the remaining traces of a colonial mentality – this element in the atmosphere has inevitably made it harder for the writer to tell the truth. He has been inhibited by the social disapproval he has sensed about him for any design that would transgress the bounds of a very restricted view of human nature and human possibilities. Now these clouds may be lifting a little. As they do, there are new opportunities for the writer.

There are some things in Canadian life that are native and special to it. But there are other things that would not be very different in Cleveland or Denver or Milan or São Paulo; and the areas of similarity are increasing. That is one reason why I have the instinct that a new strategy may come to commend itself more and more to Canadian writers. No matter what strategy he may be employing for the moment, any Canadian writer will have to wrestle with the national environment in which he lives in order to extract its secrets, so far as he can, and to know what influence it has had on him. And some writers in Canada will always want to take what is special to the Canadian scene and make it central in their work. But I suspect that other writers will be attracted by a quite different possibility. Instead of trying to refine the singularity of being Canadian, they may want to dive so deeply that what they have to say can be expressed in terms of what happens in an anonymous setting to an anonymous, or virtually anonymous, hero.

If the risks of such an undertaking are obvious, so are the advantages: it can produce a result of almost universal luminosity which can be understood anywhere. A strategy of this kind may also commend itself to some writers because of seeming to be congruent with contemporary critical views of myth and symbol. But however that may be, it would seem to be a strategy with some adventitious attractions for writers working in a country that is in one sense or another peripheral, whether the country be Argentina or Switzerland or Canada.

To make clearer the kind of opportunity that I am thinking of, I might offer one final image. It is the passport office in Ottawa, where all Canadian passports are issued. It is a nondescript office rented by the Department of External Affairs from the owners of a nondescript office building in the business district of Ottawa. But it has an importance which goes far beyond what might be suggested by its air of undistinguished bureaucratic routine. For a Canadian passport, whether genuine or forged, whether obtained honestly or fraudulently, is a very precious commodity in the eyes of many of those operating international rackets or foreign intelligence systems. When Robert Soblen jumped bail in 1961 after being convicted in New York of espionage for the Soviet Union and flew to Israel, he was carrying a Canadian passport. So was Colonel Rudolph Abel, the Soviet master spy who was exchanged for Francis Gary Powers, the U-2 pilot. So was Conon Molody, the Soviet agent who stole the plans of Britain's atomic submarine under the alias of Gordon Lonsdale.

Nor is it very difficult to understand why a Canadian passport should be so popular. Part of the explanation is that with it one can travel easily almost anywhere. Another reason for the popularity of the little blue booklet stamped in gold is that one can speak English or French or Ukrainian or Polish or Chinese and still be a Canadian. One can, in fact, be almost anyone and still be a Canadian; and to be a Canadian is to have a passport to the whole world. It is those facts which make the image of the passport office seem so important to me, make it in some moods seem even more important than the image of bourgeois and voyageur. There will always be a place for books that are redolent of a particular region or of a particular aspect of Canadian life and experience. But there will also be a place, and an increasing place I suspect, for writing which is more stripped and bare and absolute, for writing marked by little or nothing on the surface to distinguish it as Canadian and which will ultimately reveal its origin by imparting a spirit that is both adventurous and responsible and by being able to pass everywhere as true.

Or so, at least, I am inclined to think for the time being. But since I am a Canadian, it may be that by next year or next month or next week I may be thinking differently and may be tempted again to wrestle with the implacable angel of this marvelous, voiceless country.

Hugh MacLennan

After 300 Years, Our Neurosis Is Relevant

Nations, like individuals, are likely to be neurotic, and Canada's history and location have conspired to qualify her for a pretty high place on the neurotic list. The harsh loneliness of the land, the tensions between the races which were forced to share the country after they had all been defeated, the suppression of minority desires, the peculiar identification of Quebec with a strong Catholic faith opposed to the equally strong sectarianism of most English Canadians before 1940, the struggle of loyalties toward France and England, the mixed-up history of Canada and the United States – the list of neurosis-provoking influences in Canada is as long as it is familiar.

It was a list peculiarly Canadian until fairly recent times, and a list so formidable it is no wonder that our writers and artists were unable to cope with its results for a long time. Many of you are doubtless familiar with the story of the difference between a psychotic and a neurotic: the psychotic is a man who believes that two plus two equals eleven and is perfectly content with the belief, is willing indeed to bet his own life on it, but the neurotic is one who *knows* that two plus two equals four but can't stand it. This much at least can be said for Canadians. Collectively they have never become psychotic in this sense. They have never denied, when pressed against the wall, that two plus two equals four, and though they often say they can't stand it, the fact is that most of them have.

For a long time now, it seems to me, we Canadians have been willing to admit that ours is a deeply neurotic society. If talking about troubles and frustrations were all that is needed for a mature literature, we would have had

8

a huge literature already, for we have been talking about them most volubly for several generations.

But a neurotic who merely talks about himself is not only a bore to others; he is a nuisance to his own family and a burden to himself. If there is one thing an art can never afford to be, it is boring. The causes of the neuroses must be faced, admitted, and described, they must be lifted out of the dark of the mind and made visible. Within a society, it is the function and the duty of the artists to do this, and when we look back on history, we find that most great art has emerged from the agony of this self-healing process.

Out of the guilts and terrors of ancient tribal groups, at the dawn of Athenian maturity, came the Agamemnon trilogy of Aeschylus, which ends in high symbolism when Orestes' long struggle with the Furies is brought to rest in the trial before the Areopagus – in other words, when tribal vengeance was supplanted by the rule of law in Greek life. Out of the horrors of the Wars of the Roses, out of the king and queen murders and the religious frenzies which had produced – and still produced – burnings at the stake, came the artistic resolutions of Shakespeare.

In both these cases, the artistic statements were local in origin, but universal for the whole of mankind. A bridge had been built by art! The older one by the Greek Experience, the later one by the English Experience, which linked erstwhile provinces to all humanity, and provided artistic archetypes for all the human future.

But no artist, no group of artists even, can build this bridge single-handed by a mere effort of will. First they must communicate with their own people and be accepted by them. They must receive from them the assurance that they are telling the truth, or at least some important elements of the truth, about the society they share. Only then does it become possible for a nation's culture to move out across the frontiers and be accepted in the heartlands of the cultures of the world. Know yourself first; otherwise you will know no other man. Tell the truth about yourself, and then you will be telling the truth about multitudes of strangers. As with individuals, so with nations.

It will be asked, 'Has Canada reached the point of cultural development when she can turn her neurotic character to creative purposes and, in healing herself, help to heal others?'

Being myself so deeply involved in the excitement of building my own little section of the bridge, I am perhaps a poor witness in the matter. But I think – indeed to me it is now self-evident – that the familiar process of the maturing of a colony into a nation, though not by any means completed, is at least well under way.

The Group of Seven painters already belong to the history of Canadian art. They not only revealed, they made tolerable and beautiful, one of the chief sources of the Canadian neurosis – the stark, sombre, cold, and empty land in which our ancestors had to make a living in stark, sombre, and lonely ways. Advancing from this beginning, the artists working in Canada have developed a most varied work, and some of it is as truly international as any in Europe.

In literature, I believe that Canada was ready to produce some mature work in the 1930's – indeed, in the humour of Stephen Leacock, in the novels and short stories of Morley Callaghan, and in at least one novel of Ringuet, it did so. But in the 1930's the great themes which engrossed everyone's attention could not be handled here with the same authority as elsewhere. A generation was in flux and chaos, and though every facet of Canadian life was affected by the Russian Revolution, the depression, and the rise of Fascism, Canada was not at the vortex as Europe was. In those days, if Canadians were local in their themes, the themes they discovered could not interest people abroad. The final maturity of a man or a nation comes, it seems, only when his own concept of himself is at least to some extent accepted by others.

This situation began to change at the beginning of World War II and has been changing rapidly ever since. In literature there has been a steady movement forward and a great growth of genuine self-confidence. Our poets put the maple leaf behind them. Our writers forgot the old historical romances and did their best to write of the Canadian Experience with the naturalness and candour of writers in older lands. Now I truly believe the harvest is about to come in. I believe this not only from the increasing acceptance of our work abroad, but because, at this new and different moment in history, the Canadian Experience is one of immense significance for the rest of mankind. Therefore, if we talk truly about ourselves, we will be talking not only for ourselves but for others. In the particular complex of neuroses from which the rest of the world is suffering, Canada has had an acute and extremely long experience.

For not only was this country formed out of the flotsam and jetsam of three or four defeated racial and political groups; some of these groups had once been bitter enemies of one another. But they had to live here, and they had to live in peace with each other. And – more than any other new nation – they had to live in peace with the United States, and accommodate themselves in thousands of ways to American methods, American attitudes, and – these are the *mots justes* – American success and ability.

It was, after all, out of the Canadian Experience that the original concept of the Commonwealth came into being. It was out of the Canadian's capacity to live with his neuroses, to function in an environment full of unavoidable frustrations, that most of us came to the conclusion that the most important problems of life can never be solved, but merely lived with. In a remarkable line, Douglas LePan described the *voyageur* as 'Hamlet with the countenance of Horatio', and Robertson Davies said that nobody has ever packed more comprehension of the Canadian character into a single phrase. We have lived here locked up with one another in the same country, and locked up with the Americans in the same continent. This latter phrase I borrow from a letter written to me by Professor A. R. M. Lower, and it is one of the many sentences he wrote which probes to the heart of the Canadian Experience.

Well, is it not today the fate of all nations to live locked up with one another in the same world?

For this reason alone, I believe that the Canadian Experience is of more value as an example to mankind in his present predicament than the American is. For the Americans, originally, were isolationists. They sought in a new continent to escape the tensions, sins, and prejudices of Europe. By turning their schools into melting-pots, they sought deliberately to make everyone who entered their country as much like the original Anglo-Saxon stock as possible. But now isolationism is dead, and the Americans have admitted it. Unwillingly, almost tragically, they now admit themselves locked up in the same house with the Russians, Europeans, Africans, South Americans – indeed with everyone except the Chinese, and soon they will have to admit that, too. There can be no doubt that this situation is producing in them the same set of neuroses with which we have had to deal. There can be no doubt also that much of today's anti-Americanism is caused by the difficulty Americans have in believing that other people do not desire to be just like themselves. How familiar it sounds to us Canadians when we hear Americans say pathetically that if only some foreign countries would adopt *their* methods, *their* attitudes, and *their* values, the world's troubles would be over. A generation ago there were thousands of English Canadians who spoke in precisely the same way of French Canada. If only the French Canadians would be sensible like them, what a happy land Canada would be! While the French said: 'If only Quebec could live as a separate nation, how perfect all would be along our river. *Ici nous sommes chez nous.* Why can't *les Anglais* leave us alone?' But the Canadian Experience taught both these groups – and it still teaches them – that life is the art of the possible, and cannot be based on wishful thinking.

For all these reasons I believe it real and accurate to say that we can contribute a very great deal to the world *if Canada remains Canadian.* Culturally we can contribute, and politically we can contribute. If two centuries have produced such a nation as ours, now is not the time to give it up, for it was never really needed before now. We did not have to pay for political maturity with the bloodshed of a revolution, as most other countries have done. But we did pay for it in endurance, in a refusal to dramatize many personal desires which a dramatic outburst would have released. And now, perhaps, we will have to pay for it in money, just as some of us have been doing up to the present.

Speaking of the people I call the 'agents of Canadian culture' – of the writers, artists, and musicians – those who have stayed here and borne the heat and burden of the day did so for many lean years at a deliberate financial sacrifice and also at the sacrifice of a passing popular reputation. A writer who wrote solely of Canadian themes knew that the lack of interest in Canada abroad would so limit his sales that he would have to take one or two extra jobs in order to support himself. Most of us did that, and if we survived, the extra work did us good in the long run. But many of us did not survive it, and a number of potentially good writers and artists were lost to the commercial work necessary to support their families. Many of us again took the course of least resistance, and tailored our work to fit American models, American values, and – the word is a just one – attempted even to counterfeit the American Experience which was essentially different from ours in order to capture the money and prestige of the large American market.

Those hard days, of this I am sure, are now drawing to a close. It is now becoming increasingly possible for a Canadian writer, within his own terms of reference, to compete in the American and European market. Gabrielle Roy, let us not forget, was the first person not a citizen of France to be given the *prix femina*, and she won it for *Bonheur d'Occasion*, which is as Canadian as hockey night in the Montreal Forum. Jean-Paul Riopelle, Borduas, and a variety of other Canadian artists are now acclaimed in Paris. Morley Callaghan has recently been compared by Edmund Wilson to Turgeniev and Chekhov, and in that review in the *New Yorker* Wilson remarked, in effect, how odd it was to think of such a writer living in Toronto. If people would stop comparing Canadian literature, to its inevitable detriment, to Shakespeare and Racine, but would think of it solely in terms of the current international competition, I don't honestly see much reason for pessimism.

In an international society which seems capable of expressing itself only through the meetings of national states, it seems odd that there should be an air of apology here when we – as every other country has to do – consider the means of national survival. Nobody has any doubt of this necessity in French Canada. Few people doubt its necessity in other parts of the world. But in English Canada we do have doubts and I think for this reason.

Many Canadians of United Empire Loyalist origin have never been easy in their conscience that their ancestors made the right choice in 1776. In the back of their minds, and in the back of many Canadian minds which think in English, lurks the notion that we can 'join the States'. But this we cannot do for a multitude of reasons, and in their hearts all realistic Canadians know it. This particular course of least resistance must be ruled out, not on sentimental grounds, but on a basis of hard-boiled realism. In the future we might 'join the States' as part of a new version of a United Kingdom, but now, and for many years to come, this matter is academic.

Therefore the choice before us is really quite clear. We may do one of two things. We may seek ways and means, and pay for them, of making a dignified and modest success of the Canadian nation; or we may drift, as we did in the 1950's, towards the status of a northern banana republic. The latter course might give to a privileged few a soft life, but it would soon be recognized as a psychological – and quickly afterwards a political – disaster.

The attitude most of us would like to see adopted would be that of Walter Gordon – no cheap anti-American tirades, but a firm and dignified determination to do the best we can. The Americans themselves will applaud us if we do. They are the best neighbours any country ever had, and we know, if the unfortunate Cubans do not, that the genius and character of the United States can never be measured by the aims and values of their business corporations.

What we in Canada have always feared most is to be our own judges. If this particular fear is conquered, we will not, of course, be secure, because no one can be secure in the twentieth century. But we will at least give ourselves a chance of being more fruitful than we have been before.

[1961]

Pierre Trudeau

Canada and French-Canadian Nationalism

If Canada as a State has had so little room for French Canadians it is above all because we have failed to make ourselves indispensable to its future.

If we make an exception of Laurier, I fail to see a single French Canadian in more than three-quarters of a century whose presence in the federal cabinet might be considered indispensable to the history of Canada as written – except at election time, of course, when the tribe always invokes the aid of its witch-doctors.

An examination of the few nationalist 'victories' carried off at Ottawa after years of wrangling in high places will reveal probably none that could not have been won in the course of a single cabinet meeting by a French Canadian of the calibre of C. D. Howe. Let's face it: all our cabinet ministers put together would barely ever have matched the weight of a bilingual cheque or the name of a hotel.

The Anglo-Canadians have been strong by virtue only of our weakness. This is true not only at Ottawa, but even at Quebec, a veritable charnel-house where half our rights have been wasted by decay and decrepitude and the rest devoured by the maggots of political cynicism and the pestilence of corruption. Under the circumstances, can there be any wonder that Anglo-Canadians have not wanted the face of this country to bear any French features? And why would they want to learn a language that we have been at such pains to reduce to such mediocrity at all levels of our educational system?

No doubt, had English-speaking Canadians applied themselves to learning French with a quarter the diligence they have shown in refusing to do so,

14

Canada would have been effectively bilingual long ago. For here is demonstrated one of the laws of nationalism, whereby more energy is consumed in combating disagreeable but irrevocable realities than in contriving some satisfactory compromise. It stands to reason that this law works to greatest ill effect in the case of minority nationalisms: in this case – us.

We have expended a great deal of time and energy proclaiming the rights due our nationality, invoking our celestial mission, trumpeting our virtues, bewailing our misfortunes, denouncing our enemies, and avowing our independence, and for all that not one of our workmen is the more skilled, nor a civil servant the more efficient, a financier the richer, a doctor the more advanced, a bishop the more learned, nor a single solitary politician the less ignorant. Now, except for a few stubborn eccentrics, there's probably not one French-Canadian intellectual who hasn't spent at least four hours a week over the last year discussing Separatism. That makes how many thousand times two hundred hours spent just flapping our arms? And can any one of them honestly say he has heard a single argument not already expounded *ad nauseam* twenty years ago, forty years ago, and even sixty years ago?

Now this is what I call *la nouvelle trahison des clercs*: this self-deluding passion of a large segment of our thinking population for throwing themselves headlong – intellectually and spiritually – into purely escapist pursuits.

A nationalistic government is by nature intolerant, discriminatory, and, when all is said and done, totalitarian. A truly democratic government cannot be 'nationalist', because it must pursue the good of all its citizens, without prejudice to ethnic origin. The democratic government stands for and encourages good citizenship, then, never nationalism. Certainly such a government will make laws by which ethnic groups will benefit, and the majority group will benefit proportionately to its number; but that follows naturally from the principle of equality for all, not from any right due the strongest. In this sense one may well say that educational policy in Quebec has always been democratic rather than nationalistic; I would not say the same for all the other provinces.

We must separate once and for all the concepts of State and of Nation, and make Canada a truly pluralistic and polyethnic society. Now in order to do so, the different regions within the country must be assured a wide range of local autonomy, such that each national group, with an increasing background of experience in self-government, may be able to develop the body of laws and institutions essential to the fullest expression and development of its national characteristics. At the same time, the English Canadians, with their own nationalism, will have to retire gracefully to their proper place, consenting to modify their own precious image of what Canada ought to be. If they care to protect and realize their own special ethnic qualities, they should do it within this framework of regional and local autonomy rather than a pan-Canadian one. On this point the record of Quebec's treatment of its minorities can well stand as an example to other provinces with large French, German, Ukrainian, and other minorities.

I have no intention of closing my eyes to how much Canadians of British origin have to do – or rather, undo – before a pluralist State can become a reality in Canada. But I'm inclined to add that that is *their* problem. The die is cast in Canada: there are two main ethnic and linguistic groups; each is too strong and too deeply rooted in the past, too firmly bound to a mother culture, to be able to engulf the other. But if the two will collaborate at the hub of a truly pluralistic State, Canada could become the envied seat of a form of federalism that belongs to tomorrow's world. Better than the American melting-pot, Canada could offer an example to all those new Asian and African States who must discover how to govern their polyethnic populations with proper regard for justice and liberty. What better reason for cold-shouldering the lure of a Canada annexed to the United States? . . . Canadian federalism is an experiment of major proportions; it could become a brilliant prototype for the moulding of tomorrow's civilization.

If English Canadians cannot see it, so much the worse for them; they will be subsiding into a backward, short-sighted, and despotic nationalism. Lord Acton, one of the great thinkers of the nineteenth century, described, with extraordinarily prophetic insight, the error of the various nationalisms and the future they were preparing. A century ago he wrote:

> A great democracy must either sacrifice self-government to unity or preserve it by federalism. . . . The co-existence of several nations under the same State is a test, as well as the best security of its freedom. It is also one of the chief instruments of civilization. . . . The combination of different nations in one State is as necessary a condition of civilized life as the combination of men in society. . . . Where political and national boundaries coincide, society ceases to advance, and nations relapse into a condition corresponding to that of men who renounce intercourse with their fellow-men. . . . A State which is incompetent to satisfy different races condemns itself; a State which labours to neutralize, to absorb, or to expel them is destitute of the chief basis of self-government. The theory of nationality, then, is a retrograde step in history.

It goes without saying that if, in the face of Anglo-Canadian nationalism, French Canadians retreat into their own nationalistic shell, they will condemn themselves to the same stagnation. And Canada will become a sterile soil for the minds of its people, a barren waste prey to every wandering host and conquering horde.

If Quebec became a shining example, if to live there were to partake of freedom and progress, if culture enjoyed a place of honour there, if the universities commanded respect and renown from afar, if the administration of public affairs were the best in the land – and none of this presupposes any declaration of independence! – French Canadians would no longer need to do battle for bilingualism; the ability to speak French would become a status symbol, even an open-sesame in business and public life. Even in Ottawa, superior competence on the part of our politicians and civil servants would bring spectacular changes.

Such an undertaking is immensely difficult, but possible; it takes more guts than jaw. And therein, it would seem to me, is an 'ideal' not a whit less 'inspiring' than that other one that's been in vogue for a couple of years in our little part of the world.

For those who would put their shoulders to the wheel, who would pin their hopes for the future on the fully-developed man of intelligence, and who would refuse to be party to *la nouvelle trahison des clercs*, I close with a final word from the great Lord Acton:

Nationalism does not aim either at liberty or prosperity, both of which it sacrifices to the imperative necessity of making the nation the mould and measure of the State. Its course will be marked with material as well as moral ruin, in order that a new invention may prevail over the works of God and the interests of mankind.

[1962. Translated by Patricia Claxton.]

Jean Le Moyne

Coming of Age in Quebec

I owe as much to the ants as to Homer, as much to fish as to Cervantes, and as much to the poultry yard as to my formal schooling. My unremitting patience as a boy watching the ants let me penetrate the anonymity of nature and showed me countless dramas of individual risk at the very heart of the strictest collective pressures and the most basic kind of instinctive determinism. The ants taught me that fierce asceticism in the use of vital energies and that discretion in the use of a surplus, which assures the success of the individual as much as of the species. They showed me the paradoxical balance of certitudes and hazards in subsistence. They initiated me into the necessity of error and waste and into the game of hunt and share.

I learned as much from fish, which I knew better, that is to say had studied more closely and much longer. In them I saw the first faint hint of man. Through them I was present at the dawn of animal relationships with us. They instructed me in the prodigality of forms and types of behaviour. They brought the flow of water to life for me by making me feel that the living creature was half of its milieu.

It was the same with the poultry, which my father kept at great expense and to the great scandal of our neighbours, those lean and elegant poets of tennis club and golf course. I even used to go and read in the chicken yard so that the birds would forget my presence and I could study them at their most natural. On a level very close to the human, despite their reptilian ancestors, they played out before me little scenes of comradeship, politeness, humour, social climbing, and dignity. They surprised me by instinctive impulses so complex,

18

so charged with authentic improbability, that they foreshadowed the ability of certain men to give themselves over totally to the forces of life.

The roosters' behaviour in defeat or in triumph has presided over my own triumphs or defeats. And each time that I meet anew some friend, soul mate to my humanity, my gratitude, joyously rekindled, stirs in me at the level of that rich obscure life that made our geese greet each other with grave solicitude when we let them out each morning, bowing their beaks right down to the ground and trumpeting before they would eat their grain.

I loved those chickens, ducks and geese, both generally as a species and particularly as unforgettable individuals, yet it was I who put them to the knife at my father's order while he, the too tender-hearted surgeon, withdrew, majestic and downcast, once he had pronounced his condemnation like some fatal diagnosis. Unafraid, they let me catch them, and I held their burning life between my knees and with a short precise stroke of the knife let it drain away. They taught me what death was and how life is something borrowed and a debt. What a lot of them I must have killed that way, tenderly, skilfully, but without the least sentimentality. For I ate them all at my father's table, well cooked, well stuffed, well washed down, and with an excellent appetite.

Naturally, I would not have spoken of animals like this in those days. I do so now only when discussing them with poets, scholars, and philosophers. But without them, and without my intimacy with them, the unbroken, highly polished surface of Spinoza would never have given me the rich sensation of its being transformable into countless modes, and Teilhard's evolutionary thought would never have carried for me the sense of reconciliation that it does. Without them, the superanonymity of the one could never have so successfully received baptism from the superpersonalism of the other. And without this possibility of reconciliation, the tension between matter and spirit, between the collectivity and the individual, would never have been for me that healthy state of anguish (which I do not wish to forgo) but a killing disassociation, which, as I see it, is Satan's one invention.

Thanks to a certain gift of patience and contemplation and to a certain affinity for material things, I received a poetic heritage whose most precious item was that poetry that underlies all philosophy and all theology, the kind of poetry that is the flesh of thought.

But I owe even more to my father, to that solitary man of violent contrasts who was almost as impossible for himself as he was for this world. From him, from the time that we first became friends, I received, almost daily, first-hand reports on Moses, David, Jesus, St. Paul, and St. Jerome, and extremely bad reports on Tertullian, St. Augustine, Basilides, and Valentine, names as familiar in our household as those of Arthur Meighen and Alexandre Taschereau in other homes. He gave me the Bible, as a permanent habitation, as a divine inner lining for the world. He introduced me to exegesis and to church history, and from there I passed on to theology, which prepared me for philosophy. He gave me the Russian writers, the great ones, especially the inexhaustible Chekhov, but also the minor writers who are still read in the U.S.S.R. today. He gave me Homer along with my other story books, so that by the age of twelve, while caught up in the wonder of the tale, I was first exposed to the light of the Greeks. It was in them that I would later recognize the first men who were not afraid, because with the Greeks the specific characteristics of humanity take an immense step forward, becoming reason and assuming the role of synthesis and foresight in the formulation of universal laws.

At the same time as Homer, I received Cervantes and the holy madness of Don Quixote. And, since Unamuno has verified the windmills and the enchanters, I also gained for future use an antidote against intellectualism and a means of piercing the appearances of things and of reaching their meta-physical and supernatural dimensions.

A few years later I met Molière who provided me with a triple home in those three extreme plays of his in which the equivocal side of the human creature is pushed to its limit: *Don Juan, le Misanthrope,* and *Amphytrion.*

Pickwick was a prolongation of *Don Quixote* and a preparation for Rabelais.

I would rather go to the tavern with Samuel Johnson and Boswell than hang around with the French moralists who are constipated little lap dogs and never get tight. Pascal had me but I got away. Montaigne introduced me to the rigorous humanity of Stendhal, and Constant, that irrefutable cad, obliged me to accept the inconsistencies of sincerity. Baudelaire was my key to poetry as literature and my initiation in aesthetics, but after having practised him for a long time I finally freed myself from him, almost entirely because of his basic dualism.

Music was as important to me as the written word and it is present everywhere in my life. I lived through romanticism in a Wagnerian frenzy and purified and surmounted it with Schubert, while with Bach I penetrated into a world that was supremely aware, incarnate and ordered by intelligence and the supernatural, an exemplary world in every sense. If I were called on to name the summit of human creation I would say *The Art of the Fugue.* In my opinion Mozart died too young, though he showed promise.

Speaking of contrapuntalists I think of Marcel Proust and Henry James, two men close to each other metaphysically. The former gave me the sense of time as the space of hope in motion; the latter made me aware of a distinct North-Americanness, and I 'came home' from Europe.

Like others of my generation, I became embroiled in the depths of the neo-Thomist impasse and lost myself in its deep drawers where are proudly stored up the inventions of others. My final dissatisfaction with this experience has not prevented me from remembering everything about it; the intuition of being that I received from Maritain, the respect for abstraction coeval with one's respect for the human condition (as Maritain himself puts it), and the exigence of thought and art opening out onto the silence of the absolute and of death.

The Degrees of Knowledge, which is the marvellous *summum* of all this, is a work that I refer to constantly and which I never enter without feeling a twinge of nostalgia for a fine old mansion that has never really existed: philosophical security. If I have become passionately interested in the mystics and their psychology, it is mainly due to the theological charge and to the contemplative bias of Maritain's thought. And in their turn the mystics, particularly St. John of the Cross, that naked man of naked faith, have meant more to me than Freud (though he engendered Bachelard). And they have also saved me from the dance of the little second-stringers around the pit of the absurd and from the feeble little fire of gratuitousness burning in its bottom. That doesn't stop me from reading, but I re-read more, and I have all sorts of breviaries, among them Rabelais, Proust, and the Psalms.

Nearly all the thinkers, writers, and artists that I love are giants, and I know my station and my place in respect to them: a little dog under the table. But in Canada, where there are no crumbs from any table, I don't play little dog to anyone.

[1966. Translated by Philip Stratford]

Kildare
Dobbs

Canadian
Heroes?

Where are the genuine heroes, those large souls bigger than life, big enough for bronze gesticulation among traffic lights? Big enough to sustain our songs of triumphs in bed and battle, of beauty, bravery, money, fame, loves!

Our first heroes were Imperial, the wild colonial boys. Victoria, Great White Mother, sent forth a power of them from her capacious womb, fierce-whiskered militia majors and ramrod Orange drill sergeants, fire-breathing teetotal rebels, mad half-breed horsemen, dauntless editors, builders of railroads and provinces. Last and grandest of the heroes of Empire was a tycoon of telegrams and anger, none other than – let's have a big hand for him – the Beaver!

Beaverbrook with his newspapers and his millions was the colonial boy who walked with kings. No matter if he was (as some say) an evil man who took spiteful revenge on enemies; no matter if he personally was responsible for the dislike of Canadians which is now habitual with Englishmen; no matter if he was always wrong. He was a fighter and a hero. He was the subject of picturesque lies and prestige anecdotes, a capitalist lion envied by a thousand jackal entrepreneurs, a power feared and flattered, a drinker of champagne with fine women.

But it was a dying Empire the Beaver championed. After him there would be no more Imperial heroes.

Canadian independence was too cautiously won to produce figures with the glamour of Washington, Hidalgo, Bolivar. Mackenzie King was its anti-hero, a master of what Santayana called 'muffledom', the middle-class hostess's art of dealing with conflict not by resolving but by smothering and muddling it. His

22

legacy of boredom and frustration left Canada without an emotional centre. If it hadn't been for his dispiriting effect on the country, King might just have made it as a comic hero. The quintessential mother's boy who consulted mediums and astrologers, who admired ladies but could never find one quite worthy of his unguarded affection, his most passionate enterprise seems to have been the writing up of his diaries. They are among the most boring documents ever confided to the care of a nation's archives. And not only boring in themselves but the cause of boringness in others, so that a whole generation of Kingites has conspired to leave an impression of Ottawa as a kind of New-World, non-violent St. Trinian's, a breathless record of schoolgirl crushes, tiffs, and crazes. At best, King was a wily headmistress. Even his nickname sounds like something a fox-terrier might answer to: here, Rex!

But the Age of King was one of universal conflicts under whose blows at least two Canadians were forged in the heroic scale. Nurse Edith Cavell went to her death at the hands of First-World-War Germans crying, 'Patriotism is not enough!' Imperial patriots idiotically claimed her as a patriotic martyr. But she was a prophet of the post-national era, a genuine heroine. Just as heroic was the Montreal surgeon, Norman Bethune, who tended the Loyalist wounded in the Spanish Civil War and later gave his life for the Maoist cause in China.

Cavell and Bethune were Canadians, but the causes they championed were international. Perhaps all genuine Canadian heroes are international. Lester Pearson was an international hero when he negotiated a precarious peace in the Middle East which in 1957 earned him the Nobel Peace prize. But when he turned his diplomatic gifts to the service of Confederation his glamour faded.

Perhaps the office of Canadian prime minister is intrinsically anti-heroic. When Dief the Unlucky came huffing and puffing out of the west, the light of destiny burning in his mad blue eyes, how valiantly he seized the reins with his votes and his vision! Many Canadians greeted him as a hero. He would ride in his chariot of fire over the perplexities of Confederation, slay the Establishment dragon and disappear into the mists of the future, none knew whither. At last the Press Gallery had a subject worthy of their eloquence. But of course Dief the Unlucky did nothing, absolutely nothing. The Press Gallery was disillusioned. Now they'd never get to write their sagas. The hero had turned out to be a goblin.

It was too late for heroics in Ottawa. As a post-national state, Canada is a kind of business corporation — a subsidiary, some rudely add, of the immense corporation next door. Business has no business with heroics. In a sense it has no business with men; it serves abstractions like the balance-sheet, the GNP, the Economy. Man, the weakest link in the chain of production, it strives to eliminate. And if it can't do without men as consumers and taxpayers, at least it can get rid of the humanity in men, reconstruct them in a predictable mould. Hence the post-national state's jealous interest in communication and education. Call it education for citizenship, call it service, call it fostering national unity — but what it really amounts to is the Final Solution of the Human

Question. Witness the struggles of the intelligent young, caught like flies on the sticky paper of the Economy. All that's left to them of freedom and impulse is within the privacy of their own minds, or the privacy of their own private parts – drugs and orgasms, the consolations of the jail.

Here, at least, there's still room for heroism. But what if David, facing the Goliath of Philistine bureaucracy, starts to puff on a joint instead of letting fly with that slingshot? Is he a hero? Goliath will assure him that he is. He will provide him with his own newspapers, support his campaign for the right to suck his thumb, bombard him with flattering ads for psychedelic products, witty buttons, strobe-lights, multi-media workshops, beads, sandals, incense and smutty books. Goliath turns David into another market, enshrines him alongside Commander Whitehead as the newest goblin.

'You won in a fair fight,' says Goliath. 'I got to hand it to you. You certainly belong to a very, very wonderful generation.' In proof of sincerity, Goliath lets his own hair grow, studies yoga and speaks respectfully of the polymorphous perverse. He doesn't bother to confiscate David's slingshot, and in fact turns a neat profit selling him smooth round stones from the brook. David finds them fantastically interesting; in no time at all they're the rage in all Philistia.

Anyone who offers a public challenge to the machinery of the post-national state, to the bureaucracy, to the Economy, is a potential hero. If he then refuses to be bought off and lets the enemy have it between the eyes, he's a genuine hero. René Lévesque is that kind of hero, no hint of the goblin about him, as he takes on the traditional task of leading his people out of captivity. Since Confederation belongs to the forces that own the Economy, that means leading French Canadians out of the bondage imposed on them long ago by the alliance between the Empire and the Catholic hierarchy. For another genuine hero, Joey Smallwood, the Kwame Nkrumah of Newfoundland, 'Let my people go!' meant leading them *into* Confederation.

Both men have the personal attributes of heroism: passionate, brave, magnetic, witty, intelligent, and full of guile. If someone like Smallwood or Lévesque was prime minister of Canada, there would be no such thing as a crisis of national unity. But it does not seem possible for a post-national state to tolerate that kind of leadership. There are only two nations, in the old sense, in North America – Newfoundland and Quebec. The rest of us, Americans and Canadians, are a new kind of creature, members of corporations, units of the Economy. Which is why to most of us, figures like Lévesque and Smallwood seem oddly old-fashioned, fighting the battles of an earlier age. For supposing Lévesque succeeds in winning, first the national revolution and then the social revolution, a new bureaucracy, a new Economy will come into being. David will become Goliath.

Not all heroes are political. It's possible that Cardinal Léger is a hero. On the face of it he is a great churchman who, remembering that his church's task is the salvation of individual souls, has decided to save his own. Renouncing the pomps and cares of office, he disappears to serve as a humble missionary in

Africa. In choosing a leper colony, though, he introduces a goblin touch. In my own African days I helped take charge of some lepers for a time and it was obvious that, at any rate within my field of vision, leprosy was not a particularly urgent problem. Everyone believes that it's easy to catch leprosy but in fact it's not very infectious. You can live in the same hut for years with a leper and not catch it. But leprosy is a disease that history has surrounded with superstitious dread. There is something a little too glamorous – a little too safely glamorous – about choosing a leper colony. The Schweitzer touch. Yet still, to give up the princely style of a cardinal for a life of lowly housekeeping is the act of a *potential* hero. Time alone will show whether Léger is hero or goblin.

Sports heroes, show-business figures, and crusading newspapermen are, of course, goblins to a man. They are all part of the commercial illusion with which the Economy strives to console us for the humanity it is taking away from us. Why do we have so few genuine heroes? Is it because we are disillusioned?

But men have always been disillusioned. In Britain's heroic age there was a divinity that hedged a king, even rebels had the grandeur and tragedy of fallen angels. Those that entered on the Renaissance pageant were all larger than life. Yet they were mortal and the age – it was a time of endemic plague – the age remembered death. The glories of our blood and state, the poet reminded them, were shadows. Eloquent divines like Donne spoke their sombre warnings: 'It comes equally to us all, and it makes us all equal when it comes.' And a hero like Raleigh, awaiting the headsman's axe, suffered the pain of time

> Who in the dark and silent grave
> When we have wandered all our ways
> Shuts up the story of our days.

Elizabethan England, with all its pomps and heroics was an illusion that knew itself to be an illusion. The post-national state is an illusion that does not know it is an illusion because it has abolished death. Our funerary rites are all designed to conceal the fact that death has intruded. Business corporations do not die – and they are persons before the law. Far from being disillusioned, ours is an age that wallows in illusion and hysterically resists all attempts to show it for what it is.

This is the ground for intellectual heroism. The intellectual hero is one who pricks the bubble of illusion, who sees through the goblins. Despite all attempts to turn him into a goblin himself, he fights ruthlessly on. Marshall McLuhan is such a hero. Northrop Frye is another. They are both Canadians and they are both engaged in a universal conflict, champions of reality in a world of illusion.

[1968]

James Reaney

Local Grains of Sand

I've always been able to identify as a Canadian fairly easily. First of all I love the countryside where I was born and no matter what network of suburbia and gas stations are put on top of it, I could rebuild it tomorrow from a blade of grass or an old fence post. County history, township history, and old *Stratford Beacon-Heralds* matter a great deal to me. So far I've not been in a part of Canada yet where I couldn't develop anew a repeat of my original loyalty and where I didn't see some people with that sort of rootedness. In a country so physically large it is hard to think of the whole thing. A Dane or an Icelander has such a tidy neat home-shape to love. But Canadians – thoughtful patriots – see their whole nation in the local grain of sand. That feeling of a relaxed decentralized belonging *is* the Canadian national identity and it is frequently confused by Britishers and Americans with lack of national character and faceless blur. Mind you, I can remember as a child looking at a map of Canada at school and wolfing down the whole thing as *my* country. The shape of Hudson Bay, the Northern Arctic islands, the coast of Labrador and the shapes of the Great Lakes were particularly lovable. Quebec always seemed like the profile of – someone – the Duchess in *Alice in Wonderland* with the Ottawa River defining her chin and jaws, Cape Jones as her nose, Labrador as her head-dress and some unknown river (the Nottaway) as the outline of her rather pursed mouth. Ontario seems like someone in a rather grotesque rocking chair. The Arctic Islands had the fascinating fretted shapes of mackerel clouds in a sunset. Naturally I have never since known Canada as well as I did then.

'Relaxed decentralized belonging' involves playing the game of confederation according to rules that let the separate groups and loyalties, often
blissfully unconscious of each other, simmer away. Trying to separate from
it should be almost impossible; no one was ever tied in that tightly. If they
were, or think they are, *that* complaint needs an understanding and factful
investigation.

You find Canadian history dull and if you were teaching it, what would you
teach in the second term?

Better to be a nation without a history than to have too much of it as, say,
Bulgaria has. We have just enough. I can remember once at a party somebody
sneering at one of the Riel Rebellions: only seven people killed. What on earth
would he be satisfied with? Tamburlaine's pyramid of human skulls?

Our two national opposites are William Lyon Mackenzie the Rebel and his
grandson, the late Mr. King. Suppose Mr. King had one night gone to that
spiritualist in Kingston and contacted not his mother, but the grandfather!
What a berating there would have been there. 'Vision if necessary, but not
necessarily vision,' the old Rebel would have sneered at his grandson. I would
like to do a play on that sometime. Other people from the past I am fond of are:
Champlain, Brébeuf, Pierre Falcon the Métis poet, Isabella Crawford, Louis
Riel, the heretic Quaker who built that Temple at Sharon north of Toronto.
The grand mistake in the past was Sir John A. having Riel executed. Anyone
who can think up a name like Manitoba deserves to live, no matter how many
Tom Scotts he himself has hanged.

The kind of nation I have been obliquely sketching with the hope that you
will see it as good and being in existence is, of course, not always present to
everyone in Canada. It needs all sorts of help. It needs the pretence that we
are a unified nation (Air Canada & CBC, films like *The Drylanders* and 'O
Canada' and the new flag); it needs a certain amount of separatism and
minority cultures. In this regard we despise the Indian while eagerly sucking
at the symbols he evolved from a life supposedly inferior to ours. We need art.
Not Canadian art. But just art. When I think of the last twenty years here,
the thing that happened that made the most difference to me – was the
success of the Stratford Shakespeare Festival. If we can do Shakespeare that
well, we must be more awake than we had suspected. The more we do
Shakespeare, the more imaginatively awake will we be. Literature, the Bible,
and Shakespeare tell you more about the potentialities of Canada than
Canada does itself.

Some friends of mine recently trekked across the land and being products of
the Graduate School at Toronto more or less fell in with old acquaintances all
the way along. The sense of a network, of people separated by huge distances
but thinking of each other because they had once toiled through *Beowulf*
together gave my friends their first proof that Canada did exist.

You could hold a nation together by everyone eating a piece of white dog
every February. I am convinced that you get a much more interesting nation

when it doesn't have to toil at such a material identity. Cultivated imaginations (how much England owes to Jewish stories) produce a society that is one of friends, can bear all sorts of variations and knows so well what it is that it does not have to say.

[1964]

Hugh Hood

Moral Imagination: Canadian Thing

When Lord Byron was stalking across Europe, branded with a nameless and horrible curse – from Waterloo to the shores of Lake Leman to Italy to a heroic death at Missolonghi, to world fame and the impression of his personality on the next hundred and fifty years – a few poor settlers were straggling into Ontario via the trail of the black walnut, or north from Lake Champlain. There was no permanent settlement west of the lakehead. Montreal and Quebec were the tiny provincial capitals of a culture recently submerged under an invasion by one great European power and recently deserted by another. In the glorious and turbulent first quarter of the greatest of centuries, the 19th, Canada was an idea nobody had thought of.

There was no Canadian Byron. There was no Canadian Beethoven to initiate the music of world revolution, no Canadian Berlioz to create the modern orchestra and open the way for Wagner, Mahler, and 20th century music.

This century is a weak and decadent parasite on a great expansive movement in human culture. The movement began about the time of the American revolution and continued with almost undiminished force until the Russian revolution a hundred and forty years later, the great age of the romantic imagination. We never got in on any of that.

No political thinker like Burke or Coleridge or Marx; no painter like Delacroix or Goya; no spokesman for the language of democracy in literature like Wordsworth or Whitman. We had no educator like von Humboldt, not even a philosopher of reaction like de Maistre.

29

Never in the age of the Romantic movement, that tremendous complex of revolution and reaction and revolution again in every aspect of human life and thought, did a single Canadian arise to make his voice heard among the chorus of prophets.

We were clearing the country north of Brockville; thinking about building the Rideau canal; allowing British regulars, with incidental help from ourselves, to repel revolutionaries from below the border. We had no education, no poetry, no art, no science, no money to speak of – apart from certain Montreal entrepreneurs who, in 1817, felt themselves strong enough to create Canada's first bank. It's true that Montreal and Quebec had two centuries of history behind them, and Halifax was 75 years old, that the Toronto carrying place had perhaps been the focal point of a trade route since there were men in North America. But Toronto was a rickety collection of huts along a swampy lakeshore, and Montreal and Quebec were adjusting with great difficulty – or refusing forever to adjust – to British rule. Halifax was a garrison town with a culture at the level of the garrison entertainment.

In Upper Canada – when Chopin and Musset were at the feet of Mme Dudevant, and the Abbé Liszt was wowing the ladies across Europe, and Eugene de Rastignac was shaking his fist at Paris, and Julien Sorel was hatching his dream of heroic intrigue and grandeur – we had the Family Compact. It was a village in-group hugging trivial goodies to itself – not even *the* Family Compact, the great one, the Bourbon rulers of France, Spain, and the Netherlands at the beginning of the 18th century. That borrowed name tells much about our history; the grand name, as Matthew Arnold said, for the mean thing.

Where was our Byron, our Gogol, our young Tolstoy, even our Poe or Emerson? Our Washington and Jefferson? What we got was William Lyon Mackenzie or worse. Our Keats was Archibald Lampman, 60 years after the fact of Keats, and he could do you a pretty good Keats. There are few things more pathetic in our history than the sight of Lampman, with his job in the civil service, looking around for his great subject, for something to write about. With his talent, ambition, some learning, and a certain amount of leisure, Lampman might have done something. What he did was produce landscape poems, some distance after Keats, with the rich images left in and the transcendental imagination left out. He did what he could.

We were all poor, and we had no time for ideas. But we all did what we could, by and large, without vast economic resources and without the impulse of a revolutionary ideology. We worked with the moral and religious instincts (for we can hardly call them ideas) that we'd brought with us from 17th and 18th century England and France to lay the foundations of a civilized society. We began to build schools almost as soon as we pulled the last stumps from the clearings, and we quarrelled – God, how we quarrelled! – over our rights to our religions and languages, without ever managing to bring to bear on the quarrels any great statement of principle.

We missed out on every one of the great movements of ideas and feelings that swept Europe and, to some extent, the United States from 1775 (say) to 1917. We never had a genuine native Bolshevist. We had no great conservative. Sir John A. Macdonald was described by an English statesman as 'quite a gentlemanly-appearing man' and, though his nose resembled Disraeli's he resembled him in no other respect, neither in literary power nor intellectual power, nor even in slyness.

We didn't have the Romantic movement, damn it all, and we didn't have a revolution. We never understood, or even wanted to understand, the consequences to the world of that great incarnation of the hero in history, that apotheosis of the self-created man of will, Napoleon Bonaparte. We had no marshal's baton in our knapsacks, only chewing tobacco.

The twin cults of Byronism and Bonapartism, the personal and public versions of the Romantic hero, carried Europe by storm, and dominated morals, ideology, and politics almost to the present day. We find Byronism – the story of the Cain figure, the Satanic outcast – in Poe, Baudelaire, Rimbaud, Joyce, in Jay Gatsby, and in Marlon Brando, James Dean, and Bob Dylan. And we find Bonapartism in Louis Napoleon, Garibaldi, Theodore Roosevelt, a distorted and corrupted version in Hitler, and perhaps a chastened and corrected version in a certain long-nosed general whom most Canadians, French and English, resent for his intervention in Canadian affairs. Canadians don't go for Byronism or Bonapartism; we reject them the way the body rejects an alien graft.

Canadians have never formed a mass or a mass society, and we remain totally antipathetic to the psychology of the mass. It isn't accidental that one institution charged with the management of the techniques of mass media in Canadian life, the CBC, has constantly been harassed and criticized and threatened by people from all over the country. We have produced plenty of movie stars, but, like our little Byrons and our Beaverbrooks, our bush-league Napoleons, they have had to leave the country to make their grand impression. You can't make a grand impression on a Canadian. Just as our 'mass medium', the CBC, has never really been accepted by our society, so we have never had a film industry. We don't act as a mass or respond as a mass.

Everybody in this country has the psychology of a member of a minority group, and not a very important minority group either. The English Canadian feels swamped by the vast power of U.S. culture. The French Canadian feels crushed by the English Canadian, or claims to, though he's quite able to look after himself. The Ukrainians insist on their rights with the defensive, turtle-like solidarity of a minority. Minorities are suspicious, defensive, fearful of being put upon, jealous of their legal safeguards, ready to take offence. The masses are not like that. The masses are so aware of their immense power that they can never get it through their heads that not everybody wants to be just like them.

I know a very clever man, an articulate, alert, highly intelligent professor who, after he'd lived two years in Canada, asked me, 'Why does there have to be another country up here at the top of North America?' He was from the U.S., of course, and he was ready to make the mass assumption that there was no reason imaginable to live in a way different from the way people live in the States. The tendency of U.S. history has been to sink the minority in the mass – all but the one minority that won't go down, the Negroes. In Canada, the minorities – whether cultural, religious, ethnic, whether Bluenoses, Spud Islanders, Italians, Ukrainians or, God knows, French – have always and utterly refused to assimilate. And *that*, in reply to my professor friend, is why there's another country at the top of North America. This country offers an alternative life style to people who do not want to share in the benefits and deficiencies of mass society, people who do not subscribe to the personal and political ethics of neo-Romanticism.

The very idea of the masses is a Romantic idea. As understood by the political thinkers of the 19th century, Rousseau's notion of the social contract requires from the private person an abdication of his distinct selfhood, in return for the benefits of belonging to the democratic mass. Democracy, on this plan, sometimes leads straight to totalitarianism, and so do many of the leading ideas of Romantic political philosophy.

In this country, we never generated the psychology of a mass or a master race because there weren't enough of us, and we had too many cherished differences. Every time a demagogue – some tiny Napoleon like Mitchell Hepburn – rose among us and acquired control over a special group, some other group repudiated him. It is the normal condition of Canadian politics that it should be a succession of shaky compromises and infirm assertions of a status quo. Marshall McLuhan, the great apostle of the mass media, some time ago gave an interview to a U.S. mass medium – a magazine – in which he said that he enjoyed living in Canada because it was so non-contemporary that it gave him perspective on the rest of the world. Living in Canada, he thought, was like living in the 19th century in an isolated village, *not* the global village. He had the right idea, but got the century wrong. We aren't 20th century people, nor even 19th. We're 18th century men.

We can't make myths, as the last Romantics like Yeats and Joyce could, or less innocent ones like those of Hitler, and the more unprincipled salesmen of the American Dream. Imagine a Canadian Dream, which implied that every-body in the world ought to share it! Imagine a Committee on Un-Canadian Activities! You can't. Un-Canadianism is almost the very definition of *Canadianism*.

There have been two great subjects for myth making in our history: the story of the displacement of the Acadians, and the story of Louis Riel. Both are histories of the mistreatment of minority groups and therefore typically Canadian. We let one of them get away to the States, to an American poet, and we've just become aware of the mythic power of the other. I don't know how many treatments of the Riel story I've heard lately, at least half a dozen. But this myth hasn't yet come to life as a dominating force in our lives, the way the myths of the cowboy or the gangster have in the U.S. Our most talented men (we have produced no man to whom we will concede greatness) are never heroes to us; though they may be to the Chinese; we are not hero worshippers.

We are a people whose intellectual history skipped out what happened to Europe after the middle of the 18th century; our ideological framework is that of the 17th and early 18th centuries. In short, your typical Canadian, whether he be French or English, is somebody who's still fighting the doctrinal and philosophical battles of the Enlightenment.

We have no concern with the cult of the hero, with the transcendental creative imagination. What we like to quarrel about is the economics of nationalism (very 18th century, this) and the ethics of the more repressive varieties of Christianity, Catholic or Protestant. Until 10 years ago, the Roman Catholicism of Quebec was 18th century in every aspect of its style, just as spoken French in Quebec has a distinctly 18th century sound.

A student of English literature who remembers the rather palely sketched character of Sir Andrew Freeport, in the Spectator papers, will recognize there a dim but unmistakable rendering of Mitchell Sharp. Addison himself, who had all the virtues and, like us, all in the wrong order, reminds us powerfully of the Canadian prig. We are preoccupied with morals, not just our sexual morals, but all types of morals. We repress our considerable sexuality and hide our good looks in badly cut and ill-fitting clothes, as a mortification of the flesh.

The unquestioned probity of Mr. Stanfield is an 18th century virtue, that of the *honnête homme* – the good burgher, the ordinary decent man in trade. Probity is from the conscience. So is prudence, the legendary prudence of Mackenzie King and Louis St. Laurent and Pierre Elliott Trudeau, the most prudent of councillors, never mind his jazzy exterior.

The quarrel over federalism, the regions versus the central power, is a hoary question in political economy. Its various implications had been worked out by the Swiss long before the American revolution made it a pressing question to Hamilton and Jay; and it has been discussed in Canada in the terms of Enlightenment political theory, on a Newtonian model of action and reaction. What else about us is 18th century? Our conscience, our want of a modern ideology, our prejudices (goddam Pepsis, *maudits Anglais*) and even our antiquated views on linguistics.

To a contemporary linguistic scientist, the question of whether or not Canadian French or Canadian English is 'good' French or English is a non-question. The norms of language are derived from what people say, not from what some grammarian thinks they ought to say. But the prescriptive view of grammar is typically 18th century, as any history of language will show. It's a shocking thing to find men like Trudeau and Tremblay wasting their time (and ours) over whether Quebec French or Ontario English is 'good' or not. Their attitude is very Canadian. I don't know how many times I've had people from Toronto ask me dubiously, 'But the French you hear in Montreal isn't very good, is it?' What the hell does such a question mean? Nothing! Montreal French differs to some extent from the French spoken elsewhere, but not significantly in its syntax or its deep structure. Even if it did, it would still be legitimately the language of the place. Normative grammar is pre-Romantic.

Most important of all, our history froze into a pattern at the Peace of Paris, 1763, and we've been fighting ever since over the consequences of this event, the only real event in our history. Confederation wasn't a historical event; it was one more in a series of readjustments of power that had been going on since 1763 (10 years before the first of the great modern revolutions). It is *still* going on, for the very good reason that the French aren't going to go away suddenly, and they aren't going to stop looking for the best deal they can get from the other people in the country – and after all what's more reasonable than that? To want to make the best deal you can is a fundamental human need. Canadian history since 1763 has been a series of attempts by one group to get a good deal for itself at the expense of another, and a series of indignant reactions by the threatened group. Like people under an enchantment, we've been acting out the same political ritual for two centuries, while the great world outside passed us by.

The American Dream, on the other hand, was the invention of the transcendental poetic imagination as Emerson and Whitman conceived it. To put matters simply, the Jews and the Scotch Presbyterians were actuated mainly by conscience and the moral reason; the proponents of the American Dream were actuated by creative imagination and the heroic will to power, not, finally, for the betterment of man's historical condition but as the expression of an idea of absolutely unconditioned liberty. The creative imagination, as understood by its theorists at the beginning of the 19th century, was *beyond* reason and conscience; it superseded them and supplanted them by the will and the poetic-heroic capacity for totally new experience.

But what might the results be if a people like us – rich enough, capable enough, without a dreadful weight of international moral responsibility on our shoulders – were able to combine conscience and prudence with the romantic imagination and will?

Isn't it at least thinkable that there might be a human activity we could call 'moral imagination', and aren't we, the people nobody reads or pays attention to, uniquely privileged? We alone have preserved our 17th and 18th century inheritance and are nevertheless confronted every minute with what replaced it. There's nothing so fatiguing as the need to be *with it* all the time; this year's hippie is next year's . . . what? We have the chance to *refuse* to be with it, to accept and transform squareness and dulness because, somewhere in this mad world, there has to be a people who knows how and when to put on the brakes.

What we need to do is reject the mere moralism of our past – the censoriousness and exclusiveness and self-approval, the coldness of prudence and the inertia of provincialism and colonialism – and, at the same time, preserve the real integrity of conscience that your best Canadian shows. Pearson, Vanier,

Cardinal Léger. At its purest and clearest, the Canadian conscience, outmoded and faintly ridiculous as it may seem this year, is a noble power.

And then, profiting from the 150-year modern experiment of replacing conscience by imagination, reason by will – and willingly leaving out the totalitarian implications of much of even the best modern thought – we need to illuminate our conscience by poetry. We need to illuminate our prudence by the swift intuition of Blake or Keats or Rimbaud. We need to marry Byron to Margaret Laurence, handcuff Napoleon to Tommy Douglas. This sounds crazy, I know, but the results might be wonderful.

The stagnant mentality of the colonial convinces him that any place else is better than here. Some men are colonials from birth in their own homeland, convinced that their country is a worn-out and reactionary sinkhole, that the U.S. will be better. But the wise Goethe tapped his temple and said, '*Hier oder nirgends ist Amerika.*' (America is in you, or nowhere.)

Canada is filled with men who have the perpetually disappointed, self-deceiving mentality of the colonial, the conviction that Paris will be better than Montreal, London or New York better than Toronto. When one of them actually makes it to what he thinks will be his spiritual home, his letters become filled with frustration and disillusion.

You don't acquire the treasures of another country in rejecting your own; what you acquire is a sour stomach, and the flatulent prose that goes with it.

I don't say that no young artist, diplomat, student, should leave his country, Canada or whatever, for temporary or even permanent exile. I do say that the man who does this on the supposition that his own country is trivial and worthless and unworthy of his talents is in for a rude surprise. By all means choose exile, but never spit on your country and blame it for your own deficiencies.

Rid of the colonial mentality, the Canadian has a social and cultural opportunity without parallel in modern life. He can create the first modern state, the country of the moral imagination, where what happened from 1775 to 1917 and everything that went before are united, where compromise and squareness, far from being dirty words, are recognized as what they are, the vital and necessary complement of commitment and . . . what? Roundness? In a lot of ways, this is the best country there is.

[1967]

II
As Others
See Us

Hayden Carruth
Barbara Ward
Claude Julien
Ali Mazrui
Richard Crossman
Edmund Wilson
Ronald Bryden

Hayden Carruth

In Haste, with Love, to Canada

Impossible for me to separate my feeling about Canada from my recurrent desire to emigrate. There you are, you Canadians, twenty miles away. In no time I could be with you. And what more would be required? A pause at the border station, a moment to renounce my native citizenship, perhaps a paper or two to sign, an interview to endure. It could all be over in an afternoon.

Of course one's emigration fever is not constant. It rises and falls in direct proportion to the fluctuations of national ignominy at home. For me the highest pitch, at least so far, was reached on April 5, 1968 – and no, I haven't looked up that date. I don't need to, it is fixed in my memory like a stone in an arch. The evening before, April 4, we had heard the news of Martin Luther King's assassination. It had been a strange night, wild and anguished inside, ominous out. A strong south wind was blowing, hot, heavy, unseasonable. At midnight, when I went walking with my mongrel bitch, the temperature was still in the 60s. I heard snapping noises in the woods, and the wind felt steamy. I came to a huge elm limb that had fallen on the road and lay there, broken, in the flakes of its loose bark; it looked as if someone – let's say God – had flung down a great serpent on the earth with such force that it lay shattered in its blood as a sign of cosmic wrath. My bitch whimpered and ran home before me, where I found her shivering on the step.

Later that night the expected front came through, and the next morning was cold. After breakfast I drove to the village, to the post office and drug store; but then, my errands done, I did not return home, but instead drove aimlessly northward, as if compelled by some exterior force. Snow began to fall. Flocks of

39

newly arrived redwings huddled unhappily by the road. Still half numb with shock, I looked at the dismal landscape, gray fields and black mountains. Everywhere was the wreck of winter, fences broken, pavements cracked and potholed, birches bent and poplars snapped off at mid-trunk. Eventually I came to North Troy, and found myself on the hill overlooking the border stations, two squat buildings, American and Canadian, with their flags at half-mast. I stopped. I looked in either direction. Snow fluttered like a curtain on the forests and mountains. But it could not obscure the imaginary line that runs between those buildings and off in either direction, eastward, westward, dividing the land. Imaginary? You may not see it, but there are men who know where it is exactly, who can plot it to the inch, and your own relationship to it, whether you live on this side or on that side, may be a decisive factor in your life. It is likely to be even more decisive from now on.

I cannot explain my thoughts and feelings about King in a page or two. I loved him. I believed in him. It was more complicated than that, of course, but that was the essence. For me, King's program of accelerating non-violence was not only the most sensible course for American revolutionaries to adopt, it was the only course to which I myself, in this confusion of old ardors and fears that I call my personality, could commit my heart and soul. I don't really know what use the concept of sainthood has to my secular imagination, but I do know that King was a saint, the only saint America has produced in my lifetime. If his program had faltered somewhat in the year before his death, nevertheless it was still vigorous, still the focus of a tremendous effort of goodness throughout the country, and King himself had announced new programs, new approaches and emphases, that revived our hopes. Then came that afternoon in Memphis. I was shocked and heartsick, but more than that I felt cast into despair, I mean thrown right out into the bleak, lonely, anguished wastes of nihilism. It seemed to me as if the evil in American society, that immense, loathsome force, had risen and struck the one sure element of goodness we possessed. I believed then, and I still believe, that that afternoon was the end of sanity in American life.

Now I sat in my car on a hill in North Troy, looking across the snowy air to Canada. My family and I have lived in northern Vermont for some years, and like many border people we think of ourselves as in some sense dual citizens. Our nearest metropolis is Montreal. The radio station to which we listen habitually for news and entertainment is part of the CBC. In many respects we are better acquainted with public affairs in Canada than with those in the U.S. We agonize with the Quebec teachers, worry with the farmers of Ontario and Saskatchewan. We have visited briefly in both Quebec and British Columbia, and we hope to visit again at greater length. In addition, I have written occasionally for Canadian magazines, mostly in a critical spirit, and in America I have a reputation as a minor authority on contemporary Canadian literature, especially poetry. I have corresponded with a number of Canadian writers and editors.

All this means nothing, of course. If I know far more about Canada than the average American, who never thinks of Canada at all, except possibly during the play-offs for the Stanley Cup, I still know very little; and until I was invited to write this essay I had resolved to write no more for Canadians. It is so easy to be an outside critic. Too easy, and I doubt that any good purpose is served by it. Yet here I am, writing once more for a Canadian audience. All I can say is that I am trying to write now in a spirit of real humility. I shall write nothing about the follies I see, or think I see, in Canadian life, though they are numerous. I shall write instead, with acknowledged superficiality and in the broadest conceivable terms, about Canada's two great strengths. One is English, the other French, and I shall begin with the former.

Decency. Human decency, respect for the private man. Refusal to admit the means of torture, whatever torture for whatever ends. I think of those miles of little houses in Vancouver, each hedged on its thirty-foot plot – little castles. Ugly enough, God knows, tawdry and stodgy too, the essence of petty bourgeois culture. I have no difficulty whatever in sympathizing with the young radicals of Vancouver. But I would say to them, from my vantage point in a far more hideous society: 'Watch out. Don't destroy what may be your own best instrument for revolution.' Decency is a small, negative virtue; it will build no empires; all that is over and done. But with leadership it can accomplish a great deal. It can create revolutions. It already has. And as nearly as an outsider can judge it is deeply, morphologically embedded in the Anglo-Saxon part of Canadian civilization.

We had it in America once too, chiefly in New England, and we have vestiges of it still; but we long ago ruined it as a contributing element to our social evolution; ruined it, I believe, through our centuries of massacring Indians and trafficking in slaves. Canada is not guiltless in these respects. But the massive genocidal and repressionary tendencies that infiltrated the American character never gained dominance in Canada. Today we know where the power lies in America, and we know that it is absolute. General Eisenhower, in a famous phrase, called it the 'military-industrial complex'. What he meant was the oligarchy. Every day we see new segments of individual will crumble before its power. Our courts may try to hold out against it, and so may our liberal associations; but no constitutional effort can restrain a force that has evolved in a society by virtue of the society's constitutional weakness, certainly not when that force has taken control of the actual procedural centers. Only decent human hearts can do it, and we don't have enough of them. America is ruled by a tacit and instinctive alliance between corrupt oligarchs at the top and corrupt ignoramuses at the bottom. Does anyone doubt that ultimately these were the forces united behind that rifle shot in Memphis? Babylonia knew it, Assyria knew it, Greece knew it, Rome knew it. Now we know it.

Canada's other strength – still speaking in the broadest terms – is the vitality of the French nationalist renaissance. A marvelous spectacle to watch. It has a sweeping simplicity that charms the rest of us in our sophisticated quandaries; I do not mean simplemindedness, far from it, but a kind of simpleheartedness that vanished from most of western life long ago. I see it especially in the poetry of contemporary Quebec; not in all of it, since the Parisian influence is strong too, but in a good deal. It is actually Whitmanesque in the breadth and stability of its vision, in its openness and cleanliness, in its willingness to celebrate human joy and national pride. In short it is optimistic, and how rare that has become. The same quality must pervade much of the rest of French-Canadian nationalism. I hear it, for instance, in the voice of René Lévesque, in spite of his customary dry concern with practical politics. Amid the tons of obfuscation and mendacity, the plain bullshit, to which all of us in the modern world are subjected every day, this is a wonderful strength for any nation to have. It is energetic, confident, and in its way austere. Above all it is creative.

Easy enough, then, for an outsider to say that these two strengths should be working in combination, not at cross-purposes; in free and functional combination. Easy enough to suggest the great things that might be accomplished, socially, economically, culturally. But you Canadians can see them as clearly as I, and you can see the difficulties and obstacles even more clearly. I hope you make it. I hope very earnestly and warmly that you bring it off. But I urge speed. I had expected Mr. Trudeau, after assuming leadership, to say something about these issues far more cogent than any words I have heard from him so far, and to take action far more imaginative than any actions I have seen. The time is short. In our world it is getting shorter and shorter, and there can be no greater folly than delay. So do what you must. Combine. Give your indigenous peoples what they need and want, give your small black community what it needs and wants. Yes, *give* – you are rich enough, in both money and freedom. And then get on with the job.

But my desire to see you move quickly is more than the concern of a friend and well-wisher. I have an additional reason, an American reason. Obviously I did not emigrate. That morning in North Troy, as I looked across the boundary to the temptations of Canada, I realized with renewed bitterness the truth of my and everyone's predicament: a man does not choose his country, the country chooses him. Christ, wouldn't it be great to have a little yellow helicopter in which to float over the face of the globe, deciding where to settle? If I went up I might never come down. As it was, at last I turned my car around and drove back home, slowly southward again into violence and despair. That is my country.

Now over a year has passed. I have the impression that few Canadians recognize the change this year has brought to the temper of American life. Many Americans don't recognize it. Little more than a year ago we were still talking about demonstrations, marches, vigils, school integration, voter registration, etc. Now all that seems antediluvian. It *is* antediluvian. Non-violence has become as remote a dream as it was in 1941, for instance, or in 1861. We are on the edge of civil war. This is not alarmism; I know no one in our centers of social confrontation who does not believe it. The preliminary skirmishes have already been fought. Both sides are rushing frantically to arm themselves.

The production and sale of weapons has increased enormously. No one can tell, of course, when military activity will reach such a pitch that a general acknowledgment of civil war will be unavoidable. Certainly there will be no formal declaration – such an old-fashioned idea! But the time will come. And one need not be a specialist to foresee what kind of war it will be; we have plenty of other wars to look at. Right now, as I am writing, battles are under way, with bloodshed and death, in Greensboro, North Carolina, and Berkeley, California. These outbursts will become bigger and more violent, and will be repressed more violently. Then, as the cadres are organized and disciplined, the fighting will go underground, and the war will be characterized by guerrilla tactics, indiscriminate terrorism, and immense cruelty. It will be, almost certainly, a futile and terribly damaging war, just as it will be, in the final sense, unnecessary. Even now, at this late date, a few words scribbled on a piece of paper in Washington could prevent it, or at least mitigate it. But we have absolutely lost faith in the possibility that those words will be written. No wonder we are frightened and melancholy.

Soon you in Canada will be presented with a dilemma which will make your internal dilemma seem small and insignificant by comparison. This is why I urge haste in overcoming your internal dilemmas; if you can consolidate your strengths now, you will meet this greater dilemma far more reasonably and coolly than you will if you remain divided among yourselves, and you will perhaps play a genuinely constructive part in resolving it. For you must choose which side of our civil war you will be on. I don't mean, of course, that you will become militarily engaged, any more than most of us, the middle-aged white Americans, whose active roles have been pre-empted and who are needed now only as onlookers, witnesses, and civilian casualties, will become militarily engaged. But you will be engaged in nearly every other way. Neutrality will be impossible; no one in the world will evade this choice of sides, least of all you who are on our doorstep. The border will not protect you. Already the traffic across it, in connection with social disorder, is great, and it can only intensify. Ah, why aren't we left to our own problems, our own destiny? – I hear you asking it. But you aren't. You are alive, hence you are historical; and history, alas, is no respecter of nations. Soon, sooner than you wish, you will have to choose, and you will have to do it publicly and officially.

Now I come to the point at which I change tactics and tell you, boldly and bluntly, something for your own good. If, for reasons of diplomatic convenience or economic advantage, you choose the side of the oligarchs, or even if you are led by your anxieties to choose hesitantly or ambiguously or in a temporizing spirit, then you will not only betray the cause of freedom and justice everywhere, you will not only bring bitter disappointment to those throughout the world who look to Canada as a wellspring of enlightenment in these barbarous times, but you will *deny your own great sources of strength*, both of them and equally, English and French, your decency and your progressive vitality. These standards, these inner criteria, enforce your choice. Think about it. For a long time you have been able to study a country that has consistently denied itself, and you have seen the result. Take the lesson to heart. Often on the CBC I hear Canadians decry the plight of a small country jammed up against a big one. But don't you see the advantage of it? We make the mistakes first! Those of us in America who recognize these mistakes and who wear, willy-nilly and often unfairly, the rueful, inerasable mark of shame on our foreheads, look to you now with longing. For God's sake, choose the right side.

[1969]

Barbara Ward

The First International Nation

As this century moves towards its last quarter, it is quite clear that the human species is involved in an appalling institutional mess. Nothing seems to fit. Governments are too big for some purposes, too small for others. Wales and Scotland want to escape London's control, yet the whole United Kingdom needs the economic context of a united Europe. Wallonia resents Brabant but Belgium as an entity is only a small part of the Common Market. The Ukrainians are restive fifty years on from the revolution of post-national, proletarian solidarity. India could fall apart. Most post-war federations have done so.

Nor is all this turmoil simply political. Vast international businesses, usually American in origin, operate across every frontier and can achieve such business weight as almost to annul local economic sovereignty. And behind all these jostling and contradictory institutions with their claims to power lies the stark fact that all of them lack ultimate sovereignty. The dollar cannot dictate world policies for liquidity. Four times overkill cannot guarantee even super-powers full security. Capitalist markets use Communist gold. Communist stomachs need capitalist wheat. The ever tightening, thickening web of complete interdependence draws all the sovereignties great and small, kicking and screaming, into a single planetary system. But the institutions to express this unity are so frail, so dependent upon sovereign vetos of unsovereign states that they seem little more than the tribute of hypocrisy which vice pays to virtue recognizing its necessity but giving it the widest berth.

We all know the reason for the indescribable confusion. Quite suddenly in little more than a century, science and technology have shrunk the planet into a single neighbourhood of contact, communication, and common lethal danger. But knowing the reason does not automatically suggest the cure. One can say that in face of nuclear war heads, space satellites, and supersonic travel, the ultimately sovereign nation is as obsolete as those seven thousand New Guinea villages with their seven thousand separate languages. And the statement, in part, is true especially when one remembers that New Guinean villages until recently included headhunting in the next village among their inalienable rights. But can one really say nationalism has no function when one sees it act as the cement of courage among peoples like the Czechs or notices how difficult it is for African states to forge effective statehood without a national tradition to underpin it? If the new technology simply dictated a quantum jump to a world federal system, the political confusion would be less. But these simplicities are not manageable. Concrete compromises and working models of adaptation – like Solon's constitution for Athens or Simon de Montfort's parliament or late medieval Europe's fusion of language and frontiers or the visionary state-building of the Founding Fathers – are needed to get the world out of its maze of unworkable, overlapping, contradictory institutions and to offer it a number of concrete possibilities which look like a beginning to work.

Such experiments must be worked out, consciously, by governments. They are at present the central point or rendezvous of a whole range of different powers, some of which should be decentralized while others should be handed up to wider authorities. The claim to total sovereignty of a state government includes many forms of authority which are attached to it often by chance or history; a sorting out of powers is probably the essence of any fresh response to our age of unifying technology. One can think of this sorting out in abstract terms – some forms of education or culture or conservation to be devolved, for instance, certain responsibilities such as finance for world development or working capital for world trade or international security to go to authorities beyond the nation. But abstractions, even when incorporated in international charters, tend to go out through the gates of ivory. It is states and governments committing their powers and their resources to new experiment who bring in the blueprints through the gates of horn.

But the number of governments which could, in an effective way, confront and redefine the crucial problem of state authority in the modern world are fairly limited. The superpowers are too vast, too unwieldy, too locked in their own responsibilities. The great mass of new states are too poor and too shaky. It is the middle powers – Canada, Australia, Scandinavia, the Low Countries, possibly Yugoslavia, Turkey, Mexico – who occupy about the right position on the scale of influence and among these Canada has a particular aptitude for experiment. This is partly a question of her internal stresses. By reaching a bi-cultural, bi-lingual solution to the conflicts between her two cultures, she would automatically show how two 'nations' in a single community can enrich each other and not tear the place apart. She would have detached nationalism creatively from the 'nation state' and shown a way forward to the score of states – many of them new – who harbour a number of 'nations' and have found traditional federalism too formalistic a solution. Again, by encouraging the American firms which play so dominant a part in her development to invent genuinely international forms and procedures for their operations – international central direction, for instance, registration with the United Nations, even some taxes paid directly to, say, the I.D.A. – she could nudge the giants towards a creative understanding of what one might call their post-American destiny.

But it is perhaps in her external relations that the greatest opportunities lie. Of all the middle powers, Canada has the greatest resources, the most central position, the finest web of contacts and influence and, relatively speaking, the highest proportion of experts both bilingual and in each language, of any nation in the world. If all these advantages were used not to affirm Canada as a state but to develop Canada as a model-builder, then with the hindsight of history, the latter-day Solons, the creative institution-makers, the citizens who help recreate the world's image of itself might be recognized to have been citizens of Canada and Canada itself an 'Athenian' variation on an Atlantic theme.

However, setting visions aside, one can conclude that the tasks to be accomplished, if planetary society is to escape its present disorder, are already fairly clear. No civilized society can survive without some concept of law and civil power. None can survive without some institutions dedicated to the general welfare. At present, world society, like medieval Europe or China before the Chin dynasty, survives increasingly under a fragile feudal system of countervailing power between the big barons, and when one of them affirms its hold on a restive bailiwick – Czech or Dominican – there is nothing in civilized society to check the violence.

The world half-heartedly recognizes the need for alternatives, United Nations' authority, for instance, special international forces – as in Cyprus or Congo – frontier missions. But no nation or group of nations has made it its main responsibility to think through the implications of these alternatives, to offer men and resources for the building of permanent 'fire brigades' for international incidents or experienced conciliation commissions to get to the root of grievances and establish the framework for popular consultation. Can anyone doubt that a Control Commission in Vietnam strong enough to supervise elections in both zones would have made less of a catastrophic disaster of that unhappy country? As a result of United Nations action, the Congo, for all its troubles, is the only disputed state not to end up with two ideologically competitive governments.

International procedures will not be accepted overnight. But at least some steady responsible governmental voices must be raised, in season and out of season, to underline the need for alternatives, to offer to support them and to reach out to the young, to a new generation less obsessed than the present population with rival creeds or nationalities.

Equally in the field of welfare we know the facts about our hopelessly unbalanced world economy. Sixteen percent of the population (largely North Atlantic) enjoy 75 percent of the wealth and by the year 2000 the other 80 percent or so will reach nearly 6 billion with less than 2 billion in the developed zone. Unless drastic steps are taken in the next ten years to develop their economies and set them in the way of growth, those among the affluent who are now disturbed about discontented youth and ghetto cities today may live to find that more than half the world's peoples are under 25, largely alienated and living in what one could only call 'ghetto-continents'.

The facts are established even if their dangerous implications for global violence are glossed over. And some of the solutions are known as well – to transfer to the world scale some of our national institutions of welfare, to give the effective international agencies the capital needed for development via some such world tax as one percent of GNP, and improve the trade returns of poor nations by a more balanced commercial bargain – stable commodity prices, reverse protection for their manufactured exports, to introduce an element of income maintenance by making any new drawing rights at the I.M.F. available first to the poor nations. All this *can* be done. But there is no popular will or public commitment behind the programme.

Here, once again, Canada, among the wealthiest of the wealthy lands, can take on the task of leadership. It can orient its own policies towards a coherent economic strategy of world growth. It can pioneer research and training in a well-financed and fully bilingual Development Institute. Above all, it can help to form an alliance of middle states, North and South, East and West, to try to move procedures for world welfare and world conciliation from the bottom of the nations' agenda to the prime place that human survival genuinely demands.

It is a truism that one person who wants something is a hundred times stronger than a hundred who want to be left alone. A Canada prepared to pioneer with lucidity and daring the role of the first 'international nation' in history would not only have an immense impact on its fellow states. It might also transform its own political life. It could, conceivably, turn the present rather bored citizen acquiescence in modern politics into something more exciting and active, into participation, into enjoyment, into purpose, even into fun.

[1968]

Claude Julien

Europe's Last Chance

Irritation can inspire a book . . .

Irritation at hearing an academic evoke Maria Chapdelaine while ignoring the fact that one of the world's largest aluminum factories is located at Lac St. Jean, where Louis Hémon placed his sentimental heroine. Irritation at discovering in the Columbia Encyclopedia that Quebecers, however eminent they may be, 'speak a French patois'.

Such ignorance justifies real concern when the Texan in the White House brusquely reprimands the Canadian Prime Minister, holder of the Nobel Peace Prize, for daring to think he had the right to express his opinion on a policy of concern to all Western nations.

To tell the truth, Canada has mismanaged her entry onto the world scene. Since the Second World War, she has multiplied her Gross National Product almost ten times, but the only time a foreigner becomes aware of her existence is when a few firecrackers explode in an English quarter of Montreal. The irreplaceable role which Canada plays in international affairs too often goes unnoticed.

Catholics in France, quite certain that they belong to an avant-garde church, regard Quebec as a highly clerical and comfortably reactionary society. They don't realize that the secularization of Christian labour unions took place in Canada several years before it occurred in France; and they discover with amazement that the position held by the Cardinal Archbishop of Montreal in the Vatican Council overshadowed the most eminent French prelates.

49

The conceit of a certain type of Frenchman is sometimes unintentionally amusing.

It enables them to send a popular scientific journalist across the Atlantic to speak to the best Chalk River atomic scientists about nuclear research; or a large French industrial society to correspond in English with the mayor of Montreal, despite his French name.

But the Frenchman visiting Canada also finds things which annoy him. Conversations with a certain type of English-speaking Canadian provoke in him an irrepressible sympathy for the Quebec separatists. The remedy fortunately is simple: he only need listen to the impassioned speeches of the spokesmen for the most hide-bound Quebec nationalism and he will immediately feel very close to the 'damned English' with all their phlegmatic competence.

But reality is always more complicated than slogans and that is why Canadian society, despite its reputation for inherent boredom, is fascinating to analyse. How is it that two peoples, who have rejected the American melting-pot and who have attempted to live side by side in a bilingual and bicultural society, have come to be estranged from one another, to the point of casting doubt upon the federal pact which has bound them together since 1867? How is it that Quebec has succeeded in breaking down old rural and clerical structures and in rejecting archaic ideas to plunge itself into the world of big business and into the currents of modern thought? Ten years ago it appeared to dread being contaminated by such things. Can English Canada and French Canada, whether they renew their alliance or sue for divorce, avoid becoming satellites of the United States?

These questions do not interest only Canadians. For Canada possesses enormous economic potential which, if it were joined completely to the power of the United States, would prevent equilibrium between the power groups on each side of the Atlantic. Europe would no longer have any hope of making her interests prevail in the Western Alliance.

Absorbed in their linguistic quarrels, Canadians forget to think about this international dimension of their internal problems. Bound up in their own restricted interests, they only tear themselves away from morose introspection to pour invective onto their compatriots who speak the other language. Concerned only with themselves, they occasionally wake up with a start to find that they have fallen a little more deeply under the influence of the United States. But they soon sink back into a kind of torpor, for how could they effectively resist the all-powerful American giant who eats away daily their genuine independence and their true personality? Alone, they can do nothing.

But Canadians must realize that they *are* not and *cannot* be alone. Although the majority of Europeans are unaware of the fact, part of the destiny of Europe, possibly a decisive part, is being worked out in Canada. If this country of 20,000,000 inhabitants, with vast, even unknown economic resources, were to become a 'branch plant' of the United States, then the U.S., even more powerful, would no longer even pretend to treat Europe as an equal power.

It is frustrating to see English and French Canadians exhausting themselves in a struggle which is sterile because it is without global dimensions. But it is also disturbing that so few Europeans have assessed the weight which Canada can bring to bear on their own future.

Even a completely unified Western Europe would be no match for the United States, especially if the U.S. virtually absorbed Canada. In order to safeguard a certain freedom of action, Europe must gain all the support she has at her disposal in Asia, Africa, and America. And Canada occupies a prime position in this policy of expansion because of her natural wealth, her high degree of industrialization, and the ties which link her to Great Britain as well as to France. Europe would be sealing her own fate if she let herself be supplanted by the United States in Africa, if she considered Latin America as the private hunting preserve of the United States, or if she abandoned all initiative in Asia to Washington. In these three spheres of action she can consider Canada as a prime ally, as an indispensable partner because of her human, agricultural, and industrial resources.

It is also essential that Europe should not condemn Canada to meeting on unequal terms the powerful neighbour from which she is separated by the thinnest of frontiers. Only Europe can prevent the economic absorption of Canada by the United States, an absorption which would reduce Ottawa, on the political scene, to no more than a pale reflection of Washington. In return, Canada is the only Western power outside Europe which is capable of maintaining the delicate balance which oscillates from one shore of the Atlantic to the other. If the weight of Canada came to rest on the American side, then this equilibrium would be destroyed. If, however, it came to rest on the European side, then Europe would be given a chance – perhaps its last – of maintaining the balance.

Neither Canada nor Europe is thinking of severing its alliance with the United States. But Canada and Europe are struggling, sometimes successfully, sometimes not, to prevent the relationship freely established by the Atlantic Alliance from reducing them to the rank of vassals. Despite the geographical distance between them, the interests of Canada and Europe are thus closely linked. Divided, each one knowing little about the other, they remain weak and give the alliance no choice but to become a body whose only head is at Washington. United, each one lending strength to the other, they would comprise a two-sided unit which would have flexibility in the face of unknown developments, an aptitude for dialogues which would nourish a fresh vitality.

Canadians should not think badly of a European for examining their internal problems in this light. The grave crisis which overshadows the relations between English and French Canadians is of great interest in itself to the sociologist. It touches the sensitive nerve of a Frenchman who is unable to ignore the fate of these 6,000,000 men on the other side of the Atlantic who speak his language and draw upon his own cultural sources. Their presence and their vitality represent for this language and this culture a precious source of enrichment and diffusion. The Frenchman is also quite interested in seeing whether the French-speaking province of Quebec will choose secession and declare independence or whether it will play an active role in a renovated confederation, establishing communications between the two ethnic groups (on the most equitable grounds possible).

But for Europe the most important thing is to know if Canada is going to let herself be colonized by the United States or whether, reinforcing her ties with Europe, she will be of some assistance in creating a balance between the power of the United States and that of Europe. And, at the risk of hurting the feelings of French Canadians, how can one avoid telling them that if they were absorbed by their English-speaking compatriots, the European problem would still remain unchanged? For 6,000,000 French Canadians have to defend themselves not only against 13,000,000 English Canadians, but more than 200,000,000 English-speaking North Americans. But it is not against the claims of the French-speaking group that English Canadians must defend the unity of Canada. It is against the enormous power of the United States that French and English Canadians together must defend the Canadian identity.

There is no reason why a Frenchman might wish for the disappearance of French-speaking Canada. On the contrary, he delights in finding it lively, strong, and dynamic. But the interest which a Frenchman or a European might find in the eventual independence of Quebec remains purely academic. Whether Quebec secedes or obtains a more satisfactory status in the Canadian confederation; whether the Canadian nation, as a result of the conflict between French and English, disintegrates completely or manages to reconstruct her unity on a sounder basis, there is only one question which presents a real point of interest (for France and Europe): will the resources of the complex ensemble which constitutes Canada be added to those of the United States to increase the influence which they already exert upon Europe, or will they provide the help which Europe needs in order to strike up that kind of dialogue with the United States which is only possible between partners of more or less equal strength? The passion which French Canadians put into the discussion of their problems can be of interest only to themselves so long as they refuse to examine them in this new perspective. The 'separatists' – who wish for the birth of an entirely independent state of Quebec – resort to two arguments in an attempt to give their campaign a world context:

They claim to be participating in the mainstream of postwar colonial independence and compare their struggles with the fight of the peoples of Africa or Asia to achieve national independence. But whatever they say, Quebec is a colony neither of Ottawa nor Washington; and there is no guarantee that political independence will free them from American economic domination.

They proclaim their desire to integrate an independent Quebec with an international French-speaking community, which they even refer to by the curious title: 'French-speaking Commonwealth'. But they forget that, given France's manifest interest in maintaining relations with all French-speaking peoples, these relations alone will not be enough to permit France to play a leading world role in relation to the major powers. It is for this reason that France, looking beyond the narrow circle of French-speaking people, can already count on all those Europeans who express themselves in German, Dutch, or Italian; and it is also for this reason that France and Europe need Canada — the whole of Canada — and Canadians, whether they speak French or English.

In thinking that they can play a part in world affairs, the Quebec separatists show that they have a very poor understanding of them, and that they are not equipped to produce a realistic analysis of the actual balance of power. In fact they are only underlining the narrow provincialism which affects their thinking.

And yet the problems which they have are real, their revolt amply justified. The grave misunderstandings which divide French and English Canadians have reached such virulence that they threaten the very existence of Canada. But this very serious crisis cannot be examined in the restricted focus which has nourished the fallacious arguments of separatism. Will this crisis be the birthplace of a new Canadian society, stronger and more dynamic than before, capable, through its ties with the Commonwealth and with France, of not subsiding under American domination? Or will it destroy a nation, so that the United States will have only to pick up the pieces? It is not only the future of Canada and Canadians that is in question. The result of the crisis either will permit Europe to find in Canada an ally which will help to balance the power of the United States, or it will deprive the older continent of its last chance to escape the total domination of Washington.

[1968]

Ali Mazrui

A Hard Lesson for Africa

The bonds of empathy between countries which are different from each other are sometimes forged not so much by direct diplomatic or social intercourse but by comparability of human situations within their respective countries. A major problem in Canada, as in Africa, is the problem of national integration. The Canadian experience has hard lessons for Africa. One lesson is a simple one that national integration is not necessarily a matter of per capita income. Poverty and economic underdevelopment may indeed aggravate situations of inadequate national cohesion but they are not the primary cause of it except to the most determined economic determinist.

Canada might be described as an underdeveloped advanced country. It is advanced because it has attained high levels of technological and scientific sophistication and has a high standard of living. It is underdeveloped partly because the great potential it has is as yet inadequately tapped and the country is relatively under-populated. But it is also underdeveloped in the integrative sense in that the great cultural and linguistic divide within its population has not only failed to be bridged, but might conceivably be widening. This latter possibility is itself another hard lesson for Africa. It tells us that the integrative process is reversible. Progress made in fusing communities within a particular society might be negated by a sudden relapse affecting the condition of the body politic.

An alternative interpretation of the Canadian situation is to regard it as a lesson in the proposition that stability is not the same thing as national integration. In fact, the two ideals might conflict. There might be peace and

54

tranquility in a plural society where very limited integration has as yet taken place. And the stability might be shattered precisely at the moment that progress is being made to promote greater intercourse between communities. National integration, like other aspects of political development, can all too easily be disruptive. The Canadian policy might be less stable today than it was a decade ago precisely because a greater degree of integration is being achieved between cultural groups.

As Africa experiences the agonies of national construction, the Canadian example is both a hope and a warning. At the domestic level within each African country, the Canadian situation bears comparability to African ethnicity and tribal tensions. At the Pan-African level, Canada is suggestive of the continuing intellectual divide between Anglophone and Francophone Africa.

As for the position in foreign policy, Canada sometimes seems to be the Yugoslavia of the West – committed to a cause, yet always seeking to retain independence in spite of the cause.

In fact, Canada has gone further than Yugoslavia. The latter is communist in ideological conviction, and yet nonaligned in foreign policy. Canada is liberal-capitalist in ideological conviction, aligned in a formal sense with the West, and yet somehow constantly struggling to fulfil a spirit of intellectual autonomy which goes back to the grand precedent of her independence within the Commonwealth.

Perhaps the delicate balance of her bi-culturalism is the best guarantee Canada has for the survival of her intellectual autonomy in the years ahead.

[1968]

Richard Crossman

Letting People Be Different

I find Canadian politics more interesting, more fruitful, and more creative than the politics of almost any country I have studied, because it is so wonderfully varied, because it is plural. Britain, as you know, is a highly homogeneous, centralized country. There are Irishmen and there are Welshmen (but we lost out with the Irish; they got away), with whom we have had wars, but despite this we have kept a centralized homogeneous state. We are about as bad at dealing with pluralism as any nation in the world, so I can talk freely about it. In Canada I find an area which grows naturally. Unlike the United States, it does not seek to take everybody and formalize them into a united, conformist pattern. It allows people to be themselves, to be different. Canada allows provincial governments to go off into the most extraordinary heresies, heresies it of course forbids in the federal parliament as far as possible. I therefore find federal government a bit boring, but provincial government is absolutely fascinating. One travels across Canada through different kinds of government, different kinds of people expressing themselves in different ways and allowed to do so and encouraged to do so, having ideas which, expressed locally in this way, impinge on the nation so that the nation can draw from local experiments for its central planning. It is a wonderful richness and a wonderful variety. Now, I put it to you, is there not something in this provincial variety which should enable one to deal with the problem of French Canada less badly than other people have done? Of course, you can tell me this is not relevant; it is simply between English-speaking and French Canadians, and the only solution will be for the English-speaking to gang up together in fear. All I can tell you is

56

my suspicion that if that happens it is one certain way of making the problem insoluble. But I would hope that in treating this problem – which is the problem of your constitution, of your democracy, of good, ordered government – of Quebec vis-à-vis the rest of the community, you have a chance of success if you look at your variety, at your pluralism, and if you revel in your virtues.

[1964]

Edmund Wilson

A Turgenev?
In Toronto?

The Canadian Morley Callaghan, at one time well known in the United States, is today perhaps the most unjustly neglected novelist in the English-speaking world. In his youth, he worked on the Toronto *Star* – Toronto is his native city – at the time when Ernest Hemingway had a job on the same paper, and, through Hemingway, who took his manuscripts to Paris, some of Callaghan's early short stories were accepted by Ezra Pound for his little magazine *Exile*. Maxwell Perkins of Scribner's was impressed by these stories and had them reprinted in *Scribner's Magazine,* which later published other stories by Callaghan. His novels were published by Scribner's. Morley Callaghan was a friend of Fitzgerald and Hemingway and was praised by Ring Lardner, and he belonged to the literary scene of the twenties. He appeared in *transition* as well as in *Scribner's* and he spent a good deal of his time in Paris and the United States. But eventually he went back to Canada, and it is one of the most striking signs of the partial isolation of that country from the rest of the cultural world that – in spite of the fact that his stories continued to appear in the *New Yorker* up to the end of the thirties – he should quickly have been forgotten in the United States and should be almost unknown in England. Several summers ago, on a visit to Toronto, I had given me a copy of the Canadian edition of a novel of his called *The Loved and the Lost*. It seemed to me so remarkable that I expected it to attract attention in England and the United States. But it was never published in England, and it received so little notice in the United States that I imagined it had not been published here either. I found that when I talked about Callaghan, such people as remembered his existence were likely to think he was dead. When I checked, I discovered that the book *had* been published here without ever having been adequately reviewed, but that it had later sold well in paperback. A volume of Morley Callaghan's collected short stories was published last year in Toronto but not in the United States or England. This season a new novel by him – *The Many Colored Coat* – has been brought out simultaneously in Canada and in New York.

I want to talk in this review about both these two novels of Callaghan's – I have read only one of his earlier books – and to speculate first on the reasons for the current indifference to his work. This has no doubt been partly due to the peculiar relation of Canada to England and the United States. The Canadian background of Morley Callaghan's stories seems alien to both these other countries and at the same time not strange enough to exercise the spell of the truly exotic. To the reviewer, this background has much interest and charm. Montreal, with its snow-dazzling mountain, its passionate winter sports, its hearty and busy bars, its jealously guarded French culture, and its pealing of bells from French churches, side by side with the solid Presbyterianism of its Anglo-Scottish best people, is a world I find it pleasant to explore. It is curious to see how much this world has been influenced – in its language, in its amusements, its press – by the 'Americans', as they still call us, and how far – in, for example, its parliamentary politics and its social and moral codes – it rests on somewhat different foundations. But Mr. Callaghan is not writing about Canada at all from the point of view of exploiting its regional characteristics. In the second of these two novels, he does not even tell the reader that the scene of the story is Montreal. The landscapes, the streets and the houses, the atmosphere of the various milieux are known intimately and sensitively observed, but they are made to figure quite unobtrusively; there are no very long descriptions and nothing like 'documentation'. We simply find ourselves living with the characters and taking for granted, as they do, their habits and customs and assumptions, their near-Arctic climate and their split nationality. Still less is Mr. Callaghan occupied with specifically Canadian problems. The new and militant Canadian nationalism – in these novels, at least – does not touch him; he is not here concerned with the question of 'what it means to be a Canadian'. And the result of this has been, I believe, that a public, both here and in England, whose taste in American fiction seems to have been largely whetted by the perpetrators of violent scenes – and these include some of our best writers as well as our worst – does not find itself at home with, does not really comprehend, the more sober effects of Callaghan. In his novels one finds acts of violence and a certain amount of sensuality, but these are not used for melodrama or even for 'symbolic' fables of the kind that is at present fashionable. There are no love stories that follow an expected course, not even any among those I have read that eventually come out all right. It is impossible to imagine these books transposed into any kind of terms that would make them acceptable to Hollywood.

The novels of Morley Callaghan do not deal, then, with his native Canada in any editorial or informative way, nor are they aimed at any popular taste, Canadian, 'American' or British. They center on situations of primarily psychological interest that are treated from a moral point of view yet without making moral judgments of any conventional kind, and it is in consequence peculiarly difficult to convey the implications of one of these books by attempting to retell its story. The revelation of personality, of tacit conflict, of reciprocal emotion is conducted in so subtle a way that we are never quite certain what the characters are up to – they are often not certain themselves – or what the upshot of their relationships will be.

In the earlier of the two novels under discussion, *The Loved and the Lost* (not, perhaps, a very happy title), an eccentric but attractive young girl who exerts a mysterious spiritual charm, the daughter of a minister who has lost his faith, has become – as the result of a girlhood association, particularly warm and close, with the one colored family in her neighborhood – much addicted to the society of Negroes. After graduating from college in Montreal, she continues to live in that city, and goes often to a Negro night club, at which she becomes so well known to the customers and the management both that they regard her as a part of the establishment. This arouses the suspicions of her white employers and eventually makes her Negro friends uncomfortable. The former assume that she has Negro lovers and decide not to keep her on, and the latter do not know what to make of her. She evidently – though we are never told explicitly – does not sleep with either her white or her colored admirers, but she inevitably, though unintentionally, causes trouble in this little Negro world by exciting, through the fascination she exercises, the jealousies of the whites against the Negroes and of the Negroes among themselves. In the meantime, she is kind and generous to Negroes and whites alike, except when someone tries to deflect her from what is bound to appear to her non-colored friends an unsuitable mode of life, and both feel that they get from her something which is not of the conventional world and which either, with finer natures, inspires a devoted if disquieted respect or, with grosser ones, spurs them to 'possess' her and thus to get the better of something that challenges and teases and balks them without their understanding why. Having lost all her office jobs – to the scandal of her educated acquaintances – she is reduced to working in a factory, which, however, she seems not in the least to mind. She is actually a kind of saint, and yet nothing is more admirable in the novel than the way in which Mr. Callaghan never lapses into mysticism or sentimentality but always makes her a believable girl. Her way of talking, her way of dressing, her involuntary reactions to people are always of the human world, and she has moments, when lectured or importuned, of something approaching bitchiness. The reasons for her puzzling behavior are in one sense sufficiently accounted for by her first having experienced, in girlhood, a feeling of sexual ecstasy at the sight of a nude Negro boy. But this feeling had come to her, she says, as a sudden and sharp realization that 'beauty could be painful in a strange way', and one assumes that there has always been a barrier – from a kind of noble purity, apparently, as much as if not more than from racial inhibition – that has kept her from any more intimate contact. She is one of those virginal women, independent and idealistic, who elicit a wondering awe yet who pique the ego of others. The whole story is told from the point of view of a young university professor, Jim McAlpine, who has not wanted to fall in love with her but who finds that he cannot keep away from her and has been trying to make her extricate herself from the dangerous anomalies of her life yet who cannot quite understand her and is himself never able to rid himself of the suspicions of deceit and depravity that she inspires in her other acquaintances. The point is that none of these people can rise to the level of believing that such a person as she exists. In the end, a nasty brawl in the night club is provoked by her presence there, and she is raped and strangled that night by a white man who has been laying siege to her, who has set off the brawl in the night club by his brutal advances in public and who has been badly beaten up by the Negroes.

In the other of these novels, *The Many Colored Coat,* a young man named Harry Lane, personable, able and popular, and on the edge of Montreal's upper crust, has proved a spectacular success in a public relations job for a Canadian whisky distiller. He forms a friendship that to some seems incongruous with an amiable but very middle-class bank manager whose quietness and modesty and apparent good sense the young man finds reassuring in contrast to the company of those whom he is constantly, in the line of business, gladhanding and entertaining. But this middle-aged man, who seems sound and wise, is to become in his turn so beglamored by the handsome and delightful Harry that he cannot help desiring for himself a little more of the freedom of Harry's world and for his son some of Harry's advantages. An old friend of Harry's turns up, who, out of gratitude for former kindness, has made him a present of some 'Western Oil' stock. Now that a drilling is about to take place, the shares will be immensely valuable, and he will sell him some more at a dollar apiece. The manager offers Harry a loan from the bank and succeeds in putting it through, but only by misrepresenting – though Harry does not know this – the amount of his friend's security, which consists of the shares he already owns; then, rather to Harry's surprise, he asks for a slice of the stock in return for negotiating the loan. He hopes, of course, to make good the difference between the fraudulent figure and the real one from the profits to accrue from the stock. But 'Western Oil' now turns out to be worthless, and the manager is sent to jail. He kills himself in prison without having let it be known that it was he who proposed the loan and that he wanted some of the stock for himself, leaving Harry to bear the odium of having ruined the much-respected banker by inducing him to commit a fraud. Not to be liked is for Harry intolerable; it completely throws him off his base and makes him unexpectedly vindictive. But this does not help the situation. He suffers the fate of Joseph, who has been envied by his brethren for his many-colored coat – that is, for his popularity, his easy superiority. His old companions put him in Coventry, and in his vehemence to assert his innocence, to avenge himself on the dead man who has wronged him, he is carried to grotesque and almost lunatic lengths. He becomes such an obnoxious character that he can no longer have any value as a public-relations man, and his boss has to let him go. He has started a feud with a tailor, an ex-pugilist friend of the bank manager's who has always distrusted Harry and who, at the trial, has given testimony against him which, though based on a conversation misunderstood, has convinced the jury of Harry's guilt. They finally come to blows in a restaurant, and it is only when Harry, badly injured, is beginning to clear up in a hospital that he knows he has behaved ignobly. The author seems to leave him at the moment just before he is to wake to the horror of realizing that he himself, through the falsity and fatuity of his previous life, has actually shared in the guilt of his friend and let him in for his sordid disaster. The ex-pugilist, brought again into court to answer for his assault on Harry, now confesses quite gratuitously and to the horror of his lawyer that he had never really known what had happened between Harry and his friend the bank manager and that he had never had the right to judge Harry.

The danger in retelling the story of this remarkable novel is that the subject may sound so unpromising that one cannot succeed in suggesting the interest which Mr. Callaghan has made it generate. These stories are extremely well told. The details, neither stereotyped nor clever – the casual gestures of the characters, the little incidents that have no direct bearing on their purposes or their actions, the people they see in restaurants or pass on the street – have a naturalness that gives the illusion of not having been invented, of that seeming irrelevance of life that is still somehow inextricably relevant. The narrative moves quietly but rapidly, and Mr. Callaghan is a master of suspense. The first hundred pages of *The Many Colored Coat* are an excellent example of this. Nothing overtly exciting occurs; the characters – though with quietly changing relationships – seem to be following the routines of normal lives, yet you know you are approaching a climax without ever having been given a hint of what this climax is going to be. The style is very clear and spare, sometimes a bit commonplace, but always intent on its purpose, always making exactly its points so that these novels are as different as possible from the contemporary bagful of words that forms the substance of so many current American books which are nevertheless taken seriously. (The one conspicuous lapse from this standard in *The Many Colored Coat* is page 208, on which 'husky' or 'huskily' occurs three times, having previously occurred just before, on page 205, in the same general context, and on which you find the following somewhat cockeyed sentence: 'This time she was like herself as they had known her in her good days and those deep warm erotic notes came out huskily and exultant, one shoulder strap falling off, and she went on singing, her face aglow with pride and happiness, letting them see she could have sung all night.' It may happen with even a very careful writer who scrupulously rewrites and revises that there is always some page or passage which he slights – whether because it deals with something that bores him or because he knows it isn't right but doesn't know how to correct it or because of some personal anxiety which afflicted him at the time of writing and of which he shrinks from being reminded.) Mr. Callaghan's underplaying of drama and the unemphatic tone of his style are accompanied by a certain grayness of atmosphere, but this might also be said of Chekhov, whose short stories his sometimes resemble.

These books, so unconventional in subject, are at the same time expertly 'plotted'. The motivations are handled with such delicacy that one hesitates to say there are moments when this plotting seems a little contrived. Both the novels involve young men as to whom it is assumed at the beginning that they are going to marry young girls – more or less sympathetic and intelligent – of the Anglicizing upper class. In each case, this central young man is to become completely demoralized and irremediably alienated from his fiancée by something that comes from outside that class and eventually excludes him from it. McAlpine in *The Loved and the Lost* falls in love with the offbeat girl; Harry Lane in *The Many Colored Coat* is derailed by his friendship with the bank manager. Both are left adrift, almost friendless, wandering about in the streets, alone with their guilty misgivings, which it will take them a long time to allay. But the reader is troubled a little, in connection with certain turns of the narrative, by the feeling that the author has given a push to land these unreliable young men in their miserable situations. One finds it rather hard to believe that McAlpine would have left his frightened girl alone and unprotected in her room. After the ugly affair in the night club, he had, to be sure, very honorable reasons for not wanting, under the circumstances, to make love to the girl that night, when she was willing for the first time, apparently, to surrender herself to him, but he had previously seen somebody prowling about and it was obvious that she needed to be reassured. Should he not have been aware of the danger and spent the night in her room? In the case of the downfall of Harry Lane, it hardly seems probable that his fellow-townsmen – almost, it seems, to a man – should have been ready to believe the worst of him.

But one's tendency, in writing of these novels, to speak of what the characters 'should have' done is a proof of the extraordinary effect of reality which – by simply presenting their behavior – Mr. Callaghan succeeds in producing. His people, though the dramas they enact have more than individual significance, are never allowed to appear as anything other than individuals. They never become types or abstractions, nor do they ever loom larger than life. They are never removed from our common humanity, and there is never any simple opposition of beautiful and horrible, of lofty and base. The tragedies in these two books are the results of the interactions of the weaknesses and strengths of several characters, none of whom is either entirely responsible or entirely without responsibility for the outcome that concerns them all. But in order to describe these books properly, one must explain that the central element in them, the spirit that pervades the whole, is deeply if undogmatically Christian. Though they depend on no scaffolding of theology, though they embody an original vision, they have evidently somewhere behind them the tradition of the Catholic Church. This is not the acquired doctrine of the self-conscious Catholic convert – of Graham Greene or Evelyn Waugh. One is scarcely aware of doctrine; what one finds is, rather, an intuitive sense of the meaning of Christianity. An earlier novel, *Such Is My Beloved,* which was first published in 1934 and has now been reprinted in paperback, deals with a Catholic priest who both undercuts and transcends the official level of his Church – in his unworldliness, he has something in common with the girl of *The Loved and the Lost* – and who, making a certain genuine if precarious connection with the sinners he wishes to befriend but becoming an embarrassment to his bishop, is reprimanded by this superior and alienated from the objects of his solicitude: two prostitutes, who are forced to leave town. Thus cruelly driven in on himself, he loses all contact with reality, or what the world considers reality, and is sent to a mental institution, where, in his madness, he seems to touch sanctity. So the keynote of *The Many Colored Coat* is sounded by a Catholic priest – in the only scene in which he appears – who attempts, without any success, to convey to the indignant Harry Lane that his behavior is dictated by spiritual pride. But in these two most recent novels of Callaghan's, this sense of Christian moral values is introduced even more unobtrusively than the Canadian climate and landscape and the true motivations of the characters.

The reviewer, at the end of this article, after trying to give an account of these books, is now wondering whether the primary reason for the current underestimation of Morley Callaghan may not be simply a general incapacity – apparently shared by his compatriots – for believing that a writer whose work may be mentioned without absurdity in association with Chekhov's and Turgenev's can possibly be functioning in Toronto.

[November 26, 1960]

1964. Since writing the above article, I have read the rest of Callaghan's early novels, and I find that the theme of unacknowledged guilt, which figures in *The Many Colored Coat,* is central to several of them. It already appears in *Strange Fugitive* (1928), the first of his full-length fictions. This original and very curious, though unsatisfactory, book – said to be the first of the gangster novels – is the story of Harry Trotter, an almost amoeba-like creature, who, losing his job in a lumber yard and unable to find another which will give him the authority he craves, drifts along for a time, doing nothing, as he dreams of a position of power. His only way of satisfying this thirst is by an obsessional compulsion to play checkers, at which he knows he can beat his wife and friends. At one time he haunts labor meetings and sees himself as a leader but the cause of labor does not touch him. He aimlessly abandons his wife, who feels a need, unintelligible to him, of supplementing her meager life by recourse to the Catholic Church, and takes up with a woman who asks nothing of him because she sleeps with everyone else as well. Then, one evening, when walking with a friend, he sees a bootleg truck being unloaded and is seized by an impulse to hijack it. He succeeds, and he and the friend go into the bootleg business and engage in gangster wars with their rivals. Harry is quite unscrupulous and seems indifferent to the cruelty of his crimes. After murdering one of these rivals, he makes a point of attending the funeral and expressing his sympathy to the widow. But he then makes a pilgrimage to his mother's grave and has a huge and costly stone erected on it. Then he gives a gigantic dinner, which is the great high point of his life, at which everybody dances and gets drunk and which gives him immense satisfaction, for he feels that he is now a big shot. Yet he knows that he is suspected by the murdered man's friends and, after an ominous interview with them, moved apparently by a yearning for affection, he calls up his deserted wife. But he is never to see her again, for, going out with two of his pals, they are mowed down by sawed-off shot-guns. *Strange Fugitive* fails to convince because, in spite of Harry's turning to his wife and mother, he is never made sufficiently attaching, he is given no moral life. In spite of his monument to his mother, he is never actually shown either as suffering from qualms of conscience or as attempting to justify himself. The external world in which Harry moves is accurately described in detail, but he seems to be walking through it in his sleep. What the author is trying to do is present one of the lower forms of human life as, in the words of Professor F. W. Watt of Toronto University, 'a kind of automaton, unable to express himself, scarcely conscious of the passions and social forces that mold and impel him'. But we feel that it is impossible for Morley Callaghan really to imagine such a man. He cannot put himself in Harry's skin.

It is therefore a little surprising to find Mr. Callaghan returning to this theme – in his fourth novel, *They Shall Inherit the Earth* (1935) – in terms of a more complex and civilized world. Michael Aikenhead, a young civil engineer, who resents his father's second marriage, motivated by hateful jealousy, allows his stepbrother to drown and when his father comes under suspicion of having made away with the boy, who has been a great nuisance to everybody, he does nothing to correct this rumor, which is spoiling the reputation of the advertising agency for which the elder Aikenhead works and which eventually costs the latter his job. The perversity and callousness of Michael's behavior, as he goes on with his own career, his unwillingness not merely to exonerate his father but to admit to himself what he is doing, is perhaps, in such a relatively civilized man as Michael is supposed to be, even more unconvincing than Harry Trotter's insensibility to his crimes and cannot but undermine the reader's interest in an otherwise rather interesting book, which deals with Canadian life in a somewhat more various way than the author's previous novels. In between these two novels, however, the author had written another – *It's Never Over* (1930) – in which the same theme, though, perhaps, even here the story seems a little forced, is exploited in a more telling way. John Hughes, out of moral cowardice, drops a girl who is very much in love with him and whom in the normal course of things he would undoubtedly have married, because her brother, a friend of his, has been found guilty of murder and hanged. This hot-tempered friend, after serving in the war, had killed a policeman who slugged him in a speakeasy raid by crashing a chair over his head. Hughes now has an affair with a girl who has been in love with the friend and is obliged at the same time to look on at the ostracism and desperate decline of the sister. His continued association with the sister of a man who has been hanged is to lead on one occasion to her coming to see him in his lodgings, and this, when the story gets around, to the scandal of Toronto respectability, results in his being dismissed from the job in a church choir on which his livelihood has mainly depended. The fatal invisible weakness which, in so many of Callaghan's novels, is made to flaw the central character, which in this case has made John Hughes fail in loyalty, gives rise to worse and worse situations, and in the course of this he becomes demoralized to a degree which reduces him to a level far below that of the more primitive friend who had unintentionally killed a policeman. The fate of the girl he has so badly treated becomes for him a constant reproach, an accusation he cannot face; and his suppressed bad conscience is made more acute, in one of the book's best scenes, by a talk with the priest, half-drunk, who had had to officiate at the hanging and who is still deeply troubled by this. John Hughes now becomes obsessed with the delusion that it is the girl who is destroying *him*, and in his mania he is driven to decide that his only course now is to kill her. He is only prevented from doing so by the discovery that she is dying of pneumonia – which, however, leaves him little less guilty, since he himself, by his behavior toward her, has been the primary agent of her moral collapse. In *Strange Fugitive*, the local descriptions appear to be disproportionate and extraneous to the human situation. But here the rather grim environment of a Toronto intimately lived – the frozen streets, the moonlight on garage roofs, the snow slanting in from the black lake, the cathedral with its lighted cross, the brown hedge and the cinder path of the cemetery above the ravine–are not allowed to become monotonous but are made most effectively to merge with the uncomfortable personal relations, the insoluble emotional problems, the stifled guilt that at last takes possession in the dark lie of an insane fixation.

This condensation of a local atmosphere is very much less in evidence in Morley Callaghan's later books, where the locality is taken for granted and only very lightly sketched in. But it is a feature of *The Varsity Story* of 1948. This story is unique among Callaghan's books. It is the only one of his works in which the main subject is a local institution: the University of Toronto. One imagines that it was written in response to some suggestion on the part of the University itself, of which Mr. Callaghan is a graduate. It seems clear that he had wished, affectionately, at the same time to criticize and to celebrate. In order to accomplish this, he invents for his real university an imaginary president from New Zealand, who is at first rather contemptuous of Toronto: 'Pictures like this one [a landscape painting] had built up his expectations of the country. He had dreamed of brooding northern landscapes. That first summertime he had gone on a fishing trip to the north shore of Lake Superior and there in the blue Algoma hills had looked upon this sombre operatic country and felt its remote loneliness, and had seen the great hills rising like cathedrals against the slashes of light made by the setting sun. In the loneliness he had found grandeur. The whole countryside, the northland, the prairies, the deep rivers, accentuated in his mind his belief that in such a land and among its people there would be a poetry, a wildness or a harsh strength. He had seemed to hear the music of Sibelius. Even the extremes of climate, the unbearably hot summers and the fiercely cold winters, suggested an extreme of character in the people, a vigour, a passion. But in this city and at this university he had felt only a dismal lack of passion. Even among the students who should be so alive and so open to intellectual stimulation, and among the Faculty men, too, he had found a peculiar mildness and a lack of true affability and charm. As a city Toronto had a reticent coldness. In other Ontario towns and in the West they jeered at Toronto. But he had soon learned that many of these places were simply smaller Torontos. The more bitterly they mocked at Toronto the more conscious they seemed to be that the Toronto spirit was a skeleton hidden in their own closets.'

But as the New Zealander gets to know the place better, he comes to find it more interesting and sympathetic; yet is puzzled at not being able to discover what kind of ideals the University represents, what general purpose it proposes to serve. The point is that the University of Toronto differs from our universities in the United States in being composed of a number of colleges which are dominated by different faiths and different points of view. There is a Catholic college, St. Michael's; an Anglican college, Trinity; an Evangelical college, Victoria; a non-denominational humanities college, University; and a School of Practical Science. The new president finds this confusing and cannot pin the professors down to any clear definition of what they are trying to do; but he finally comes to the conclusion that this cluster of colleges, which are dedicated to often mutually exclusive ideas, are the facets of 'a giant crystal', each of which is 'an aspect of the truth', which together, for the poet or philosopher, may contribute to some larger comprehension of life. This crystal is made to take shape among the gray skies and stones of Toronto, among its fogs, snows and drizzling rains, through which the facets glint and which are invested, not as in *It's Never Over* with the malaise of a coming horror, but with the dignity of human strivings. It is rather impressive evidence of Morley Callaghan's power as an artist that, in a book undertaken, apparently, for a definite practical purpose, he is able to perform this feat.

My further reading of Callaghan's novels has suggested another reason from the one proposed in my article for their relative unpopularity. Almost all of them end in annihilating violence or, more often, in blank unfulfilment. The bootlegger of *Strange Fugitive* is left riddled and dying in the street; the

ex-convict of *More Joy in Heaven,* who has been doing his best to go straight but
has found himself unable to free himself from his old underworld connections,
shoots a policeman and is shot by the police. John Hughes of *It's Never Over,*
who has shabbily abandoned one girl, becomes eventually odious to the other
and is dismissed by her without much sympathy: 'It was such a cold wind it was
more important Lillian should not miss the car than that they should go on
talking.' John still has his serviceable voice but he does not know how to use it:
he only knows that he must go somewhere else; and Sam Raymond, in *A
Passion in Rome* (1961), who, discarded by the nightclub singer whom he has
rescued from alcoholism and established as a star attraction, can only hope to
make up for the failure of his early aspirations as a painter by also going
somewhere else and becoming a top photographer – an ambition in which the
reader has no confidence that he will succeed. Marion Gibbons, in *A Broken
Journey,* who is supposed to be highly sexed, feels constrained to renounce her
two lovers, and leaves one of them lying half-paralyzed among the wilds of a
northern lake. He has, to be sure, a sympathetic brother who will look after him,
perhaps get him back to civilization, but one is not left with any suggestion as
to what will become of either of them. The young professor of *The Loved and
the Lost,* who had failed to stay with Peggy Sanders on the night when she was
raped and strangled, is seen in the last pages desolately tramping the streets as
he looks for a little church, from which he hopes for some consolation but
which he is not able to find; the ex-publicity man of *The Many Colored Coat* is
also left roaming the streets with no discernible future. In fact, the little
drawing on the title page of *The Loved and the Lost* of a man in an overcoat,
with his head bowed and his shoulders hunched, walking past a café in a
snowstorm, might serve as a frontispiece for a number of Callaghan's novels.
Even President Tyndall of *The Varsity Story,* after a public affirmation of faith
in the value of the University, on the eve of his departure for the war, is – it
seems to one, quite unnecessarily – made to fall a victim to the Toronto winter
and be prostrated with an influenza which the doctor fears may turn to
pneumonia and from which the reader is sure that this good man will not
recover. The only positive ending in these novels is that of *They Shall Inherit
the Earth,* in which the sinner expiates his sin, under the influence of his
lower-class Ukrainian wife, one of the meek who shall inherit the earth, by
confessing it to his father and restoring their broken relations. As for the saints
or near-saints of these novels, the too-innocent priest of *Such Is My Beloved* is
consigned to an insane asylum, and the Negro-haunting heroine of *The Loved
and the Lost* is headed for her own destruction. All these endings have their
moral point: recognition of personal guilt, loyalty in personal relationships, the
nobility of some reckless devotion to a Christian ideal of love which is bound to
come to grief in the world. But they are probably too bleak for the ordinary
reader, who may already have been disconcerted by beginning what seems to be
an ordinary novel – a love story that does not go quite smoothly but which one
does not expect to be wrecked or the story of a sympathetic sinner who in the

end ought to be redeemed – and then finding that there is something not just temporarily but fundamentally and permanently wrong and that matters are getting out of hand, with no hope of escaping disaster. But only a very sober, self-disciplined and 'self-directed' writer could have persisted, from decade to decade, in submitting these parables to the public. They are almost invariably tragic, but their tragedy avoids convulsions and it allows itself no outbreak in tirades.

[1964]

Ronald Bryden

How To Live on the Margin

The first piece of Commonwealth literature I read, I now consider, was a letter addressed to Jennifer, the advice-to-the-lovelorn columnist on the Trinidad newspaper where I worked as a sub my first year out of school. 'Jennifer', a pretty Guianese divorcée whose own love-life certainly seemed triumphantly unlorn (it was autumn 1945 and the island was full of British and American naval officers hanging about to be demobbed), had gone on a week's holiday to Barbados, and our features editor had dumped the column on me. I must have shown my outrage, for he relented enough to offer, smiling gloomily, his help with any problems beyond my experience. I took the letter straight to him. The writer sought Jennifer's advice about her 'fiancé', a taxi-driver with whom she had lived for four years and borne two children. He had found another woman, made her pregnant and brought her home to their two-roomed house. The woman was foul-mouthed and harsh to the children, and the man demanded that she be cooked for. 'Oh God tell me what to do,' the letter ended, 'for I shame in front of my children till I feel I would kill myself.'

It was a familiar situation in an island of minimal housing and the common-law unions customary in the West Indies since the days when slaves were forbidden to marry, lest it check their breeding. I had never had its anguish brought home to me; the letter did so. I handed it to the features editor dumbly, pale with shock and appeal. 'We can't use that,' he said, glancing over it. 'If there's nothing else in the post, get one of the girls to dig through the syndicated fashion stuff and recipes. Cook up some query about original ideas

70

for a Christmas wedding, the section could use something seasonal. Brides-maids in red, perhaps, with holly in their hair.'

I should have kept the letter and printed it in the little Sunday magazine section I was later given to edit. Its purpose, said a neat box on the front of the first issue, was to encourage West Indian writing, and indeed we managed to publish each week, among the crosswords, horoscopes, and articles about English actresses which we bought from the Beaverbrook papers, a short story contributed by a local author. Several were submitted by a gaunt young Guianese who used to lounge around the office in a pale green sports shirt chatting up the secretaries. They were lurid fantasies about the Guianese hinterland, full of murders, incest, and adjectives. They had a certain comic-strip compulsion, but one forgot them the moment one finished them, as one usually forgot how to spell his name, Edgar Mittelholzer. It wasn't until *A Morning at the Office* appeared that I realized he could write, and why he'd spent so much time lounging on our desks.

I dreamed of discovering a great natural writer, and did so. He was a Tobago schoolmaster who sent in a brilliant little sketch about a pig who got into the village church at night and convinced the entire population it was a ghost. It caught the villagers' speech and humour perfectly, and was vivid, riotous, and not a word too long. I wrote enthusiastically asking for more, and received a heavy envelope by return of post. It was packed with stories about the pirates – Teach, Morgan, and the like – who had cruised Tobago's coast in the seventeenth century. They were all swordplay and ornate oaths; their charac-ters never spoke, they quoth; they were dignified, carefully written and totally dead. I coaxed one or two more village sketches out of him, but he preferred Teach.

At the end of the year, I left for Canada to read English at Toronto University. There, confronted for the first time with the need to think why I liked books instead of just liking them, I began to see what had been wrong with the West Indian writing I encountered. It sounded as if it had been written somewhere else, a long way away. It made the hinterlands of the Guianas sound like darkest Africa, instead of a short flight inland from the busy, dirty streets of Georgetown. It made the old French houses of Port of Spain sound, not as if we walked under their scrawny iron balconies every day, but like something we'd once seen on a tourist-folder. It refused to deal with the things which interested us. It tried to isolate the things which (we hoped) might make us interesting to people living in London, Paris, or New York.

It was the same thing which was wrong with most of the Canadian writing I now met. The classics of Canadian literature, it turned out, were all about trappers, settlers, frozen wastes, and the great bleak North. No one I ever met in Canada had ever been in the North. The enormous majority of my friends, the enormous majority of Canadians, lived in sprawling neon-lit cities indis-tinguishable from the sprawling neon-lit cities a few miles the other side of the United States border. But Canadian poetry, like Canadian painting, seemed to be all about blazing sumachs in the autumn wilderness, the great geological ribs of the northern tundra. Canadian novels tended to be historical, or else about stark, Gothic immigrants and their wives going mad on prairie farms. The difference was that Canadians, wry, well-educated and world-minded, knew this about their literature and laughed at it. There was a fine, subterranean corpus of obscene parody of Robert Service, and a lot of excellent satire, descending from Stephen Leacock, on the national cults of gaunt homestead and hirsute northland. But the humour was as provincial as the official romanticism. Naive Canadian writers tried to prove there was something uniquely interesting in Canada. Sophisticated ones confessed, with a defeated smile, that there was nothing interesting about Canada at all.

I once went to listen to a lecture on Canadian drama by Robertson Davies, the bearded Ontario wit who had then written half of it. Shrewdly, he declared that the greatest dramatist of Canadian life was Chekhov. 'I'm going home to write a play,' the girl I'd taken declared afterwards, 'about three spinster sisters on an Ontario peach-farm who spend their lives dreaming of going to Toronto. Only the end will be more Chekhov than Chekhov – I'll let them get there!'

I know all this is a commonplace now in talking about colonial literatures. Everyone agrees in reviling the bad old days when Commonwealth writers wrote as if their aim were to please and impress an English examiner several thousand miles away, falsifying their perspective to suggest a metropolitan one, desperately trying to prove that they possessed not only all the amenities and sophistications any one else had, but something specially and uniquely exotic of their own. I bring up my experience of it only because I've never been convinced that the revulsion has dealt with the real problem involved. Both Canada and the West Indies have now produced writers of world importance, but for their cultures in general the problem stands – and it is one which British literature may also face shortly.

Our trouble was that we wrote on the margins of history, trying to visualize ourselves from history's centre. We wanted to see ourselves with the eye of history, and at the time this happened to be the eye of an English schoolmaster. I don't think this is an impulse which can be brushed under the carpet of nationalism. History does have centres which shift from age to age, and one's position in respect of them is part of one's reality, one's relevance and literary vision. Mass communications have made the world more provincial, not less so, and increased the difficulty of writing in a province without falling into the self-deprecation or over-compensation which has been the defeating distortion of colonial literature. Even as good a writer as George Lamming is capable of juggling West Indian speech so as to claim for it the rhythms and richness of Shakespeare's and Hardy's choruses. Even so fine a poet as James Reaney can raddle the drab hues of Canadian rural life in order to find in it values as statuesque or Jacobean as those in Eugene O'Neill and Tennessee Williams. The pressures are great to wear holly in one's hair.

How does one live on the margins of the world yet make one's imagination the centre of it as a writer must do? Probably the answer is first to recognize and accept the problem — I find it no accident that the profoundest discussion of this has come from the one really great writer the West Indies have produced, in V. S. Naipaul's *The Middle Passage*. West Indians often complain that Naipaul 'looks down' on his compatriots. I'd say myself that the author of *A House for Mr. Biswas* was one of the tiny handful of Commonwealth writers — Dan Jacobson, Derek Walcott, Hugh MacLennan, a few others — who have accepted that one may be provincial yet central to one's world; that there is a private self beyond the one whose 'interest' and relevance are defined by history, and that the war of these two is a major theme for modern literature. Provincialism is a deprivation; recognized, it becomes tragic — as Chekhov saw so early, a general and increasing tragedy of our time — and the democratic miracle of tragedy is that it can make any man the centre of the world.

To admit deprivation is the first step toward claiming equality of opportunity, a possible equality of fulfilment. The writer on the margins who pretends that his culture is self-sufficient, rich and flavoursome cuts himself off from any real connection with history, any international validity for his work, by denying the shape of the world as it is today. It is a world centralized by airlines and airwaves, of which huge tracts have been turned into cultural suburbia. Living in suburbia may be preferable, healthier than living in the metropolis, but only if you make your address work for you, knowing what to take from the centre, when to take it and when to leave it alone. To do that, it is necessary first to admit your position.

The woman who wrote 'Jennifer' for advice knew there was a centre to the society whose fringe she inhabited: from that centre she needed recognition, a standard, a public reality. She also knew her unhappiness was the heart of history. It took a special confidence to write her letter. The same tragic confidence will be increasingly necessary to Commonwealth literature, including Britain's in the coming years.

[1965]

III
Travellers
and Exiles

Malcolm Lowry
John Hirsch
Pierre Trottier
Kildare Dobbs

Malcolm Lowry

Letter to a Brother

Dollarton, B.C., Canada
—or perhaps I should spell it Dolorton
[Fall, 1950]

Dear old Stuart:

A towering sea is bearing down upon me. Gulls are balancing in the gale. A black cormorant is struggling low over the waves against the wind. All around me is a thunderous sound of breaking, smashing, trees pirouetting and dancing, as a full gale smashes through the forest. What is this? A seascape – or a suggestion for program music, as for Sibelius or Wagner. No: this is the view out of our living room window, while we are having our morning coffee. What I see is quite unbelievable, even for you, unless you have seen it – and where else would you see, but here, a house that is built in the sea and where the problems – and noises – are those that beset the mariner rather than the normal householder? It is wonderfully dramatic – too dramatic, even for me, for us, in some respects, for we now live under the shadow, at any moment, of losing it. This I've told you before. We only live here by grace of being pioneers, and Canada, alas, is forgetting that it is its pioneers who built this country and made it what it was: now it wants to be like everyone else and have autocamps instead of trees and Coca-Cola stands instead of human beings. In that way, for it has little culture at all, it could destroy its soul: that is its own business, no doubt – what we mind is that it threatens to destroy us in the process, an eventuality that it now becomes my duty to try and avoid. Have I mentioned that this is supposed to be a begging letter, even if addressed to one who can do naught, and is hamstrung even as I? One of those letters that you see, or may see one day, under a glass case in a museum – just as this house that we fear to be thrown out of someone may make money out of one day – for I am the only Canadian writer ever to be placed in the *Encyclopedia Britannica* – a sort of begging letter at least, though I don't know on what moral grounds I am presumed to be begging for what upon one plane of reasoning would certainly seem to have been once at least intended to be mine; begging being something I understand that even the tycoons of Canada may be driven to from their neighbouring country as an alternative to stealing, a practice I am inhibited from less on moral grounds than fear of the consequences and plain incompetence.

All this, in my usual direct fashion, you may take to refer to the crucificial position of a writer in Canada.

First I shall give you – an important item in the technique of such letters even when one understands perfectly well the utter fruitlessness of it – a list of my accomplishments, immediately followed of course by a similar list of catastrophes.

Have written and completed in collaboration with Margerie a detailed movie script – adapted from a novel you won't have heard of – upon which we worked, sometimes with the temperature below zero in the house, some fourteen hours a day – it was so cold at one point we couldn't take off our clothes for a fortnight.

Succeeded in having the *Volcano* published in translation in Norway, Denmark, Sweden, and France – in the first and last countries put into an edition with the classics of the world.

Seen it hailed as the greatest masterpiece of the last ten years in the French translation in Paris.

Been put in the *Encyclopedia Britannica*. (For how long? Are you comfortable there, Malcolm?)

Well I could go on with these, but I think it's time now for a few catastrophes, sometimes transcended catastrophes.

Operation for a chronic condition of my legs. Successful and expensive.

Continued anxiety – partly responsible for condition when you met me – of thinking one had T.B. Tests showed I have had T.B. at some time or other – when? – and am liable to it: but have it no longer. Have conquered anxiety neurosis on this score.

My monthly income is now little more than $90 – that has the purchasing power of little more than a fiver in the old days, and I am not exaggerating. Rent makes sympathetic and contradictory fluctuations of course, but you would be lucky merely to rent anywhere these days for $90 a month, without food – let alone live.

A notice of eviction that seems final, but with just a bare possibility of reprieve in it: but it scarcely seems possible it can last more than a few months.

Margerie ill – with ourselves still in the dark as to what is really wrong with her: x-rays, brain tumor still suspected, treatment that must be continued, begins to put us into the category of the starving. Much may be done with oatmeal. I begin even to think of the saying, 'Home is the place where, when they have to, they take you in.' But where indeed is that, unless here? Her mother lives 2,000 miles away in America, mine 10,000. And we have no friends in Canada save three fishermen in like case, a cat, five wild ducks, two seagulls, and, of course, a wolf.

In my case the possibilities of work are or were three: teaching, radio, newspaper work. The first requires at least a year's negotiation and a complete rededication of one's life – and probably going to the Prairies, since the English are hated in B.C. The second pays starvation wages and moreover requires a car, while the third not only does that but would be senseless because what I do anyway to attempt to augment the income makes more money and comes into the category of free lancing. In short there is no possibility of a job where we live – short of turning sailor again or working in a sawmill – for taking one would mean abandoning the really practical hope we cling to in regard to our serious work, and also our house: and indeed at the moment we haven't got money even to *move* anywhere else. Even if I could get a labourer's job the cost of transportation would swallow the money we save by living in the house. And writing is a whole-time job or nothing, so it would mean quitting. Margie can't augment matters by getting a job herself because she's not well enough: besides, we do our work together. And for the same reason, however willing to turn my hand to anything, I couldn't leave her long enough in the wilderness by herself. In short it's better to stick to one's guns: only it seems that begging is a standard part of writing, or is about to become so. You may therefore count this as work, for it's my all too valuable time, not counting yours. It may interest you to know that there is a long broadcast tonight or tomorrow night on the subject of Malcom Lowry, Canada's greatest most successful writer, which we can't listen to because our radio has run down and we can't afford to replenish the battery. The unkindest cut of all. Despite our love I have been warned that for Margie to live another winter under these conditions is very dangerous during the coldest part.

Losing the house under these callous conditions – and they are totally callous and selfish – would be a blow considering all the others – having lost it by fire and rebuilt it ourselves – of such psychological importance that if we had our way we wouldn't live in Canada at all any more. Well, we don't expect our way. The object is to live at all.

John Hirsch

On Becoming Canadian

I am not a Canadian by birth; I came here after the Second World War from Hungary where I was born and was brought up in an extremely chauvinistic and nationalistic kind of a country where, as a child, I was taught that the world is God's hat, and Hungary is the flower on it. Later on, I discovered that I certainly was not part of this flower because being a Jew, I was quickly thrown off the flower and even the whole hat. I was also taught at school that Rumanians are untrustworthy and Hungarians are the most truthful people in the world. Czechs are liars, Serbs are thieves, Germans are robbers, Russians are uncivilised and so on ad infinitum and ad nauseam. Only Hungarians were people really worth talking to and worth living with.

I came to Canada trying to be Canadian because I lost my home and I lost my country. I tried my best, I think; but nowadays I find myself in a very difficult position. First of all, in Quebec now, I am regarded as an Anglo-Saxon, which I find hard to believe. In Toronto, I'm looked upon as a westerner in spite of my Hungarian accent; I am expected to ride on the back of a buffalo. When I go to Edmonton, I am called an easterner. In Vancouver, they don't even talk to me. I really don't know where I fit in as a Canadian.

I made a point of going across the country as soon as possible after I had arrived; and seeing the land gave me my first and most deeply felt impression of what this country is about. I had to know the land I was going to live in; not Manitoba, not the prairies, but the whole of it. It seemed to me as I travelled that most Canadians did not know this country at all; consequently they could not have a feeling about it. There was nothing to grasp because they did not grasp the physical realities of this place.

I was born in a handkerchief of a country, where you could travel from one place to another, one border to another, in one day. To me, Canada was overwhelming; and there were two ways to cope with it as a human being: either to run away, because it was simply too great to do anything in it; or to try to stretch oneself. And I wanted to stretch. I needed a place; I needed a place where I could move mountains or carry larger stones than Sisyphus, and here was the place for it. I realized that the very lack of drums and trumpets, the non-existence of slogans and parades, with nobody telling me what I'm supposed to believe as a Canadian, the very lack of being pasted all over with slogans, gave me a kind of a freedom for my mind and for my spirit and my creative energies that I had never experienced before in my life. I also realized that I am living in a rich country, which I haven't done before, and as an artist, I found that, for me anyhow, anything could be possible here.

[1965]

Pierre Trottier

Return to Winter

Thanks to a long and uninterrupted stay abroad I was able to escape six Canadian winters. Thus it was not without some anxiety that, back home once again, I faced the prospect of January for the first time in six years. It was not so much the physical cold that I feared (for I was well aware of the efficiency of central heating in our houses) as much as the doping of the spirit, that strangulation or crushing of the soul under the weight of the opaque snow. In short, I feared a sort of internal frost and was upset at the very thought that the cold could undermine the foundations and pull apart the stones of my personal museum, the museum of my memory, which, for some years, had received the attention of so much of my leisure time, my energy, my reflection, and my love.

The problem for me was one that went far beyond that of once again picking up on winter sports which, I was advised, would divert my mind from the long and passive wait for the arrival of summer. In order to avoid drowsiness, I was told, be active, go skiing! I couldn't help thinking that this sounded too much like the slogans we heard in secondary school: to keep your mind off evil thoughts, participate in sports! Down with sombre delectations! *Mens sana in corpore sano!*

I am not one to prize highly the wholly negative tone of such precepts and advice, which are the products of that antinomic way of thinking which, having postulated a given behaviour, enjoins one to act in opposition to it. (This is like playing a game of checkers with you using the white squares and your opponent the black ones.) Thus, I cannot fathom how activity can overcome passivity, or sport, troubling thoughts, or winter sports, winter. To put it more precisely, I don't think that sports activity, which I respect a great deal, ought to flow from any theory of physical activism, any more than poetry should from verbal activism. The prevention of drowsiness, evil thoughts, or silence is similar to fire prevention, and the suggestion of activism for me smacks of the type of advice given to one by a fireman: the fire hose can douse the flames but it can never rebuild what has been destroyed. The fear I felt at the thought of returning to the Canadian winter was a fear of firemen who extinguish the fire burning beneath the snow and ice, a fear of the mortifying silence of these snow-bound spaces, the fear of winter as absence, of winter as an excuse for inaction, of winter as an alibi, as confession and penitence, as a refuge for a bad conscience, as an escape, as a scapegoat for our inability to exist.

The fact is that our winter has a broad back. It has served us well, just as the *maudits anglais* have done, as a masochistic instrument of self-flagellation perfectly suited to our faulty morals. We have used winter to create a beautiful myth with which to apologize for our tardiness in regard to history, progress, civilization, culture, art. Like so many little Sisyphuses rolling snowballs which keep slipping back onto us from one winter to the next, we are in a good position to shrug our shoulders in a gesture of resigned impotence and say, 'Well, what do you expect in a climate like ours . . .' Our winter, though, has paid us back in kind. It has readily accepted its double role of judge and justifier. Before its tribunal, our fear of living, our inability to exist, our lack of substance on this earth, all receive their absolution and condemnation: absolution for all our failings of the past, and simultaneous condemnation for those of the future. Peace be with you, my son, and sin again! Our winter whitewashes us, without ever giving us a taste for true colour, but only for that of the colour print.

Of course our climate is not a tender one. Yet neither was the sea that brought to England's shores barbarians – Angles, Saxons, Jutes, Danes, and others – until at last the British people set out to plant on that same sea their own vocation and grandeur. In my view, we must establish what it is we can build upon the ice and snow, and in this regard, we must first see winter as it really is, that is to say, demystified and stripped of its double role of judge and justifier. Isn't it really necessary to cleanse ourselves of the hangovers of primitive and superstitious paganism which suggest the presence of some avenging demiurge behind the functioning of the elements of nature?

Even though having missed six Canadian winters did not entirely free me from a kind of fear which I explained above, I did return from abroad with a new outlook. With my new gaze, I took in December, then January and February, and I discovered that after some days of sombre anger came others of peace and brilliance which, while they did not lessen the cold and its exigencies of dress, nonetheless gave equal play to the sunlight, against a background of a very pure blue sky. For our winters are not grey and surly as are those of Europe. On the contrary, if one excepts a minority of stormy days, our winters are remarkably clear and bright. The temperature and the snow certainly belong to a northern climate, but the sun doesn't, in so far as the European concept of the north is concerned. It is even somewhat Mediterranean. Thus, given sunshine of this nature, and with the problem of heating our homes resolved, one is surely able to think and not only dream or rock oneself to sleep amidst thoughts of guilt-ridden nostalgia. Think about what? Why about the space we occupy, the space on which Borduas reflected, for example, particularly when executing his white and black canvases and later, near the end of his life, in his monochromatic works in which the desert is not so much a lack or an absence but rather a desert that has a rigorous and stark quality that is accepted by the artist, and given shape by him.

When I speak of reflecting on our spatial dimension, I do not mean that we should study it logically, and analyse, dissect, measure, and imprison it in an idea or concept. I am not talking about drawing up a property assessor's report. What I have in mind is the verb *penser,* which in a derived meaning gave *pensum,* meaning weight. (Denis de Rougemont talks about this somewhere.) *Penser notre espace* means to take cognizance of the space around us, to be present in it with all our weight instead of allowing ourselves to be abstracted from it, drawn away from it, or inhibited from facing it by our faulty morality which is in fact a morality of abstraction, withdrawal, and inhibition. Perhaps we deserved this type of morality. In any case, we inherited it. But surely this country does not deserve it. For we live on a continent that requires a morality of possession and not one of withdrawal. *We,* and not our country nor its winter, must change. I recall several extremely cold days in that winter which I had tasted again after a lapse of six years. Nothing in the sky disturbed the peace and brightness. The sky was anything but cloudy, as our morality might suggest. It was not an Italian sky, which reflects too much sea and the almost tangible brightness of which clings to every object, evoking in the soul of the viewer an ancient dream of beauty and love. No, it was not a sky which might have given birth to Venus. This Canadian sky, reflecting the snow, was of a paler blue than that found in Italy, but seemed translucent before the infinite which traversed it and descended from it, as if calling for a human presence on the earth as an act of faith. In principle, the sky always represents the infinite, but I maintain that in Canada it does so more than elsewhere. However that may be, since those days of February and of a winter finally understood or at least understandable, this sky has for me become one of possibilities, just as have winter, ice, and snow, which I no longer regard as burdens, prisons, or tortures, but rather as a new form of freedom. The desert sky also beckons through the infinite for man's presence and faith, but there the shape of liberty is that of the absence of everything, while in the Canadian winter it takes the form of a reduction to essentials and of a meditation. With an eye to what? With an eye to the thunder of the waters of the thaw, the bursting of buds, the explosion of spring. For in our country spring is indeed an explosion while elsewhere it is a gentler and more gradual blossoming.

Thus, since it is in the bosom of winter that this explosion is born, death and whiteness and virginity – no longer seen as so many sterile negations in the style of conceptual thinking – can be interpreted as real, concrete, and fruitful. Moreover, since winter makes the earth hard and prevents inhumation, it represents the refusal of death in so far as it is finite. Winter is the season of the return to the infinite, to the incomplete that is man, for whom the flowers and fruits, having completed their cycle, offer unbounded possibilities. It is also the season of the return from the infinite in the Christian mystery of God made into man. Return to, return from: these two expressions mean basically the meeting between the infinite which is in God and the infinite which is in man and which, in the final analysis, are made to link up and touch one another. Now, a meeting requires a presence. Here I come back to the principles of the immaculate conception of which I spoke in an earlier chapter, to say that there will be such a presence and a meeting of the two infinities, of God and man, in that capacity for immaculate conception on which I hinge my definition of our winter and its indispensable condition of fertility which hides behind its exterior of death, whiteness, and virginity.

[1963. Translated by Ben Shek.]

D*

Kildare Dobbs

Running to Paradise

The sound of a train whistle at night – now reincarnate as a diesel klaxon – is the key experience of North Americans, so often written about that it may have become too familiar to mean much. Yet not to me, an immigrant when I first heard it. A lonely sound. I imagined the train rushing on into the dark, past sleeping farms and fields, through forests and by lakes and across the vast prairies to the west, running westward, running to the far mountains and beyond them to an ocean on the other side of the world. It spoke rather of voyages than journeys, seafaring overland, an ocean of loneliness scattered with villages and cities like lighthouses winking from shores of sleep. The Canadian sound, suggesting the vastness and emptiness of a country still in the future, it was hinting at a destination as yet unimagined. That is the place I am restlessly faring to, riding westward, running to Paradise.

'Aida,' the train sang through its steel nostrils, running westward from Toronto, myself stretched snugly in a roomette. *'Aiii-da.'*

Aida wasn't opera, but a mnemonic given me by the sales manager. For I was now one of the travelling fraternity, the boys on the road: the sample cases stuffed with books and bibles out there in the porter's care attested me a book salesman, a bible man. *Aida* was how to sell books, or boots or toothpaste or whatever. A, I, D, A. A for Attention. 'The bookseller, he sees a lot of salesmen. He's heard it all before. You got to go in there and grab his attention, okay?' Okay. And I for Interest: once you had your man's attention, you had to hold his interest. Then you came to D for Desire. The next step was to awaken desire. . . . 'Let's keep this discussion on a decent level, shall we? Desire here is

86

for the product, which in your case is books. You got to make the customer want what you're selling.' Which in my case was also bibles. (But I'm coming to that.) After desire — then A for Action! This was what you had joined for. Close the deal and make the sale. Nothing to do but write up the order and mail it.

Aida, Muse of Salesmanship, invoked with Attention, pursued with Interest, wooed with Desire, possessed in Action — it was she who led me into the cities of the West, into the *châteaux* of railway hotels with hot and cold gracious living, the principality of bell captains and sample rooms, territory of the taxi-meter and the expense claim. In some of those hotels (the Paralyser of C———for instance), a whole floor was given over to salesmen. The corridor was cluttered with what appeared to be big black coffins. In these, I was told, the garment salesmen carried not corpses but their wares. Theirs seemed a gruesome trade. Once I lay awake half the night in the next room to a pair of garment salesmen who had invited in two women. At first it sounded fairly genial: much laughter and the clink of glasses. Later it changed. There was a drone of female talk from one side of the room; on the other side the men had their heads together. Not my idea of fun. Much later the women, frustrated perhaps, began to scream abuse at the men, demanding at last that a taxi be called.

Drinking with old John Lush in his prairie city, I learned Aida's hidden mysteries. He was, as they say, a valued customer, and the visits of book-travellers were the most exciting events in his year. Unlike the girls who work in candy factories, he enjoyed the product he dealt in: he would dream over the *Memoirs* of Casanova of an evening before he went to bed, and from the way he handled the samples you could see he liked a good read.

John was a man who had in youth been visited by an experience much like that of Saul of Tarsus on the road to Damascus. He had been training for the Ministry. Zealous and devout in his studies, he believed he had forsaken the world. And then one evening, on his way back to his lodgings from a lecture on Predestination, he became conscious that a woman was smiling at him from a doorway. 'I saw the light!' From that moment his life changed. 'It was a red light.' He drowned his theology books in the river.

All this he imparted as we knocked back a bottle of Scotch in my hotel room. I'm afraid I was a disappointment to him, though he gave me a good fat order to keep my employer happy. He was accustomed to more lively entertainment than I offered. 'Do you know Charley Magnum?' he said wistfully. 'He used to travel for Green Press.' I remembered meeting him. A little black-haired goat of a man, ugly as sin. He was blind drunk at the time, roaring out obscene songs.

'That's the fella.' John seemed pleased. He shook his head, shocked and delighted at the memory of Charley Magnum. He assumed a more demotic turn of speech, coarsening his accent to signify that we were boys together. 'The times we had. Well, sir, they fired him. Yes, sir, after fifteen years of his carryon they gave him his marching orders. I never saw a fella like him.' He began to cough and creak with laughter. I filled his glass again. 'Hey, whoa there! Oh well, okay. . . . I sure miss Charley. First thing when he came to town he'd call me up and say, "Come on over the room, I got something for ya." So I'd climb right in a cab and come over. Well, he'd pick up the phone and grin like a devil – homely little bugger he was too – and he'd say, "Whaddya want John – a woman?" *Jeesus* – well, I've been married a good many years. I'm past all that. But – "Whatsa matter, John?" he'd say. "Hell, give the cat a canary, it's on the house!" '

John was obviously pleased at these courtesies, though he felt (since his retirement to marriage) that he could not take advantage of them. 'God, Charley could get away with murder! One time, on our way to his room in the hotel, the corridor was half blocked by a chambermaid. She was bending down with her back to us, fixing her vacuum-cleaner or something. And Charley, he just went right up to her and gave her a tremenjous smack on the ass. She let a squawk and shot up with her hand on it, mad as hell. A redhead, not bad either. I walked away pretty quick, but before she could say a word, Charley leaned over and said something to her. Don't know what it was, but would you believe it, the next thing I saw was that girl taking her vacuum-cleaner into Charley's room. . . .'

It was at about this point that John and I went through my book catalogue. (Action!) Later he told me that Charley had turned up once at his house with a woman – a terrible female. 'Who was that dreadful creature?' John's wife wanted to know after they had left. 'I think,' said John, honest even in adversity, 'it was a chambermaid from the Grand Prairie Hotel.'

These things I learned from old John over a period of some hours, the Scotch giving way at last to a case of beer. In a thickening fog of booze and reminiscence we transacted our business. The names of eminent authors, some Canadian, were mentioned eruditely or brushed rudely but knowledgeably aside as beneath the notice of civilized bookmen. Hours after John had left, stepping high like a man walking through long grass, I was grimly writing out titles, prices, and (incorrect) totals.

Aida had not deserted me. A for Alcohol, she began in her new dispensation, I for Incofluence, D for Drunk. And lastly A for Alcohol again. In my end (as we reading-men like to say) is my beginning.

Aida worked all right for the books, once I had got through my head what she really stood for. It was the bibles that defeated me. *Biblical,* I discovered, was not the same as *bibliophile,* certainly had no connection, etymological or otherwise, with *bibulous.* The bible accounts were dry; not only dry but the cause of dryness in others. A for Alcohol was out. It would have to be A for Attention. But how to attract it? Bible-selling is a bitterly competitive game. Since all the texts are the same (with a few exceptions, latter-day freaks such as Revised Versions, modern translations, and texts 'designed to be read as literature' – heretical no doubt), the Word as dedicated to King James I, what the bible man has to put across is their format. Paper, print, binding, zip-fasteners, yapped edges, not to mention more spiritual considerations such as price, discount, service, and shipping dates – these are the subjects that interest the bible-buyer.

How could I hope to talk convincingly of such matters? There were about three hundred bibles in my list, all with code numbers which to adepts revealed at a glance whether they were bound in Persian Morocco, Full Morocco, Pigskin, Goatskin, Rexine, Rhinoceros hide, or whatever; whether yapped, zipped, warped, or wrapped (don't ask me, I'm a stranger myself); whether printed in Pearl, Onyx, Chasuble, Urim, Thummim, or Bourgeois (this, one thing I knew, was pronounced 'Boorjoys'); or whether equipped with indexes, cross-references, maps, concordances, introductions, translators' prefaces, baptismal certificates, confirmation documents, driving licences, charts, questions, answers, apocryphas, pseudepigrapha, illustrations, pop-ups, or singing covers.

From a mine so thoroughly exploited, what jewel could an ignoramus like myself hope to extract and hold shining before the case-hardened buyer of a fundamentalist church-chandler? True, I had the advantage of having read the book, parts of it several times. There was the example of the Moderator of the Church of Scotland, that grim black figure, like a crow among peacocks, at the pomp and glamour of the Queen's coronation. 'Here is Wisdom,' he had said, moving, bible in hand, to the centre of my TV set. 'This is the Royal Law. These are the lively Oracles of God.' I knew enough about blurb-writing to recognize first-class work. But after all, the Moderator wasn't putting across merchandise. To introduce a note of that sort into the sales situation would have been an embarrassing reminder of those money-changers' tables in the Temple.

After a few kindly rebuffs, so cleverly administered that I was lucky to leave the various premises without having actually *bought* some of the competing merchandise, I decided to use physical violence. Bursting into a religious-goods store in the next prairie city on my itinerary, I seized my most expensive bible-sample in both hands, bent it double to show the beautiful suppleness of its fine leather and India paper, thrust it under the nose of the buyer.

'Smell that!'

Backed up against a bookcase, the poor woman capitulated on every point: A, I, D, A. She gave me a splendid order. It wasn't till later that I found out from my home office that her credit was shot. I wasn't supposed to have called on her at all.

Perhaps it was not my destiny to sell holy writ. I could *read* it with pleasure, a refuge from the duller non-fiction among my current samples. And I read:

Where shall wisdom be found?

But I was seeing Canada, a limitless territory rising from imagination into fact, and now sunk down to memory. The prairies – before I set eyes on the prairies I imagined them a region of unspeakable desolation, as dreary and oppressive to the spirit as they appear on the back of a dollar bill. Now that I had seen them – I knew them to be a region of unspeakable desolation, as dreary and oppressive to &c. &c. There is a sense in which the paradox is true, that travel narrows the mind. Yet you could see what it was about the region that had prairie people by the heart. It was like the open sea, that wide flat land under the vast sky, a brown sea now, though winter would soon cover it in greyish white, its loneliness more than earthly, more than mortal. Like the loneliness of God (I told a prairie poet in a fit of Aida-induced confidence) before he made the universe. The poet nodded enthusiastically. 'You're right, you're *right* – that's just it!'

I had to go and spoil it for him. 'The only trouble is, he couldn't stand it. . . . He made the universe.'

Between hotels – from the windows of trains or airliners – it was possible to catch a notion of the country. The hotels, like the cities, tend to merge into each other in memory, so that the commercial palaces of Winnipeg, Regina, Saskatoon, Edmonton, Calgary, now seem all one hotel, and the cities themselves – for all their several peculiarities – one city. Smaller cities are more distinct. Moose Jaw, with its heroic public library; Medicine Hat, crouched in a sort of amphitheatre in a bend of its river; Lethbridge, haunted by the sombre figures of Hutterites, black-suited, black-bearded, accompanied by women like Victorian dolls in their long skirts and headkerchiefs. But the land – as you went westward it changed. At first flat in the continental doldrums, it began to take on a long undulation, like the heavy groundswell of the Western Ocean. Gradually over hundreds of miles it continued to work itself up by ever shorter and steeper waves into a flurry of foothills till at last it broke over the horizon in a storm of jagged mountains, the icy peaks of the Canadian Rockies.

At the Paralyser Hotel, for me the climax of the foothills, I drank late with my brother-traveller Ken Tupper. My room was by the freight yard of the railroad; we could hardly hear ourselves speak above the metallic clank and clash of shunting trains. At three a.m. Ken phoned the desk and made his polite enquiry. 'What time does the hotel leave for Vancouver?'

For we were impatient to get to the Coast – that by now almost mythical destination. That first time I went by train, climbing slowly till dark by the boulder-strewn Bow River and through the forested passes, looking up with awe at bare crags of the terrible mountains – those mountains that men from flat country fear and feel oppressed by, though to me, brought up in view of Mount Leinster, nostalgic and exciting – and staring, at night-fall, at the last of the sun touching faintly a distant white peak.

And I woke to a new light, the soft, changing light of British Columbia, its green grass and blue distances that drew me like a song. Running still westward to the sea, an Irish melancholy came over me, that pleasant sadness which was one of the seven deadly sins of the Middle Ages. Accidia now took Aida by the hand, enfolded her in a damp and mildewy embrace, stifling her voice so that in Vancouver's Stanley Park I almost forgot her in contemplation of captive king penguins. My employers, bookmen to the backbone, roused me with a telegram: SIT NOT UPON THE ORDERS OF YOUR TAKING BUT MAIL AT ONCE.

Still I was running westward. I took ship for Victoria, some hours away on Vancouver Island, and there checked in at the hotel which is like no other. I had the feeling that they did not care for salesmen, particularly bookmen and biblemen.

The bellhop picked up my suitcase. I began to walk toward the main elevator. 'No, sir!' he called to me. 'Not that one. This way, sir.' I turned. He was heading in the opposite direction. I followed him for some distance to a smaller, meaner elevator. We mounted one floor, emerged and walked about a thousand yards or so along a corridor. Then we came to a staircase and walked *down* two floors. From there we began a second long march – I don't know how far, but I would say at a guess at least a mile – along another corridor or tunnel. We might have been in a mine. I had that feeling of being at a great distance from the world.

The bellhop let me into my sample room. It was a vast chamber, carpeted in decaying green felt, and equipped all round with display counters. In a distant corner was the bed I hoped to sleep in. 'Good-bye, sir,' said the bellhop, pocketing his tip.

I shivered.

Some time later I decided to pick up my mail. Back I went along the tunnel, up those two flights of stairs, along that thousand yards of corridor and down one flight in the little elevator. Somewhat breathless, I asked the desk clerk for my mail.

'It will be delivered to your room, sir.'

'But I want to pick it up now.'

'I'm sorry, sir. It will be delivered to your room.'

I could see that they didn't want fellows like me hanging round where the guests could see us. I turned away, and reluctant to face that descent into the earth again for a while, looked about me for something to do. A notice caught my eye. TO THE GLASS GARDEN. A hand pointed in the direction of a conservatory. I followed it.

There was a fountain like a sort of giantess's *bidet,* ornamented with encaustic tiles. Near it a door opened on a garden, pleasant with lawns and flowers. Another notice pointed into the garden. Out I went and along a path that led to some trees. To one of them was attached a third sign indicating the way to the Glass Garden (whatever it was). I followed. It led me to a blank wall – or wooden fence. I could see no way through it. And so, of the Glass Garden I may not speak properly, for I was not there.

Did I dream this? Was it a trap set for me by the hotel – as paranoia whispered at the time? Or was it a hint, perhaps, that that country I was running to, and still seek, was not to be found? Aida had led me to this, of that I was convinced, so that I realized at last that I was not her favourite. I gave up (or was given up) as a bible man and book salesman.

Months afterwards, on a journey of another sort, a journey made for pleasure, I drove by night farther to the west – to Point No Point on the Pacific Coast of Vancouver Island. As I got out of the car I could hear it, loud as guns in the darkness, the crash of surf from the main deep. I walked down to the shore, behind me the black forests – and behind *them* the whole of Canada and the world and my life, before me the gleam of the Pacific, the waves running over sand and pebbles to my feet, the heavy drum of the surf beating on my brain. I looked out to the open ocean.

　　And the sea saith, It is not with me.

[1962]

IV
A Sense of the Place

Farley Mowat
Charles Bruce
Anne Hébert
Naim Kattan
William Kilbourn
Douglas Fisher
W.O. Mitchell
Roderick
  Haig-Brown
Farley Mowat

Farley Mowat

Newfoundland: "T'ree Hunnert Year Gone By"

It is hard for Canadians to comprehend the antiquity and tenacity of the human roots in this rock-grit island, stuffed into the broad maw of the St. Lawrence Gulf. My own forebears came out to Upper Canada about 1800 and I used to pride myself on being a real native son until I came to Newfoundland to live. One day during my first year here I was poking about in a graveyard at Ship Cove (a fishing village of half-a-hundred families on Conception Bay) when I came across a headstone dated 1650. The name of Dawes was still readable. The discovery fascinated me and I had to share it with someone, but the only person around was a venerable grey-beard scything hay between the graves. I called him to me and pointed to the stone.

'Just think of that!' I said in awe. 'Three hundred years ago a man named Dawes died here. I wonder where he came from, and who he was.' For a moment the old man looked at me suspiciously as if he feared I was pulling his leg; but then he realized that I was only another ignorant Mainlander, and he stooped to humour me. 'No need to wonder, me son. He were Johnny Dawes, he were. Borned and died in Ships' Cove. Belonged here, like his pore old dad afore him. Like me, ye might say . . . Uncle Jim Dawes is me name, an you cares to know.'

And I remember another occasion when Howard Morry of Ferryland took me up to a Gaze – a lookout on a hill overlooking the wide grey waters of the Western Ocean – to tell me the story of how his great-great-great-great grandmother used to come up here to watch for the return of her husband's

95

sailing vessel after a three or four month voyage to the Azores and Portugal. That was in the early 1700's.

Howard is a fisherman of about eighty, who looks and acts about forty, and who knows the entire history of Ferryland from its first use as a summer fishing settlement around 1500 better than most of us know the history of our newly built commuter suburbs. As with most Newfoundlanders of his generation, history means something to him because he is, and knows he is, a part of it.

'I'll tell ye how it is with us. There was no larnin' in the outports until just a few years back. Most people couldn't read nor write. But my, how they could talk! As youngsters we used to sit by the hour listening to the old people yarn. We heard stories from two and three hundred years ago that was just as fresh as if they happened yesterday. Aye, that's how it was. But 'tis all changing now. The history of this Island, kept alive inside our heads for a dozen generations or more, is going to pass away in one generation now that Confederation's come.' Without knowing it, Howard was reflecting the ambivalence that so many Newfoundlanders feel about the changes that came with joining Canada.

Discovered in 986 by Greenland Norse who made an abortive settlement in the north part, Newfoundland began to take shape as a European entity in the west as early as 1450, by which time Basque and Portuguese whalers and fishers were regularly sailing to the Grand Banks, into Belle Isle Strait, and probably to most of the good harbours that ring the island. The early history is dim, principally because until the 1700's it was illegal to settle in Newfoundland. The wealthy west coast fish merchants of England had engineered such laws in an attempt to prevent the establishment of a native fishery in the 'New Land'. But laws are mostly made to be broken. By 1510 runaways from fishing ships – the Masterless Men, as they are known in tradition – had spread like a slow, silent tide into remote Newfoundland bays. They lived hard lives in a hard land – but they lived. There were six thousand miles of rock-ribbed, sea-roaring coasts to hide them, and here they built their little 'tilts' of sod or logs, concealing themselves from strangers and passing ships, getting a little 'country meat' from the land, but subsisting mainly on the fish they caught from open boats. Historians have ignored these early planters, remembering only the grandiose attempts of men like Lord Baltimore, which mostly failed. Nevertheless by 1550 a large part of the Newfoundland coast was occupied and these early 'liveyers' (people who 'live here' – a name still in use on the Labrador coast) slowly increased in numbers.

The odds against them were terrible. Starvation was the common lot through the first three centuries of Newfoundland's recent history, and chronic hunger filled most of the fourth. But a steady flow of new blood came in from Ireland, the Southern Counties of England and the Channel Islands, in the form of indentured labour brought over by great English and Jersey merchant companies to man their fishing factories. These indentured people, men and women both, were practically slaves and a good many of them slipped quietly off to seek freedom in the secret little coves. The English outporters met French fishermen-settlers and Mic Mac Indians and, since all men were equal before the sea, marriages took place freely across the lines of race and blood.

So the Newfoundlanders early evolved into a unique people – a true 'People of the Sea' who eventually ringed the island with more than thirteen hundred outports, ranging in size from two or three families to as high as fifty. Most of these settlements had no contact with one another or with the world outside except by water.

They struggled for survival as few human beings in our time have had to struggle. In small open boats the men fished the year round, with time off for gruelling voyages in small schooners carrying salt cod to Europe and the West Indies; while the women 'made' (dried and treated) the salt cod which was the great product of the northern seas. Every September at 'settling up time' the salt fish was carried to the merchant who bought it, at his price – not for cash, but as payment against the debts, the endless debts, of the fisherman and his family.

The merchant class of Newfoundland held the people in a deadly vice; as inescapable and as ruthless a trap as any that was ever devised by a trader to ensnare a simple Indian. From its beginnings until as late as the 1950's in some remote outports, a man was born, grew up, and died in debt to the merchant.

The long centuries slipped by and a score of times Newfoundland became a battlefield, usually between French and English, during which the outporters often lost all they possessed and had to start again with nothing but their hands. During all those years nothing really changed. The system remained the same. The poor stayed desperately poor, and the rich grew fabulously rich. St. John's was the only real town the island boasted, and it was the home of the great merchants – the 'Water Street men'. Even as late as 1950 St. John's had more millionaires per capita than any other city in North America, including the capital of Texas! And in 1949 the majority of the people of Newfoundland still knew grinding poverty.

Here is the way it was: 'In the thirties – the "Hard Times", we called it – there was nothing to be had. The merchants would give out no more credit and the people had no money, of course. Fish was a glut. Nobody would buy our fish. People all up and down the coasts were starving. Nobody will ever know how many children died, but a good many grown men starved to death. If there happened to be a doctor handy, he'd write it down as heart failure, which was true enough. The government gave out the dole – six cents a day for a family and you took it "in kind", and the kind, often enough, was rotten or weevily flour. My people were a little better off than most, and many's the time neighbours would come out to our kitchen for a feed. I mind how they smelled. My mother told me: "Son," she says, "That is the smell of poverty. Don't you forget it." I knew one man, poor fellow, set out to ask for help from the relieving officer one day in winter time. But he froze to death on the way. When we found him, all he was wearing was a pair of trousers and a jacket made of wore-out flour sacks. He had no socks – only a torn pair of rubber boots on his feet. . . .'

Hard times! Yes. But a Newfoundlander was used to hard times, having known little else for centuries. He begat immense families, often fifteen to eighteen children, but it was rare for more than a handful of them to reach maturity, and when they were grown-up the sea would take its toll of the men – 'Bridegrooms of the Sea', they called the drowned – while tuberculosis took a toll of the women – a heavy toll.

It was like that right up until Confederation in 1949. And yet when union with Canada was mooted, the 'Water Street men' fought a bitter battle to prevent it. They preferred things to stay as they were. But they lost. One day in April of 1949 Newfoundland ceased to be the oldest European settlement in North America and became the youngest of the ten Canadian provinces. And an ancient mould was shattered, almost overnight – not by a bomb or by a similar catastrophe, but . . . by the baby bonus!

The baby bonus accomplished in a few years what the merchants had been able to prevent through three or four centuries. It brought cash, and therefore a measure of freedom to the people. Its effect was unbelievable. My neighbours in the outport of Burgeo, where I now live, never tire of recalling what happened.

'Before my wife got her first bonus money,' one of them told me, 'nobody in our family had ever seen a five-dollar bill. If we saw five dollars in silver in a year – that was a lot. Everything we sold went to one merchant, and everything we bought had to come from him. He owned us, do you see?'

Here is how things now stand in this old Island after 18 years of being part of Canada. Nobody starves to death anymore, not even children. Nobody, or at least not many people, die because of a lack of medical services. For the first time, every child can learn to read and write, even if the educational standard is much lower than on the Mainland. Men who never had anything to lean on except their own strong muscles can now draw unemployment insurance, sick benefits, or relief assistance, while their wives gather in the baby bonus cheques. Old people, who used to survive (or try to) on a government pension of $120.00 a year are now so relatively affluent that they hardly know what to do with their money. The population is exploding; not because more children are being born, but because a lot more of them are surviving.

It all looks very good indeed. And yet there is a shadow over the paradise created by Confederation. Having tasted the fruits of the Canadian way of life, more and more and more Newfoundlanders are turning their backs on the pitiless grey sea which made them what they were. The truly vast Newfoundland merchant marine, mostly under sail, as late as 1939 had about five hundred sailing vessels operating out of Newfoundland ports, many of them engaged in the trans-Atlantic salt fish trade, while others carried cargo to and from Canadian and Caribbean ports. But employment in the fisheries has fallen sharply as, indeed, it must. Where once fifty men, working for starvation wages, could land a certain weight of fish, now four or five men, better paid and operating a modern dragger, do the same job.

Standards of living go up, and the number of acceptable jobs at these new standards, go down. The birth rate goes up, and there are not enough jobs available even for those presently employable. And so Newfoundland, once noted as the greatest exporter in the world of salt fish, is now exporting men and women as its major produce. They go because they must, and because the new generation will not accept the kind of life their fathers knew.

But more than the physical presence of the new generation is being lost. The tough, impervious core of courage, resourcefulness, ability, endurance, and personal pride that was a product of the evolution of the outport man and woman – the byproduct of adversity – is disappearing in the interval between one generation and the next.

Newfoundland demonstrates with pitiless clarity the terrible paradox of our times: as we make life easier, more tolerable, less demanding, so do we weaken the sustaining fabric of pride and strength which made us men in the first place.

In Burgeo, as in most of Newfoundland, the older men still go fishing in their little boats, although there is no longer any need for men of sixty or seventy to endure the cold seas and the cutting gales. They go because they love the life, not for the money that is in it. But they know they are the last of their kind – that the young fellows who are their sons and grandsons will soon be gone from the little outports; from Heart's Ease, Pushthrough, Fransway, and all the others. They know that in the past ten years more than three hundred outports have died, or been abandoned. They know that the young people will go to the Mainland, where they will become real Canadians – whatever that may be; but they will have a feeling that these men of a new age will somehow be less than the men their fathers were. The sons and the grandsons will be Canadians, but for men like Harvey Pink, the celebrations that took place on the Mainland in 1967 had but little meaning.

'Yiss, me darlin' man; we's had our Cen-teen-ial, ye might say – t'ree or four hunnert year gone by . . .'

[1967]

Charles Bruce

Atlantic Cadence

A bemused Montrealer went home from Prince Edward Island not long ago with a fish story. On a golf course in the 'Garden of the Gulf' he had found a fellow traveller fly-casting the water hazards for speckled trout. Successfully, at that: he planned to continue fishing the course instead of playing it.

From the reviewing stand, the day they hooked Cape Breton to the Nova Scotia mainland via the Canso Causeway, the Queen's representative – Lieutenant Governor Alistair Fraser – could see the giant scar on his hill of rock from which had come 10 million tons of fill for the road to the isle. As a private person he was already suing Ottawa (there was some unofficial chortling about the Queen suing the Queen) for a better deal than the pittance set by expropriation. Eight years later he would win his case.

Through the smoking car window of an east-bound express sliding down a New Brunswick Valley two passengers peered out at a river full of logs. 'Now who,' said one – obviously a native son home for a look – 'who, d'you s'pose, owns all that wood?' His companion considered and said: 'Don't know. Might be God. Might be the government. Likely it's K. C. Irving.'

These irrelevant notes are set down here merely because they seem to have in them something of the casual realism that colours the weave of Maritime life. And because, really, there is no other safe way to start a story about it.

Anyone who tries to catch the essence of Maritime Canada in words, many or few, had better be careful. All the more so if he happens to have been raised there: visitors can be excused; our own should know better. So I come to the writing of this piece with all the hesitancy of an Upper Canadian approaching the pronunciation of Apohaqui or Necum Teuch.

The hazard lies in what Stewart MacNutt (a Prince Edward Islander who went to college in Nova Scotia and teaches history in New Brunswick) has called 'a land-sea economy of intense diversity'. Vivid in my own mind are the feel of a scythe in timothy, the creak and thump of row-locks in fog, and the far-off thudding of a one-cylinder boat engine. What haunts someone else may well be the growl of a pulpmill, the whine of a lathe, Saturday night in a coal town or the ceaseless wind on Tantramar. To generalize is fatal.

If there is one thing known in common it must be the sound of water, the many sounds of water: surf on a hundred beaches, from Bay Chaleur down the coasts of New Brunswick and The Island, round the headlands of Cape North, down the eastern and southern shores and round the coast of Fundy to Passamaquoddy and the edge of Maine. The grumbling sigh of calm bays at night, the rush of millbrooks and the soft slap on the shores of lakes. The sound of rivers that run to the beat of their names, Matapedia and Kennebecasis, Medway and Margaree . . .

Down on the Eastern Shore of Nova Scotia, Helen Dacey Wilson grew up in Wilson's Cove. 'When I was a very small child,' she writes, 'my father and his brothers owned a pulpmill. When this was lost during the depression, Papa supported his family by lobster fishing in season, and by cutting and hauling wood in the winter. We had a small farm too, just large enough to keep the family in meat and vegetables.' I wish William Moorsom and Thomas Chandler Haliburton could be resurrected to read Helen's book.

A captain of engineers in the English garrison at Halifax 140 years ago, Moorsom spent his spare time on horseback travelling 'vile cowpaths dignified with the name of roads' to look at the country, and in smoky kitchens observing the people, rather than in the more lurid pursuits common to the military gentry of the time. He liked the province but he had a criticism: These people didn't understand 'the great principle of the division of labor'. Their ignorance made them depend partly on land, partly on water, instead of attending wholly to the one while their neighbours looked wholly to the other.

Haliburton, born and raised there, friend of Joe Howe and creator of Sam Slick, made the same kind of comment. Of my own country, at about the same time as Moorsom, he remarked: 'As the adjoining fisheries presented a prospect of support, with less labor and fatigue, they applied themselves alternately to the cultivation of the soil, and catching fish. To this unprofitable system, not only they but most of those who have subsequently settled there, have always adhered. . . .'

Neither Moorsom nor Haliburton ever 'held' a plough or hauled a killick in his life. Moorsom came from a land where the hedger doesn't ditch, Haliburton from the Annapolis Valley, a fertile place where a living from the land was sure. They both missed the point: there are regions and times and circumstances in which a man must turn his hand to anything. Diversity, adaptability: they are the Maritime inheritance.

Back in the settlement days German farmers were set down on rocky shores where they must learn to fish or starve. They fished. Disbanded riflemen to whom an axe was a strange tool, and Scottish crofters used to gorse-covered hills and open moors, found themselves in uncleared woods. They cleared it. It was, indeed, a land-sea economy of intense diversity.

Times, of course, have changed. Giant pine grew a new breed of men along the St. John and the Miramichi. Men converted wood into wind-ships and sailed them round the world. The 140-mile crescent of Prince Edward Island, where in 1771 a governor 'never met with such an increase of potatoes', turned more and more to farming. Steel and coal brought in a measure of industrial specialization within walking distance of Cape Breton's misty glens and the Pictou county hills. Today an upsurge of mechanical industry finds motor cars assembled in Nova Scotia scooting over Canadian roads, base metals from New Brunswick's North Shore in the fabric of world construction. With more to come.

Through it all the inheritance remains. It has always been of vast import-ance on the ground where it first flourished. What has not been fully realized, even by those who possess it, is the part it plays in the continuing existence of Canada as a whole.

For beyond that flickering ring of surf there is another community – or rather, an extension of the first – grown from the seed of these provinces that has blown elsewhere: to New England and across the continent to the West and the North.

The characters are many and various, but the plot of the story is plain. The people who settled the Maritimes were adventurers and refugees, Acadians slipping back from exile, British-American victims of American expulsion, Scots kicked off their hills to make room for sheep, home-seekers fed up with life in the ancient lands. They sowed their flesh when the frontier was a mile from the beach and the river, when the nation we know was less than a gleam in the eye of time. They built a home, a headquarters. They pushed the frontier back. This done, their sons and grandsons, many of them, roved to new frontiers; and the adaptability learned in this land of intense diversity served them everywhere.

In the days before the combine ended 'Harvest Excursions', Maritimers brought up to rowboat and crosscut were welcome in the West because they could also handle horses. And among the sheepskin coats from central and eastern Europe (the accepted cliché for western settlement) there was many a mail-order mackinaw from Rexton and Guysborough and Murray River. Pick up an old snapshot album, east or west. You may well find a postcard showing First Street North in Vermilion, Alberta, next to a snapshot of lobster pots at Shediac, N.B. The face of a man on the driving board of a drill seeder north of Regina looks up at you also from beside the flywheel of a one-lunger at Queensport wharf.

They live and move and share the broadening life of the Canadian nation. On prairie farms, in school-house and pulpit, in mines tucked into the crevices of granite hills. The life and the colour.

I know that in some ways it is dangerous to stress these things. There is a school of thought that deplores this kind of movement, regrets the fact that these provinces have not been able to keep all their children home. Without doubt, within limits, this is a valid point. No doubt also there were gentlemen in England then abed who viewed with alarm the colonizing voyages of Raleigh and Penn.

It is chiefly a story of expansion, not exodus. One and a half million men and women and kids people the land enclosed by the ring of surf. Within that other boundary, traced by bloodlines, flesh, the sound of voices, that sweeps round Wainwright and Estevan, Prince George and Dawson Creek, who knows how many?

Both communities are peopled by as varied a crowd as ever drew breath. Both have cast up names that live in the national lore. Dunn and Aitken and Killam, the business colossi who reached the peak of their power away from these provinces, and Irving who did it at home. Borden and Bennett and Yvon Durelle. Joe O'Brien, the harness-race driver from that island of spuds, foxes, and fast trotting horses. Giant McAskill and giantess Anna Swan, and Lucy Maud Montgomery. Charlie Gorman the skater and Charles Roberts the poet. Hugh MacLennan the novelist and Alex Colville, stippling on panels the heart of the people and the land . . .

That second community of course embraces many who have gone outside the borders of Canada and the Commonwealth (Cyrus Ching the adviser of presidents and Cyrus Eaton the connoisseur of thinkers) but their numbers in Canada are vast, their stories varied. As one having in it much that is typical (though it records a success that few reach or hope to reach) I like the story of John MacIsaac as Ma Murray, the journalistic high priestess of the North, has told it in the *Alaska Highway News*.

From the Cape Breton settlement of Dunvegan MacIsaac worked his way west and north to the Yukon. There he heard of a caterpillar buried in silt at Mile 800 of the new Alaska Highway, for sale as army surplus where it lay. With Eric Steeves (a New Brunswicker of that ilk) he set up frames, winched it out, cleaned it up, and was on his way. Profits from his first road-building job went into new machinery. The breezily articulate Mrs. Murray thus celebrated MacIsaac's parlaying of an abandoned cat into a million dollar business: 'He moved machinery and men into the United Keno Hill for building roads. He moved over to Cassiar and built roads there. He built roads into mining properties and there wasn't a job in the Yukon too tough . . .'

But there is a side to this migration that should never be forgotten. A while ago I found a school register for the year 1834, thirty years before Tupper brought in free schools in Nova Scotia. Twenty house-holders were listed, along with their children. What caught my eye was this: most of these families had sent offshoots to establish the name and the family in other parts of Canada and the world. But, with one exception, every surname is still there, stencilled on the mailboxes of Rural Route One.

Better than any federal-provincial pact, this is the measure of Maritime involvement in the national dream. For blood, though it may be no thicker than politics, is more adhesive. On the evening of the Canso Causeway opening (Fraser, incidentally, earmarked a large chunk of that rock-money for Dalhousie University) I dropped in at a country parlour and found other visitors there. From five provinces and two states, sons, daughters, and grandsons, nieces and nephews and cousins of the families listed in the old school register. I had just read a book by a female American who asserted after a trip to the Maritimes that 'Atlantic Canada . . . is parochial, because it has been driven in on itself . . . left slumping in a backwater.' Obviously she had run into a chronic complainer or an old-timer with a lump in his cheek that was not tobacco. Equally obviously she had never been around Rural Route One in the home-coming season, when two aspects of Maritime life – its continuity and its cosmopolitan flair – are most evident to the eye and ear.

There is no special mystique about all this, despite considerable literature and art, native and otherwise, that depends heavily on the ancient and the quaint. Maritimers possess the same wry humour and common sense, seasoned here and there with irascibility and braggadocio, that make up human nature anywhere. (Let me quote again, from another Eastern Shore woman, Joyce Hemlow of Liscomb, who teaches English at McGill: 'Man is a creature richly compounded of elements, deeps and motives other than reason, as it takes no heap of manuscripts to show.') It is just that here these things are concentrated to an essence, as they are in any country still open to the sky: the rancher on the windy plains of Medicine Hat, who said, 'it blew so hard it would give a gopher the heartburn,' is kin to the Islander who remarked of a dour neighbour that 'his looks mightn't stop a clock but they'd sure slow it down'.

Dilute the essence three to one to arrive at the brew they serve under smoky canopies in the all-industrial regions of the world.

[1967]

Anne Hebért

Quebec: The Original Heart

This province is a country within a country. Québec the original heart. The hardest and deepest kernel. The core of first time. All around, nine other provinces form the flesh of this still-bitter fruit called Canada.

The creation of the world took place on the rock of Québec. Face to the river. Adam and Eve were Louis Hébert and Marie Rollet. The first dwelling. The first land tilled. The first sheaf of grain reaped. The first bit of bread. The first child brought into life. The first body laid in earth.

The first written word. It was in 1534: 'In the name of God and of the King of France.' A cross planted at Gaspé by Jacques Cartier. The vocation of writing begun in the wilderness wind.

And then we were surrendered to time. Time followed its course. By turns we were shaken or lulled by time. Like logs drifting down rivers, we slipped by. A defeat in the heart. A rosary between the fingers. Like the dead. Musing on the song of Lazarus. But see the thought give way to the word. The word becomes flesh. To possess the world. To seize and name the earth. Four and a half centuries of roots. The tree, no longer subterranean, admittedly in the light. Erect. Confronting the world. The Tree of Knowledge. Not in the centre of the garden. Those soft prenatal limbs outside paradise, in the accursed open land. At the hour of birth, a gate opens upon the round and total world.

The right of the adult to be and to do. His man's heart to take and to speak. His man's work to build and to proclaim.

'In Québec nothing changes.' Once this was truth. Immobile, peasant-like. Beneath the snow, or the summer sun. Yet no Sleeping Beauty can pass

105

unchanged the test of slumber. Beneath so many dreams and sorrows a duty is discerned. Take up thy bed and walk. The heaped-up treasure-hoard cracks and splits. Reclaim the heritage from foreign imposts.

The river is salt like the sea. Waves beat upon seaweed-laden shores. Here the wind blows free for ten leagues around. The adventure is boundless. Who can merely tell of it? One must shout it, hands forming a loud-hailer. The two banks narrowing together are thickly black with trees. It is on no human scale. Here man may labour only. Whoever speaks will speak savagely. With a voice of earth and water mixed.

Helter skelter land of wood and sea. North bank. South bank. Kamouraska, Saint-Vallier, Cap à l'Aigle, Saint-Jean-Port-Joli, Ile aux Lièvres, Rimouski, Father Point, Sainte-Luce, Anse Pleureuse, Coin du Banc, Pic de l'Aurore, Gros Morne, Cloridorme, Ile Bonaventure.

Sea birds by thousands encrust the rock. Lift. Wheel. Raucous cries on the swell of the sea. Gannets, grebes, cormorants, gulls. Beneath the wind the rock seems to shake itself, like a wild beast attacked by superbly fantastic swarms of bees. Above, the sky.

A hundred thousand lakes. Streams with the strength of a river. Forests entangled by dead-falls. An axe in the hand like a cane. The tracks are those of caribou. Mosquitoes smoke upon your body like your own breath.

Burnt-over land as far as the eye can see. New growth of birch on the green moss. Long tendrils of moss, drawn from the soil, like garlands with fine sandy roots. Gathering blueberries. The barrens laden with blue fruit. That silvery mist clouding the fresh berries. That was when I was a child. Now the reign of the birches is threatened. The face of Charlebois is pitted by dead birches. Sad little white bones against the green of the forest.

Calm lakes, like water in the hollow of a hand. Lake Edward. We children were forbidden to go near the water. 'Your hair the colour of the fallow deer, your body of peacocks' – hunters might fire in error. The midges, the blackflies ambushed us. Thousands of needles. Was that the sound of a moose? It crosses the lake, swimming. As if it ploughed a mirror. Deer! A deer in the hayfield! A prodigy of a leap! There it is, out of range. Sheltering in the black spruce.

Sainte-Catherine. Each summer's end a brown bear ventured from the forest. Prowled the edges of the fields. While the golden hay assumed the colour of fresh-baked bread. Children saw enormous tracks in the sand of the little strawberry woods. Games were erased. Sand castles crushed. The children gravely enchanted. As if in the night an heraldic beast had come from the high plains of the Countess de Segur, née Rostopchine, claiming her tribute in Canadian land.

Sainte-Foy. Named for a bitter victory. There where the city, the new university city, now expands. During my childhood it was a little wood. A whole summer of holidays. A brook. Green grass-snakes. Symphonies of tree-frogs. Strawberries bordering the fields. Orchards. Apples succeeding apples – the green, the white, the transparents, the Fameuses. Four houses thick-shelled with white brick. Each with its garden and its orchard. The road was called the Avenue of the Four Bourgeois. It was the country.

Québec. That city where my parents were born. Where my ancestors prospered and were undone. The city is lived in. Above. Below. The city is ours. We need only plainly speak its name, this city. City on a crag. City of the New World. Upper Town. Lower Town. The secret province. Homogeneous. Certain of its identity. Dreaming behind its jalousies. Taking its time. Sauntering through the narrow streets. Through the summer evenings. Releasing in full bloom the beauty of its daughters.

The long length of Dufferin Terrace. Rue Saint-Louis, rue de la Fabrique, Esplanade, rue des Grissons, rue des Glaçis, ruelle du Trésor, côte à Coton, côte de la Négresse, Latin Quarter, rue Dauphine, Jardin du Fort, Jardin du Gouverneur, rue sous le Cap, Petit Champlain. Little by little the aristocratic quarters move from the old city. A whole floating population camps within the walls. The tall dwellings divide into rented pigeonholes. They sell souvenirs. The port overflows with shipping. Whirlpools of gulls. Vast gates of the water. The sea begins. Clerical bands and coifs. A city of terraces and convents.

Sugar and syrup from the Beauce. Honey from Saint-Pierre-les-Becquets. Mushrooms from Waterloo. Cider from Saint-Hilaire. Brome Lake duck. Valcartier turkey. Real geography is learned at the table, in the breaking of bread.

Boucherville, Varennes, Verchères, Contrecœur, Saint-Antoine-de-Tilly, Sorel, Saint-Jean-sur-Richelieu. Old villages of the French régime. Fine stone houses in the style of manors. Elms, of all trees the most civilized; maples; an amiable river. A domesticated landscape. Ripe and reassuring age.

Rapid, rugged ice hockey. The log drive, perilous leap without a net, on rivers in full flood. Twenty-five thousand white geese alight on Cap Tourmente. Take to the sky. Perfect formations. Passing above Québec. Their faraway raucous yelping, solid, unhearing, almost unreal, dominating the whole autumnal night sky – if you have never heard it, you have never felt the strange sensation of physical envelopment in a dream, never escaped above the earth.

Once this city was called Hochelaga. François-Xavier Garneau wrote of it, 'a half-hundred wooden habitations, fifty paces long and twelve to fifteen wide. In each house, walls hung with skins skilfully sewn together, several rooms opened upon a square room containing the hearth. The settlement was surrounded by a triple palisade.' This city was called Ville-Marie. There mass was celebrated by the light of fireflies. 'Should every tree on Montreal Island become an Iroquois, it is my duty there to found a colony, and I will go.' Thus spoke Maisonneuve. This city is called Montreal. More than two million inhabitants. A vigorous, enterprising life. Creates. Defies. Struggles, gains, loses, rejoices in its destiny. Multiplies. Becomes complex. Accepts or rejects. Melting pot. Cultural broth. Constructs. Demolishes. Reconstructs. A perpetual factory. A city which had no age. Which burns its past. Of which its present pride is its future. At the high heat of its energy. At the peak of its endeavours. Victorian Sherbrooke Street is earth-bound. Vive Dorchester Boulevard and its proud, fine skyscrapers. The calm of Westmount's little streets: Mount Stephen, Oliver, Kensington. Men, ideas, politics, commerce; business, the arts and daily life assert themselves, confront each other. With the rhythm of neon. Flashing in the immense city. By day as by night.

Country of water. Of the tumultuous strength of water. Untamed water harnessed. Like a hot-blooded team. Proud water tamed and mastered. The powerhouse of La Gabelle. The Beauharnois dam. Manicouagan. The greatest workshop in the world. Man's all-powerful hand set over the energy of the water.

Asbestos. Noranda. Bourlamaque. Gagnon. Arvida. Matagami. The darkness of the earth is opened. The black heart of the earth delivers up its treasures. Asbestos, copper, gold, zinc, aluminum, iron. The shadows are heavy. The miner's lamp scarcely lights the depths of the workings. The patient slow efforts of the young master of the premises. Claiming his entire share.

To seize this province in flagrante delicto, in the very act of existence. To understand. To do it justice. To put it into words. The task of a poet. The honour of living.

[1967]

Naim Kattan

Montreal Comes of Age

When I first got there fourteen years ago, Montrealers were not yet in possession of their city. It was a migratory city, where nothing, not even the most ancient walls, seemed there to stay. Vast, pervasive gas stations side by side with grocery stores: people stopped in these places; they didn't occupy them. These men and women accepted life in the transitory. You told yourself that the heart of the city wasn't there, that the geographical centre was fleeting and unreal, that you must look elsewhere for the throb of life. And then, walking from one quarter to another, you found distinct communities – weighed down by the past, nostalgic in the present, and towards the future feeling a mixture of indifference and uncertainty. You wanted to satisfy yourself with this accumulating wealth by taking possession of it. And you perceived that these weren't quarters at all, but villages placed end to end, added one to another without making a totality. You went from the charming to the sordid, from the exotic to the commonplace. There were English, living in the dream of a great empire but accepting their own role as 'colonials'; French, aspiring to remake an America in their own style, letting the traces of the past rot away, turning their backs on the pre-Conquest city – still there but hideously disguised; Jews reconstructing, in the framework of the new continent, an ever-receding Europe; Italians, happy at having risen above the misery of their native land, persisting in a loyalty to it that was often anachronistic and sometimes desperate.

'The secret of this town has got to be somewhere else,' I told myself. These people, in spite of their differences – no, because of them – *must* want to get

E 109

together. Yet the movie theatres were French, English, sometimes Italian, and (just lately) Greek. No neutral ground. No shared places for everybody to rub shoulders and at least see each other, even if they didn't speak. This cluster of villages extended even into the cafés and restaurants.

I went to look for the physical face of the city. Montreal stretches between the river and the mountain: the perfect place for space to translate the dreams of men. I spent a lot of time walking on the mountain. I hardly ever met Montrealers there, or rather only a new species, my own – the ones who had chosen to be here, who had picked Montreal as their home, mostly Europeans. These strollers were undoubtedly looking for a bit of countryside in the heart of the city. They hadn't yet got used to the idea of going out of town to find themselves, of going elsewhere, were it only to crowd into restaurants or hotels oddly like the ones where they lived. 'Elsewhere', for them, was the city itself. One had no right to its secret if one turned one's back on it. But one was all the more a foreigner when among foreigners who had been there always, or for a long time anyway.

And then I discovered the river bank. How often I have walked along the shore from Verdun to Senneville. But the Montrealers, shut into their villages, didn't even know the river was there, that they could walk to Verdun and sit on the banks. Some Sunday afternoons you found a few solitary people there, often of the same kind that abounded on the mountain, who found in the wild, untamed waters of that inland sea an image of the force and power they were looking for. There too you went from village to village; from Lachine to Dorval, from Pointe-Claire to Saint-Anne-de-Bellevue. But these were settings that gave the city a frontier. These clusters of population born on the edge of the river surrounded the city and gave it the solidity that the stores and gas-stations deprived it of. So the city had boundaries; it knew them and seemed to love them. Montreal had all the elements of a city, but wasn't yet one in the minds of its inhabitants.

And then, as if everybody had passed the word through the villages, the explosion happened. You would have thought it had been planned, that there had been secret meetings, that unknown powers were laying foundations and drawing up plans. At last Montreal was coming out of limbo, being born in broad daylight.

All along Dorchester Street, old houses revealed their decrepitude – not that they were really old, but they belonged to an era when merchants lived on the edge of the village, seeking a comfort that nowadays seems anachronistic. It was as if these houses were razing themselves to the ground of their own accord and the skyscrapers were replacing them – a speculator's dream. But it also seemed as if the speculators sensed which way the wind was blowing, and were responding as much to a collective need as to the profit motive. In New York – on Wall Street as on Park Avenue – the skyscrapers bear witness to a power that demands expression. In Rio de Janeiro the wall of skyscrapers along Copacabana reflects the desire of men to insist on their own presence amidst excessively pervasive natural enchantments. In Montreal, the skyscrapers answered a need for solidity. The city was asserting its permanence. Willpower and dream had suddenly coincided. The metropolis abruptly detached itself from a pseudo-aristocratic Britain, a France beyond recall, an eastern and central Europe of which only pale shadows remained. Montreal proclaimed itself an American city. But America is perpetually being discovered, and Montrealers just now are sketching a rough portrait of one of its many faces.

And behind the skyscrapers near the harbour a buried city was being brought to light: Old Montreal was being born, for this new city can realize its own youth only by discovering its past. To accept itself as American it must restore its links with its French ancestors and make friends anew with a contemporary France.

It is on its own conditions that Montreal is an American city – in the assertion of its triple character as a francophone, European, and international city. Even when one declares, with a straight face and without sarcasm, that Montreal is the second French city in the world, one cannot fail to recognize that it is more a matter of an ardent desire, of a dream even, than of a blinding reality. But a francophone city Montreal is, by the majority of its people and above all by their will to preserve their language and culture. All the same, its relation to France is not that of a provincial town to the country as a whole. The country Montreal belongs to is Canada; its continent is America. Nevertheless it is a city that cannot dispense with its family connection with Paris. But this link is real only in so far as one takes account of the differences and the autonomies. Montreal has to affirm its francophone character in tension and with an effort, for it is not taken for granted. It is constantly disputed, because this city is anglophone too, and – to an increasing extent – European. The tension between the francophone city and the European and anglophone one is not the tension of adversaries – still less of enemies – where the issue must be a victory and a defeat. This is a tension that can be overcome and transcended only by a synthesis, in which the city's francophone character, instead of being challenged by its Europeanness, will be enriched and under-lined.

Already a start has been made. And the city is no longer a collection of villages; it is now a concourse of human groups seeking to form a community. They can still tear the city apart or prevent it from growing, from reaching its full strength. They can also make it a model environment, unique in North America. Expo 67 proved that it is not merely desirable but also possible. In this great global happening Montreal declared itself an international city. Not a cosmopolitan city, lacking an individual character, but an international city with a character of its own, welcoming all contributions and fusing them in a common spirit which makes the city into this ideal place where men meet and feel less alone; where they live side by side and from their neighbourly proximity there springs an event; where community life renders possible the dream of happiness.

Montreal asserts its modernity without denying its past. A city that welcomes the citizens of the whole world because it knows how to remain itself. A young city, because it respects its own antiquity even as it passes beyond it. A city in process of becoming, which points to the future while accepting the present.

[1968. Translated by Ivon Owen.]

William Kilbourn

Tory Ontario

I knew an American lady in Oakville who was a lifelong member of the Daughters of the American Revolution and the Imperial Order of the Daughters of the Empire, and to the end of her days she remained fiercely proud of both. I remember school children in Dundas who solemnly intoned their morning vows to the British connection in words very like those being addressed to the Stars and Stripes in other classrooms across the border. 'I pledge allegiance to the Empire, one and indivisible . . . ,' their oath began. Ontario has always been a bit like that.

Thrust down into the heartland of the United States, between the American midwest and industrial north-east, the old thickly-settled part of the province has spent nearly two centuries becoming a thoroughly American society, all the while fiercely fighting off Yankee invasions and influences with ringing protestations of loyalty to things imperial, royal, and British. 'As loyal she began,' says our provincial motto, 'so shall she ever remain.' It was altogether fitting that the Red Ensign, that glorious amalgamation of assorted heraldic shrubbery with the Union Jack, should reach its final resting place in 1965 as the provincial flag of Ontario. We have never allowed ourselves to forget that our first settlers were exiled from their homes for their loyalty to King and Empire during the American Revolution. The first farming in Ontario was done by war refugees along the banks of the Niagara River in 1779. The Loyalists' settlements along the St. Lawrence, on the Bay of Quinte and the Detroit river followed in the 1780s, never far at first from the shadow of the military forts. They were joined by soldiers retired on half pay and by the lairds and squires from Britain – Thomas Talbot, the Lake Erie baron, the tribal chief Archibald MacNab, John Galt and Tiger Dunlop of the Canada Company who received their vast estates in return for the hundreds of settlers they brought out. The Gaelic-speaking Glengarry Fencibles, the first Roman Catholic regiment in the British Army since the Reformation, came out to settle Glengarry County, and their chaplain and leader, Alexander Macdonell, became an ecclesiastical pillar of the Family Compact in Upper Canada second only to Bishop Strachan. Even the Indians were Loyalist. Led from their home in American territory by the chief of the Six Nations, Joseph Brant, who spoke with the accent of an 18th century English gentleman, they took up land along the Grand River. One of their tribe, Pauline Johnson, a century later wrote anti-American popular verse:

> Oh the Dutch may have their Holland
> And the Spaniards have their Spain
> But the Yankees to the south of us
> Must south of us remain.

But remain they did not. Encouraged by the promise of land, from the beginning thousands of Yankee farmers poured in to settle beside the Loyalist exiles and the emigrants from Britain. By the time the War of 1812 actually brought invading American troops into the province, three-fifths of Upper Canada's scattered population of eighty thousand was already made up of newly-arrived Americans. They brought Yankee ways and attitudes with them, and they helped make Canada that turbulent and vulgar democracy which even Nova Scotian radicals like Joseph Howe looked on with distaste and were so reluctant to join in 1867. John A. Macdonald did not find them the easiest sort of people to manage. Speaking of the province of Canada in the eighteen-fifties, which at that time combined what were to be Ontario and Quebec, he said, 'The western peninsula must not get control of the ship. It is occupied by Yankees and Covenanters, the most yeasty and unsafe of populations.' Such 'unsafe' elements provided the chief constituency for the Clear Grits and George Brown's Toronto *Globe*. Many of them had fought or sympathized with William Lyon Mackenzie and the rebels of 1837.

Though they were soon outnumbered by Orangemen and other later British arrivals, Americans continued to cross the border. In the mid-nineteenth century, much to the province's benefit, American craftsmen and entrepreneurs came to invest the skills and capital that started many of Ontario's first foundries and manufacturing plants. And later still, American union organizers and branch plant presidents have been familiar figures on the Ontario scene. Ontario society of course was bound to have a North American flavour anyway, even without the influence of the United States. The frontier itself and the hard life of pioneer farming imposed a rough social equality of their own. They allowed for little of the leisure and dignity needed for a landed aristocracy to take root.

Nevertheless Loyalist sentiment in Ontario has always been predominant. The memory of a people fighting for their homes in the War of 1812, against invaders who burned farm buildings and the little colonial parliament houses at York, was reinforced by the armed invasions after the 1837 rebellion and the Fenian raids of 1866, and by a good deal of aggressive talk by American politicians right down into the twentieth century. With Loyalism there has been a basic conservatism which the radical Grit tradition has rarely been able to break through. Egerton Ryerson and his Methodists very early on turned Tory. George Brown's sympathies and thinking moved gradually towards those of the urban businessmen to form a new kind of Ontario conservatism, which has really lasted ever since. The victory of the United Farmers of Ontario in 1919 was the last fleeting protest of the pioneers. And the new urban radicalism has seriously threatened to take over only once, with the C.C.F. upsurge in 1943.

One thing both radicals and conservatives did have in common was the conviction that French was a foreign language; they could get equally enthusiastic about capturing Louis Riel or enforcing conscription in Québec. Canadian nationalism is still in many ways Ontario nationalism writ large, but it is now more apt to take the form of decorating our buildings with *avant garde* Montreal art or demanding French language instruction in the primary schools. We have even discovered, along with the recognition at last of Québec's claim for a special status in Confederation, that Ontario itself never has been an exclusively British domain, and itself has claims to being bicultural. Not only was it part of New France, the land of Champlain and the *coureurs de bois* and the Jesuit martyrs, but it also has more people of French descent than any place else in the new world outside Québec.

Other cultures than our two official ones were also an early presence. The Mennonites came from Pennsylvania about 1800 and Waterloo County is still thoroughly German. Italians and Ukrainians have been coming to Ontario for three generations. But it was Canada's great postwar influx of European immigrants, over half of whom came to settle in Ontario, that really made the point clear.

The newcomers also contributed to the province's cultural coming-of-age. They helped transform the shops and parks and restaurants, the universities and the theatres, and make things grow that were not there before. The provincial capital itself became suddenly a great cosmopolitan city. Yet the curving twin towers of Toronto's new city hall in no way contradicted the values of their neighbour, the venerable shrine of the Law Society of Upper Canada, a living symbol of Ontario's Loyalist tradition. The new city hall in fact bespeaks that civic pride and respect for order that has made Metro Toronto a world-famous experiment in local government and kept Toronto to the very core one of the few viable big cities in North America.

The whole society of Ontario is predominantly urban. By the 1961 census seven of the fifteen largest metropolitan areas in Canada were situated in the province. Yet the first and lasting image of Southern Ontario is still the pastoral one. It is a mild and temperate land, between the lower edge of the Rocky Shield and the rim of the Great Lakes, full of Holsteins and lush fields, cedar swamps and slow meandering rivers – the Speed and the Thames and the Avon, this land of the weekly newspaper – *The Grand River Sachem, The Dundalk Herald,* land of lawns and verandahs, giant shade trees and weathered brick Victorian houses, the land that grew the Oslers and the Masseys. There are the Scottish stone towns, like Fergus and Perth, the cathedral and university towns, Kingston and London and Guelph, the estates like Jalna, the lakefronts and main streets like Mariposa's. There are the regional accents of the rolling Caledon hills, the flat black-loamed acres of Holland Marsh, the sandy tobacco counties above Lake Erie, the warm peninsula of peaches and grapes and cherries beneath the Niagara escarpment. And lurking behind and beneath, half hidden through it all, the roads and meeting places, the portages and town sites, the names and the legends inherited from the original, the deepest possessors, the Indians.

[1967]

Douglas Fisher

Ontario's Ancient North

One night back in late 1965 a convivial mob surged into a small Toronto hall. Several lonesome migrants from Port Arthur had hired the hall and advertised a 'Lakehead reunion' by word of mouth. The response bowled them over. The chattering throng hated to leave and did so vowing more and bigger reunions.

Such re-kindling of a small community's spirit at the heart of Ontario's urban sprawl could just as easily be gathered from ex-residents of Sudbury or Kapuskasing or the Sault. Like the Maritimes before it, Northern Ontario has a continual population flow, especially of its youth, mostly to the metropolitan south.

In this century the region has staged from frontier to development to stability and, in much of it, to stagnation. The chambers of commerce and the politicians keep the style and clichés of the past — 'inexhaustible resources', 'the treasure-house of the continent'. Northern Ontario has been 'next year' and 'next generation' country. But now there's a shrillness. The demands, claims, and plaints no longer have the swagger. There has never been, of course, a coherent regional movement of any kind. Just a similarity in hopes and grieving of each of its towns and subsections!

This is the striking paradox of Northern Ontario: the climate and landscape, the people and their work, are so much alike but there is no entity, merely a scatter of locales.

The Ontario government declares that Northern Ontario is that shield-shaped bloc, roughly 500 miles deep from Hudson Bay to the Upper Lakes and the French River, and 1,000 miles wide from Quebec to Manitoba. It divides the bloc in two: Northeastern Ontario with three sub-regions: the Clay Belt, the Nickel Range, and Algoma; and Northwestern Ontario with three massive parts: the Lakehead, Fort Frances, and Kenora.

The area is Russian or Texan in scope but the low, rocky terrain, the dearth of mighty, navigable rivers, the scattered and partial nature of the merchantable timber, the vicious winters and the brief growing season all have inhibited widespread or intensive settlement. All but the boggish thickets of the Hudson Bay rim is Canadian Shield country. The children's texts acclaim the Shield as the world's greatest mineral storehouse but the keys to it are expensive and the riches buried at random.

The toughest task in Canadian development through the fur-trade era to 1830 and through the railway-building age to 1914 was to bridge Northern Ontario to reach attractions westward. The provincial government did not turn to its north until the mid-90s. Its first endeavour was to collect old survey reports of federal geological parties which had made canoe sweeps through the region in the '70s and '80s. Significantly, these geologists had had unknown country before them. The lore and maps recorded long before by the Northwesters and the Bay company were filed in Beaver House, London. Each generation in each part of Northern Ontario has had to have its past rediscovered for it, usually from records in London or Toronto or Ottawa or Winnipeg. As yet its two new universities, Lakehead and Laurentian at Sudbury, have not taken up the tasks of interpreting the region or collating information about it.

Any gold camp, logging chance, paper-mill, railway point, Indian reserve, or trading post in Northern Ontario is much like another. Indigenous local leadership across this variety, whether it be economic, political, or social, is frustrated by the large scale of economic enterprise. This is particularly true of railroads and mining companies. Neither enterprise has taken a keen interest in and responsibility for the social and political life of the area or its parts, except to evade municipal demands for taxes. Each northern town has looked with querulous aspiration and exasperation to Queen's Park in Toronto. The departments of Highways, Education, Mines, and Lands and Forests provide the main administrative channels for local needs and wishes. Despite the earnest of good intentions proclaimed at each provincial election, there has been little decentralization of administration towards the north.

Each community has had its colourful characters, especially its strong men, but there have been few regional spokesmen and no concerted political action from the whole. Every once in a while a secession movement pops up – e.g. Cochrane or the Lakehead or Kenora – but it never has more than a few wild disciples. C. D. Howe, Sir James Dunn, and Roy Thomson started on the road to power and wealth in Northern Ontario. Each came as an adult, attained a certain scale, and then moved on to bigger leagues.

The lack of a past, the separateness, the distance, the boom and bust of mining and logging, and the mixed ethnicity of the people have made for open local societies, an intense community life, and a frenetic liveliness. The Moose, the Masons, the Elks, the Royal Order of the Purple, the Eastern Star, the Lions, the Kinsmen, the Foresters, the Dante Clubs, the Prosvita Societies, the Legion, and a clutch of sporting clubs preoccupy the communities. They make for vociferousness, not brooding. It was symbolic that the impostor professor, MacDonald, not only held a university post at the Lakehead for two and a half years but was treasured for a host of community works.

Movement, boom, depletion, completion, and change! These are intrinsic to railroading, road, hydro, and rail construction, mining, logging, and lumbering. At first strong backs were more essential than skills. Thus the Finns, Swedes, Balts, Italians, and Ukrainians found places in the flood years of immigration. Most of the merchandising and professional people came from old Ontario. The engineering and techniques were drawn from the U.K. and the U.S.

Such diversity allied with the isolation, the rawness, and the dreams to make communities which bridged their people without a set class structure or a strong administrative grouping to control them. Any tendency to company dominance, always likely – especially in the Sault with Algoma Steel and in Sudbury with INCO – tended to dissipate with the flow and variety of folk. One doesn't regiment or keep down railroaders or loggers or miners very easily.

There are about 25,000 native Indians in Northern Ontario. They have been scattered, either as nomads, on tiny reserves, or in the shack-town fringes of the villages and towns. An Indian problem only emerged in the sixties. Typically, most of the whites underplay it, in part because there hasn't been a strong colour-line against intermarriage, mostly because the Indians have been so inconspicuous as a pressure group.

French Canadians came early into the region, most of the first-comers being assimilated. Later migrants of the '20s and '30s clustered together, retaining their language, in settlements along the north line of the C.N.R. west to Hearst, around the Porcupine, and in the Nickel Range. Aside from the odd airing of educational grievances they have not riven towns apart. Few seem to sense themselves as outliers of Quebec and neither Montreal nor Hull nor Quebec City is their inspiration or cultural reservoir.

Even in ridings where the French are in the majority, Social Credit has not elected members. The C.C.F., and its successor the New Democratic Party, has been a more successful dissident. In most of the region, an election means a three-way fight; a slight edge goes federally to the Liberals and provincially to the Conservatives. The personality of the candidate means more and party label less than in most of Canada.

Northern Ontario is more highly unionized than any other part of the country. A consequence is a high wage-level. This factor, added to the mobile bent of the out-of-work, and the decamping of the young and educated, has hidden the slow growth of jobs and inhibits any diversification of industry based on a labour surplus.

The high cost of transportation is the continuing bugbear of each locality. Everybody is conscious and combative about freight rates. Thus the theme of politics most of the time has been for better, cheaper transport. At first it was railroads, then roads, then air services. The other main theme has been the control and use of Crown lands, especially timber limits. Despite recurring uproar, delegations, and briefs galore, the apportionment of leases has never favoured the small local operator. The big enterprise, financed and directed from the south, has been consistently more effective as a lobby.

In recent Ontario politics Northern Ontario has spawned three major scandals: highway contract deceits, the franchise manoeuvring of Northern Ontario Natural Gas, and the Windfall bubble at Timmins. In each case the enticers to skulduggery were from the outside. The distances and the remoteness of the region made such plots both possible and attractive.

Tourism, becoming the summer dormitory of the south, is the surest aspect of the future but mineral prospects remain the 'some day' dream. Despite the sobering ratio of a thousand prospects for each producing mine, mineral production, especially of iron ore, moves ahead.

In its parts, Northern Ontario has a future of change and development. But a rich diversity of industry is most unlikely. The fresh friendliness of its original melting-pot mix will continue to fade as the best-trained young folk are lost and the new immigrant surges go to the big cities. Though a youngish area, many of its towns are prematurely aged. The clearest reflection of this age was seen in 1958. The 'northern vision' of John Diefenbaker had its worst response in Northern Ontario. Why? They had heard it all before.

[1970]

W.O. Mitchell

A Boy's Prairie

Here was the least common denominator of nature, the skeleton requirements simply, of land and sky – Saskatchewan prairie. It lay wide around the town, stretching tan to the far line of the sky, shimmering under the June sun and waiting for the unfailing visitation of wind, gentle at first, barely stroking the long grasses and giving them life; later, a long hot gusting that would lift the black topsoil and pile it in barrow pits along the roads, or in deep banks against the fences.

Over the prairie, cattle stood listless beside the dried-up slough beds which held no water for them. Where the snow-white of alkali edged the course of the river, a thin trickle of water made its way towards the town low upon the horizon. Silver willow, heavy with dust, grew along the riverbanks, perfuming the air with its honey smell.

Just before the town the river took a wide loop and entered at the eastern edge. Inhabited now by some eighteen hundred souls, it had grown up on either side of the river from the seed of one homesteader's sod hut built in the spring of eighteen seventy-five. It was made up largely of frame buildings with high, peaked roofs, each with an expanse of lawn in front and a garden in the back; they lined avenues with prairie names: Bison, Riel, Qu'Appelle, Blackfoot, Fort. Cement sidewalks extended from First Street to Sixth Street at Mac-Taggart's Corner; from that point to the prairie a boardwalk ran.

Lawn sprinklers sparkled in the sun; Russian poplars stood along either side of Sixth Street. Five houses up from MacTaggart's Corner stood the O'Connal home, a three storeyed house lifting high above the white cottage to the left of

121

it. Virginia creepers had almost smothered the veranda; honeysuckle and spirea grew on either side of the steps. A tricycle with its front wheel sharply turned stood in the middle of the walk.

Brian walked back towards his home. He did not turn down Bison Avenue where it crossed the street upon which the church was, but continued on, a dark wishbone of a child wrapped in reflection.

The wind was persistent now, a steady urgency upon his straight back, smoking up the dust from the road along the walk, lifting it and carrying it out to the prairie beyond. Several times Brian stopped: once to look up into the sun's unbearable radiance and then away with the lingering glow stubborn in his eyes; another time when he came upon a fox-red caterpillar making a procession of itself over a crack that snaked along the walk. He squashed it with his foot. Further on he paused at a spider that carried its bead of a body between hurrying thread-legs. Death came for the spider too.

He looked up to find that the street had stopped. Ahead lay the sudden emptiness of the prairie. For the first time in his four years of life he was alone on the prairie.

He had seen it often, from the veranda of his uncle's farmhouse, or at the end of a long street, but till now he had never heard it. The hum of telephone wires along the road, the ring of hidden crickets, the stitching sound of grasshoppers, the sudden relief of a meadow lark's song, were deliciously strange to him. Without hesitation he crossed the road and walked out through the hip-deep grass stirring in the steady wind; the grass clung at his legs; haloed fox-tails bowed before him; grasshoppers sprang from hidden places in the grass, clicketing ahead of him to disappear, then lift again.

A gopher squeaked questioningly as Brian sat down upon a rock warm to the backs of his thighs. He picked a pale blue flax-flower at his feet, stared long at the stripings in its shallow throat, then looked up to see a dragonfly hanging on shimmering wings directly in front of him. The gopher squeaked again, and he saw it a few yards away, sitting up, watching him from its pulpit hole. A suave-winged hawk chose that moment to slip its shadow over the face of the prairie.

And all about him was the wind now, a pervasive sighing through great emptiness, unhampered by the buildings of the town, warm and living against his face and in his hair.

Then for the second time that day he saw a strange boy – one who came from behind him soundlessly, who stood and stared at him with steady grey eyes in a face of remarkable broadness, with cheekbones circling high under a dark and freckled skin. He saw that the boy's hair, bleached as the dead prairie grass itself, lay across his forehead in an all-round cowlick curling under at the edge. His faded blue pants hung open in two tears just below the knees. He was barefooted.

Brian was not startled; he simply accepted the boy's presence out here as he had accepted that of the gopher and the hawk and the dragonfly.

'This is your prairie,' Brian said.

The boy did not answer him. He turned and walked as silently as he had come, out over the prairie. His walk was smooth.

After the boy's figure had become just a speck in the distance, Brian looked up into the sky, now filled with a soft expanse of cloud, the higher edges luminous and startling against the blue. It stretched to the prairie's rim. As he stared, the grey underside carded out, and through the cloud's softness was revealed a blue well shot with sunlight. Almost as soon as it had cleared, a whisking of cloud stole over it.

For one moment no wind stirred. A butterfly went pelting past. God, Brian decided, must like the boy's prairie.

[1947]

Roderick Haig-Brown

British Columbia: Loggers and Lotus Eaters

Flying into it, as most modern visitors are likely to, from any direction except the west, the province is a spectacular array of mountain ridges, seamed and furrowed with snow, more or less heavily timbered on the lower slopes, the deep and narrow valleys floored by the reflected blue or steel-grey of the long lakes. Settlements are scattered and tiny, the few roads to be seen climb out of nothing into emptiness. Then there is the long let-down over the widening green of the Fraser delta, black city smog clinging along the mountain slopes, and the luxurious spread of settlement at the edge of the Gulf of Georgia. At night the transition is even more dramatic, from occasional dim and tiny lights scattered through black immensity to the jewelled glare of neon and mercury vapor and ribboned headlights laid out in a pattern of unlikely beauty for miles on every side.

As a quick impression, it conveys as much truth as any other. But people are living and working out among those mountains, along those narrow valleys, out over the spread of the interior plateau, up the long coastal inlets. The rich glow of lights, the formidable concentration of settlement down in the southwest corner of the province is the yield of a hundred years of men burrowing into the mountains, stripping trees from the timbered slopes, raking the coastal seas, fighting the inland rivers, threading narrow ways through the canyons, chancing cattle among the gentler hills and kindlier valleys. Nearly a million people live on those eight hundred square miles of delta lands and the same lands produce ninety-seven per cent of the dairy products and fifty per cent of the farm value that comes from the whole province. Considerably less than a million people are scattered over the other 365 thousand square miles, where the mountains rear up and the lakes form and the rivers run down.

British Columbia was a hard place to discover and a hard place to explore. The first explorers were more concerned with finding a passage to China and the Indies through the upset scenery than with finding anything useful in the country itself. In fact they were singularly unimpressed with the looks of the place and at times quite bitter about it. Captain George Vancouver, who put an end to the myth of the Northwest Passage in the early 1790s and explored the entire coast of British Columbia in the course of doing so, was addicted to such phrases as: 'the shores put on a very dreary aspect, chiefly composed of rugged rocks, thinly wooded with small dwarf pine trees', thus anticipating the scathing 'rocks and Christmas trees' of later coast settlers. In June of 1792, among the islands at the northern end of the Gulf of Georgia, he found 'as gloomy and dismal an aspect as nature could well be supposed to exhibit', though he was again thankful for the trees which 'screened from our sight the dreary rocks and precipices that compose these desolate shores'. As a writer he lacked the angle that makes the tourist folder.

Alexander Mackenzie, who came to the province by land, was somewhat more phlegmatic about it all; but even he, his canoes broken and his men numbed with cold and half-drowned, had few doubts about the quality of the first stream he found across the continental divide: 'The evil nature of our small river, which we called the Bad River, was such that we were four full days longer in reaching the big water.' Simon Fraser, discovering his great river, had rough words for it: 'I scarcely ever saw anything so dreary; and seldom so dangerous in any country . . . whatever way I turn, mountains upon mountains, whose summits are covered with eternal snows, close the glooming scene.' Even David Thompson, the kindliest and most receptive of all the explorers, had his moments of doubt on the western slope of the Rockies: 'The scene of desolation before us was dreadful, and I knew it. A heavy gale of wind, much more a mountain storm, would have buried us.' And then, as he and his men came down into the floor of the Columbia Valley: 'We are pygmies among the giant pines and cedars of this country, some of them forty feet in girth and reaching two hundred feet without a branch.'

This inhospitable land that so overawed the early explorers was supporting at this time a native population of at least seventy thousand people, many of them in some degree of comfort and security, with a high level of cultural advancement. It took another eighty years, annihilation of the sea otters, decimation of the fur seal herds, the discovery of gold, reduction of the native population (through disease) by some sixty per cent, union with Canada and a transcontinental railroad to build a white population comparable in size to that of their aboriginal predecessors.

As settlement developed it gradually became apparent that this was, after all, a rich and generous land; there were soft and gentle places among its awesome mountains; the mountains themselves had a beauty that inspired affection as well as fear. Richer than gold and more lasting were the zinc and lead of the Kootenays and the copper of the Coast Range. More valuable than beaver skins were the great Douglas firs and red cedars of the coastal forests and the salmon that ran to every river and stream. Farmers boldly dyked and drained the flood plain of the Fraser delta and found themselves with land that would grow almost anything; others in the Okanagan Valley were soon growing tree fruits of superb quality. A pioneer's life was never, anywhere, made up of roses and rapture or lilies and languor, nor even of beer and skittles, but in British Columbia it had worthwhile compensations. The climate was kindly enough, at least in the southern parts and along the coast. Work in the woods or the mines or the fisheries was a source of ready cash, while the dream of independence in the small farm or logging operation, the fishboat or trapline was never too far from probability. For recreation, there were fish to be caught in the streams and lakes, game to be hunted in the hills. Signs of growth and development were evident everywhere and in spite of periodic setbacks no British Columbian doubted them. Logging companies grew massive with the power of steam and sawmills worked into the night; the 'white Empresses' of the C.P.R. sailed for the Orient from Vancouver and the proud fleet of coastal steamships grew ever larger, faster, and more luxurious; mines became richer and more sophisticated, the Fraser valley grew the finest dairy products, the Okanagan the finest fruit in the world.

It is rather easy to think of the development of British Columbia as a series of engineering triumphs; the Cariboo Road of Colonel Moody's Royal Engineers, the driving of the C.P.R. through the Fraser canyons and the passes of the Rockies and the Selkirks, the Fraser valley dykes, the logging railroads – often little miracles of ingenuity – the Hell's Gate fishways, the Aluminum Company's Kemano project, the miles upon empty miles of hard-topped highways built in the years since World War Two, the great hydro projects under construction on the Columbia and at Portage mountain – all these represent a good measure of the faith needed to move mountains and confirm the impression of the early explorers that this was indeed a difficult country. But engineering miracles are commonplace on the North American continent and reflect little of the individuality and meaning of a state or province.

In British Columbia there has always been a gallantry about the job and a shoddiness about the end result. The logger, the province's true aristocrat, stands large and bold against the background of his ravaged acres. The hardrock miner, courageous, skilful, and hard handed, moves on, leaving his ghost towns and tailings and abandoned millsites as scars upon the hillsides. The fisherman, proud and independent, struggles in the chaos of a disorganized industry. Farmland, brought to full fertility through three or four lifetimes, makes easy money for the real estate speculator. The construction worker manoeuvres his mighty machines in frantic haste through mud and dust and rock to leave behind him drowned and derelict forests, arrogant mills, and ill-planned cracker-box towns. Enormous log rafts among the coastal inlets, the seine boat fleets, white-face cattle driven down the Chilcotin or spread over the rolling hills of the Nicola Valley, tourists flanked by huge dead fish, loneliness of deep forest and mile-high glacier, gold of poplar and tamarack, desolate black of spruce, reflections in quiet lakes, rock and snow reared against the sky, surge of Pacific surf and watery glint of muskeg miles, all these things, too, are the pictured, familiar face of British Columbia.

Yet far more than all this, the province is an idea of pleasure and rich living, elegant houses hung on the rocks in West Vancouver, money made from nothing, as it always has been, in the big buildings downtown, retirement in Victoria, pleasure boats, year around golf, equitable climate generally, and in contrast with the rest of Canada, easy living.

The other side of this picture is the province's long tradition of militant unions, from the time of the early coal miners to the International Wood-workers, United Fishermen, United Mine Workers, and many others of today. Owing much to British trade unionism and the British Labour Party it has been, for the most part, a strong and successful movement, balancing the easy successes of capital let loose in the broad and fruitful field of natural resources. From the time of Amor de Cosmos and his war upon the 'Family-Company-Compact', this view has had expression in the legislature, though usually in opposition. Without its counterbalance and the determined humanity of such men as Ernest Winch, who sat in the B.C. Legislature from 1933 until his death in 1957, the province would have been little better than a playground for economic imperialists, with the spoils going unfailingly to the strong.

Even as it is, British Columbia remains something of an anachronism. Until the last few years the mountains had effectively restricted development to a few favourable areas. Modern machinery and modern technology have suddenly opened up new areas and these are among the last on the continent available for old-fashioned industrial empire-building. Stakes, in the form of capital investment, are high; but the returns, in the form of long-term claims on natural resources, are almost beyond calculation.

Living out the final stages of nineteenth-century concepts in the latter half of the twentieth century, it has so far spared little attention for much beyond physical development. The pragmatic values of education are recognized in some degree and the university at Point Grey has become a great, though overburdened, school; it is now supported by two younger institutions, the universities of Victoria and Simon Fraser, and a growing list of regional colleges. The province's greatest collective artistic endeavour, the Vancouver International Festival, has faded into steady decline through lack of municipal and provincial support. Yet the province has better artists in almost every field than it deserves or is aware of, and in this may be the real promise of change and growth. British Columbia has the wealth, energy, and newness to become the most enlightened and humanitarian of all the provinces. If the vision has become blurred in the rush of prosperity, it can still be renewed in the calmer times of consolidation.

[1967]

Farley Mowat

The Canadian Arctic

The first difficulty that must be mastered in coming to grips with the Far North is to decide just where 'north' begins and to ascertain its boundaries. Modern man has tried to evade the issue by separating the northern regions into sections, like a layer cake, so that he can deal with each part as a separate entity. Ask a scientist for a definition of 'north' and you are instantly ears deep in boreal, subarctic, and arctic zones, in isotherms, degree-days, and permafrost limits. The truth is that the region has no arbitrary southern boundary except in so far as one exists in us as a state of mind. The situation is akin to that of an astronaut shot up in a rocket. At what point does he enter space? At no *point*, but only when he has become aware that he has entered an alien environment.

Since Canadians generally regard the Far North as an alien environment, they enter it when they leave their familiar world of the South behind them. The entry takes place in the upper reaches of the broad band of sombre coniferous forest that stretches across the entire breadth of Canada. Beginning near the Yukon–British Columbia border, this transition region slopes southeastward to Hudson Bay near Churchill where it swings sharply south paralleling the coast around James Bay. It then angles northeastward across Ungava to reach the Atlantic in the general vicinity of Nain on the Labrador coast. At its southernmost point (the top of James Bay) there are polar bears, seals, tundra, and caribou, although the region is eight hundred miles south of the Arctic Circle. The North embraces the arctic zone but it is not limited to that region, nor to the Yukon and the Northwest Territories. It includes a sliver of northern Alberta, rather more of northern Saskatchewan, a goodly bite of northern Manitoba, a nibble of Ontario, a large part of Quebec, and the upper portion of Labrador.

It comprises a huge section of the earth's surface. Measuring from the north tip of Ellesmere Island (less than five hundred miles from the North Pole), the northern land mass strikes southward nearly two thousand miles to Cape Henrietta Maria on Hudson Bay – roughly the distance between Montreal and Calgary! And from the Alaska-Yukon border to Cape Dyer on the coast of Baffin Bay it stretches about the same distance east and west. It encompasses about one million, seven hundred thousand square miles – nearly half the total area of Canada.

The Canadian North reaches from Atlantic to Pacific but, more important, it extends almost to the heart of the Arctic Ocean. Canada *fronts* on this third ocean, which is a true mediterranean sea, in exactly the same way that North Africa fronts on the European Mediterranean. This is a startling idea but one we would be well advised to get used to since Asia, Europe, and North America all face each other across the almost land-locked polar sea and it is here that the three continents lie closest together. The orientation we get from looking at standard maps that show the North Pole at the top of beyond is arbitrary and wrong. This is *not* the way the world really is. The polar region is actually the *centre* of the northern hemisphere, and the geographic centre of Canada is in the Keewatin tundra 250 miles north-northwest of Churchill. Consequently when we turn our back on the North in the belief that there isn't much of interest in that direction, we are turning our backs on Europe and Asia, as well as on a great part of our own country. So far only the military men, preoccupied with death and destruction, have grasped this vital fact. When and if Canadians have the sense to appreciate its peaceful significance we may become a nation at the centre, instead of remaining a sycophantic satellite at the back door of the United States.

One of the particularly cockeyed misconceptions we have about our North is that it is all of a piece – or, at the most, of two pieces: a bleak expanse of frozen sea and a dreary wilderness of frozen plain. The truth is that the Arctic displays as much variety as any other great natural realm on earth. Stretching from central Labrador to Baffin Island, the up-tilted eastern edge of the Canadian Shield forms a shaggy range of glacier-encrusted mountains that are as formidable, as massively overwhelming in appearance, as anything in the Rockies. There is nothing to match them in eastern North America; yet they are almost unknown to us. They form the eastern wall of the North. Far to the westward, beyond the Mackenzie River, rise range after range of mountains that culminate in the St. Elias Range whose glacier-shrouded peaks soar to nearly twenty thousand feet in Canada and twenty-four thousand in Alaska. This is the western wall. Between these walls sprawls the worn and pitted face of the Canadian Shield composed of some of the oldest rocks on earth and so eroded by the work of the eons that only the time-smoothed stubs of its once-mighty mountains remain as undulating hills, giving relief to the naked, ancient rock. Here, in the Shield country, lies the greatest assemblage of lakes upon our planet. Between the western edge of the Shield and the risers of the Yukon Cordillera lies a broad tongue of lowlands that extends north from the Great Central Plains of North America, and down it one of the world's greatest rivers, the Mackenzie, carries the waters of the Peace, the Liard, and many lesser rivers to the Arctic Ocean.

North of the mainland lies the Arctic Archipelago, some nine hundred thousand square miles of lands constituting the largest island group in the world. These islands, too, have their variety. Some are mountainous, others are low and grassy plains, still others are bald stone and gravel deserts. Surrounding them lies a complex of sounds and channels as intricate as the most sophisticated maze.

Contained within the arctic lands of Canada is the vast inland sea of Hudson Bay in which the British Isles could be sunk without a trace. East of the main northern land mass a tremendous ice river carried on the Labrador Current flows down through Baffin Bay and Davis Strait, stretching an arctic tentacle as far south as Nova Scotia. The polar ocean is itself a species of 'land', for it is perpetually ice covered and, though the ice moves, men can and do travel over it, and four-engine aircraft can land upon it.

Although the bone structure of most of the North, the Canadian Shield, is perhaps five million years old, much of the land looks raw and new. This is because a mere ten thousand years ago the entire region, except for the northwestern corner, lay buried beneath a gigantic ice sheet. The dome of the Keewatin District ice sheet was two miles thick. Its own titanic weight made the ice sheet plastic and it flowed implacably in all directions outwards from several high-domed centres. It scoured and gouged the ancient rocks, shearing off the surface soil layers and leaving behind an incredibly intricate pattern of water-filled valleys, basins and deep coastal fiords. When the ice eventually melted it left the land littered with debris that ranged from barn-sized boulders to vast fields of shattered rock, and it embossed the naked bones of the country with a complex design of morainic ridges, drumlins, and long sinuous eskers of sand and gravel.

The ice had another, unseen effect. It deep-froze the rock beneath it, producing what we call permafrost. In the extreme northern islands permafrost penetrates fifteen hundred feet into the primeval rock. Even as far south as northern Manitoba the ancient frost remains, unyielding, only a few feet below the shallow surface layers that thaw in summer.

Remnants of the ice sheet itself also survive. In the wall of the eastern mountains some sixty thousand square miles of ice crown the heights and fill great valleys. Other remnants of ice persist in the mountains of the west.

Another generally held misconception about the North is that its climate is so hostile that only polar bears and Eskimos can endure it. Yet winter blizzards on the western prairies can match, in ferocity if not in intensity, the worst weather the North produces. Northern residents who have subsequently endured a winter at Saskatoon or Winnipeg have been heard to refer with nostalgia to the North as 'the banana belt'. Surprisingly, it is a dry world with very little rain or snowfall. Winter snows often lie deeper in Toronto or Montreal than in most parts of the North. Although not even the Yellowknife Chamber of Commerce would call northern winters balmy, they are as bearable as – if longer than – the winters at Ottawa, and the summers can be lovely. There are only two true seasons: winter and summer, the transitions between them being so brief as to be negligible. Near and north of the Arctic Circle the midsummer sun never sets and temperatures sometimes persist in the comfortable sixties and higher for days on end. In winter above the Arctic Circle the sun vanishes for weeks or months, but this 'long night' is seldom really dark. The Northern Lights often give a pervading luminosity and the glitter of the stars in a lucid atmosphere combined with bright moonlight provides enough light for almost all normal activity, including hunting.

The concept of the Far North as a lifeless land is another of our more grotesque illusions. Its southern fringes include the upper reaches of the taiga forests – mainly black and white spruce, larch, birch, and poplar. The northward-marching trees of the taiga grow sparser and more stunted until they fade out in the vast open plains called tundra. There is no absolute line of demarcation between taiga and tundra – no real 'timberline'. The two regions interpenetrate like the clasped fingers of gigantic hands. There are pockets of tundra deep inside the forest, and oases of trees far out on the sweep of the tundra. Nor is the tundra all of a kind. There is alpine tundra high on mountain slopes, shrub tundra close to the taiga region, sedge tundra to the north, moss-and-lichen tundra still farther north and, on the extreme northern islands, fell-field tundra where vegetation finally gives up its stubborn attempt to occupy the remote lands that lie surrounded by unyielding polar ice. But in summertime most tundra regions boast an array of flowering plants of infinite number and delight. Although they are small, they mass in such profusion that they suffuse hundreds of square miles with shifting colour. They form a Lilliputian jungle where hunting spiders, bumblebees, small and delicate moths and butterflies abound. Black flies and mosquitoes abound too, alas, and there is no evading the fact that they are the bane of summer in the North.

Birds breed almost everywhere. Mammals of many species, ranging from squat, rotund lemmings to massive muskox, occupy the lands. The seas are home to whales, seals, obese walrus, and sinuous white bears. The seas are also rich in fishes as are the numberless inland lakes. For those with eyes to see, the North is vitally and vividly alive. Long, long ago, men of other races out of another time recognized this truth and learned to call the northern regions 'home'.

[1967]

V
Peoples: First Canadians and New Canadians

Edmund Carpenter
Joseph Mitchell
James Eayrs
Larry Zolf
Mordecai Richler
George Woodcock

Edmund Carpenter

The Eskimo and His Art

In the mid-winter of 1772, in the desolate Canadian tundra, Samuel Hearne and his native companions saw the track of a strange snowshoe. They followed it to a little hut where they discovered a young woman sitting alone. She told of her capture by a hostile band, the murder of her parents, husband, and infant, and of her escape nearly seven months before. Living alone, without seeing a human face, she supported herself by snaring small game.

'It is scarcely possible to conceive,' observed Hearne, 'that a person in her forlorn situation could be so composed as to contrive, or execute, anything not absolutely essential to her existence. Nevertheless, all her clothing, besides being calculated for real service, showed great taste, and no little variety of ornament. The materials, though crude, were very curiously wrought, and so judiciously placed as to make the whole of her garb have a very pleasing, though rather romantic appearance.'

From northern Scandinavia, across the tundra and taiga of Siberia, Alaska, and Canada, to the ice-bound coast of East Greenland, men have lived for thousands of years. It's a hard land. The earth never thaws. It's snow-covered most of the year. Nothing grows. The mystery is not that men should be tossed by chance into this desolate waste; it is, rather, that within this prison of ice and wind they are able to draw from themselves images powerful enough to deny their nothingness.

Nowhere is life more difficult than in the Arctic, yet when life there is reduced to its barest essentials, art and poetry turn out to be among those

135

essentials. Art to the Eskimo is far more than an object: it is an act of seeing and expressing life's values; it is a ritual of exploration by which patterns of nature, and of human nature, are revealed by man.

As the carver holds the unworked ivory lightly in his hand, turning it this way and that, he whispers, 'Who are you? Who hides there?' And then: 'Ah, Seal!' He rarely sets out to carve, say, a seal, but picks up the ivory, examines it to find its hidden form, and, if that is not immediately apparent, carves aimlessly until he sees it, humming or chanting as he works. Then he brings it out: Seal, hidden, emerges. It was always there: he didn't create it, he released it: he helped it step forth.

I watched one white man, seeking souvenirs, commission a carving of a seal but receive instead a carving of a walrus. Another, who wanted a chess set, though his explicit instructions were clearly understood, received a set in which each pawn was different. *Ahmi*, 'It cannot be known in advance' what lies in the ivory.

Eskimo has no real equivalents to our words 'create' or 'make' which presuppose imposition of the self on matter. The closest Eskimo term means 'to work on' which also involves an act of will, but one which is restrained. The carver never attempts to force the ivory into uncharacteristic forms, but responds to the material as it tries to be itself, and thus the carving is continually modified as the ivory has its say.

This is the Eskimo attitude not only toward ivory, but toward all things, especially people: parent toward child, husband toward wife. Where we think of art as possession – and possession to us means control, to do with as we like – art to them is a way of revealing.

In the Eskimo language, little distinction is made between 'nouns' and 'verbs', but rather all words are forms of the verb 'to be' which itself is lacking in Eskimo. That is, all words proclaim in themselves their own existence. Eskimo isn't a nominal language; it doesn't simply name things which already exist, but rather brings both things and actions (nouns and verbs) into being as it goes along. This idea is reflected in the practice of naming a child at birth: when the mother is in labor, an old woman stands around and says as many different eligible names as she can think of. The child comes out of the womb when its own name is called. Thus the naming and the giving birth to the new thing are inextricably bound together.

The environment encourages the Eskimo to think in this fashion. To western minds the 'monotony' of snow, ice, and darkness can often be depressing, even frightening. Nothing in particular stands out; there is no scenery in the sense in which we use the term. But the Eskimo do not see it this way. They're not interested in scenery, but in action, existence. This is true to some extent of many people, but it is almost of necessity true for the Eskimo, for nothing in their world easily defines itself and is separable from the general background. What exists, the Eskimo themselves must struggle to bring into existence. Theirs is a world which has to be conquered with each act and statement, each carving and song – but which, with each act accomplished, is as quickly lost. The secret of conquering a world greater than himself is not known to the Eskimo. But his role is not passive. Man is the force that reveals form. He is the force which ultimately cancels nothingness.

Language is the principal tool with which the Eskimo make the natural world a human world. They use many 'words' for snow which permit fine distinctions, not simply because they are much concerned with snow, but because snow takes its form from the actions in which it participates: sledding, falling, igloo-building, blowing. These distinctions are possible only when experienced in a meaningful context. Different kinds of snow are brought into existence by the Eskimo as they experience their environment and speak; the words do not label something already there. Words, for the Eskimo, are like the knife of the carver: they free the idea, the thing, from the general formlessness of the outside. As a man speaks, not only is his language *in statu nascendi*, but also the very thing about which he is talking. The carver, like the poet, releases form from the bonds of formlessness: he brings it forth into consciousness. He must reveal form in order to protest against a universe that is formless, and the form he reveals should be beautiful.

When spring comes and igloos melt, the old habitation sites are littered with waste, including beautifully designed tools and tiny ivory carvings, not deliberately thrown away, but, with even greater indifference, just lost. Eskimo are interested in the artistic act, not in the product of that activity.

A carving, like a song, is not a thing; it is an action. When you sense a form emerging from the ivory, you release it; when you feel a song within you, you sing it. The Eskimo word 'to make poetry' is the word 'to breathe'; both are derivatives of *anerca*, the soul, that which is eternal, the individual breath of life. A poem is words infused with breath or spirit: 'Let me breathe of it,' says the poet-maker and then begins: 'One has put his poem in order on the threshold of his tongue.'

' "My Breath" – this is what I call this song,' said Orpingalik, 'for it is just as necessary to me to sing it as it is to breathe,' and then began: 'I will sing this song,/A song that is strong . . .'

'Songs,' he added, 'are thoughts, sung out with the breath when people are moved by great forces and ordinary speech no longer suffices. Man is moved just like the ice floe sailing here and there out in the current. His thoughts are driven by a flowing force when he feels joy, when he feels fear, when he feels sorrow. Thoughts can wash over him like a flood, making his blood come in gasps, and his heart throb. Something, like an abatement in the weather, will keep him thawed up. And then it will happen that we, who always think we are small, will feel still smaller. And we will fear to use words. But it will happen that the words we need will come of themselves. When the words we want to use shoot up of themselves – we get a new song.'

Uvavnuk, delighting in the joy of simply being moved by nature, sang:

The great sea
Has sent me adrift
It moves me
As the weed in a great river.

Earth and the great weather
Move me,
Have carried me away
And move my inward parts with joy.

Here the phrase translated 'moves me' also means 'to be in a natural state': to be moved by nature is to be in nature, to belong there. Emotions are expressed as physical responses: anger — *loosening-of-bowels*, fear — *tightening-of-sinews*, joy — *floating-of-viscera*. Man is small, no more than a weed moved endlessly by the current, but intensely aware of the forces acting upon him and delighting in even the most trivial:

And I think over again
My small adventures
When with a shore wind I drifted out
In my kayak
And thought I was in danger.
My fears,
Those small ones
That I thought so big
For all the vital things
I had to get and to reach.

And yet, there is only
One great thing,
The only thing:
To live to see in huts and on journeys
The great day that dawns,
And the light that fills the world

Toothless Kukilasar told of starvation, of children born and husbands lost, of new lands and faces, and concluded: 'How happy I have been! How good life has been to me!' She had not conquered life, nor been rewarded by it, but life had acted upon her, spoken through her, and this gave her joy.

All Eskimo speech has a musical quality, and for heightened emotional expressions the speaker moves easily into song. Eskimo often talk and sing to themselves. To them, thinking and speaking are one: there is no purely inner experience. Members of our culture who are indifferent to literacy also do this: the lone child talking to his toys, the drunk, the angry man who walks away mumbling, the senile, the insane. Momentarily or permanently, all have reverted to an earlier, perhaps more basic philosophy, in which individualism plays little part and thought is conceived of as an external experience.

The Eskimo language contains no distinct first person pronoun, which in English is so important that we make 'I' upper case, an honour otherwise restricted to gods and kings. Eskimo does provide a suffix to indicate participation of self in experience, but generally Eskimo avoid even this, and use an impersonal person: 'One has driven his spear into a walrus.' Yet, despite the absence of individualism in our sense, there is often spectacular achievement, and though there is no 'I', there is great dignity.

Carvers make no effort to develop personal styles and take no care to be remembered as individuals, but simply disappear, as it were, behind their works. Their goal is not to develop unique art styles, not to present personal views, nor even to bring to fruition biases peculiar to them personally; rather, it is to express to perfection a timeless tradition, breathing into it *the carver's* 'breath of life' so that each form is fresh, though the grammar is never violated.

I recently travelled across Siberia, studying arctic art. The contrast was remarkable: here was the most completely non-literate art tradition known, seen against a setting of total literacy. For Soviet Russia is the final, most sterile expression of literacy, with all the worst of the Renaissance and none of the freedom and hope and release of that incredible experiment. Everything is segmental and replaceable – especially people: Napoleon's citizen army at last! Everything visual requires a single point of view – a review position, like Stalin reviewing troops; all painting is in three-dimensional perspective; every plaza is to be viewed from X. One cannot enter into an experience, complete it, modify it, interpret it. All communications: high-definition, exact, with the same meaning for everyone. Dictionaries are popular. Lectures involve learning the correct, single meaning: copy it, memorize it. Da Vinci, yes; Miro, no.

The phonetic alphabet and all its derivatives stress a one-thing-at-a-time analytic awareness in perception. This intensity of analysis is achieved at the price of forcing all else in the field of perception into the subliminal. For 2,500 years literate man lived in what Joyce called 'ABCED-mindedness'. He won, as a result of this fragmenting of the field of perception and the breaking of movement into static bits, a power of applied knowledge and technology unrivalled in human history. The price he paid was existing personally and socially in a state of almost total subliminal awareness.

The Eskimo artist emphasizes all-at-onceness. For him there is no subliminal factor in experience; his mythic forms of explanation explicate all levels of any situation at the same time. Freud makes no sense when applied to him. The carver leaves nothing hidden, suppresses nothing. He employs X-ray techniques, carving an animal with its rib-cage open and an inner being exposed, or with its ribs and vertebrae etched on its surface; he delights in visual puns that show the many dimensions of a being; he uses multiple perspective, observing an experience with the eyes of many. At the same time, he never expresses thoughts openly, but rather drops slight hints, not to censor or suppress, but rather to force his audience to participate, to join in the creation, to complete. There is freedom in all this; nothing is presented ready-made.

A distinctive mark of Eskimo art is that many of the ivory carvings, generally of sea mammals, won't stand up, but roll clumsily about. Each lacks a single, favoured point of view and hence a base. They were never intended to be set in place and viewed, but rather to be worn and handled, turned this way and that.

In Eskimo tales, the narrator speaks only of things you can touch and see. He constantly chooses the concrete word, in phrase after phrase, forcing you to touch and see. No speaker so insistently teaches the general through the particular. He has mastery over the definite, detailed, particular, visualized image.

The Eskimo language, being polysynthetic, favours such construction. Phrases are not composed of little words chronologically ordered, but of great, tight conglomerates, like twisted knots, within which concepts are juxtaposed and inseparably fused. Such conglomerates are not 'verbs' or 'nouns' or even 'words'; each is a linguistic expression for an impression forming a unit to the speaker. Thus 'the house is red' in Eskimo is phrased 'the-house, looking-like-flowing-blood-it-is'; the sequence may indicate a kind of subordination, but 'red' is felt and treated as a substantive. Such parts of speech, though they follow one another, are remarkably independent, with the result that Eskimo is jerky; it does not flow. What we call action, Eskimo see and describe as a pattern of succeeding impressions.

I ran an experiment with a number of Eskimo. I sketched on paper some twenty figures, each oriented in a different direction. Then I asked each individual to point to the seal, the walrus, the bear. Without hesitation or moving the paper, all located the correct figures. But though I had made the drawings I found it necessary to turn the paper round towards me each time to ascertain the accuracy of their selections. Similarly, when handed a photograph, they examine it as it is handed to them, no matter how it is oriented.

The value we place on verticality (it influences even our perception) stems from the strength of literacy in our lives. Children must be taught it. Natives do not know it. And when the mentally ill in our society withdraw from the burdens of literate values, and return to non-vertical, non-lineal codifications, we call them child-like, and even note parallels with primitives. To lack of verticality can be added multiple perspective, visual puns, X-ray sculpture, absence of background, and correspondence between symbol and size: all examples of non-optical structuring of space.

Auditory space has no favoured focus. It's a sphere without fixed boundaries, space made by the thing itself, not space containing the thing. It's not pictorial space, boxed in, but dynamic, always in flux, creating its own dimensions, moment by moment. It has no fixed boundaries; it's indifferent to background. The eye focuses, pinpoints, abstracts, locating each object in physical space, against a background; the ear, however, favours sound from any direction.

The familiar Western notion of enclosed space is foreign to the Eskimo. Both snow igloos and skin tents lack vertical walls and horizontal ceiling; no planes parallel each other and none intersect at 90 degrees. There are no straight lines, at least none of any length. Rectangles are unknown. Euclidean space is a concept unique to literate man. Eskimo, with a magnificent disregard for environmental determinism, open up rather than enclose space. They must, of course, create sealed-off heat areas, but instead of resorting to boxes, they build complex, many-roomed igloos which have as many dimensions and as much freedom as a cloud.

I know of no examples of an Eskimo describing space primarily in visual terms. They do not regard space as static, and therefore measurable: hence they have no formal units of spatial measurement, just as they have no uniform divisions of time. The carver is indifferent to the demands of the optical eye: he lets each piece fill its own space, create its own world, without reference to background or anything external to it. Each carving lives in spatial independence. Size and shape, proportions and selection, these are set by the object itself, not forced from without. Like sound, each carving creates its own space, its own identity; it imposes its own assumptions.

In literate society, to be real a thing has to be visible. We trust the eye, not the ear. Not since Aristotle assured his *readers* that the sense of sight was 'above all others' the one to be trusted have we accorded to sound the role of dominant sense. 'Seeing is believing.' 'Believe half of what you see, nothing of what you hear.' 'The eyes of the Lord preserve knowledge, and He overthroweth the words of the transgressor' (Proverbs 22: 12). Truth, literate man thinks, must be observed by the eye, then judged by the 'I'. Mysticism, intuition, are bad words among scientists. Most thinking in literate societies is done in terms of *visual* models, even when an auditory one might prove more efficient. We employ spatial metaphor even for such inner psychological states as tendency, duration, intensity. We say 'thereafter', not the more logical 'thenafter'; 'always' means 'at all times'; 'before' means etymologically 'in front of'; we even speak of a 'space' or 'interval' of time.

To the Eskimo, truth is given through oral tradition, mysticism, intuition, all cognition, not simply by observation and measurement of physical phenomena. To them, the ocularly visible apparition is not nearly as important as the purely auditory one.

The Eskimo view of self isn't as clearly demarcated as ours, and its precise limits often vary according to circumstances. They don't reduce the self to a sharply delimited, consistent, controlling 'I'. They postulate no personality 'structure', but accept the clotted nature of experience – the simultaneity of good and evil, of joy and despair, multiple models within the one, contraries inextricably commingled. Where literate man regards an 'alias' as deceiving, representing something other than the 'real' self, every Eskimo has several names, each a different facet of himself, for they assert that man's ego is not a thing imprisoned in itself, sternly shut up in boundaries of flesh and time. They say that many of the elements which make it up belong to a world before it and outside it, while the notion that each person is himself and can be no other is to

F

them impossible, for it leaves out of account all the transitions which bind the individual consciousness to the general.

The most interesting Eskimo masks known to me are great composite, mobile puns: the same lines serve to depict Walrus-Caribou-Man; turned slightly, one form may be emphasized, but the others are never lost. There is no need for shape-shifting; all relevant forms are already present.

Such a mask expresses the variety and infinite subtlety of personality, its power of preserving due proportion between diverse and opposite elements.

[1970]

Joseph Mitchell

The Mohawks in High Steel

Abridged by the editor from an article first published in the *New Yorker*, September 17, 1949. Reprinted by permission. Copyright © The New Yorker Magazine, Inc.

In the early years at Caughnawaga, the men clung to their old, aboriginal Iroquois ways of making a living. The Jesuits tried to get them to become farmers, but they would not. In the summer, while the women farmed, they fished. In the fall and winter, they hunted in a body in woods all over Quebec, returning to the village now and then with canoeloads of smoked deer meat, moose meat, and bear meat. Then, around 1700, a few of the youths of the first generation born at Caughnawaga went down to Montreal and took jobs in the French fur trade. They became canoemen in the great fleets of canoes that carried trading goods to remote depots on the St. Lawrence and its tributaries and brought back bales of furs. They liked this work – it was hard but hazardous – and they recruited others. Thereafter, for almost a century and a half, practically every youth in the band took a job in a freight canoe as soon as he got his strength, usually around the age of seventeen. In the eighteen-thirties,-forties, and -fifties, as the fur trade declined in Lower Canada, the Caughnawaga men were forced to find other things to do. Some switched to the St. Lawrence timber-rafting industry and became famous on the river for their skill in running immense rafts of oak and pine over Lachine Rapids. Some broke down and became farmers. Some made moccasins and snowshoes and sold them to jobbers in Montreal. A few who were still good at the old Mohawk dances came down to the United States and travelled with circuses; Caughnawagas were among the first circus Indians. A few bought horses and buggies and went from farmhouse to farmhouse in New England in the summer,

143

peddling medicines – tonics, purges, liniments, and remedies for female ills – that the old women brewed from herbs and roots and seeds. A good many became depressed and shiftless; these hung out in Montreal and did odd jobs and drank cheap brandy.

In 1886, the life at Caughnawaga changed abruptly. In the spring of that year, the Dominion Bridge Company began the construction of a cantilever railroad bridge across the St. Lawrence for the Canadian Pacific Railroad below Caughnawaga village. In obtaining the right to use reservation land for the bridge abutment, the Canadian Pacific and the D.B.C. promised that Caughnawagas would be employed on the job wherever possible.

'It was our understanding that we would employ these Indians as ordinary day laborers, unloading materials,' an official of the D.B.C. wrote. 'They were dissatisfied with this arrangement and would come out on the bridge itself every chance they got. It was quite impossible to keep them off. As the work progressed, it became apparent to all concerned that these Indians were very odd in that they did not have any fear of heights. If not watched, they would climb up into the spans and walk around up there as cool and collected as the toughest of our riveters, most of whom at that period were old sailing-ship men especially picked for their experience in working aloft. These Indians were as agile as goats. They would walk a narrow beam high up in the air with nothing below them but the river, which is rough there and ugly to look down on, and it wouldn't mean any more to them than walking on the solid ground. They seemed immune to the noise of the riveting, which goes right through you and is often enough in itself to make newcomers to construction feel sick and dizzy. They were inquisitive about the riveting and were continually bothering our foremen by requesting that they be allowed to take a crack at it. This happens to be the most dangerous work in all construction, and the highest-paid. Men who want to do it are rare and men who can do it are even rarer, and in good construction years there are sometimes not enough of them to go round. We decided it would be mutually advantageous to see what these Indians could do, so we picked out some and gave them a little training, and it turned out that putting riveting tools in their hands was like putting ham with eggs. They were natural-born bridgemen.'

After the D.B.C. completed the Canadian Pacific Bridge, it began work on a jackknife bridge now known as the Soo Bridge, which crosses two canals and a river and connects the twin cities of Sault Ste. Marie, Ontario, and Sault Ste. Marie, Michigan. This job took two years. Old Mr. Jacobs, the patriarch of the band, says that the Caughnawaga riveting gangs went straight from the Canadian Pacific job to the Soo job and that each gang took along an apprentice. Mr. Jacobs is in his eighties. In his youth, he was a member of a riveting gang; in his middle age, he was, successively, a commercial traveller for a wholesale grocer in Montreal, a schoolteacher on the reservation, and a campaigner for compulsory education for Indians. 'The Indian boys turned the Soo Bridge into a college for themselves,' he says. 'The way they worked it, as soon as one apprentice was trained, they'd send back to the reservation for another one.'

By 1907 there were over seventy skilled bridgemen in the Caughnawaga band. On August 29, 1907, during the erection of the Quebec Bridge, which crosses the St. Lawrence nine miles above Quebec City, a span collapsed, killing ninety-six men, of whom thirty-five were Caughnawagas. In the band, this is always spoken of as 'the disaster'.

'People thought the disaster would scare the Indians away from high steel for good,' Mr. Jacobs says. 'Instead of which, the general effect it had, it made high steel much more interesting to them. It made them take pride in themselves that they could do such dangerous work. Up to then, the majority of them, they didn't consider it any more dangerous than timber-rafting. Also, it made them the most looked-up-to men on the reservation. The little boys in Caughnawaga used to look up to the men that went out with circuses in the summer and danced and war-whooped all over the States and came back to the reservation in the winter and holed up and sat by the stove and drank whiskey and bragged. That's what they wanted to do. Either that, or work on the timber rafts. After the disaster, they changed their minds – they all wanted to go into high steel. The disaster was a terrible blow to the women. The first thing they did, they got together a sum of money for a life-size crucifix to hang over the main altar in St. Francis Xavier's. They did that to show their Christian resignation. The next thing they did, they got in behind the men and made them split up and scatter out. That is, they wouldn't allow all the gangs to work together on one bridge any more, which, if something went wrong, it might widow half the young women on the reservation. A few gangs would go to this bridge and a few would go to that. Pretty soon, there weren't enough bridge jobs, and the gangs began working on all types of high steel – factories, office buildings, department stores, hospitals, hotels, apartment houses, schools, breweries, distilleries, powerhouses, piers, railroad stations, grain elevators, anything and everything. In a few years, every steel structure of any size that went up in Canada, there were Indians on it. Then Canada got too small and they began crossing the border.'

A while back I spent an afternoon with one of them at the old Brooklyn saloon where the Caughnawagas congregate. Orvis Diabo, whose Indian name is O-ron-ia-ke-te, or He Carries the Sky, is squat and barrel-chested. He has small, sharp eyes and a round, swarthy, double-chinned, piratical face. Unlike most other Caughnawagas, he does not deny or even minimize his white blood. 'My mother was half Scotch and half Indian,' he says. 'My grandmother on my father's side was Scotch-Irish. Somewhere along the line, I forget just where, some French immigrant and some full Irish crept in. If you were to take my blood and strain it, God only knows what you'd find.' He was born a Catholic; in young manhood, he became a Presbyterian; he now thinks of himself as 'a kind of a free-thinker'. Mr. Diabo started working in riveting gangs when he was nineteen and quit recently at fifty-four because of crippling attacks of arthritis. 'I heated a million rivets,' he says. 'When they talk about the men that built this country, one of the men they mean is me.' Mr. Diabo owns a house and thirty-three acres of farmland on the reservation. He inherited the farmland and rents it to a French Canadian.

'I feel very low in my mind,' he said. 'I've got to go back to the reservation. I've run out of excuses and I can't put it off much longer. I got a letter from my wife today and she's disgusted with me. "I'm sick and tired of begging you to come home," she said. "You can sit in Brooklyn until your tail takes root." The trouble is, I don't want to go. That is, I do and I don't. I'll try to explain what I mean. An Indian high-steel man, when he first leaves the reservation to work in the States, the homesickness just about kills him. The first few years, he goes back as often as he can. Every time he finishes a job, unless he's thousands of miles away, he goes back. If he's working in New York, he drives up weekends, and it's a twelve-hour drive. After a while, he gets married and brings his wife down and starts a family, and he doesn't go back so often. Oh, he most likely takes the wife and children up for the summer, but he doesn't stay with them. After three or four days, the reservation gets on his nerves and he highballs it back to the States. He gets used to the States. The years go by. He gets to be my age, maybe a little older, maybe a little younger, and one fine morning he comes to the conclusion he's a little too damned stiff in the joints to be walking a naked beam five hundred feet in the air. Either that, or some foreman notices he hasn't got a sure step any longer and takes him aside and tells him a few home truths. He gives up high-steel work and he packs his belongings and he takes his money out of the bank or the postal savings, what little he's been able to squirrel away, and he goes on back to the reservation for good. And it's hard on him. He's used to danger, and reservation life is very slow; the biggest thing that ever happens is a funeral. He's used to jumping around from job to job, and reservation life boxes him in. He's used to having a drink, and it's against the law to traffic in liquor on the reservation; he has to buy a bottle in some French-Canadian town across the river and smuggle it in like a high-school boy, and that annoys the hell out of him.

'There's not much he can do to occupy the time. He can sit on the highway and watch the cars go by, or he can sit on the riverbank and fish for eels and watch the boats go by, or he can weed the garden, or he can go to church, or he can congregate in the grocery stores with the other old retired high-steel men and play cards and talk. That is, if he can stand it. You'd think those old men would talk about the cities they worked in, the sprees they went on, the girls that follow construction all over the country that they knew, the skyscrapers and bridges they put up – only they don't. After they been sitting around the reservation five years, six years, seven years, they seem to turn against their high-steel days. Some of them, they get to be as Indian as all hell; they won't even speak English any more; they make out they can't understand it. They like to talk about religion. A miraculous cure they heard about, something the priest said – they'll harp on it for weeks. They're all amateur priests, or preachers. They've all got some religious notion lurking around in their minds.

'And they like to talk about reservation matters. The electric-light company that supplies the village had been trying and trying to get the Indians to name the streets and lanes. The meter-readers are always getting balled up, and the company had offered to put up street signs and house numbers free of charge. The old men didn't want street names; they were raising holy hell about it. It wouldn't be Indian. And they were discussing the pros and cons of a waterworks system. They're eternally discussing that. Some want a waterworks, but the majority don't. The majority of them, they'd a whole lot rather get behind a poor old horse that his next step might be his last and cart their water up from the river by the barrel. It's more Indian. Sometimes, the way an Indian reasons, there's no rhyme or reason to it. Electric lights are all right and the biggest second-hand car they can find, and radios that the only time they turn them off is when they're changing the tubes, and seventy-five-dollar baby carriages, and four-hundred-dollar coffins, but street names and tap water – oh, Jesus, no! That's going entirely too damned far.

'On the other hand, there's things I look forward to. I look forward to eating real Indian grub again. Such as *o-nen-sto*, or corn soup. That's the Mohawk national dish. Some of the women make it down here in Brooklyn, but they use Quaker corn meal. The good old women up on the reservation, they make it the hard way, the way the Mohawks were making it five hundred years ago. They shell some corn, and they put it in a pot with a handful of maple ashes and boil it. The lye in the ashes skins the hulls off the kernels, and the kernels swell up into big fat pearls. Then they wash off the lye. Then they put in some red kidney beans. Then they put in a pig's head; in the old days, it was a bear's head. Then they cook it until it's as thick as mud. And when it's cooking, it smells so good. If you were breathing your last, if you had the rattle in your throat, and the wind blew you a faint suggestion of a smell of it, you'd rise and walk.

'And another thing I look forward to, if I can manage it – I want to attend a longhouse festival. If I have to join to do so, I'll join. One night, the last time I was home, the longhousers were having a festival. I decided I'd go up to the Catholic graveyard that's right below the longhouse and hide in the bushes and listen to the music. So I snuck up there and waded through the thistles and the twitch grass and the Queen Anne's lace, and I sat down on a flat stone on the grave of an uncle of mine, Miles Diabo, who was a warwhooper with the Miller Brothers 101 Ranch Wild West Show and died with the pneumonia in Wheeling, West Virginia, in 1916. Uncle Miles was one of the last of the Caughnawaga circus Indians. My mother is in that graveyard, and my father, old Nazareth Diabo that I hardly even knew. They called him Nazzry. He was a pioneer high-steel Indian. He was away from home the majority of the time, and he was killed in the disaster – when the Quebec Bridge went down. There's hundreds of high-steel men buried in there. The ones that were killed on the job, they don't have stones; their graves are marked with lengths of steel girders made into crosses. There's a forest of girder crosses in there. So I was sitting on Uncle Miles's stone, thinking of the way things go in life, and suddenly the people in the longhouse began to sing and dance and drum on their drums. They were singing Mohawk chants that came down from the old, old red-Indian times. I could hear men's voices and women's voices and children's voices. The Mohawk language, when it's sung, it's beautiful to hear. Oh, it takes your breath away. A feeling ran through me that made me tremble; I had to take a deep breath to quiet my heart, it was beating so fast. I felt very sad; at the same time, I felt very peaceful. I thought I was all alone in the graveyard, and then who loomed up out of the dark and sat down beside me but an old high-steel man I had been talking with in a store that afternoon, one of the soreheads, an old man that fights every improvement that's suggested on the reservation, whatever it is, on the grounds it isn't Indian – this isn't Indian, that isn't Indian. So he said to me, "You're not alone up here. Look over there." I looked where he pointed, and I saw a white shirt in among the bushes. And he said, "Look over there," and I saw a cigarette gleaming in the dark. "The bushes are full of Catholics and Protestants," he said. "Every night there's a longhouse festival, they creep up here and listen to the singing. It draws them like flies." So I said, "The longhouse music is beautiful to hear, isn't it?" And he remarked it ought to be, it was the old Indian music. So I said the longhouse religion appealed to me. "One of these days," I said, "I might possibly join." I asked him how he felt about it. He said he was a Catholic and it was out of the question. "If I was to join the longhouse," he said, "I'd be excommunicated, and I couldn't be buried in holy ground, and I'd burn in Hell." I said to him, "Hell isn't Indian." It was the wrong thing to say. He didn't reply to me. He sat there awhile – I guess he was thinking it over – and then he got up and walked away.'

[1949]

James Eayrs

Canada's Black Fact: From Pullmans to Reservations to Igloos

In the rhetoric of Confederation, the phrase *le fait français* finds frequent use. It recurs in the reports of royal commissions, it resonates through Parliament's halls. The expression 'Black Fact', however, is virtually unknown. Few Canadians, until very recently, found much time to think about the Afro-Canadians in their midst.

Partly because there were not too many to think about. The census of 1961 lists less than 33,000. The census of 1971 will list none at all, as it is no longer to take note of the racial origins of Canadians. But there is likely to be by then anywhere from 75,000 to 100,000, depending on the number of immigrants from the West Indies. That is a dramatic rate of increase, but from a base so tiny as not in itself to justify those prospective Canadian Stokely Carmichaels who are already preaching 'Black Power', let alone those prospective Canadian Enoch Powells who are readying to rant about 'Black Peril'. For the foreseeable future, the number of Afro-Canadians will remain a small fraction of the population as a whole, a minuscule portion of the Canadian mosaic.

Partly because of prejudice, the forebears of the majority of Afro-Canadians came to this country as political refugees, escapees from that slavery which during much of the 19th century was a fact of life in the United States but not in British North America. As many as 50,000 travelled on the 'Underground Railway' – the clandestine escape route by which they made their way to formal freedom, and beyond.

The Negro came to Canada to become a free man. He became instead an invisible man. After abolition, little marked him off from his neighbour Negro in the northern states save the latter's better job prospects and higher living standards. Prejudice, humiliation, deprivation, degradation, all existed here as there. All were harder to bear here than there, for Negro Canadians, being scattered and isolated and few, did not have the solace of community. Dresden was hardly Harlem.

By the turn of the century the Negro began to return in large numbers to the land he had so lately fled. He left behind him a dispirited people. Fortunate the Canadian Negro who found work upon the railway – though if he found work it would not be up front with the engine but behind in the Pullman where the porter's job was exclusively his own.

The Canadian public, travelling or otherwise, could not care less and would not care more. It would not care to this day but for events outside its native land, mainly in the United States. It is the 23,000,000 Americans styling themselves, with varying degrees of militancy and pride, Negro, black, or Afro-American, who have aroused Canada's conscience and stirred Canada's fears. It is the American black community, now goaded by a volatile combination of hope and frustration to a pitch of awareness and assertiveness unknown to its history, which has brought the Canadian black community to the attention of a largely indifferent Canadian public. It is the black fact in the United States which has made Canadians confront the black fact in Canada.

And for once a Prime Minister of Canada has led his people in their new concern, rather than bobbing along in the wake of opinion. 'I am less worried about what is over the Berlin wall,' Mr. Trudeau mused aloud last November, 'than about what might happen in Chicago or in New York or in our own great cities in Canada.' Events since then have shown how proper a priority this is. The smoke from Sir George Williams University last month was not the same smoke that hung over the burning ghettos of Watts and Washington and Detroit. But the fire from which it rose feeds on the same tinder and is fanned by the same prevailing winds. And the frontier has proved to be no kind of firebreak at all.

In a matter so momentous, metaphor must clarify or is best discarded. I am not at all implying that white student discontent is part and parcel of the black fact. That white students have been influenced and inspired by the example of black militants is incontestable. Their tactics of sit-in and confrontation are tactics pioneered by Martin Luther King and his followers in the Southern Christian Leadership Conference when they desegregated lunch-counters and buses in Alabama 13 years ago. Their rhetoric is one part Red Guard and two parts Black Panther. But tactics and rhetoric are only life styles, the hemlines of revolution. They are far from being life itself.

The life situation (as distinct from the life style) of white students in either country is as far removed from the life situation of black people in either country as is privilege from oppression, a head-cold from double pneumonia, a computer from an abacus. White students who make them out to be the same – hoping to claim black circumstances as their own the better to extenuate extremism – indulge themselves in fantasy. No blacks make them out to be the same. When Eldridge Cleaver writes that 'black and white, the young rebels are free people', he does not mean that only recently both were slaves together. Most blacks have nothing to lose but their chains; most white students, nothing to lose but their marks. 'The task is still to be out in the university, in the lounges, the cafeteria, the mezzanine . . .' So *The Sir George Student*, in unconscious parody of a more famous call to arms, sternly counselled its militant readership. Medgar Evers made a rougher scene. The student as nigger is not to be compared with the 'nigger', who is unlikely to be a student, let alone have lounges in which to study, lounge, or merely wage guerrilla warfare.

Nor is the black fact to be compared with *le fait français*. In spite of everything by which they differ – the catalyst of culture, the heritage of history, the ties of church and family, above all the colour of their skin – there are those among the disaffected of French Canada who see themselves and Afro-North Americans as struggling in a common cause, as united in a common enterprise. It is one thing for black militants to reach out to the people of a tenuously defined third world. They need all the help that they can get. Who would deny them what psychological support – there'll be no foreign aid – may come from Africa, China, Cuba, and other 'liberated areas'? But this does not excuse French-speaking radicals in their self-deception. To imagine, as some do, that their hang-ups with the English are in any way akin to the monumental injustices befalling Negro Americans is a symptom not of persecution but of persecution mania. It is a failure of the historical imagination. It is of a piece with the *gaffe* of a separatist leader who, not long ago, sought sympathy from an audience in France by telling how, as a young man in the Gaspé during the early 1940s, he was forced to speak English to draw money from his bank. He may have wondered why they were not more deeply moved by this tale of tyranny *à la Canadien*. It was because many in his audience were then trading wits, and lives, with the Gestapo, and that to them English was the language of liberty.

What, finally, of Métis, Indians, and Eskimo? Are they a part of the black fact in Canada? They are, most emphatically; as are any Canadians forcibly deprived by their society of the right to life, liberty, and the pursuit of happiness. The phrase is an American phrase, but it is none the worse for that. Without it the contradiction between North American ideals and North American realities would not be so starkly clear. And without the grim reminder from the south we might still be oblivious to the inhuman conditions of our north. Of the black Canadian in our midst – Métis, Indian, Eskimo, Negro – we would be saying what Auden wrote of another citizen:

Was he free? Was he happy?
The question is absurd;
Had anything been wrong,
We should certainly have heard.

[1969]

Larry Zolf

Boil Me No Melting Pots

When the Fathers of Confederation built this country in 1867 there was universal agreement among *all* Canadians, English- and French-speaking, that there was no place for the American Dream on the northern half of this continent. In 1776 we embraced the United Empire Loyalists and rejected George Washington's Revolutionary Army by force of arms. We booted Uncle Sam in the pants in 1812 and slapped his wrists in the Fenian Raids of the 1880s. We rejected slavery and provided sanctuary for American Negroes fleeing that 'peculiar institution'.

We rejected republicanism, the American idea that the People in and of themselves can shape their own ends and destinies. We countered Jacksonian Democracy with the Responsible Government of a constitutional monarchy and made it plain to our southern neighbours that there were higher forces shaping our destinies than the untutored rabble of the untouched West. And while we did agree with the Yankees that life and liberty were inseparable, we differed in our pursuit of happiness. In Canada, that pursuit didn't necessarily entail *égalité* and *fraternité*. We flatly rejected the American egalitarianism of the Western Frontier and the American fraternity of the melting pot.

Canada was conservative country, the land of particularity. That particularity known as Anglo-Saxon British Canada was prepared to tolerate the particularity of French Canada and the Slavic-German-Jewish-Oriental particularities of the Golden West, provided all accepted the British Monarchy, the British Connection, the British Rules of the British Game as summum bonum underlying all these particularities.

152

This then was the lay of this land in the year 1926 when an obscure ex-Czarist draft-dodger and obscure ex-infantryman in Alexander Kerensky's Revolutionary Army decided to emigrate to these shores. That dashing, mustachioed, bulbous-nosed Polack of the Judaic persuasion was none other than Yoshua Falk Zholf, son of Reb Yisroael Zholf, husband to Freda Rachel Zholf, father to Meyer, Reisel and Judith Zholf, and father-to-be to son-to-be yours truly.

My father was a dreamer. In his youth he dreamt of a Russia where life and liberty were inseparable, where a Jew could freely pursue happiness. In 1914 he was a draft-dodger, moving from city to city and village to village. When the Czar was toppled in February 1917 and Alexander Kerensky proclaimed liberty and equality, my father came out of hiding, drafted his own personal revolutionary manifesto, and presented it to a recruiting officer in Kerensky's army. It read:

To:

The Russian Revolutionary Army.

Dear Sirs:
Whereas, I Falek Zholf, have hitherto refused to shed my blood for the bloody Czar Nikolai the Second, enemy of my people, and,
Whereas, the great Revolution has freed my people, and all other peoples that inhabit Mother Russia, I today present myself in payment of my holy debt of loyalty to the Fatherland.

My father's revolutionary dreams of brotherhood quickly came to naught. He was sickened by Kerensky's execution of soldiers with Bolshevik sympathies and sickened by the Bolshevik execution of nationalists. Soon he and his family were threatened by the vicious anti-Semitism of the Polish Government of Pilsudski and Sikorski.

Still my father continued to dream. There was the pastoral dream of life on the land in communion with the sky and the stars and all that but the Polish Government took his land away. There was the dream of pioneering in Palestine but the Zionists wanted only single men. There was the dream of America, the new homeland of his three brothers, but the Goddess Liberty had shut her eyes and gates to Europe's teeming, huddled masses.

Suddenly along came Canada, the British colony that dreamt no dreams, and offered Pa, the peasant, a chance to join the Galician garlic-eaters that were cultivating the flatlands of the Canadian Golden West.

All this is by way of introduction to a fundamental confusion in my father's life which led to a subsequent fundamental confusion in my life. My father ultimately drifted into Winnipeg and renewed an occupation he once pursued secretly in Poland at some risk to his own life — the teaching of Jewish liberal-socialist values to Jewish children. He became first a teacher and then the principal of the Isaac Loeb Peretz Folk School in Winnipeg. This school was a branch of a school system and school curriculum whose central headquarters was in New York City.

Herein lay the rub. My father, unaware of all the trouble Sir John A. and the Fathers had gone to, just naturally assumed that Canada was part of the American Dream. His admission to this country he regarded as a miracle. He looked on Canada as a place that Americans sent people to that it didn't really want to have *now* but might take in later on, provided that while here they were always on good behaviour. In a sense, he regarded Canada as America's Australia − a temporary penal colony for temporary undesirables.

As my father's English was not very good and his reading material was strictly confined to Yiddish books and newspapers that came from New York, it was not surprising that Pop was soon to regard Winnipeg as just another borough of Gotham on the Hudson.

The more he read his New York Yiddish newspapers the more he got excited by the American Dream! Who could blame him? The New York papers told of Jewish wonders that poor old Pop could scarcely have imagined in the dreary Polish village that was once his home.

Not only could Jews own land in the U.S.A., but, miracle of miracles, wonder of wonders, Jews were actually trusted in America. In the Soviet Union they were purging Trotsky, Kamenev, and Zenoviev. In America they were electing Herbert Lehman Governor of New York State. Didn't Roosevelt have a Morgenthau in his Cabinet? Weren't Felix Frankfurter, Sam Rosenman, and Ben Cohen FDR's bosom buddies? America was indeed the land of milk and honey; its streets were paved with Jews.

It was natural, almost proper, that my father should have passed the American Dream on to me − his youngest and the first to be born on the very soil of Canada-America. Until I was 13 years old, I was enrolled in the day school section of the Isaac Loeb Peretz Folk School. My father was my teacher. There I learned to read from a Yiddish Dick and Jane− Max and Molly primer. It was in Yiddish that I first read *Huckleberry Finn, Tom Sawyer, Rip Van Winkle,* and *Moby Dick.* For extra grabbers my father threw in a Jewish Children's History of the Life and Times of Eugene V. Debs, the Life and Times of Samuel Gompers, and the Life and Times of Emma Goldman. At the tender age of nine I knew that Franklin D. Roosevelt was God the Father, David Dubinsky of the International Ladies Garment Workers Union was God the Son, and Sidney Hillman of the Amalgamated Clothing Workers of America was God the Holy Ghost.

At the tender age of 12, I won my first essay contest. The subject was Statue of Liberty poetess Emma Lazarus, as described by the then Wunderkind of Winnipeg, borough of Manhattan, in these immortal words:

'Emma Lazarus was not only a daughter of Israel but a daughter of the World.'

The next year I capped my success with a bar-mitzvah speech-triumph that extolled the virtues of Meyer Levin, bombardier of Captain Colin Kelly's Spirit of America and the only Jew decorated for bravery at Pearl Harbor. Knowing a good thing when I saw it I spoke these immortal words:

'Meyer Levin was not only a son of Israel, he was a son of America.'

And so was I. As I listened in my teens to my father telling horror stories of gas ovens and lamp shades and watched his heart slowly breaking as the news drifted in of the death of his entire family overseas, it was nice, almost comforting, to cast your eyes south of the border. There I could thrill to the athletic exploits of Barney Ross and Hank Greenberg. I could drool at the succulent beauty of Bess Myerson, Miss America 1946. I could cry tomorrow with Lillian Roth and call my house a home with Polly Adler.

I can remember staying up all night with the old man, crying and cheering as Harry Truman, who gave us Israel, was given four more years. In high school I defended America in the Korean War and argued that West Germans were good and East Germans bad. In college, NATO was groovy, the Marshall Plan divine, McCarthyism a minor aberration.

Today, as I reflect on the validity of the American Dream for me then and now, a certain sense of nostalgic silliness seems to overtake me. I can understand the validity of the American Dream for my father. In the bitter anti-Semitism of Czarist Russia and Sikorski's Poland he was sub-human. In Auschwitz and Dachau he and his fellow Jews were not human at all. In the American melting pot he was not only human, he was an involved participant, an equal.

As my father saw the American Dream, to be Jewish and human was to be American. Today as I see the American Dream operating in Black America and Yellow Vietnam, I am forced to conclude that somehow to be *really* human is to be neither Jewish nor American. Today the Jewish community in America is indeed a participant and more than an equal in the power élite of White America. The Jews are close to the top in education, affluence, status. But to Black America the Jew is as much Whitey as anyone else. The lessons of persecution and humiliation that the Jew picked up on his way to affluence and success he is not prepared to pass on to the Negroes way, way below. The American Jew lives in a white neighbourhood, worships in a white, cavernous temple, eats white kosher Chinese food at white Chinese restaurants, has white directors for his white bar-mitzvah movies. He likes it that way and is sure *everyone* will understand.

Having richly benefited from the American Dream, he is eager to pass on the message, not the benefits, to those less fortunate people abroad. The patriotism of today's American Jewry is awesomely wholesome. American-style democracy has been good for the teeming, huddled Jewish masses. How can it help but be good for the teeming, huddled masses of Vietnam? Our Hebrew boy, Walt Whitman Rostow, is today's Emma Lazarus, offering Lyndon Johnson in Statue of Liberty drag as sanctuary to the misguided peasants of South-East Asia. Our Hebrew boy, Dr. Edward Teller, Pop to the

H-bomb, is today's real-life Dr. Sivana, just itching to say 'Shazam' and watch the world disappear.

I must admit that my stomach feels queasy when I hear Nicholas Katzenbach and Dean Rusk gloating over the Viet Cong kill toll, the damned dead of American-style democracy. I must admit to a similar type queasiness when I hear Jews gloating over Six-Day War Arab losses, the damned dead of Zionist-style democracy, even though I know you can't compare the two and that Nasser will fry me whenever he gets the chance. I also feel queasy whenever I hear bigots, Birchers, and Lubor Zinks praising to the skies the Jewish victory over 'Arab Communism'.

It saddens me to see how the American Dream and the melting pot has coarsened and vulgarized my racial confrères. The gentleness of East European Jewish Hassidism, the sweet music of the soft, humane Yiddish culture is no longer there. I guess I prefer the schlemiel wisdom of Gimpel the Fool to the Sammy Glick-shtick of Norman Podhoretz. I'd rather walk the crooked, narrow streets of Chagall's shtetl than drive through Forest Hill or Shaker Heights.

That brings me to the lay of this land in 1968. Canada has not yet bought the American Dream. It's still conservative country, the land of particularity. I know the Hebrew particularity ain't quite as yet the equal of other particularities. I know that living here is still a trip backwards in the Time Tunnel.

Still, I'm glad to be here and to be a Canadian, whatever that word means. I'd rather be somewhat of an outsider in Canada than an equal, accepted participant in the American Nightmare.

I am aware that we have avoided American pitfalls more by accident than by design. I realize that we don't have America's responsibilities and therefore her problems. Well, huzzah, I'm glad we don't and to hell with the reasons.

Huzzah, we're not in Vietnam. Huzzah, we won't go there. Huzzah, we never will. Huzzah, we have no Watts-Newarks-Detroits. Huzzah, we don't intend to build them.

I'm also aware that my country is in a state of disarray and flux. The old order is crumbling and all institutions are open to criticism and review. I like that. In my own little way, here in Canada, I can be a minor revolutionary, albeit a gutless one, a sort of chicken-hearted Trotsky.

I know that my country has not quite made up its mind what it wants to be. It has ceased being British and, thankfully, has not yet become American. If there is anything still valid to the British heritage left us by the Fathers of Confederation, let it be this:

Let the country continue to be a land of un-American activities. Boil me no melting pots and dream me no dreams. Worry not, rumour has it that God is Dead. If so, he can't bless America.

[1968]

Mordecai Richler

"The Jewish beavers of this land will help make the Maple Leaf a symbol of greatness."
(Dr. S.I. Katz, O.B.E.)

The ghetto of Montreal has no real walls and no true dimensions. The walls are the habit of atavism and the dimensions are an illusion. But the ghetto exists all the same. The fathers say: 'I work like this so it'll be better for the kids.' A few of the fathers, the dissenters, do not crowd their days with work. They drink instead. But in the end it amounts to the same thing: in the end, work, drink, or what have you, they are all trying to fill in the void.

Most of the Jews who live at the diminishing end of the ghetto, on streets named St. Urbain, St. Dominic, Rachel, and City Hall, work in textile or garment factories. Some are orthodox, others are communist. But all of them do their buying and their praying and their agitating and most of their sinning on St. Lawrence Boulevard, which is the aorta of the ghetto, reaching out in one direction towards Mount Royal, and past that (where it is no longer the ghetto) into the financial district and the factory slums, coming to a hard stop at the waterfront. In the other direction, northwards, St. Lawrence Boulevard approaches the fields at the city limits; where there is a rumour of grass and sun and quick spurious lovemaking.

All day long St. Lawrence Boulevard, or Main Street, is a frenzy of poor Jews, who gather there to buy groceries, furniture, clothing, and meat. Most walls are plastered with fraying election bills, in Yiddish, French, and English. The street reeks of garlic and quarrels and bill collectors: orange crates, stuffed full with garbage and decaying fruit, are piled slipshod in most alleys. Swift children gobble pilfered plums, slower cats prowl the fish market. After the water truck has passed, the odd dead rat can be seen floating down the gutter followed fast by rotten apples, cigar butts, chunks of horse manure, and a terrifying zigzag of flies. Few stores go in for posh window displays. Instead, their windows are jammed full and pasted up with streamers that say ALL GOODS REDUCED or EVERYTHING MUST GO.

Every night St. Lawrence Boulevard is lit up like a neon cake and used-up men stumble out of a hundred different flophouses to mix with rabbinical students and pimps and Trotskyites and poolroom sharks. Hair tonic and water is consumed in back alleys. Swank whores sally at you out of the promised jubilee of all the penny arcades. Crap games flourish under lamp posts. You can take Rita the Polack up to the Liberty Rooms or you can listen to Panofsky speak on Tim Buck and The Worker. You can catch Bubbles Dawson doing her strip at the Roxie Follies. You can study Talmud at the B'nai Jacob Yeshiva, or you can look over the girls at the AZA Stag or Drag.

Conditions improve on the five streets between St. Lawrence Boulevard and Park Avenue. Most of the Jews who live on these streets market what is cut or pressed by their relations below St. Lawrence Boulevard. Others, the aspiring, own haberdashery stores, junk yards, and basement zipper factories.

The employer and professional Jews own their own duplexes in Outremont, a mild residential area which begins above Park Avenue. They belong to the Freemasons, or, if they can't get into that organization, to the Knights of Pythias. Their sons study at McGill, where they are Zionists and opposed to anti-Semitic fraternities. They shop on St. Lawrence Boulevard, where the Jews speak quaintly like the heroes of nightclub jokes.

In the spring of 1952 the B'nai B'rith published a report saying that anti-Semitism was on the decline in Canada and that the Jews joined with the great prime minister of this great country in the great fight against communism. The uranium market boomed. Dr. S. I. Katz, O.B.E., told the Canadian Club that 'The Jewish beavers of this land will help make the Maple Leaf a symbol of greatness.' But the spring passed fast. Those balmy days which had accounted for the melting of the snows turned longer and more hard. The sun swelled in the sky and a stillness gripped the ghetto. When the heat was but two days old everyone seemed to have forgotten that there had ever been a time of no heat. This was partly sham. For, secretively, the people of the ghetto gloated over every darkening cloud. They supposed that tomorrow there would be rain, and if not tomorrow then at least the day after that. But the sky was a fever and there was no saying how long a day would last or what shape the heat would assume by night. There were the usual heat rumours about old men going crazy and women swooning in the streets and babies being born prematurely. When the rains came the children danced in the streets clad only in their underwear and the old men sipped lemon tea on their balconies and told tales about the pogroms of the czar. But the rains didn't amount to much. After the rains there was always the heat again. The flies returned, the old men retreated to their beds, and all the missing odours of the heat reappeared with a new intensity.

The heat first appeared in June when it was still too soon to send the family up north for the summer. But, just the same, things were not too bad. Not too bad until the weekends came along. The weekends were hell. All week long you could at least work but when the weekends came along there was nothing to do. You were on your own. You were free, so to speak.

So on Saturday afternoons the well-to-do Jews walked up and down Decarie Boulevard, which was their street. A street of sumptuous supermarkets and banks built of granite, an aquarium in the lobby of the Snowdon Theatre, a synagogue with a soundproof auditorium and a rabbi as modern and quick as the Miss Snowdon restaurant, neon drugstores for all your needs and delicatessens rich in chromium plating. Buick convertibles and Cadillacs parked on both sides: a street without a past. Almost as if these Jews, who had prospered, craved for many lights. Wishing away their past and the dark. Almost as if these Jews, who had prospered, regretted only the solemn sky, which was beyond their reach. Sunny by day, and by night – star-filled: a swirl of asking eyes spying down on them. Watching. Poking fun at their ephemeral lights.

The neither rich nor poor Jews walked up and down Park Avenue – a few of the nervy ones attempting Decarie Boulevard. The poor and the elderly kept to St. Lawrence Boulevard. Each street had its own technique of walking, a technique so finely developed that you could always tell a man off his own street.

The Decarie Boulevard Jews walked like prosperity, grinning a flabby grin which said money in the bank. Notaries, lawyers, businessmen, doctors. They wore their wives like signposts of their success and dressed them accordingly. The children were big and little proofs, depending on the size of their achievements.

'Lou, meet the boy. Sheldon. He just won a scholarship to McGill.'

'Don't say eh? Mm. Hey, I hear talk you're gonna expand the factory. That increases your risk, Jack. You come round first thing Monday morning and I'll fix you like a friend. For your own good. You owe it to your family to protect yourself.'

The wives exchanged small flatteries.

'Jack's going to buy a Cadillac. *You* try to stop him.'

'Me, I don't live for show. Lou doubled his life insurance instead of buying a new car this year. He says you can never tell. . . .'

Park Avenue was different. It had once been to the prospering what Decarie Boulevard was to them now. But the prospering had built a more affluent street for themselves to walk on, a bigger proof, where, twenty years hence, they would again feel the inadequacy of the neon, the need to push on and to flee the past and install brighter lights again. Meanwhile, the new ones, the intruding *greeners,* were beginning to move in around Park Avenue. Here, they mixed with the middling Jews. Knowing the right people was important. The aspiring walked without certainty, pompous and ingratiating by turns.

On St. Lawrence Boulevard the Jews, many of them bearded, walked with their heads bent and their hands clasped behind their backs. They walked looking down at the pavement or up at the sky, seldom straight ahead.

[1955]

George Woodcock

Encounter with an Archangel

I first knew the Doukhobors as shadowy figures of legend in my English childhood, when my father would compensate for a dull life in a small town beside the Thames by weaving nostalgic threnodies on his young manhood in the Canadian West. Evenings on the prairies, with the great pink-bellied hawks settling down; Cobalt in the silver boom; fishing camps on the pristine shores of the northern lakes; and the great winter fires of the cities when burnt-out buildings became palaces of ice. Against such scenes the necessary characters moved in the cinema of my brain with the exaggerated gesticulation of Japanese actors. Lefty Louis and Zip the Blood shot it out with the police from a Winnipeg streetcar; Charlie Chaplin clowned through the one-elevator hamlets with Fred Karno; Chinese in blue gowns and pigtails scurried along Portage Avenue; strange Russians cleared snow in the prairie towns and were given to stripping in public, regardless of sex.

I realized the Doukhobors were something more than eccentric shovellers of snow when I read Tolstoy and Kropotkin and discovered that for these great Russians the Doukhobors were a group of admirable peasant radicals – Nature's anarchists. During the thirties I found in Doukhobor anti-militarism a strain that appealed to my own pacifism, and I accepted Tolstoy's impression of a libertarian sect who took their Christianity neat and had turned their settlements into Utopian communes. Like Tolstoy, I was unaware that this simple view took no account of certain fundamental aspects of Doukhobor philosophy and practice. Unlike Tolstoy, I learnt my error.

When my wife and I returned to Canada in the spring of 1949, I found that

161

on Vancouver Island, where we settled, there was a small group of Doukhobors who had migrated from the interior of British Columbia and had founded a colony at Hilliers, sixty miles north of the village where we were clearing land and carpentering a house in search of that Tolstoyan *ignis fatuus*, the marriage of manual and mental work.

The people of our village talked reluctantly about the Hilliers community, yet even their hostile comments told us something. The leader of the group – a heretical offshoot – was a prophet who called himself Michael the Archangel. He openly preached the destruction of marriage, and this our neighbours vaguely envisaged as a complex and orgiastic pattern of shacking-up which provoked and offended their Presbyterian imagination at one and the same time.

Since Hilliers was near, we could easily go there to see for ourselves, but we knew already that chronic bad relations with the Canadian authorities had made the Doukhobors distrustful of strangers. However, I wrote to the community, and by return I received a letter from the secretary, whose name was Joe. He not only welcomed my interest, but invited us to stay at Hilliers as long as we wished. I was a little surprised at the enthusiastic tone of his letter, but the reason became evident once we reached Hilliers.

One day in August we set off northward. For lack of money, we hitch-hiked, and it was late afternoon when the last driver turned off the seacoast road into the broad valley, hot and still of air, where Hilliers lies in the lee of the hard mountain spine that runs down the length of Vancouver Island. The older, non-Doukhobor Hilliers was a whistle-stop on the island railway, and the entrance to the community stood opposite a siding filled with boxcars. A high cedar fence faced the road. A large board had been nailed to it. UNION OF SPIRITUAL COMMUNITIES OF CHRIST, it said, in Russian and English. The wide gates stood open; looking between them, the eye encompassed and then recognized with some surprise the unconscious faithfulness with which a Russian village of the Chekhov era had been reproduced. Low cabins of logs and unpainted shacks were scattered along a faintly marked trail that ran between grass verges to end, a furlong on, at two larger two-storeyed houses standing against the brown background of the mountains, with the grey bubble of a communal baking oven between them. Each cabin was surrounded by a picketed garden, where green rows of vegetables and raspberry canes ran over the black earth in neatly weeded symmetry, and ranks of sunflowers lolled their brown and yellow masks towards the light.

An old woman with a white kerchief shading her face was hoeing very slowly in the nearest garden. She was the only person in sight, and I went up to her fence. Could she tell me where to find Joe? Her English was so broken that I could not follow what she was trying to tell me. By this time our arrival had been noticed in the cabins, and a little wave of younger women in bright full petticoats, and of blond, crop-headed small boys, came towards us hesitantly. There was nothing of the welcome we had expected. Inge spoke to one of the women. 'Joe ain't here', she answered. 'He's at the other place.' She waved vaguely northward. A pick-up truck drove in through the gates, and two young men got out. The women called to them, and they talked together in rapid, anxious Russian. Then one man got back into the truck and drove off, while the other came up to us. He was dark and nervous, dressed in an old blue serge suit with chaff whitening the wrinkles. 'I'm Pete,' he said. 'Joe's brother. Joe's coming.' He paused. 'Afterwards . . . you'll see Michael . . . Michael Archangel,' he added hesitantly, and then fell silent. The small boys gave up interest and went to play on the boxcars.

Joe was so different from Pete that it was hard to believe them brothers — blue-eyed, wiry, jumping out of the truck to run and pump our hands. 'Michael Archangel knew you were coming. A long time ago,' he shouted. I had written only a week before. 'A long time ago?' I asked. Joe looked at me and then laughed. 'Yes, before you wrote!' Then he grabbed our rucksacks, helped us into the truck, and drove wildly for a couple of miles along a rough track beside the railway to a large old farm house in a quadrangle of shacks and barns surrounded by propped-up apple trees that were ochre-yellow with lichen. 'This is the other place,' Joe explained. 'Most of the young people stay here. The old 'uns live up there with Michael Archangel.'

We went into the kitchen. Two young women, fair and steatopygous as Doukhobor beauties are expected to be, were preparing the evening meal. A small girl showed us to our room, and stood, avid with curiosity, while we unpacked our rucksacks and washed our faces. Then Joe took us around the yard, showed us the new bakehouse on which a hawk-faced old man like a Circassian bandit was laying bricks, and tried to entice us into the bathhouse. I looked through the doorway and saw naked people moving like the damned in the clouds of steam that puffed up whenever a bucket of water was thrown on the hot stones. In a couple of seconds I withdrew, gasping for breath. The bricklayer laughed. 'You never make a Doukhobor,' he said. 'Add ten years to your life,' said Joe, coaxingly.

When everyone stood in a circle around the great oval table for the communal meal we began to see the kind of people the Doukhobors were. There were twenty of them, singing in the half-Caucasian rhythm that penetrates Doukhobor music, the women high and nasal, the men resonant as bells. Most had Slavonic features, their breadth emphasized among the women by the straight fringes in which their hair was cut across the forehead. But a few, like the bricklayer, were so un-Russian as to suggest that Doukhobors had interbred with Caucasian Moslems during their long exile in the mountains before they came to Canada. They sang of Siberian and Canadian prisons, of martyrs and heroes in the faith. 'Rest at last, ye eagles of courage, rest at last in the arms of God,' they boomed and shrilled.

The singing was solemn, but afterwards the mood changed at once and the meal went on with laughter and loud Russian talk; now and then our neighbours would break off repentantly to translate for our benefit. The food was vegetarian, but the best of its kind I have ever tasted; bowls of purple borscht, dashed with white streaks of cream, and then casha, made with millet and butter, and vegetables cooked in oil, and pirogi stuffed with cheese and beans and blackberries, and eaten with great scoops of sour cream. Slices of black bread passed around the table, cut from a massive square loaf that stood in the middle, beside the salt of hospitality, and the meal ended with huckleberries and cherries.

Afterwards Joe and Pete took us to drink tea in a room they used as an office. It was furnished with a table and benches of thick hand-adzed cedar, but a big blue enamel teapot served instead of a samovar. This was the first of a series of long conversations in which the ideas of the community were imparted to us, principally by Joe, who spoke English more fluently than anyone else at Hilliers. Except for a few phrases, the details of the dialogues have become blurred in my memory during the thirteen years that have passed since then, but this, in substance, is what we were told on the first evening.

The community began with the experiences of Michael Verigin, a back-sliding Doukhobor. Michael had left his home in the mountains, opened a boarding-house for Russians in Vancouver, and prospered there. After a few years Michael began to feel the malaise which many Doukhobors experience when they go from their villages into the acquisitive outside world, and he returned to the mountain valley of Krestova. Krestova is the Mecca of the Sons of Freedom, the fire-raising and nude-parading radical wing of the Doukhobor sect. Michael rejoined the Sons of Freedom and was regarded with deference because he bore the holy name of Verigin and was a distant cousin of Peter the Lordly, the Living Christ who presided over the Doukhobors' first years in Canada, and died mysteriously in a train explosion during the 1920s.

'Then Michael had a vision.'

'A dream?'

'No, a vision. He was awake, and he said there was a voice and a presence.'

'He saw nothing?'

'That time he didn't. The vision told him he was no longer Mike Verigin. Michael the Archangel had gone into him. He was the same man, but the Archangel as well.'

'How did he know it was a real vision?'

'He just knew.' Joe looked at me with the imperturbable blue-eyed confidence of a man used to assessing the authenticity of supernatural messages. 'The vision said Michael must prepare the world for the Second Coming.'

The Second Coming did not mean the return of Christ. According to Doukhobor beliefs, Christ is returning all the time in various forms. The Second Coming meant the establishment of God's earthly kingdom and the end of time and mortality.

As the chosen pioneers in this great mission, the Doukhobors must purify themselves. The Archangel began by proclaiming that they must renounce not only meat and alcohol, but also tobacco and musical instruments. A radio was playing loudly in the kitchen as Joe explained this. 'That's O.K.,' he reassured us. 'A radio ain't a musical instrument.'

Above all, the lust for possession must be rooted out. This meant not only a return to the traditional communistic economy from which the Doukhobors had lapsed under evil Canadian influences, but also the destruction of that inner citadel of possession, marriage. No person must have rights over another, either parental or marital. Women must be liberated, sexual relations must be free, families must wither away.

Two or three hundred of the Sons of Freedom, mostly seasoned old veterans of the nude marches and the pre-war internment on Piers Island, accepted the Archangel's teaching. Their neighbours showed disagreement by burning down the houses of those who followed Verigin. At this point the Archangel very conveniently had another vision.

Two of his followers must visit Vancouver Island. There they would find a town where a clock had stopped at half past two, and then they must proceed eastward until they saw a white horse by the gate of a farm. Joe and another man went on the expedition. They found the clock at Port Alberni, and the horse by the gate of a three-hundred-acre farm that was up for sale at a knockdown price. And, for what the fact is worth, I should record that after I had heard Joe's story I happened to visit Port Alberni, and there, on the tower of a fire-hall, I saw a dummy clock whose painted hands stood unmoving at half past two.

The farm was bought with the pooled resources of the faithful, and Michael the Archangel led two hundred of his disciples on the exodus to Vancouver Island. Immediately after leaving the mainland he added to all the other prohibitions a ban on sexual intercourse – to conserve energies for the great task of spiritual regeneration. Complete freedom was only to be won by complete self-control. So much for the stories of Free Love rampant!

I wanted to find out the actual nature of the power that enabled Michael the Archangel to impose such restrictions. Tolstoy once thought that, because they opposed the state, the Doukhobors lived without rulers. Other writers had suggested that the Living Christs, like Peter the Lordly Verigin and his son Peter the Purger, had been rulers as powerful as any earthly governor.

'He is just our spiritual leader,' Joe explained blandly.

'But he still seems to have a big say in your practical affairs.'

'It depends on what you mean by *say*. He gives no orders. We are free men. We don't obey anybody. But he gives us advice.'

'Do you always accept it?'

'If we know what's good for us, we do.'

'Why?'

'Because we know Michael the Archangel is always right.'

'How do you know?'

'We just know.'

The next day we met the Archangel. He had sent a message early that morning summoning us to his presence, and Joe drove us to the hamlet where we had arrived originally. The Archangel's house was one of the larger buildings, but we were not allowed to go in. We waited outside. The Archangel would meet us in the garden.

A tall man in his late fifties came stepping heavily between the zinnia borders. A heavy paunch filled his knitted sweater, and his shining bald head loosened into a coarse, flushed face with a potato nose, a sandy moustache, and small eyes that glinted out of puffy sockets. It was a disappointing encounter. The Archangel bowed in the customary Doukhobor manner, but without the warmth most Doukhobors put into their greeting. He shook hands limply. He spoke a few sentences in Russian, welcoming us and wishing us good health, and he affected not to understand English, though we learned later that he was effectively bilingual. He picked two small pink roses from a briar that ran along the fence and gave one to each of us. In five minutes he was gone, retiring with dignified adroitness and leaving all our intended questions about archangelic power unanswered. Joe led us away, loudly declaring that the Archangel had been delighted with us, and that he had given many messages which he, Joe, would transmit in due course. Our whole relationship with the Archangel took on this elusive, indirect form, with Joe acting like a voluble priest interpreting and embellishing the laconic banalities of the oracle.

For the rest of the second day we wandered around the community, talking to the people we encountered. I pumped the handle of a primitive hand washing-machine, and learned from the girl I helped a curious instance of Doukhobor double-think. A spaniel bitch trotted over the yard, followed by a single pup. 'She had four,' the girl volunteered. 'Did you give the rest away?' 'No, they were drowned.' 'I thought you didn't believe in killing.' 'We didn't kill 'em. That Mountie sergeant drowned 'em for us.' She chuckled, and quite obviously felt no guilt for merely condoning a killing someone else had carried out.

Under the prophetic discipline there were certainly signs of strain. I found empty beer bottles under the bushes in a corner of one Doukhobor field, and in the shelter of the ten-feet plumes of corn which were the community's pride a young man begged a cigarette and smoked in hasty gulps to finish it before anyone came into sight. Yet there was also an atmosphere of dogged devotion. Much of the land had been irrigated, and it was growing heavier crops of corn and tomatoes and vegetables than any of the neighbouring farms, while the houses were surrounded by rows of hotbeds and cold frames where melons and gherkins ripened. The younger people talked constantly of schemes for new kinds of cultivation and for starting up light industries, but the younger people were so few. There were too many children, too many old visionaries.

Sunday was the climax of our visit. Our arrival had coincided with the community's first great festival. In the afternoon the only child so far born there was to be handed over to the care of the community as a symbolic demonstration against conventional ideas of motherhood and the family. Since the Archangel had forbidden fornication, we were rather surprised that a child whose very presence seemed to defy his will should be so honoured. From my attempts to discuss the situation I gained an impression that the Doukhobors applied a rather Dostoevskian equation – considering that, if the ban itself was sacred, so must be the sin against it. 'Free men ain't bound by reason,' as one young man rather unanswerably concluded a discussion on this point.

The day began with morning service in the bare meeting house. Flowers and plates of red apples had been brought in, and the sunlight played over the white head-shawls and bright cotton dresses of the women. Bread and salt stood symbolically on the small central table, and also a great ewer of water from which anybody who happened to feel thirsty would stop and drink as the service went on. The women ranged to the right of the table and the men to the left. On entering the hall each person bowed low from the waist, and the bow was returned by the whole assembly; the salutation was not to the man, but to the God within him. The Archangel stood at the head of the men, benign and copiously sweating; despite his celestial nature, he did not attempt to offend Doukhobor precedent by acting like a priest. Today, in fact, as a child was to be the centre of the festival, the children led off the service, choosing and starting in their sharp, clear voices the Doukhobor psalms and hymns for the day. Almost every part of the service was sung, and the wild and wholly incomprehensible chanting of the two hundred people in the small meeting house produced in us an extraordinary sense of exaltation such as I have only experienced once since then, in a church full of Zapotec peasants at a festival south of Oaxaca. At the end of the service, we all linked arms at the elbows and kissed each other's cheeks, first right then left, in traditional token of forgiveness.

Later in the day we reassembled in the open air, forming a great V with the bread and salt at the apex. The singing rose like a fountain of sound among the drooping cedar trees, and between lines of women waving flowers and men waving green boughs the mother carried her child to the table. She was one of the young women we had met at the farmhouse on our arrival. As she stood there, her fair face grave and melancholy within the white frame of her head-shawl, she looked like the dolorous mother of some naïve ikon. The singing ended, the old hawk-faced bricklayer prayed before the table, and the mother, showing no emotion, handed the child to another of the women. The Archangel began to speak, in high, emotional tones; Pete, standing beside me, translated. The child would be named Angel Gabriel. The fruit of sin, he contained the seed of celestial nature. It was he who would fulfil the great destiny of the Doukhobors and lead mankind back on the great journey to lost Eden.

The women brought out pitchers of kvass and walked among the people as the orators began to speak. Emblematic banners were unfurled before the assembly. One, representing women dragging the ploughs that broke the prairies during the hard early days of the sect in Canada, was meant to celebrate the coming liberation of the sect from all forms of bondage. Another, covered with images of clocks and other symbols of time, was carefully expounded by the Archangel, who found in it the fatal dates that charted the destiny of the world. Then everyone spoke who wished – elders and young women; a Communist lawyer who had come in from the blue; even I, under moral coercion, as the enquiring Tolstoyan I then was. It was hot and tedious work as the sun beat down into the bowl among the mountains and Sunday trippers from Qualicum Beach gazed in astonishment through the palisades.

We walked back to the farmhouse with a Canadian woman who had married into the Doukhobors. 'You've seen what Mike wants you to see,' she said, bitterly. 'You don't know all there is to know about that girl. Today they've taken her child. Now she'll go to stay up in Mike's house. They won't let her talk to anyone, and they'll pay her out in every way they can for having a child by her own husband. Purification! That's what they talk about. I call it prison!' The mother of the Angel Gabriel was not at the evening meal, and we never saw her again. We asked Joe what had happened to her. She had gone willingly into seclusion, he answered, for her own good, of course.

Indeed, Joe had much more important things to talk about in that last conversation. 'You have a great part to play in the future of mankind.' He fixed me with a sharp, pale eye. 'Michael's vision has told him that the end of the world is very near. Now we have to gather in Jerusalem the hundred and forty-four thousand true servants of God mentioned in the Book of Revelation. This time Jerusalem will be right here.'

'Here? On Vancouver Island?'

'On this very spot.'

'But how do you *know*?'

'We ain't worrying. We just know. And the Archangel had a vision about you. He knew you were coming a long time ago. He knew you were a writer. He knew you were being sent here so you could tell the world what we're doing.'

I must have looked at him very dubiously for he flapped his hands reassuringly. 'I ain't asking you to do it. Nor is Archangel. We just know you will. You'll write about us, and people will come to us, and then you will come back and be marked with the sign and live for ever among the servants of God.'

We left the next day. The Archangel saw us once more in his garden, gave us a white rose each, and said we should meet again before long. 'It's a prophecy,' Joe whispered.

And indeed it was. One day, months later, I was broadcasting in Vancouver when Ross McLean, who was then a radio producer, said he had heard Joe was locked up in the court house. I went over, but I could not see him. The Mounties were holding him incommunicado. But as I was leaving the station Michael the Archangel was brought in, and for a couple of minutes, in that grim barred room, I was allowed to talk to him. He was pleased to be recognized, and even willing to talk a little English. 'I am free soon,' he said, as he was led away to the cells. Not long afterwards he and Joe were sentenced on some rather nebulous charges of disturbing public order. And a few months later Michael the Archangel Verigin died in jail.

Ten years afterwards we drove through Hilliers, turning off our road on a nostalgic impulse. The palisade was still there, opposite the railway siding, and for a moment everything looked unchanged. But inside, where Jerusalem should have been rising, there was only the ghost of what we had seen on the day the Angel Gabriel was named. Most of the buildings had gone, but falling fences and squares of thistles still marked out the theocracy where the Archangel had ruled.

[1963]

VI
Patterns: Mores, Religion, and Life Styles

Jean Le Moyne
Pierre Berton
Christina Newman
Adrienne Clarkson
Jean Le Moyne
Gordon Sheppard
Don Owen

Jean Le Moyne

Religion in French Canada

French Canadians are one of the European groups that came to America to undertake a totally new human experience. Transplantation into the midst of a wild, harsh, and immeasurably vast land forced them, of necessity, to adopt a youthful outlook and began to work profound changes in them. Conquest of the land and the first steps they took to humanize it obliged them, in their isolation, to accept a terrible asceticism and to accept such privations as not only moulded character permanently but marked them from the very start. Later, when they re-discovered their European origins and began to evolve rapidly, they discovered a universal difference; they saw, as it were, that they were no longer themselves. The race continued to be essentially a French invention, but French Canadians discovered that more and more they must invent themselves. Their ancestral heritage did not cease to be any less vital and present to them but it was no longer the only frame of reference. The French of Canada were now obliged to refer to their North American roots and from them to develop toward a future classicism of unforeseeable forms.

In the indispensable, intoxicating, and cruel light of his European culture, the French Canadian often finds it extremely hard to remain faithful to an experience that is still so limited, whose expression is ordinarily so bereft of nourishment, and that so rarely reaches a universal level. He may consent to consign himself anew, as his pioneer ancestors did, to spiritual and intellectual poverty but not without a feeling of keen bitterness, nor without having to surmount a crushing sense of inferiority. He becomes touchy, tries to find compensations, asserts himself energetically in a naïve and blustering way. He lays the blame on the fatal authority of history, resentfully accusing the English and nostalgically cursing the French.

Along with the rest of our society, the Catholic Church in French Canada has kindred deficiencies. It is no further advanced than any of the other social orders in the elaboration of a style it could call its own. From this point of view we are at one with our clergy; we speak for each other; we mutually deserve each other in the strictest sense. None the less there exists, as we will see, a justifiable hostility towards the church and a great temptation to make the clergy a scapegoat responsible for difficulties that are quite normal and are also experienced by our English compatriots. It is this hostility that explains in part the French-Canadian appetite for raw clergy whom they gobble up with a kind of mad, masochistic, maniacal greed that many observers, even ones who are indifferent to our faith, find astonishing and irritating. This emotional transfer makes the most of whatever evidence comes to hand from plentiful and immediate sources. But a concern for justice and truth requires that we distinguish here between the drama of our clerical heritage in Quebec and the drama of our North American situation, for the latter encompasses the former, pre-dates it, and surpasses it.

From being a small, precarious, and neglected colony on the bottom rung of the provincial ladder, we were suddenly conquered, isolated, and surrounded by foreigners. It was the clergy then, our only real *élite*, who very naturally espoused our cause, expressed our will to be, our French obstinacy, which now was linked by circumstances to our faith. It was they who, teaching us to fall back on our traditional virtues and possessions, guaranteed our survival. This admirable story is well known and one can easily imagine how strictly faithful to themselves the authorities must have been to reach the goal of that first and indispensable numerical affirmation.

The danger was that, constantly menaced yet constantly encouraged by success, authority would tend to prolong its licence unduly, would exaggerate its dominion and degenerate into clerical self-sufficiency. Even so, having once saved us from the peril of extinction, the ecclesiastical authorities kept up the habit but thereafter tended to save us from life. Having once experienced a well-founded fear, they henceforth applied this fear to illusory objects. Authority began to fear everything outside itself and to develop a radical xenophobia, the logical consequence of which was, if not to reject what was human, at least to adulterate and diminish it. It fulfils a host of indispensable functions and renders eminent services with a generosity that the state would certainly be incapable of. But it taxes us invisibly. The church serves but she is an exclusive servant. She serves without mercy like Ubu in chains. She administers from an inaccessible château where only those whose interests mysteriously coincide with her own are granted audience. Commerce and finance have invented that prize sucker, the consumer; she conceived the despicable layman, the fringe-Christian, that poor spiritless soul whom she disdainfully regards from the pinnacle of her overweening pride in her own purity, while he splashes around in the mire of the world.

By affinity she allies herself with reactionary and authoritarian elements in society that are mad on the question of survival, and she dreams of a happy concubinage with them, ignoring the lessons of history. There is no shortage of would-be Francos among us here (they run to type, even to the size), and one shudders at the thought of what would happen if French Canadians constituted themselves an independent state.

Our unique safeguard is a circumstantial one, the fact that we share this country with an Anglo-Saxon Protestant majority. It is Protestantism that keeps us different and maintains the equilibrium. It represents unshakable reality, and its free thought serves us, indirectly, in lieu of a revolutionary tradition. It saves us from the corruption, the bogging down, and the sterile violence that have been the lot of Catholics in Latin America. It keeps alive the hope of a possible evolution, of a gradual liberation, and of our entrance into an adult Catholicism that will be no illusory reform but a true renewal creating a new and original religious habitation. And it will not be new with the damnable newness of heresy but new in the sense that within the holy and living orthodoxy of the Catholic Church the people may be prompted to sing forth freely, as children of light, a new hymn. Protestantism nullifies at the root the dangerous xenophobia of our survivalists. The risk inherent in its very inconsistency invites us to explore a wider world, enlarges our horizons, and counteracts our obscurantist tendencies.

I do not intend this to be a defence of Protestantism, and it should be clearly understood that I am speaking strictly from within the church, without the least urge to be elsewhere, thanks be to God. I am simply singling out one major feature of the Canadian situation. As two social groups engaged in crucial questions, Catholic and Protestant elements react on one another without knowing each other and force each other to accept a mutual *modus vivendi* in accordance with the spirit of compromise that characterizes this country. As far as we are concerned, the permeability of the Protestant world helps us by exposing us a little more fully to other human adventures. The Protestant habit of free inquiry, replacing for us (and very poorly at that) a true Catholic maturity, does constitute a temptation to disaffection that it is impossible to resist effectively because of the dual nature of our nation.

When I learned to read two angels were assigned to my company: a good one on the right and a bad one on the left. As long as I live I will never forget the sight of one of my schoolmates, overcome with fright and indignation, striking out madly at empty space on his left.

The self-sufficient left-hand angel sneered conspicuously at every fault committed, whether trifling or of some indefinable gravity, while the good one, one of the see-all-do-nothing variety, went to squeal to Jesus who, planing his little cross, wept already over his future death, staged by us, little Judases that we were, assassins, hangmen, little torturers all, at seven years old. And what image could we supply for the heavenly joy occasioned by the spectacle of our virtues? The only available images of religious excellence were those disconsolate saints, those eye-rolling wonders the like of which were never seen on this earth.

We were schooled in the law and taught the ABC of sin.

The living, everyday Christ was never taught us. Nor the Christ of Easter. We only saw him on the cross or at the Second Coming; either dead to man or catastrophe for the world.

[1966. Translated by Philip Stratford.]

Pierre Berton

The Religion of Work and the Dirtiest Job in the World

On my seventeenth birthday, which fell on July 12, 1937, one of the worst years of the Depression, I went to work for pay and there was jubilation among my friends and relatives. In an era when jobs were scarce I had a job; and having a job was the goal of everyone in those days. Having a job in the Thirties was a bit like having a swimming pool in the Sixties; it conferred status. It didn't really matter what the job was. It could be unrewarding, mindless, foolish, unproductive, even degrading – no matter: it set you apart as a paying member of a society whose creed was that everyone must work at something, and the harder the better, too.

My job was in a mining camp in the Yukon some 1,500 miles from my home in Victoria, B.C. I worked ten hours a day, seven days a week, and I was paid $4.50 a day plus my board. Almost everybody who learned about my job had the same thing to say about it: 'It will make a man out of you!' And when the job came to an end at the start of my university term, almost every adult I knew examined my hands to note with satisfaction the heavy calluses. Back-breaking work was considered to be a high form of human endeavour. A man who worked hard couldn't be all bad, whether he was a convict breaking rocks in a prison yard or an executive neglecting his family by toiling weekends at the office.

I worked for three summer seasons at that same job and it was commonly held that I was 'working my way through college', another laudable endeavour in a society which believed, and still believes, that every individual must pay his own way regardless of position, health, mental ability, or physical condition.

177

The first year I worked on a construction gang; the following years I worked on the thawing crew, engaged in preparing the ground for the actual gold mining that was to follow. Thawing permafrost with cold water is a fascinating process to almost everyone except those actually employed in it. As far as I know, it is the world's muddiest job, involving as it does the pumping of millions of gallons of cold water into the bowels of the earth.

And so we toiled away, up to our ankles, our knees, and sometimes even our hips in a pulsating gruel of mud and ice-water. The men who drove those points into the rock-like soil were soaking wet most of the time, for it was difficult to add extension or withdraw a point without water spurting in all directions. All day long they laboured, with their fingers curled around the handles of their slide hammers, their torsos rising and falling as they drove each pipe inch by inch into the earth. When a point became plugged it had to be hauled up and unplugged while the ice-water squirted in their faces. Each man was logged on the amount of footage he had driven in a day, and if that footage was seen to be too low he could expect to draw his time slip that evening. There was a story current in my day that the general manager had come out from Dawson on a tour of inspection and seen a man standing immobile in the distance. 'Fire that man!' he cried. 'I've been watching him and he hasn't moved for half an hour.' Later it was discovered that he *couldn't* move; he was up to his hips in mud.

When you work for ten hours at hard labour, whether you are seventeen or fifty-seven, there is precious little time or energy left for anything else. We rose at six, performed our swift ablutions, wolfed an enormous breakfast, and headed off for the job which had to begin at seven. At noon we started back up the valley slopes through the mud to the messhall, wolfed another vast meal, and finished it just in time to head back once more. At six we were finished, in more ways than one. I have seen men so tired they could not eat the final meal of the day which was always consumed in silence and at top speed. (It was said that any man who stumbled on the messhall steps on the way in found himself trampled by the rush coming out.) When this was over, large numbers of men of varying ages simply lay down on their bunks utterly fagged out, and slept. There was nothing else to do anyway: no library, no recreation hall, no lounge, no radio or films – nothing but a roadhouse five miles distant where you could buy bootleg rum. Civilization was represented by Dawson, forty miles away; we never visited it. We were like men in a prison camp, except that we worked much harder.

Under such conditions any kind of creative act or thought is difficult. I remember one man, a German immigrant, who was trying to learn to draw by correspondence. He had some talent but in the end he had to give it up. He was too tired to draw. I had brought along a pile of books required in my university course for summer reading, but most of the time I found I was too tired to read. Those who did not immediately go to sleep after supper spent their spare time washing their work clothes or lying in their bunks indulging in verbal sexual fantasies. I often wondered if this was what the adults meant when they said that mining camp life would make a man of me. Certainly I learned a great deal more from these sexual bull sessions than I had at my mother's knee. It was not until many years later that I discovered most of it was wrong.

It is difficult to describe the absolute dreariness and hopelessness of this kind of job. The worst thing about it was that there was no respite, since – in a seven-day-a-week job – there were no breaks of any kind to look forward to until the coming of winter rendered further toil impossible. There was one wit among us who used to leap from his bunk once a week, when the bull cook banged the triangle at 6.00 a.m., crying jubilantly: 'Thank God, it's Sunday!' This always provoked a bitter laugh. Without any change of pace, time moves sluggishly; without any break in the routine, a kind of lethargy steals over the mind. The blessed winter seemed eons away to all of us.

Yet for me, in my late teens, life in this mining camp was immeasurably easier than it was for the others. There were men here in their sixties who had lived this way all their lives. There were men in their prime with wives and children to support – families they did not see for half of every year. There were all kinds of men here and few who were really stupid. I worked with immigrants from Austria, Germany, Switzerland, Italy, Sweden, Norway, and Denmark, as well as with Canadians. Most were intelligent and a great many were extremely sharp and able. All were industrious. Each had displayed enough courage and independence to somehow make his way several thousand miles to the one corner of North America where a job of sorts was comparatively easy to get. But all had one thing in common: according to my observation, none had been educated up to his ability.

There were many men in that mining camp easily capable of obtaining a university degree; and there were many more who might have completed high school and then gone on to technical school. I saw them each evening, lying on their bunks and trying to force their hands open – hands that had been curled into almost permanent positions around cold pipes; I saw them each morning, shambling down to that grotesque mudpie of a valley; during the day I saw them – scores of ant-like figures, bend double over their slide hammers, struggling in the gumbo, striving and groaning; and the thought that came to my mind was ever the same: 'What a waste of human resources!'

For this 'job', which everybody had congratulated me upon getting, which was supposed to be so ennobling, which was to make a man of me, was actually degrading, destructive, and above all useless. It was degrading because it reduced men to the status of beasts. There was one wag who went around with his zipper purposely undone and his genitals exposed. 'If I'm working like a horse, I might as well look like one,' he'd say. It was destructive because it reduced a glorious setting to a black obscenity. And it was useless because the gold, which was mined at such expense and human cost, was melted into bars and shipped to Fort Knox in the United States where it was once again confined below ground. Every manjack of us knew this; it was the subject of much bitter banter and wisecracking; each of us, I think, was disturbed by the fact that we were engaged in an operation which was essentially unproductive. If we'd been growing wheat, we would at least have had the satisfaction of knowing our labours were useful. The whole, vast, complicated operation seemed to me to be pointless: even the stockholders failed to profit by it greatly; for years the company was forced to pass its dividends. Would we or the nation have been worse off if we had stayed drunk all summer?

The one valuable asset that I recovered from my mining camp experience was status. It allows me to use a line in my official biography which I notice is seized upon joyfully by those who have to introduce me when I make after-dinner speeches: 'During the Thirties, he worked in Yukon mining camps to help put himself through university.' When that line is uttered the audience is prepared to forgive me almost anything: outlandishly radical opinions, dangerous views on matters sexual, alarming attitudes toward religion. I am pronounced worthy because, in that one sentence, is summed up the great Canadian myth: that work – *any* work – is the most important thing in life, and that anybody who is willing to work hard enough can by his own initiative get as far as he wants.

[1967]

Christina Newman

Two Snapshots of Capital Culture: Ottawa Man Ottawa Farewell

Ottawa Man

In most Canadian cities a young man on the way up tries hard to make other people notice him. He's brash, he's bombastic, he's got bezazz. Success, he knows, comes to the man who stands out in the crowd. But there's one city in this country where following that formula could mean not personal glory but self-destruction. That city is Ottawa. There, it's well known that success, in civil service circles, comes to the man who looks just like everybody else (everybody else important, that is). For the Ottawa man on the rise what's *de rigueur* is urbane anonymity. It's a curious but irrefutable fact that the people who do the people's business move upward to the higher echelons by being reserved and seemly, distinguishable only to the educated eye.

This is why the city had developed a unique character type who can only be called Ottawa Man. Young men of ambition in the nation's capital relentlessly pursue a single goal: to turn themselves into Ottawa Men. When they make it, they become a special variety of the human species, as alien to a Montrealer as a Mau Mau, as alien to a Torontonian as a Turk.

By definition the Ottawa Man is inconspicuous. He's also highly educated (very often in England as well as Canada), formal in manner, meticulous in speech. He's a snob, but a nice snob, a gentle man who nothing common does or mean (he never gossips). He is most like himself when he unavoidably fetches up – at an airport, perhaps – next to a Toronto Man, whom he regards as crass, vulgar, and probably in advertising.

G*   181

The Ottawa Man is likely to be *in* External (Affairs, that is) or Finance, or even Trade and Commerce; but he can't be found *at* the Queen's Printer, Agriculture, or Veterans' Affairs. In brief, all civil servants are by no means Ottawa Men; and you can be an Ottawa Man in other, if allied, lines of work – in the CBC, administration of course, the Canada Council, UNESCO. The Ottawa Man is well but not lavishly paid. He aspires to a deputy ministership, the China Desk, or the permanent delegation at the U.N.

For tourists who may want to spot him, or careerists who may want to emulate him, this is the Ottawa Man, 1962, an all-Canadian sociological phenomenon:

★ *Dress:* He wears a navy blue suit with a vest, carries an umbrella (black, furled, with wooden handle), lets his hair grow rather too long. His glasses have gold or tortoise-shell rims, and his large, brown briefcase (not attaché case) is always bulging and worn about the handle. He never wears button-down shirts, narrow ties, summer suits, or snap-brim hats.

★ *Conversation:* Unlike men elsewhere in Canada, he seldom uses slang. You'll never hear him say 'fink' or 'impact-wise', or *anything* like that. You will hear him say (constantly), 'So I've heard,' or 'I'm told by,' or 'I explored this point with Mike.' He will not discuss partisan politics with any but intimate friends, and you will see him smile at an anti-Diefenbaker joke only if he knows you fairly well. When he does loosen up, however, it will come out that he thinks John Diefenbaker is an upstart and that he regrets the Fall (of 1957). Most of the time he's apt to talk about constitutional fine points, the coming crisis in Central Africa, and the Pilkington commission on broadcasting in Britain. He *still* talks about the Rowell-Sirois report.

★ *Women:* He never appears with the big, built blondes in bouffants who are popular elsewhere; he doesn't even dream about them. His wife tries for the little-brown-hen look: shiny clean undyed hair, cashmere sweater, string of pearls, black silk dress, white kid gloves, old beaver coat – maybe a small, tatty mink stole. She knows what to do at a formal dinner, she belongs to the National Gallery Association, sits on the Toy Testing Committee, and ushers at the Ottawa Choral Society.

★ *Taste:* He drinks sherry, wine, ale, or Scotch, not martinis, manhattans, or daiquiris. He never drives a big new car; he has a Morris or Austin or Vauxhall, or perhaps a '55 Ford with the insignia removed. His house has a log fireplace, a study, comfortable chairs (some leather), frayed Oriental rug, and no TV or hi-fi in sight. He doesn't know who Ben Casey is, and he's barely heard of Harold Town, though he owns an A. Y. Jackson and may very well possess a faded lithograph of the skating pond at Rideau Hall in 1872. He never talks about Pierre Berton, the Diners' Club, Norman Mailer, or the Nouvelle Vague.

★ *Leisure:* He skis at Fortune in winter, plays tennis in summer, walks (literally) in the Gatineau in the fall.

★ *Entertainment:* He doesn't go to bars, dine in restaurants, listen to jazz. He knows how much his friends earn (it's in the Blue Book of departmental estimates though he never has to look it up) and they all make about what he does, or within, say, $500. He knows no local Ottawa people; in fact he sees almost nobody except other Ottawa Men and people from Abroad. He gives many small dinner parties (often featuring one black, brown, or yellow guest from Abroad, who comes with his Oxford accent and his wife, in a sari). Once a year he gives a large cocktail party at which his guests, unlike those in other parts of Canada, do not stay beyond the specified hour (six to eight p.m.) or get high, or talk to strangers. Ideally, his parties have the steward from the Speaker's chamber at the bar, and are catered by a Miss Minnie and her sister, who provide asparagus sandwiches, radish rosettes and hot lobster canapés, and wear black dresses with frilly white aprons. They're professional caterers, but they aren't in the phone book and they don't come to just anyone. Only Ottawa Men.

[1962]

Ottawa Farewell

The first time I recognized the existence of the Establishment in Ottawa was about a year after we arrived here. We were invited to a small dinner at the Rideau Club, given by a gentleman journalist for a deputy minister and his wife and a St. Laurent vintage Liberal Cabinet minister's widow. We were sitting decorously in the lounge over brandy discussing how marvellous the Brie used to be at Vincent Massey's Sunday evening supper dances when Paul Martin (then the titular second-in-command of the Liberal Opposition) ankled by and attempted to make conversation. They were perfectly polite but completely cool to him, and after he moved uneasily on the Liberal minister's widow arched her pale brows and whispered, 'Did you see his socks?' and, I thought to myself, 'Holy Toledo! He doesn't belong and what's more he knows that they know he doesn't belong.'

This particular scene couldn't happen now; the Rideau Club doesn't matter much any more, the St. Laurent government's glories are no longer talked about and Paul Martin has gone gracefully to the Senate (after, as some of his friends said bitterly, the Establishment had cost him the Liberal leadership). But the élitist attitude implicit in that exchange still dominates Ottawa. The Establishment's style may vary slightly, and its personnel may change, but it continues to function on the twin bases of caution and exclusion.

There are, of course, those who resist it (in addition to those who are deliberately excluded from it), who never become Ottawa Men no matter how brief or long a time they stay here. They fall into four categories:

(1) Most French Canadians, or at least those who plan to return to the Province of Quebec. (I once tried to figure out why a French Canadian we

knew was so out of the Establishment mainstream even though he had an important title; it hit me that he liked to say, 'I enjoy life.' Nobody with any sense in Ottawa enjoys life.)

(2) Certain Western Canadians who have spent the first part of their working lives in the West and are consequently too open, too plainly alive, to be fitted into the mould.

(3) All Jews, who, no matter how skilfully they are passing as short-haired natives of WASPland, are forever indicating by small spurts of laughter or brief glitters of eye that underneath the vest there still beats the heart of a *mensch*.

(4) A miscellaneous group of the bright and the young who use Ottawa as a training ground, come here to learn and to change things, soon realize there is a lot to be learned and almost nothing that can be changed, and, having made their valuable connections, get out before middle age and the System overtake them.

At this time last year, most people would have added a fifth category: Pierre Elliott Trudeau. But, *hélas,* it's beginning to look as though they were wrong. After eleven months in power Trudeau seems not so much to be changing Ottawa as being changed by it. Ottawa is showing once again its fantastic ability to absorb divergents. (Those it can't absorb it destroys, as it did John Diefenbaker and Walter Gordon.)

The Trudeau group came in dedicated to the belief that the government could be changed, that the system could be streamlined, made a truer reflection of the country, infused with new ideas, new men, new purpose. Indeed, it became enmeshed in policy reviews, task forces, critical flow charts – all factors contributing to a further dehumanization of the governmental process, a further exclusion of the governed from the magic circle of the governors.

Last year we needed 'new guys with new ideas'; this year we have Mitchell Sharp in External, Bud Drury in Treasury, Gordon Robertson, as the Clerk of the Privy Council, and Bob Bryce as the Deputy Minister of Finance – all key members of the old, old Establishment, all key members of the new, new government.

While there are many more French-speaking ministers, many younger ministers (all of them with tight-buttoned lips), and a new group of advisers who are technocrats rather than generalists (the Harvard Business School rather than Oxbridge in their background), they are turning out to be as decorous in their persons and as cautious in their ideas as the crustiest members of the old Establishment might have wished.

In fact, some days it seems as though nothing has changed, at all. One bright February noon, I was walking along Wellington Street and saw, alive and well and whistling 'The British Grenadiers' through his moustache, a man mounting the steps to the Rideau Club clad in a coonskin coat that just cleared the top of his buckled galoshes. I couldn't help murmuring in gratitude, 'Oh Ottawa, fare thee well!'

[1969]

Adrienne Clarkson

The Female Style in Politics: A Bird in a Gilded Cage

For the tide that must be taken in the affairs of men, most politicians usually approach the riverbank with hip waders or scuba-diving outfits, their copies of Machiavelli neatly packaged in polyethylene. This, one suspects, Judy LaMarsh could never do. *Why* she didn't do it is something we can go into later, but it is very and often painfully clear that the frank political feminine soul which sings out in *Memoirs of a Bird in a Gilded Cage* is one which does not protect itself much. Consequently the book is remarkable not as much for its revelations as for its atmosphere of vulnerability. It is probably not the first time that a political memoir has been used as therapy by the writer, but it may be the first time in Canada. What has been labelled as gossipy ('no one ever bought a round [of coffee] for everyone at the [Cabinet] table') is really the therapeutic obsession with detail which often accompanies the recall of a total situation that was traumatic. The lack of coffee being laid on for members of Cabinet comes to stand for all the disillusion that she found in being a Cabinet minister at all. The lack of bathroom facilities for her in the Department of National Health and Welfare building, the failure of Mrs. Pearson to send flowers to Mrs. Michener, the insistence of certain junior Ministers' wives to a right of place at the Vanier funeral, curtsying during Centennial celebrations – they add up to the minor irritations on which huge dissatisfactions build.

To stare at these details and dismiss them loftily as the unimportant trivia of the feminine mind is to miss the whole point. The pattern of the details makes up a pointillist design of frustration and genuine disillusionment which one

185

rarely sees so honestly revealed. And it must be remembered that it is in defence of nothing. The Hon. Pierre Sévigny, of the Gerda Munsinger affair, wrote *This Game of Politics* and petulantly gossiped a great deal, and defensively; we all knew *why*. Judy LaMarsh writes a book full of personal revelations and opinions, and the critics (especially the press gallery with their unspoken code of gentlemanly behaviour – no one should mention that anyone else was drunk) double over biliously in their attempt to dismiss her as a hysterical woman; in fact, they usually assume that their readers think of hysteria and femininity as synonymous and play on this association. For some unknown reason, attention to human detail is considered to be feminine, and on this point Miss LaMarsh's book is the most feminine to emerge about the Canadian political scene. And what a relief it is to read someone saying things as a participator and not an observer. I was there, she says stoutly and crossly, and this is what I saw.

Nowadays, we are used to the analysis of events of importance from the so-called detached observer – the political pundit whose high official sources of information depend upon him for political advancement, the television journalist who must have a story to fill that hour even though nothing may have happened in seven days; in our style of instantly transmittable non-events, we value impartiality and objectivity as though we did not know of electronic tape editing or the exigencies of a highly political press. A political reporter gives us History, we think, because he has been able to go with his tape recorder to every Cabinet Minister and get the whole story. Judy LaMarsh tells us of the Canada Pension crisis but it is only her point of view as the Minister in charge, and we can dismiss it. I have no doubt that many Cabinet doors were closed to her in the way they wouldn't be to that tape-recording journalist; but to me, that is what makes her story so intriguing. She has only her side to tell and she spills it forth conversationally, and without another motive than an overwhelming need to say out loud that this was how it really was. It is thoroughly enjoyable to have a politician's-eye view of other politicians, and the highly personal assessment of their value as people and as functionaries is easily established as relative, because the personality writing the book is strong. In this way, the book is fair to the reader, for you are never deluded for a minute into thinking that what you are reading is political history or even considered opinion; it is the testament of the involved and embattled partici-pant – emotion recollected in agitation.

When I see her during the CBC crisis of 1966, scorned by the high administrators on the one hand and manipulated by the clever young producers on the other, she is even more dramatic than she gives herself credit for. She may think she knows which of them has God and Creativity on his side, but you know from everything you've read up to that point that she tends to be more sympathetic to people who are nice to her. Walter Gordon, 'Ben' Benson, and Jean Marchand take her off to lunch like one of the boys and she assesses them in varying shades of brilliant, incorruptible, and patriotic; there is something transparent and appealing about these judgments; they are the aspects of a naïve and affectionate nature which is easier to keep track of than an attempt at genuine historical perspective, or the assessment of a government as a failure in radicalism. It is history with a human, rather than a systematic, flaw.

And what does she stand to gain from it all? It won't get her the judgeship that Pearson refused her, nor is it likely to elongate her to the moribund ranks of the Senate. Nor do I think she wouldn't have written the book if she had gotten either of those dubious honours. For it is a book which just had to be written; it is as compulsive and inconclusive and contradictory as all such spontaneous documents are. The events and the judgments are not the centre of attention; Judy LaMarsh is. It is a self-portrait of appalling honesty, some stridency, and frequently ungrammatical freshness.

What it may mean for the prospects of women in political life in Canada is another matter. Will it mean that a future Prime Minister will hesitate to appoint even a token woman to his Cabinet for fear that the ashtray situation will leak out? I don't think so; Prime Ministers who think in terms of token women have clearly braced themselves for such ordeals and can dismiss them as petty. What is more saddening and faintly mysterious is to see through this particular woman Cabinet Minister's eyes the powerlessness of a Cabinet position. In the case of the CBC, she says she wanted to change things, but she couldn't; who wants to work up through the grass roots of the Liberal party for twenty years and discover that they are powerless? Would it have been any different if she hadn't been Judy LaMarsh or are they all as powerless and just ashamed to say so? Until someone else reveals themselves in the same terms, we won't know.

[1969]

Jean
Le Moyne

The Strong Women of Quebec

In 1665, when a royal decision was finally taken to send troops to Canada, the country was showing signs of dangerous fatigue. The weakness of the colony is seen mainly in relation to the Iroquois menace, but locally it was eclipsed by an incredible fertility. 'Those who have been settled for some time in this country,' writes Marie de l'Incarnation, 'have so many children that it is marvellous to see how they thrive.' Talon, in 1667, sending in a report like a horse dealer's, states that the country 'is fruitful in natural-born Frenchmen, the women bearing nearly every year.' De Meulles adds in 1683: 'They commonly have ten or twelve children and quite often more, and it is surprising to see how they proliferate.' Dollier de Casson waxes lyrical celebrating the vigour and longevity of the women. He recalls that from 1666 to 1672 only one woman died in Montreal and, in a prophetic vein no doubt, exclaims that in New France 'the female is almost immortal.'

The first shipments of *les filles du roi* began to arrive after 1663, and the tender cargoes continued to come until 1673. Hand-picked, dowered by the king, these marriageable young women were not long left languishing. In the words of Marie de l'Incarnation they were 'married off by the score'. In a few days, a few weeks, or at the most a few months, they were generally all matched.

No matter what allowance one makes for the customs of the times or however much one insists on the strict supervision that prevailed over these unions and the girls' freedom of choice, the fact remains that this organized stampede to the altar was absolutely abnormal.

188

An effort of imagination is necessary to see the human side of these statistics, to see it, for example, in the crude list sent by Colbert to Talon to announce the dispatch of 'four hundred stout fellows, fifty females, twelve mares, and two stallions'. One must try to imagine young girls rudely transplanted to a distant, formless world, then confronted instantly with perfect strangers with whom they were to enter into the most important engagement of their lives. They came deliberately for that – granted. They took a cool view of the whole situation – all right. But was that coolness, which is a form of solitude, ever certain to be replaced by the desired warmth?

Whatever the case, these odious manipulations of youth immediately paid off in cash returns, and Talon manufactured enough people to disconcert history.

Here, then, is the experience that man and woman have made of each other and of themselves in this country according to those who, by definition, speak the mind of all: a love that is blocked, forbidden, tarnished, and tainted, a feeling of anguish before the other partner, the rebuff of liberation and possession, the uselessness of human help or of recourse to God, downfall and death for having wanted to embrace one another as lovers or as man and wife, for having wanted to make something of the couple. What an extraordinary irony when one thinks of the history of conjugality among us! Three centuries full of triumph for the family, full of the sacramental blessings of marriage. Three centuries spent in faith and piety, sheltered from revolutions, scepticism, perversions, sheltered from everything, to end in this unhealthy havoc! The experience of procreation that we turned into a pseudo-mystique was a preparation for the over-scrupulous race we have become, an intimidated race, haunted by the flesh as if we had never known it and as mistrustful of it as if the only way to save it were by yielding to the vertigo of perdition. If we have lost the capacity to enjoy our promises or our promised ones, it is because we have lost our joy.

Someone else has eaten our joy and somewhere else.

In the very first words of a terrible and magnificent story whose symbolic charge is explosive, Anne Hébert hands us the key to our alienation. *Le Torrent* is the story of a child who lives alone with a guilty mother who is hardened by remorse and pride and is as strong as a man. Claudine wishes her son to become a priest, for she hopes thereby to win the redemption of her own sin and her own rehabilitation into society. But François refuses and, in a fury, the mother strikes her son so hard that she deafens him to all earthly voices. A wild horse, which is freed by François and which combines all the powers of life, sex, revolt, and death, kills Claudine. With his mother's money François buys a nameless woman and calls her Amica, the friend. One day Amica runs off with Claudine's money and François throws himself into the torrent, a place that has long exerted a fascination over him. The story begins with these words: 'I was a child dispossessed of this world.'

These hints point to a universal context, and if we trace it back in history to the time of our origins, we find ourselves in a period dedicated to the liquidation of the uniformity of the Middle Ages, in a period that is essentially dualistic. Now dualism is the greatest heresy, the only one that can justly and directly be called Satanic. It begins in Adam, our link with creation. It breaks the unity of things visible and invisible, joined in man by the substantial union of flesh and spirit. Henceforth it condemns these two to be torn apart by unholy desires and to be constantly reconstructing a harmony that is ceaselessly compromised. Now Christian orthodoxy possesses in Christ the principle of a unity that is infinitely superior to Adam's and against which nothing shall prevail. But the orthodox themselves are not safe in their psychology, in their metaphysics, or in their morals; they, too, can be poisoned and unconsciously contradict salvation, for salvation is to choose everything, that is to say, the assumption of the material and the visitation of the spiritual. As a result of Adam's sin, the haughty spirit mistrusts matter, which has now become opaque, and makes it the seat of evil and despises the earth that it should interpret and possess. And since it knows matter through the instrumentality of the body and since the body expresses itself by means of sex, the spirit impregnates sex with fear and shame.

History is made up of pulsations from these poles, and the more mind develops, the more exigent the conditions of unity will become; at one and the same time the convergences become more comprehensive and the estrangements vaster, the harmonies richer and the discords more violent.

It is our misfortune to be a tributary to the main current of dualism that swept through the classicism of seventeenth-century France. Historically, our country began at the time when the new casuistry was attempting vainly to free man from an excessive responsibility, at the time of the Jansenist reaction, at the time when Pascal was inaugurating our modern age of anxiety and Descartes was proposing his sovereign divorces to the Western world. It was also the time when a new type of man appeared, the bourgeois, the prophet of 'the average'. It is the bourgeois who goes into mourning for joy, dresses in black and turns over to woman, as though it were an immoral game, the pleasure of ornamenting the body. He distinguishes himself from her to assert his difference, for he is really intimidated and incapable of freely risking exchanges with her or of allowing any resemblances between the sexes. And since it is still a man's world, all the blame, the reproaches, the mistrust, and the severity are directed against woman — chief object of desire and chief victim.

So we undertook the conquest of this New World while at the same time we hated and refused the world. Our natural drives were slowed down and frustrated at their source and in their overflow. We multiplied greatly though rejecting the flesh, in the intimacy of a secret intellectually grasped though not understood. When we loved we did so with a defective intimacy that made the need of woman become something forbidden. And we deceived ourselves by entering into a union in which the wife was the mother.

But we came here accompanied by men and women of God, that is to say, beings at unity with themselves in proportion to their sanctity. Their presence among us is a prophecy over us, and their inspired piety has given us the protection of a supernatural inoculation.

The Precursor, our patron, is a solitary man of whom Jesus said, 'Among the children of man there has never been one greater than he.' But this child 'grew and waxed strong in spirit'. And after he had reached his full stature he said of Christ and himself, 'He must increase but I must decrease.' Implicitly or explicitly one must, of necessity, want oneself and love oneself before one can give oneself in charity; one must possess the world before one can make a valid sacrifice of it. And woe unto them who anticipate on earth or in heaven, and who leave holes in reality behind them. They omit hope, the virtue of time, which knows how to abide patiently in the mind, even if it cannot operate with immediate efficacy through asceticism.

The widow, Marie de l'Incarnation, is the exact contradiction of a maternity closed in upon itself like a prison or closed on childhood like a trap. Her solitude weds God. Her son, abandoned, moves in conformity with his mother's intuition from frustration to a maturity that he will, in turn, freely dedicate to God's work. Though they come to pass in quite different ways, the same acts of self-abandonment are no less decisively required of the great number of us whose vocation it is to fulfil the couple, that is to say that we must put ourselves, under God's blessing, into each other's power to the exclusion of all other powers of the flesh.

[1966. Translated by Philip Stratford.]

Gordon Sheppard

Violence and the French-Canadian Male

Hubert Aquin, whose soul is on fire, not on ice, is the great imaginative writer of Quebec revolt. But he is much more than that. He's probably the greatest writer this country has yielded to its memory. *Prochain episode,* his first novel, revealed this extraordinary talent; *Trou de mémoire,* his second novel, confirms and develops that talent in a heroic story about the perplex of the humanist revolutionary. For M. Aquin is a loving revolutionary writer who writes of revolution with passion tempered by civilized torment, which goes straight to the heart of our matter.

As it appears from his writing, what brought M. Aquin to violent revolt was not simply a desire to establish an independent French-speaking Quebec or a Marxist state, nor even to serve mistress anarchy. It was a passionate love of women colliding with lack of the male pride that alone can make true love possible.

The terrible, guilty secret of the French-Canadian people is the weakness of their men and the strength of their women. They have the Conquest, the Church, and themselves to thank for that. Together, the Conquest and the Church humbled the French-Canadian men, making most of them weak, miserable, seldom capable of generosity or tenderness; while their women, used to conquest and supported by a Church that made a hero of the Virgin Mary and fellow-women out of celibate priests, became the splendid rocks of this society – which humbled the men still more.

If Marie-Claire Blais is the female voice of the tortured soul of Quebec, Hubert Aquin is its male cry of rage, demanding the return of male pride so

192

that he and his fellows can manfully seek, find, and enjoy life's greatest gift to man – the loving woman, who must be loved with generosity and tenderness.

And M. Aquin implies that to do this he thinks (or thought) that the French-Canadian male must gain independence for Quebec by violent means, not just because this is the only way it can be achieved, but also because revolutionary crime will blood them into manhood. 'Life begins with crime,' writes Pierre X. Magnant, hero of *Trou de mémoire*. '. . . The revolution is the greatest crime of all.'

M. Aquin's two novels are a testament to the torment of this sensitive, immensely gifted man, as he, playing the hero in detective stories, uses literature like a Herman Kahn psychodrama to make his demands for violence triumph over his humanism, oscillating constantly between the real and the fictional, searching for help in the histories, philosophies, literature, customs of many men and nations, and in drugs, psychiatry, and geography. And he does this in language, now sober, now comic, always rich, that must be among the most brilliant in the French language.

In *Prochain episode*, the jailed hero distracts himself by inventing an espionage story in which he is an F.L.Q. agent, detailed to carry out a political assassination in Switzerland. But he is too romantic about it, his victim escapes, his blonde lovelady, K (a female Kafka?), disappears, and the hero returns home to Montreal and arrest.

At the end, the hero (M. Aquin) resolves to be less quixotic in his next (prochain) episode of the Quebec revolution; from now on, to revolt without ratiocination or romanticism. And then he will find his lovelady again. Public commitment must procede private epiphany, as Dante knew.

But in *Trou de mémoire* he shows more subtle, more profound understanding of the revolutionary's dilemma, because he has made this novel's act of violence less Bondish, more personal, more relevant to the Quebec context.

The hero, Pierre X. Magnant, Montreal pharmacologist and revolutionary, rapes Joan, an English-Canadian biochemist, in order to 'conquer' her; instead, he is conquered once again, and they become lovers. Finding his subjection to her too painful to bear, and wishing to try out his theories about violence, he finally drugs and murders her in what his political ecstasy calls 'le crime parfait', his first revolutionary act. Yet murder proves no more effective than rape as a way to freedom and dignity. Quite the opposite, for he discovers with dismay that his victim has entered his being and obsesses him, that by killing Joan he has killed his future chance for love. Victor and victim alike are vanquished by violence.

What must be the fate of a man who sees so much to caution his emotion, whose head must constantly fight his heart? Suicide? Madness? M. Aquin chooses both, as his drugged and hallucinating Pierre X. Magnant confesses this story by writing it as a novel in which, with increasing delirium and incandescent scholarship, he vainly tried to sustain the theory of violent revolt against the soul-destroying reality he now knows. Relief comes only with suicide, later on.

So far, you assume that *Trou de mémoire* is a one-sided exploration of the revolutionary psyche and the effects on revolutionaries themselves of the violence they do to others. And then, near the end of the book, with a stunning reference to *trompe-l'oeil* in a Holbein painting, M. Aquin makes you see that his terrible insight is meant to apply to the English rape of French Canadians (by conquest and hidden violence). The *trou de mémoire* (lapse of memory) results from the traumatic shock of rape, and any person, any nationality subject to violence is prey to the same mental and cultural derangement.

Like Nabokov of *Pale Fire*, M. Aquin tells his politico-literary story in the guise of an intellectual thriller, with footnotes, exegesis, and text supposedly by four authors who, the style suggests, are all Pierre X. Magnant masquerading to hide his pain.

Given the conclusions of *Trou de mémoire*, how long will it be before French-Canadian men have regained their pride and rejoined the confident community of men who know how to love their women? And will it take a generation of French-Canadian men willing to kill or be killed, and will it take much English-Canadian blood, and mutual hate? Are we Canadians faced by a dilemma that has No Exit but only playing room?

Even though he is a romantic revolutionary fighting for his manhood, M. Aquin has had the courage and the civility to force his mind through the consequences of his revolutionary passion, and to present us his reflections in great art. It must have been an agony for him. That this noble book was written by such a committed man is an honour to him and to us. We all must try to understand how to be worthy of it. We can begin by honestly examining our own violence, one to another.

[1969]

Don Owen

Leonard Cohen: The Poet As Hero

I first met Leonard Cohen in the late 1950s, when he used to come down to Toronto with Irving Layton for the poetry readings that were held in the old Greenwich Gallery on Bay Street. There was a considerable literary scene in Toronto at that time, and once a month the gallery would be filled with Harris tweed jackets, Viyella shirts, Karen Bulow ties, baggy grey flannel trousers, and desert boots, mixing it up with peasant blouses and skirts with lots of crinolines under them. I didn't spend much time with Leonard on those evenings, though – held back, I suppose, by a certain resentment that he was coming on so strong on my turf. I could get used to the idea that he was a better poet than I was, but he always seemed to leave the gallery with the most interesting woman there, the one I'd spent all evening trying to get up enough nerve to say hello to.

When I moved to Montreal a while later I started hanging out in the coffee houses on Stanley Street that Leonard also frequented when he was in town. He was still in his Golden Boy bag at that time. He was plump and handsome and had published his first novel, *The Favorite Game*, and all the pretty girls loved him. I'd see him come smiling along Sherbrooke Street with either Robert or Morton, his two old childhood friends. They'd be dressed impeccably in dark grey Brooks Bros. suits and button-down Oxford cloth shirts, on their way to the Ritz for a drink and dinner. It was too easy to resent what looked so good and you couldn't be part of.

In spite of myself I got to know and like his quiet wit and easy generosity. When one of the girls that hung out on Stanley Street became pregnant by a

195

guy who quickly left town when he heard the news, Leonard went around and dug the money out of whoever he thought had some, giving the largest amount himself to help her out. His generosity also included being loyal to old friends who had become bores, and loving to those who had no reason to expect it.

If Leonard's easy to be with, it's not something he's always able to feel about others. If the going gets rough he might make a quick remark that nobody has to understand or laugh at, and depart abruptly for the corner drugstore to buy half a dozen strawberry ice cream cones. But though he insists on being free, he does make a point of returning for at least his share of the suffering. Leonard's very concerned with the idea of taking his share of the pain, the necessity of losing at least as much as you win. His songs are a kind of therapy he engages in to keep from going nuts while confronting his losses. This is the tragic view of life, that you are free to the extent that you are able to confront your own death.

I became one of a group of friends who met frequently in Robert Hershorn's apartment way up on Pine Avenue, a house on the hill with a white verandah, overlooking the city. Nearly everyone played an instrument – bongo, harmonica, guitar – and the music would go on till dawn. Leonard occasionally would sing one of his poems. Some of those moments are captured in spirit on the records, though the mood of 1961 was much gayer.

Then Leonard would decide that he had work to do. There would be a dinner party at the Athens restaurant on St. Lawrence Main with plenty of ouzos and retzina, and then he would be off in the morning to Greece. He would be gone for a few months or a year, and with each successive return would be thinner and more pained looking. Everything else about him would have increased.

If you listen to a Cohen song long enough it seems to lose its meaning. In the 'Stranger Song', for instance, the stanzas almost cancel each other out. It's his way of insisting that nobody's to blame for the separation and loneliness.

Leonard's been writing and singing songs for a long time, since long before Bob Dylan came on the scene. But he kept going back to Greece to write his books, and few people got a chance to hear what he was doing. Had he gone to New York in the first place, Dylan might have felt no need to change his name from Zimmerman. In this context I'm reminded of that interview Beryl Fox did with Leonard a few years ago on *Seven Days*. It went something like this:

BERYL: Now that you've become a singer, are you thinking of changing your name?
LEONARD: Yes, I'm thinking of changing my name to September.
BERYL: (incredulous) Leonard September?
LEONARD: No, September Cohen.

Leonard decided to deliver his application for a Canada Council grant in person. He was broke, but he borrowed enough money to hire a huge black limousine with uniformed driver. With the glass partition firmly shut, he spent the trip in the back seat with a friend, getting stoned and having a hell of a good time singing and playing music. When they arrived in Ottawa they somehow managed to get their hands on a wheelchair, and took turns pushing each other in and around and about the Canada Council offices, serenading the secretaries and causing a big uproar. It was from this visit that he got money to go back to Hydra and write *Beautiful Losers,* in which there is a very funny scene concerning two men being driven to Ottawa in a large car. I found *Beautiful Losers* difficult to read, it was so word-bound and awkward, and I didn't feel that the author understood the material that he was dealing with. But I was touched by the painful break between the erotic and the spiritual in the book. It isn't until much later, in the song 'Suzanne', that Leonard's work reflects some resolution of this conflict.

It's very Eastern, this idea that the erotic is at the very core of the spiritual, and that if you give yourself wholly to another person's mind, the bodies will take care of themselves. It takes a great deal of courage to confront the sexual fear that separates us all. In part, it's this sexual courage that makes Leonard so popular with the kids, who make fewer distinctions in sexual matters than we do.

Only drowning men can see him. This line suggests Leonard's notion of the religious idea being a technique for remaining sane in the face of despair. I suppose this is connected with the fact that I now hear about Leonard's being involved with Scientology. The thought of Leonard's holding those two cans in his hands appalls me, but I suppose it's the result of his commitment to the idea of exploring everything. I expect he'll do what he's always done, go right through it and out the other side. If I have any reservations, it's for his increasing band of admirers, few of whom are as quick on their feet as he is.

In the last few days I've met two young girls who both claimed to be in love with Leonard. One of them told me that she left her home in Vancouver and came East with the express purpose of having an affair with him. I asked her if her name was Marita, because I remembered something that occurred a few years ago. We were sitting in a sidewalk café in Montreal, talking about growing old, when Leonard took out his felt pen and wrote on the concrete wall that ran beside our table:

Marita
Please find me
I am almost thirty

It's possible that our generation (Leonard's and mine) is the first one ever to be so deeply influenced by the generations coming after it – the Beatles, Dylan, hippies and flower children, the New, New Left. In many ways we are less their teachers than they are ours.

[1969]

VII
Policies: Relating to the New Romans

Jack Ludwig
Leonard Beaton
Harry Johnson
James Eayrs
George Grant

Jack Ludwig

Canada: Kept Woman or Free?

The question of Canadian–U.S. relations will always be a delicate subject. The peaceful, friendly rapport between two countries disproportionate in financial, industrial, and military power calls for flexibility, tact, and good taste. It would be vulgar for the big United States to flex its muscles, ignore Canadian wishes, behave as if North America were its turf because its money and its firepower guarantee North American safety.

It would be equally vulgar for smaller Canada to bait the United States for its mere largeness, or its vigour, or its international successes. Yet a country like the United States, committed – perhaps over-committed – in so many areas and carrying, as it feels, the new white man's burden, may consciously, or unconsciously, commit itself to actions which affect not only Canada's security and well-being but our sense of ourselves as a national entity, our very sovereignty. Not that Canadians are so very clear, and unanimous, about what does and does not affect our national definitions: the various responses to the U.S. anti-ballistic-missile program indicate we are not all one.

But far more important than head-on clashes and stern confrontations is the matter of style – the day-to-day actions and reactions of two countries which during the course of 24 hours may have hundreds, thousands, of transactions large and small, crucial and insignificant. Being the smaller country, Canada could, perhaps, become paranoid about the United States and its possible encroachments. Or, from another point of view, querulous, terribly anxious to please, or, if not that, to avoid displeasing. Too much of that sort of thing, though, and a small country can end up behaving like – if I may be pardoned

201

the example – a kept woman, keen to anticipate demands long before they are even formulated. Or, if I may change the metaphor and make an honest woman of my country, a harried mother who keeps shushing the kids to make sure they won't disturb busy daddy.

I've always suspected that fear of U.S. displeasure might be the greatest invention to excuse laziness and inaction – a marvelous built-in cutoff one can point to as the obstacle to explain the undone. I've always suspected, too, that this same fear is used to keep Canadian imaginations sleeping, Canadian vitality at a low, almost hopeless, ebb. A sovereign country doesn't have to go out of its way to tweak its neighbour's nose, but neither should it rest paralysed in areas important to its own welfare, its own sense of destiny. Whom Canada has diplomatic relations with is, quite obviously, only Canada's concern; whom Canada trades with, too. Canadian cultural exchanges have to be arranged in Canada, with Canadian understanding about what is to be accomplished. All this, too, is a matter of taste and style. When the United States, in its worst days, assailed Albert Einstein and Thomas Mann as nothing more than 'dupes' and – again I ask forgiveness – 'Comsymps', it would have been the height of international folly for Canadians to accept such definitions.

And yet, at this moment, another U.S. term, 'deserter', is clearly being accepted by us – if the action of our immigration men at border points is seen for what it is.* The United States, of course, is free to label anyone who leaves its armed services a 'deserter', but when such a person presents himself at a Canadian immigration entry-point the U.S. definition ceases to apply. If it does not, Canada has cavalierly – and, I insist, quite unnecessarily – ceded part of its significant function as a sovereign nation to a foreign power, friendly though that power be. That person is an applicant for admission to Canada. If he wants to be thought of as a refugee, that is his business, and this definition does not have to be accepted either.

I think what I worry about most is the possibility that we will lose the habit of behaving independently. Pressures from the United States, real or imagined, must be resisted, with cool. The United States, in that way, develops the habit of consultation, consideration, and respect for sovereignty and even neutrality. The metaphor we search for is so simple: a man must be master even in his own small house.

[1969]

---

*Shortly after this was written the Minister of Immigration did a complete about face and began allowing American deserters into Canada. – Ed.

Leonard Beaton

Declaration of Independence

No country on earth has foreign relations quite like those of Canada. The country is too large to feel the small country sense of withdrawal; it is too small to have a power position of its own; situated between the United States and the Soviet Union, it either has no security problems or insoluble ones; and it is richer and more world-minded than almost any other country. Designing a Canadian foreign policy is an almost pure exercise: virtually nothing is dictated by geography or economics except perhaps a general commitment to wider world trading. And yet the character of the people has created a remarkable international fact: Canada was the only country in the western hemisphere which decided in 1939 that Hitler had to be dealt with and did something about it; she was one of the inventors of the North Atlantic alliance which made North America and Western Europe effectively a single military fact for a generation; she was an inventor of the Colombo plan and so of aid programs as they have been known; she is the largest and most significant country to decide that support for the United Nations as an organization should be a continuing object of policy; and she is the only major government still putting some effort into the Commonwealth. The list could be greatly extended. If it were not for the fact that Canadians insist on conducting their debates about both national and international affairs in the context of an obsession with the United States, the world would have come to regard Canadian foreign policy as an impressive edifice worthy of study.

The trouble is that Canadians have become intellectually colonized. When this country really was a colony, the inhabitants were independent and

203

opinionated: now that it has enjoyed a long and prosperous independence, it no longer seems capable of thinking for itself on many important subjects.

There is a strong critique of Canadian policy to be made. We are in NATO but we take no part in assessing and re-assessing the Soviet threat. If there is a Canadian contribution to the debate about what the dangers are, it is well concealed. On central issues like the promotion of a European union, Canada has accepted, as prophecies, half-baked and imaginary policies invented by lightweights at Harvard and in the State Department and reflecting a ludicrous American view of their own history. Canada's richest, most historic, and most rewarding single relationship – that with Britain – is now conducted for all practical purposes through the United States. If the U.S. throws Britain and France into each other's arms and alienates herself from both, Canada will have done nothing to stop it; and she was apparently ready to allow her relations with these countries to be wrecked by a Texan cowboy advised by intellectuals which quite minor Canadian universities would recognize as second rate.

Yet an independent Canada situated between the United States and the Soviet Union should have views, for example, on the development of the strategic nuclear confrontation. Canada did not participate in (and probably did not understand) the great debate about counterforce. Nor has any Canadian government shown any sign of thought about the problem of how nuclear weapons are to be controlled by the various members of the western alliance, even during the fantastic episode of the American advocacy of a NATO multilateral force. Where is Canada in the great debate about ballistic missile defence? The combination of the Bomarc affair and the NATO re-equipment with tactical nuclear weapons showed how completely out of touch the political leaders of the country were. Technical appreciations loaded with American political content regularly flow into Canada as abstract truths. Canadians looking for a foreign policy should attack this inability to participate in the great issues.

In spite of her moral pretensions, Canada has given no lead on the real dilemmas – especially those which relate to the use of force in the world. Is it enough that there should be a threat to the peace for the world to be concerned? What we do care about 500,000 Indonesians, or the slaughter in Biafra, or the slow spread of chaos in one area after another? Perhaps nothing: and certainly the Americans, the British, the Russians, the French have nothing to offer. Should non-proliferation be backed by force? Do the countries of Latin America or Eastern Europe have a right to align themselves with whom they will (and, for that matter, lend their soil for allied missiles)? How can nuclear weapons be safely organized? If Canada wants to make an impact on the world she should be using her incredible combination of wealth, intelligence, political experience, and almost total lack of obligations to try to develop views on these issues and become identified with them before the world.

The sad thing is to see Canada's potential being thrown away in the petty prejudices of the border state: the Poland of the Americas. Canada is utterly different psychologically from the United States. That is why she exists. Her relationship should be vigorous, obviously allied, but inevitably at arm's length because Canadians think differently, have different relationships and a different history. She must build her own relations with the middle powers of the free world with which she has so much in common: primarily Britain and France but also increasingly Japan, Germany, and Italy. We live in a mass of working political, military, and economic institutions and if Canada wants influence she will find it within them. At the moment, these institutions are mainly in the non-Communist world. In the years to come, the East Europeans and Russians will probably gradually opt in.

Yet Canada is not well-equipped for the organization game. At the moment, the world sees her as a mild and dependent variant on the United States with wheat and nickel to sell but no real political *point d'appui*. By supporting the continentalism of the Americans in Europe, in Asia, in Latin America, and in North America, the Canadian government is placing itself outside the great debates. An independent Canadian foreign policy will have to shape another and more realistic environment in which to function. Otherwise, it will just be posturing. Canada to be independent must look to herself, to her enfeebled capacity to understand the world, to her deepening division from Britain and Western Europe, to her ignorance of modern political-military problems, to her dependence on Washington for so many things Washington does not have to offer. Quiet diplomacy is, of course, euphemistic nonsense: Canada and the U.S. do not have the relations of independent powers seeking a common mind. But it is a comfortable substitute for hard work and real responsibilities. Anything more than posturing will cost money and effort. It is a hard thing for politicians under pressure to decide to do unless they can see the promise of tangible results. That is why in the final analysis Canada remains a large small power rather than a small large power. Changing this will take ambition and effort.

[1968]

H

Harry Johnson

Unlovely Canadianism

As I understand it, the nationalist position is that Canadian national identity and independence – frail plants of a very recent growth – are being threatened by insidious influences emanating from the United States, influences both cultural and economic, which if not resisted will inevitably lead to the absorption of Canada by the United States, culturally and economically if not politically. Further, it is argued, these influences should be resisted by using government action to foster forces Canadian and frustrate forces American, because forces Canadian are by definition valuable and ought to be protected and promoted. By implication forces American are not valuable, though nationalists often try to avoid saying so specifically.

The nationalist position seems to me to beg a number of questions. The first question concerns the meaning and extent of the national identity and independence that are alleged to be threatened. It seems to me that the nationalists often tend both to underestimate the extent to which there exists a Canadian national identity, and to confuse independence in the sense of having the power to take independent action with something quite different – 'independence' in the sense of choosing to take action different from the action of other countries, usually the United States. So far as national identity is concerned, I have no doubts at all that a Canadian is an animal recognizably distinct from an American, not just in the way he pronounces 'out' or 'about' or 'twenty' but also in his attitudes and general character. My confidence on this score is the result of having observed Canadians in different international contexts, and listened to people of other nationalities discussing Canadian

206

character and behaviour. I won't say that the qualities I think of as typically Canadian are altogether admirable – in addition to seriousness and a fairly high level of competence, they include a certain provinciality of outlook, signs of inferiority feeling, and a tendency at meetings either to orate at a high moral level or to keep quiet and then grumble afterwards about not being listened to – but they are recognizable as a distinct national mixture. So far as national independence is concerned, both my brief acquaintance with Canadian constitutional history and my observation of the Canadian role in international affairs give me no cause to doubt that Canada is an independent country in the only reasonable meaning I can give to that word. I do not think that Canadian independence is impaired in any way when Canada's political leadership decides that Canada's best interests lie in supporting policies initiated by the United States; and I cannot understand the belief of various Canadians I know that Canadian independence can only be demonstrated by opposing American policies. It also seems to me that in many cases – for example, on the question of recognizing the People's Republic of China – Canadians fall into the immature habit (or perhaps adopt the debating trick) of blaming Canadian policies of which they disapprove on American domination when the plain truth is that the alternatives they desire are simply unpopular in Canada.

The second question is how, precisely, Canadian identity and independence are threatened by the United States. With respect to the threat to national identity, the nationalist usually points to the consumption of American goods and the practice of the American standard of life in Canada, and to the wide circulation of American communications media in Canada. This is not a convincing argument, especially to an economist. What the nationalist sees as a 'penetration' of Canada by the United States, the economist sees as an expression of the preferences of an opulent society. That the taste for American-type goods, ways of life, and communications and advertising methods has been spreading rapidly all over the world as incomes have risen, and that they have been instituted in countries subject to very little direct American influence, make it difficult to argue that American penetration and not simply affluence is the explanation. One may deplore many features of the affluent American style of life, but I do not think one can deny either that it is what people want to buy, or that it does contribute to human comfort and pleasure. Nor do I believe that the deplorable aspects could be removed by forcing people to buy Canadian goods and magazines instead of American – the Canadian producers would simply produce the same types of goods, and probably not as well.

With respect to the threat to Canadian independence, the nationalist usually points to the proportion of imports from the United States, and of American ownership of Canadian enterprises, as if these themselves were a proof of 'domination' by the United States; in some ways, on the contrary, they represent Canadian exploitation of the United States. For example, the half-billion or so dollars of corporate income taxes that Canada collects from

American direct investments here comes more or less directly at the expense of the United States Treasury; and the United States government has heavily subsidized Canadian resource development through the depletion allowances. Aside altogether from that sort of question, neither imports of American goods nor imports of American capital acquire voting rights in Canada, so Canadian independence as embodied in the sovereignty of Parliament can hardly be threatened that way; and it is very hard to see why the economic dependence of the United States on Canada which is the other side of Canadian economic dependence on the United States – that is, of the interdependence between the two – should make the American Government more rather than less anxious to put pressure on Canada.

The fundamental questions about the nationalist position concern the validity of the assertion that closer economic relations with the United States, through mutual trade and through American investment in Canada, mean that Canada must inevitably be absorbed by the United States. It seems to me this assertion assumes a degree of economic determinism in politics going far beyond anything the facts of history would warrant. Nations have in the past practised free trade, or at least had lower barriers to trade than they now have, without losing their national identity or feeling an overwhelming urge to submerge themselves in political union with a larger country. If it were true that economic integration leads to a loss of identity, how could one explain the survival of minority and regional groups inside national boundaries, such as the Scotch and Welsh in England or the French Canadians and Nova Scotians in Canada? I would be very surprised indeed if closer economic integration between the United States and Canada led to a Canadian demand for political integration; rather, I would expect that closer economic integration, by enabling Canadians to achieve a standard of living closer to that of the United States, would make them better able and more willing to use the political sovereignty of their country to pursue political and social policies appropriate to their own conceptions and requirements.

Contemporary Canadian nationalism seems to me to be riddled with chauvinism in its constant harping on the idea of Canadian-ness rather than goodness as the objective, and its assumption that if you make things more Canadian you automatically make them better. There are, in my view, a great many accomplishments that Canadians can and should be proud of; but they should be proud of them because they are accomplishments, not simply because they are Canadian. There are also some things in Canada that Canadians should be ashamed of, and could do something about – slums, town planning, water pollution, technological unemployment, race discrimination in immigration policy, to name a few.

This brings me to the question of anti-American feeling in Canada, a subject on which the Canadian talent for genteel hypocrisy comes to its finest flower, with eminent Canadians loudly expressing their admiration and warm friendship for the American people while advocating schemes for depriving some of them of control of their property, and professional explainers of Canada to the Americans begging the Americans not to be offended by the nasty anti-American remarks they are about to hear, because we're just having a friendly argument among ourselves, and really we love them.

It is this two-faced character of anti-Americanism in Canada – the desire to enjoy the emotional jag of indulging in hatred, envy, and greed while maintaining the pretence that one is being very restrained and reasonable and that Americans not only should not be offended but should in fact approve – that I find particularly repugnant to me as a Canadian. It seems to be a characteristic which distinguishes Canadian anti-Americanism, to its discredit, from anti-Americanism elsewhere in the world; and, paradoxically enough, it seems to confirm what it seeks to deny, the similarity of Canadians to Americans, for the desire to be loved in spite of one's obnoxious behaviour is a deeply ingrained American characteristic.

Anti-Americanism in Canada rests almost entirely on assertions convincing only to those already convinced. Yet it is a latent element in the Canadian national character, apparently always available for mobilization. I would suggest that it is closely connected with a certain immaturity in the Canadian national character, expressed in the unwillingness to accept the fact that Canada is, except from the geographical point of view, a small country. Unlike the citizens of other small countries bordering on large countries, Canadians are not prepared to content themselves with the advantages that can be derived from small size, but set themselves the impossible aspiration of equalling the United States, and, still more impossible, of getting the United States to treat them as equals. Thus anti-Americanism becomes a way of evading recognition of the inconsistency between Canadian aspirations and Canadian possibilities, and finding emotional consolation for inevitable failure.

The economic measures advocated by the nationalists fall into two categories: increased protection for Canadian secondary industry, and the forced insertion of Canadians into the ownership and management of American enterprises in Canada. I have three reasons for doubting that the advocacy of these measures is in the Canadian national interest.

In the first place, it is extremely questionable whether these measures will produce the benefits to the Canadian people that are claimed for them. They are more likely to have the effect of benefiting particular groups of Canadians at the national expense.

The most predictable effect of higher protection is that Canadians in the protected industries will have higher incomes, or be able to get away with a less efficient performance, than they otherwise would, and this at the expense of the general Canadian community. The most predictable effect of Canadianization of American subsidiaries is that some Canadian capitalists will obtain higher dividend and directorship incomes than their enterprise and business knowledge hitherto entitled them to, and that some Canadian employees of American firms will be paid more than their competence hitherto justified, at the cost of some discouragement to American investment in Canada and some reduction in the efficiency of the operations of already established enterprises.

Not only is it very doubtful whether protectionism and 'Canadianization' will produce the national benefits claimed for them: the philosophy of economic nationalism which they represent seems to be the opposite of what is called for if Canada is to make the most of her opportunities in the modern international economy. That economy is characterized by the rapid spread and progressive development of industrial production, which demands efficiency and flexibility if a country is to compete on the world market. It is also characterized by the belief on the part of the major industrial countries of Europe and many of the underdeveloped countries that the small size of their national markets prevents them from reaping the full potential gains of industrial development; hence their desire and willingness to expand their markets by entering into arrangements for free trade areas and common markets. Both the spread of industrialization and the formation of larger trading groups offer a threat and a challenge to the advanced economies of North America – Canada and the United States – which were shielded from keen international competition, from the war until just a few years ago. The alternatives are to face the challenge confidently, actively joining in the process of extending the area of international competition; or to retreat from international competition into protectionism. Protectionism is the natural first choice of a private enterprise system which has gone soft from easy living in a period of boom, but its likely effects would be to impair the vigour and efficiency of Canadian industry, impede adjustment to the new circumstances of international competition, and in the long run retard the rate of economic growth. There are good reasons for believing that much of Canadian industry could adjust to and hold its own in modern international competition – it has more capital, skill, and modern technology at its disposal than many of its emerging competitors – and if the protectionist argument that what restrains Canadian industry is the small size of the Canadian market is valid, it suggests that Canada would gain in efficiency from the greater access to large foreign markets that participation in freer trade arrangements would entail.

My third reason for believing that the advocacy of protectionist and Canadianization measures has not been in the Canadian national interest is that, by attributing the high unemployment of the past few years to the absence of sufficient tariff protection and to American investment in Canada, the nationalists have helped to divert attention from the fact that the depressed condition of the Canadian economy is to a substantial extent the result of the economic policies pursued by the Government and the Bank of Canada. In so doing, the nationalists have helped the authorities to evade a searching public discussion of those policies, which would have been a much more useful contribution to the growth of Canadian national independence than the fostering of anti-American sentiment could ever be. Canada has had a golden opportunity to show her capacity for intelligent economic policy in the past few years; if she has instead chosen to fritter it away, it is Canadians who must bear the responsibility – and Canadian nationalism which has helped to disguise that fact from the Canadian people.

[1961]

James Eayrs

The Undefended Border

The striking thing about Canadian-American statecraft is that Canadian and American statesmen really do believe that Canadian-American relations are more virtuous and better than ordinary international relations. They really think this to be true – in spite of all the insults and the injuries, the quarrels and the wars, by which the history of the two countries has been marked and marred since 1817. 'There is nothing which gives both Canada and the United States more joint and mutual pride,' declared a former American Ambassador to Britain in 1922, 'than to point to the 5400 miles (including Alaska) that divide the countries without a gun or sentry.' Forty-four years later, Mr. McNamara pridefully pointed to the same illusion. 'There is not the remotest set of circumstances, in any imaginable time-frame of the future, in which our two nations could wage war on one another. It is so unthinkable an idea as to be totally absurd.'

But I don't find it so absurd. Mr. McNamara knows very well that the waging of war has many dimensions, of which those involving the salvo of missiles and the infliction of fall-out are among the least likely and the least useful. Even the more modest methods of applying force to the conduct of international politics are not always the most expedient or cost-effective. There are other, more economical, ways of compelling a country to come to terms with you, on terms selected by you, than to souse it with napalm or to send in the marines. You buy up its resources. You buy out its institutions. You drain away its rivers. And you drain away its brains. Little by little, national independence seeps slowly southwards. It happens so stealthily, it takes place so painlessly, that the victim

212

does not notice. But one day he tries to exercise his independence and finds it isn't there – like the decapitated swordsman in the Thurber cartoon who, protesting he's fit to carry on duelling, is told to try to blow his nose.

All this is not to say that Canada lies prostrate as the consequence of a campaign of psychological and cultural and economic warfare subtly waged against her by Washington. It is to say only that these methods of coercion by which the government of one country ordinarily attempts to influence the governments of others are clearly available to, and just as clearly indulged in by, the governments of our two countries. I am not at all disheartened to think it so. I would be disheartened to think it otherwise. For if it were otherwise, it would indicate that our respective countries are not what I fervently hope they are and ought to be: different countries, separate countries, foreign countries. Countries whose policies towards each other are happily free from those techniques of statecraft employing high degrees of coercion. Countries whose governments may say of each other as Samuel Johnson once said of a companion: 'He is my great and good friend; we differ not at all, except in the matter of opinion.' I'll come back to that.

Among those Canadians actively interested in foreign affairs – a group which, until recently, might be numbered on the fingers of a severely mutilated hand but which now is growing both in size and competence – among this group there is going on a kind of debate – a debate about how our government ought to be conducting its all-important business of influencing what the United States government is doing in and to the world.

Notice there's no argument to speak of over the fact that influencing the United States is the most important mission of Canadian foreign policy. Almost all of us agree that this is our prime purpose. The debate is over methods, not over the mission itself. What is the best way – the most effective way – of keeping the Americans on course?

Opinion on the answer to this question breaks sharply into two schools. One calls itself the school of quiet diplomacy. It takes for its teacher the former Prime Minister of Canada. It takes for its text the report of the former Canadian Ambassador to the United States and the former American Ambassador to Canada – the so-called Heeney-Merchant Report, entitled 'Canada and the United States: Principles for Partnership'. There are many principles enunciated in this document, but for purposes of the great debate they boil down to two. One is that foreign policy should be left to its professional practitioners. The other is that its professional practitioners should be left alone to conduct foreign policy in private. Both principles are enunciated within a single sentence of the Heeney-Merchant Report (paragraph 81): 'It is in the abiding interest of both countries that, wherever possible, divergent views between the two governments should be expressed and if possible resolved in private, through diplomatic channels.' Enrolled in the school of quiet diplomacy are, as you might expect, the quiet diplomatists of the Canadian

H*

Department of External Affairs, together with a few academics who, for the most part, received their training and acquired their prejudices as members of that Department.

They call themselves the quiet Canadians, but I like to call them, with as much pejorative intent as I can muster, the 'smooth Canadians', as in the whiskey advertisements. The world of the smooth Canadians, and the methods they commend, are the world and methods of traditional, old-fashioned, secret diplomacy – swaddled in green baize, bundled in red tape, shrouded by the Official Secrets Act. It is a world as comfortable for its inhabitants as it is frustrating for those who are left outside. For as long as it prevails, the outsiders are effectively prevented from scrutinizing the actions of the insiders. Since they do not know, and cannot tell, what the insiders are doing, who are outsiders to criticize? How are outsiders to criticize? The sting of criticism thus deftly removed, the insiders are free to ply the crafts of state – competently or incompetently as the case may be.

Until not too long ago, the insiders had things pretty much their own way. It is only in recent years – I think fair to say in recent months – that the school of quiet diplomacy has been challenged by a more raucous and unprofessional band of outsiders, made restive and uncomfortable by their suspicion that within the portals of quiet diplomacy competence is distinguished by its absence. These rough Canadians, among whom I would be proud to be counted, are by no means certain that the best way to influence the policy-makers of the White House and the Congress is by keeping things quiet and keeping things dark. They are concerned that to talk in tones as dulcet and decorous as those in which diplomatists are accustomed to address each other may mean that Canadian complaints go unheard and Canadian suggestions unremarked. They repose some trust in the homely aphorism that the squeaky wheel gets the grease. They have heard, and are inclined to believe, the proposition that nice guys finish last. Their grumbling has grown to the point that, from his lofty eminence, the Prime Minister himself had to pay them some attention. In an open letter addressed to those of my colleagues at the University of Toronto, some 400 in all, who were presumptuous enough to urge upon him a more forcible disaffiliation of Canada from the American war in Vietnam, Mr. Pearson thus extolled the virtues of the old school:

> Confidential and quiet arguments by a responsible government are usually more effective than public ones. . . . Too many public declarations and disclosures run the risk of complicating matters for those concerned. . . . The more complex and dangerous the problem, the greater is the need for calm and deliberate diplomacy.

That, Mr. Pearson conceded, 'may sound like an expression of timidity to some of the proponents of political activism at Canadian universities and elsewhere today. I can only assure them with all the personal conviction at my command that in my view it is the only way in which results can be achieved.'

I find it a curious paradox that there should come out of contemporary Canada, at one and the same time, the advanced theory of communications associated with Marshall McLuhan, and the obsolete conception of diplomacy practised by Lester Pearson. Perhaps some future historian of ideas will be able to elucidate the paradox. Meanwhile, to an era of international politics which President Johnson has himself described as the decade of urgency – an era in which one might say the missile is the message – the style of quiet diplomacy seems curiously unsuited.

For it will be a fact of life during the decade of urgency, as it's been a fact of life in the decade just past, that nice guys *do* finish last, while the squeaky wheels of the international system – the bitchers and the groaners, the whiners and the wailers – get the grease in whatever form desired. To my mind there comes at once the example of de Gaulle. By that example I don't expect you to be persuaded, if only because opinion in this country has been blinded to the achievements of Gaullist diplomacy by anger. But maybe you will accept the example of West Germany. The Germans under Adenauer, even more under Erhard, were the most compliant and docile of America's European allies. Their influence, as a consequence, was like that of a lapdog upon his master. Only under Kiesinger and Brandt, when the preternatural docility of Bonn's foreign policy gave way to a more normal assertion of national interest, has Washington begun to pay attention.

In this respect, Washington's relations with Ottawa differ not at all from Washington's relations with Paris, or with Bonn, or with Conakry, or with wherever. The great beast of state has too thick a hide, too many preoccupations of its own, to prick up its ears attentively whenever a Canadian minister sidles into one of the antechambers of power and there, quietly, courteously, diffidently, decorously, recites from his confidential brief his confidential case. It may have been like that in the good old days – the days when the State Department, as George Kennan recalls with much nostalgia, 'was a quaint old place, with its law-office atmosphere, its cool dark corridors, its swinging doors, its brass cuspidors, its black leather rocking chairs, and the grandfather clock in the Secretary of State's office' – and, he might have added, recalling the incumbent of that time, the grandfather figure in the Secretary of State's office. But it's not like that any more. The atmosphere is less that of a law-office than of bomber-command; the corridors are neither cool nor dark; cuspidors are out and computers are in. And in place of Charles Evans Hughes we have Dean Rusk. Dean Rusk, of whom Arthur Schlesinger has written: 'When Assistant Secretaries brought him problems, he listened courteously, thanked them, and let them go; they would often depart little wiser than they came.' Where American diplomatists fail to make an impression on so experienced a stone-waller, who are Canadian diplomatists to succeed? You have to go higher than that, speak louder than that.

The case against going higher and speaking louder is said by the smooth

Canadians to be made, with chilling finality, by two experiences of Canadian-American relations during the 1960s.

The first of these occurred early in 1963, at a time when Canadian diplomacy, especially towards the United States, was neither smooth nor quiet. We'd refused to put the Canadian component of NORAD into a condition of emergency alert over the Cuban missile crisis, to which our government's first reaction was that Washington had fabricated the evidence. And we'd continued to refuse to equip Canadian forces with nuclear weapons. For these policies, accompanied by a good deal of public posturing in defiance of all of the precepts of quiet diplomacy, John Diefenbaker earned the contempt of the President and the wrath of the State Department which, finally expressed in public, led to the overthrow of the Diefenbaker Government in the House of Commons. There, some have said, is what happens to high posture policy-makers in Canada when they collide with policy-making in the United States. I don't think that's what *necessarily* happens to them. Mr. Diefenbaker was vulnerable to other pressures and for other reasons. It is still possible to challenge the United States and get away with it, but you have to be nimble and you have to be quick. Like the mythical small bird which feeds by picking food from between the teeth of the crocodile, you had better be pretty expert in knowing when crocodiles close their mouths. Mr. Diefenbaker had lost his sense of timing.

The other experience took place early in 1965 when Mr. Pearson, putting his precepts about quiet diplomacy to one side, remarked in a speech at Philadelphia that if the Americans really wanted to negotiate with North Vietnam, it might be wise to stop bombing them for a few days to see what happened. Mr. Pearson met Mr. Johnson the next morning and, judging from some of the accounts of their meeting, it did not go well. Mr. Johnson seems to have treated Mr. Pearson less like the Prime Minister of Canada and more like one of his pet beagles, whom he was wont to pick up by the ears and beat on the buttocks when they misbehaved. Here again, argue some smooth Canadians, is what happens to Canadian Prime Ministers when they so far forget themselves as to speak their minds in public over their misgivings about American policy.

I do not think this conclusion follows. What really upset the President about the Prime Minister's intervention, I think, was that it took him by surprise. Mr. Pearson acted not so much out of turn as out of character. He was expected to speak smoothly, and it was nettling and rattling to have him speak roughly. A public figure with a reputation for frank and fearless speech – it is not easy to think of many, for politicians are people who tend occupationally to talk through an excess of meal in their mouths, but one might mention Menzies or de Gaulle – such a figure can hope to get away with speaking frankly and fearlessly. Where you get the worst of all possible worlds is by carefully cultivating a reputation for discretion only to destroy it by occasionally blurting out your troubles when these become too intense to be borne in silence. To act the part of the quiet Canadian, you've got to keep quiet all the time. But if you keep quiet all the time, you won't be heard, and your case will go by default.

If you haven't much of a case to begin with, that it goes by default is no great loss to the world. There was a time, and it wasn't very long ago, when a Canadian party leader could cut short his speech on foreign policy by observing: 'I did intend to say something about the St. Lawrence Waterway, but I do not think I should trespass much longer on the time of the House . . . I cannot, however, refrain from saying something about the position of truck transportation on Prince Edward Island.' Or when, during one of the great crises of the modern world – Munich – the House of Commons devoted 27 minutes to foreign policy and eight hours to a tariff on asparagus.

But this emphasis is changing. We are not yet able to match in Canada the enormous resources poured into foreign policy research by the American universities, the American foundations, the American departments of government, and by the Central Intelligence Agency. But we are beginning to muster not merely our own distinctive set of attitudes on such issues as foreign aid, and arms control, and China, and Cuba, and Vietnam – attitudes, after all, are easily come by, and don't solve any problems – we are beginning to assemble not attitudes only, but the expertise and experience by means of which attitudes are made over into ideas, and emotions into solutions. And here I would like to pause to pay tribute to the generosity and enlightenment of those American philanthropists who have done much more than any Canadians to guide us to maturity in this respect. The spectacle of Fords and Rockefellers and Guggenheims helping to create in Canada, and elsewhere in the world, the means with which to break the American stranglehold upon area specialties and strategic analysis is no doubt gleefully pounced upon in certain quarters as yet further evidence of the contradictions by which monopoly capitalism is being torn apart: but to me, I confess, it is a most agreeable manifestation of the flowering of the liberal spirit.

Slowly, then, but surely, we Canadians are acquiring the means for coming to our own independent appraisal of what makes for conflict or co-operation among nations. For Canada this is a good thing. And I'm well aware that this observation cannot interest Americans very much. Americans are much more interested, and properly interested, in whether it is a good thing for the United States. So I will put it this way. From the American point of view, it is a very good thing indeed that there should be in North America another country, a foreign government, experimenting in the laboratory of co-existence – experimenting reliably, trustworthily, responsibly, but with a certain daring and imagination, in ways that American opinion and American inhibitions might not easily permit. From this point of view, if Canada didn't exist, Washington might find it useful to invent us.

In principle American policy-makers often make this point. It is implicit in their praise of diversity, with which they are sometimes very lavish. In one of his last speeches, President Kennedy appealed to his countrymen to help make the world 'safe for diversity'. Dean Rusk was once made to say (by Arthur Schlesinger, who wrote the speech for him): 'We seek a world of free choice in which a great diversity of nations, each faithful to its own traditions and its own genius, will learn to respect the ground rules of human survival.' And the present American ambassador to NATO prefaces a recent book with a poem by Phyllis McGinley:

> *Rejoice that under cloud and star*
> *The planet's more than Maine or Texas.*
> *Bless the delightful fact there are*
> *Twelve months, nine muses, and two sexes.*
> *And infinite in earth's dominions*
> *Arts, climates, wonder, and opinions.*

There could not be a more civilized outlook for the representative of a Great Power.

The trouble is that these sentiments are more easily preached than practised; and often they're not even preached. Where the Kennedy Administration favoured sermons praising diversity, the Johnson Administration liked sermons praising unity. Hubert Humphrey chose to preach such a sermon out in Fulton, Missouri, in March, where he told us that we should resist 'the temptations . . . for unilateral action', and told us further: 'We cannot afford the luxury of division.' I like to think that that's what one lemming told another lemming as they swam together out to sea. If you want a really impressive demonstration of unity, look at the Gadarene swine.

That's why, rather than following the established Canadian-American tradition of belittling our border, rejoicing in its fragility, celebrating its permeability, I am glad that it is there. It enlarges the area of human freedom, and not for governments only. Edward Gibbon, in his *Decline and Fall,* sees 'the division of Europe into a number of independent states, connected . . . with each other by the general resemblance of religion, language and manners', as 'productive of the most beneficial consequences to the liberty of mankind'. First and foremost among these consequences he puts the possibility of political asylum. In such a Europe, the conscientious objector of those times might 'easily obtain, in a happier climate, a secure refuge, a new future adequate to his merit, the freedom of complaint, and perhaps the means of revenge. But the Empire of the Romans filled the world, and when that empire fell into the hands of a single person, the world became a safe and dreary prison for his enemies.' I was put in mind of this passage when I read, in the current issue of *Ramparts* magazine, of the young American who, having come to Canada to avoid the draft, remarked: 'I don't feel any stranger moving to Toronto than if I had moved to Kansas City – only freer.' Well, I'm glad to hear it. (We too have our skyscrapers seven storeys high – about as high as a building ought to go.)

[1967]

George Grant

To Be a Citizen in North America

I speak as a Canadian nationalist and as a conservative. It is necessary to start here for the following reason. To speak of the moral responsibility of the citizen in general is impossible; the question entirely depends on the kind of régime in which one is a citizen. The United States is a world empire – the largest to date. Its life at home is controlled by mammoth corporations, private and public, and through these bureaucracies it reaches out to control a large proportion of the globe and soon beyond the globe. Now Canada moves more and more to being a satellite of that empire. And Canadians live much of their lives under the same imperial bureaucracies. The institutions of Toronto are much the same as those of Detroit. Yet despite this there is a sense in which we still have more citizenship here than in the U.S. because we have some political sovereignty, if we fight for it. Traditional democratic means – the vote and support for political parties – have more meaning in our smaller sphere. Political choice is both more real and more possible in Canada. This might be truly useful to the world, if we in Canada could use it to see that North American relations with Asia did not always simply follow Washington.

What is it to be a citizen in North America in this era? Let me start from the position of the New Left in North America. How can a conservative not feel sympathy with their outrage against the emptiness and dehumanization that North American society produces?

But when the New Left speaks of overcoming these conditions by protest, I think they are indulging in dreams and dangerous dreams. When they speak as if it were possible by marching and sitting to turn North American society

219

away from being an empire protecting its interests in the world by violence, I disagree.

For several centuries the chief energies of Western society have been directed to the mastery of nature – at first non-human nature and now human nature. The motive of this pursuit was that men should be made free. It has gained men great victories over natural necessity. Who can doubt that? But at the same time, it has subjected men to the forces of the artificial necessities of the technological society. 'The further the technical mechanism develops which allows us to escape natural necessity, the more we are subjected to artificial technical necessities.'

I do not see why anybody should believe that by some dialectical process of history there should suddenly spring out of this technological society a free and humane society. First Western men and now men everywhere in the world are driving with enormous speed to the building of this technological strait jacket. That technological apparatus is now autonomous and produces its own needs which are quite detached from human needs.

The supreme example of the autonomy of technique is surely the space programme. If it is possible for man to do something it must be done. Vast resources of brains, money, materials are poured out in the U.S. and U.S.S.R. to keep this fantastic programme proliferating. And it is accepted by the masses in both societies not only as necessary but as man's crowning glory. One leader of the U.S. space programme said that as we cannot change the environment of space, we will have to change man. So we are going to produce beings half flesh, half electronic organs. If it can be done, it must be done and it surely will be done. This is what I mean by the autonomy of technique. The question whether technique serves human good is no longer asked. It has become an end in itself.

The New Left said: Look at our triumphs in the South; we will now carry these triumphs of citizen action into new fields of social revolution. What was forgotten is that the powerful people and institutions of North America were more than willing that the society of the white South should be broken. The civil rights movement had behind it all the powerful forces of the American empire. It marched protected by federal troops, it had the blessing of the leading government figures. It was encouraged night after night by N.B.C. and C.B.S. There was violence from the white South, but the white South is not an important part of the American power élite. It will surely be a different matter when the protests are against some position which is dear and close to the American liberal establishment. Anyway, dissent and protest are themselves bureaucratized in our society. They are taken into the system and trivialized. They are made to serve the interests of the system they are supposed to be attacking, by showing that free speech is allowed.

I am not advocating inaction or cynicism. I do not deny for one moment the nobility of protest or that justice is good and that injustice is evil and that it is required of human beings to know the difference between the two. To live with courage in the world is always better than retreat or disillusion. Human beings are less than themselves when they are cut off from being citizens. Indeed one of the finest things about the present protest movements in North America is that they try to give meaning to citizenship in a society which by its enormity and impersonality cuts people off from the public world. Anybody who lives within a university must know that the students who care enough about the world to protest are much finer than those who are interested in public affairs simply because they want to climb within the system and use it to gain recognition for their egos. Indeed how much finer are those who protest than those who crawl through the university simply as a guarantee of the slow road to death in the suburbs. In our monolithic society, the pressures upon the individual to retreat from the public sphere are immense. The new politics of protest have tried to overcome those pressures and to give new meaning to citizenship. Nobody should attack them for that.

What I am arguing against is the politics based on easy hopes about the future human situation. The most dangerous quality of the politics of Utopia is that it can easily turn into despair. If people have vast expectations of hope about a society such as ours, they are going to be disappointed and then their moral fervour can turn rancid and bitter. Moral fervour is too precious a commodity not to be put in the service of reality.

If protest is to be effective in this era, then those who are in the forefront of protest must combine with their action the deepest and most careful thought. The central Christian platitude still holds good. 'The truth shall make you free.' For in the long pull freedom without the knowledge of reality is empty and vacuous. The greatest figure of our era, Gandhi, was interested in public action and in political liberty, but he knew that the right direction of that action had to be based on knowledge of reality – with all the discipline and order and study that that entailed.

Truth-seeking is of course hard to accomplish in this society. Our universities have at many points retreated from it into fact-gathering and technological mastery – the knowledge industry. Most of our social scientists have used the idea of a value-free social science to opt out of the battle over what constitutes the good society, and spend their time in discovering techniques for adjusting people to the system. The philosophers have often opted out to play clever professional games. Much of the religious tradition seems a worn-out garment not able to help in the search for truth. Above all, what may hold people from the search for the truth is that the human situation in the totally realized mass world may be so unpalatable that we simply do not want to face it.

We in North America are the society that has most completely realized the dominance of technique over every aspect of human life. Every year we are moving with prodigious speed to the greater and greater realization of that system. All other societies move at various speeds to the same kind of society we are creating. We are the first people who will have to learn what it is to be citizens in a society dominated by technique. Because that system is most fully realized with us, we are the first people who can look it in the face and we are called upon to see it for what it is and not fool ourselves about it. We must face the laws of its necessity – its potential to free men from natural necessity, its potential for inhumanity and tyranny. We must not delude ourselves and we must not throw up our hands. We must define our possible areas of influence with the most careful clarity. Where in this mammoth system can we use our intelligence and our love to open up spaces in which human excellence can exist? How can we use the most effective pressure to see that our empire uses moderation and restraint in its relations with the rest of the world? I end where I began, that our greatest obligation as Canadians is to work for a country which is not simply a satellite of any empire.

[1965]

VIII
Politics:

(a) **Three P.M.s and a Joker**

Marshall McLuhan
James Eayrs
Peter Newman
Bruce Hutchison

(b) **Choices for French Canada**

Claude Ryan
René Lévesque
Fernand Dumont

(c) **A Political Style for English Canada**

Gad Horowitz

Marshall McLuhan

The Man in the Mask: Pierre Trudeau

The Mohawk is at home in high steel because he has no visual orientation, no point of view. He doesn't get dizzy on a girder on the 40th floor because he doesn't focus on distant points either vertically or horizontally. Only literate societies use points of view. The man without a point of view 'goes through the vanishing point'; he goes from 1-degree vision to 360-degree, which is not visual but acoustic space, i.e., total involvement and equilibrium. This, of course, is the pattern for the new business 'conglomerates' brought on by information speed-up. The single business with its limited goals or objectives is finished just as parties and policies are finished in politics. Pierre Elliott Trudeau, Prime Minister of Canada, anticipated the 20th century by his French-Canadian tradition. French Canada doesn't have an 18th century or a 19th century to obscure its awareness of the 20th. Backward societies always begin with the latest.

The story of Pierre Trudeau is the story of the Man in the Mask. That is why he came into his own with TV. His image has been shaped by the Canadian culture gap. Canada has never had an identity. Instead, it has had a cultural interface of 17th-century France and 19th-century America. After World War II French Canada leapt into the 20th century without ever having had a 19th century. Like all backward and tribal societies, it is very much 'turned on', or at home in the new electric world of the 20th century. Japan, of course, is a much greater instance of the same dynamic. The tribal and oral Japanese are as much at home in the new electric age of software information as the Eskimo hunter. Nineteenth-century countries like England, English

225

Canada, and the United States are having a bad time in the new electric age. Russia, of course, is trying to have a 19th century.

Trudeau grew up straddling two cultures, perfectly at home in both:

'Aren't you some sort of Communist?'

'No, I'm a Canoeist.'

This aristocratic 'Simon Templar', unique in any political establishment, is a Trimmer, like a canoeist, like a glider pilot, like a man on the high wire. He is as tribal as the Beatles. His image is as corporate and mask-like as a member of a Mozart dance group and as earthy and casual as an American Negro. He is as cool and as indifferent to power as he is deeply concerned with the orchestrating and conducting of the numerous components and emergent factors of his rapidly changing world.

Trudeau's book on federalism is a collection of essays, a mosaic. It is a series of navigational markers and warnings for those who, like himself, delight in skilled and complicated action:

> The only constant factor to be found in my thinking over the years has been opposition to accepted opinions. Had I applied this principle to the stock market, I might have made a fortune. I chose to apply it to politics and it led me to power – a result I had not really desired, or even expected.

The man who goes against the current can steer. His rudder is in play. With the unconcern of the enormously erudite and the socially assured man of wealth, Trudeau can say, 'It goes without saying that the top levels of our society suffer from paralysing inertia.' He correctly assumes that all the top-level experts in any field of endeavour are hopelessly copeless in their involvement in fragmentary aspects of their situation. No American President, past or present, can approximate his range of awareness or his reading of men and affairs. Yet, as Richard Steele said of the ideal gentleman, 'He undervalues the world with good breeding and goes to heaven with a very good mien.'

It is only one of the many fortunate features of Trudeau that he is indifferent to the power that results from the bureaucratic congregating of the misguided somnambulists that make up ordinary human society. If his were a private opinion or point of view, it would be insufferable. Instead, it is the fruit of a great corporate European tradition deeply imbued with Christianity and other-worldliness. That is why Trudeau can be playful and spontaneous at all times, in private and public conduct.

The essays in the present book are written at the level of Edmund Burke's best meditations. For example, Burke said, 'The first right of every man in civilized society is the right to be protected against the consequences of his own stupidity.' Trudeau is always aware of the consequences that emanate from any kind of policy or program. He is completely aware of the political consequences of speeded-up electric information or software in retribalizing our entire world. The clash between these two great trends has destroyed the American identity since TV.

Canada never had a unified national identity or goal, and so has nothing to lose in the TV age. The TV generation has neither identity nor goals. Its instinct is to plunge into tragic violence as a means of creating a new identity or image. Trudeau suggests federalism in place of this tragic strategy: and federalism is the cool, casual interface of numerous components minus the old 19th-century drive for goals and gains.

Pierre Trudeau would find no difficulty in coping with the American dilemma of the Negro, who is being urged to detribalize by the educational and business establishment while experiencing the thrill of retribalization and ethnic superiority to the white man via his superior TV image. Peter Drucker pointed out years ago that any Negro in a truck was the equal of a white man. On color TV any Negro is the superior of any white man. His corporate mask, integral and iconic, is suited to the iconoscope and dissolves the adjacent white image into insignificance.

It is our own new technology that has created black power. The somnambulist response to this positive Negritude and assurance is the negative backlash, white power. It is this tragically misunderstood situation that only the trained perceptions of a Trudeau could resolve. American culture has long ago abolished the possibility of a Trudeau in its confident drive for goals and power.

[1968]

James Eayrs

The Scrutable Canadian: Lester Pearson

So few political leaders get out on time. Everything conspires to keep them in office long past their prime and their ability to do it justice. Colleagues and confidants may privately yearn for 'the old man' to step down before he makes a fool of himself and a wreck of his country; but they characteristically keep such thoughts to themselves, fearing that should they confide them to their leader they will be misunderstood, or chewed out, or fired – or, indeed, all three. Driven back upon his own judgment, the aging leader finds there only reasons for prolonging his incumbency. He thinks of himself as indispensable, of his life's work as still incomplete. What might he not yet do for his country, given only a few more months – or years? It is not as though his successor could do just as well. Which among these brawling underlings is to succeed him anyway? Which of them is worthy to succeed? And what does he do in his retirement? To whom will he give orders, what will there be to plan? The surfacing to private life, after the pressures of politics, involves a period of decompression too sudden, too painful, to look forward to. And why should he, of all men, willingly bow his head before the scimitar of time?

The results of this interrogation are apparent in the record. Not one of the Prime Ministers of Canada – Mr. Pearson excepted – has made a graceful exit. Macdonald died in office. Laurier, St. Laurent, Diefenbaker led their parties to defeat. Borden hung on in low spirits and ill health. The final year of the reign of Mackenzie King was marred by an idiosyncrasy verging upon senility. It is the same in other countries. There is the example of Churchill. There is the example of Adenauer. And there is the example of de Gaulle, who replied to a

228

question about his retirement in the following words: 'Perhaps tonight, or in six months, or in five years. If I wanted to make some laugh and others groan, I would add that it might be in 10 or 15 years.' There is something to be said, after all, for that amendment to the American Constitution which prohibits a President of the United States from seeking re-election after two full terms in office.

So Mr. Pearson, whose critics accuse him of indecision, made one of the hardest decisions of them all. He made it in the right way and at the right time – not under pressure to retire but under pressure to remain, when there was still work for him to do, when he still had much to give.

Appraisals of the Pearson career already have become a flood, and in them a number of misconceptions have appeared. A couple of these, while minor and of little consequence, may nevertheless be corrected. It is being said that he entered diplomacy forty years ago from an already 'illustrious' – to quote one commentator – and 'distinguished' – to quote another – career in university teaching. Mr. Pearson's record as a history don at the University of Toronto was, as he would be the first to admit, neither illustrious nor distinguished. It was simply barely begun. It is possible that, had he stayed in academic life, he would have become a great professor. It is possible that he would have become something less than that. In those days students did not, as they do today, grade their professors and publish, sometimes to their edification, more often to their embarrassment, the results. One of his students was sufficiently impressed by him to marry him. But that is something else again.

It is also being said, or implied, that his entrance to the Department of External Affairs was easy and automatic. That does the departmental examiners too much credit. It is true that he led the list of applicants. But the list was a short list, and his position at its head was not undisputed. One of his examiners – Vincent Massey – questioned the wisdom of his admission on the grounds that there was 'something curiously loose-jointed and sloppy about his mental make-up which, as a matter of fact, is reflected in some measure in his physical bearing'.

A third misconception is of greater consequence. Among the appraisals which have thus far appeared, that of Bruce Hutchison – Canada's political laureate – is likely to carry the most weight among the public of today and the historians of tomorrow. That is unfortunate, for it is a singularly wrong-headed appraisal. Mr. Hutchison is one of those writers who cannot bear to have his subject-matter straightforward. Canada, in his hands, becomes an unknown and largely unknowable country. Mackenzie King, similarly, is the incredible Canadian. And Mr. Pearson, predictably, the man nobody understands. 'To judge him,' he insists, 'we must look down a very deep well. The complex nature of the man resists analysis.' And again: 'His real meanings and ultimate intentions were known only to himself.'

This is true only in the sense that we all of us move in a mysterious way. But that is not the sense in which Mr. Hutchison intends it. I do not know of any evidence to confirm his belief that Mike Pearson, of all the complicated and serpentine characters that have presided over our country's destiny for its first hundred years, needs to be singled out for attention as especially inscrutable. So far from that, I should have thought our Prime Minister to be one of the most scrutable Canadians ever to attain high public office. He owes his unparalleled success – unparalleled in diplomacy, at any rate, whatever may be said of his success as a politician – to a readily identifiable combination of causes. One of these – perhaps the first of these – is enormous personal talent, particularly a talent for conciliation. Another is good luck – Machiavelli's *fortuna*, which so disposed herself to assure that the future Prime Minister was throughout his career at the right place at the right time with the appropriate skills for the next job to be done. And the last of these – or is it after all the first? – is a sunny and uncomplicated temperament, a disposition to take things as they come, rendering him immune, or nearly so, to the temptation to become preoccupied by intrigue or ridden by ambition – that 'vaulting ambition, which o'erleaps itself'.

[1968]

Peter Newman

The Diefenbaker Legend Will Live On

When he stood up that last night in Maple Leaf Gardens, his forehead corded with excitement, and called on Conservatives to give 'loyalty in the rank and file' to their new leader, John Diefenbaker was performing the closing rites to probably the most incredible, easily the most spectacular, certainly the most tragic career in Canadian politics.

Here, on display for one final, luminous moment was the greatness and the courage, the rhetorical ardor of the man. Yet it was also a poignant occasion, full of regret for the less self-destructive course he might have chosen and the opportunities he had missed.

Watching him there, a man of lacerated ego and exhausted sensibilities, one could not but wonder how the long sweep of history will deal with the Diefenbaker phenomenon. Only this much seemed certain: that if the historians of the future write off John Diefenbaker as merely the last gasp of a Prairie protest movement that managed briefly to attain national prominence – that if they dismiss him so lightly, the historians will be wrong.

Like most statesmen, Diefenbaker leaves behind him as he moves into the retirement phase of his life a reputation compounded more of myth than reality, though in his case, the two may never be disentangled. But a politician's greatness must be judged as much by his impact on the country's conscience as by what he did or left undone.

Most men lead short political lives and leave few followers. But John Diefenbaker's name will be reckoned with long after the events which gave birth to his brief flowering have been forgotten.

231

What will survive in the nation's folk memory will be the stride and stance of the man, the quality of his courage, the biblical cadence of his rhetoric. These will be the seminal elements of the Diefenbaker legend. Here was a politician who filled the space around him; whatever ground he stood on was *his*.

It was always easy to satirize his rages and caricature his crusades, but the spirit – the sheer guts – that took him so much further than the many politicians who had started with so much more, these qualities made the Prince Albert politician a man apart.

The legend of John Diefenbaker grew out of his resonance with the moods and weathers of his followers. His passion for the homely, awkward, and shattering small truth made him a political poet who could evoke the glories of a simpler past when the Red River carts still creaked along the Battleford trail and buffalo bones littered the horizonless prairies. He became a champion of society's drop-outs, a guerrilla fighter whose lonely assaults on the proud fortress of sophisticated Canada lent hope to the discontented and promise to the dispossessed. He gave tongue to the sense of affront felt by those good and honest pioneers who had won the country and were now losing it to the slick, new, rootless generation of the big cities.

The John Diefenbaker of the election platform soaked up the mood of rural Canada and as he gave it off a wave of electricity flowed through his audiences.

The grand theme of his campaigns – that glory shines the brightest through outrage – succeeded as long as he was able to engage a majority of the nation's voters in his own persecution complex. This was the basis of his 1957 and 1958 electoral victories, when he legitimately could claim to be the chief articulator of an angry Canada, fed up with the arrogant Liberal government that operated like an IBM machine which badly needed re-programming. He excited a political response in a larger proportion of Canadians than any politician before him and once in office managed to bring the federal government into a more meaningful relationship with the average citizen.

Even though he eventually dissipated the magnificent mandate he had been granted, his monument will always exist within Canada's Conservative Party. He single-handedly rescued his party from oblivion and was the first Tory to beat the Liberals three times since Sir John A. Macdonald. During his stormy stewardship he transformed the character of Canadian conservatism, so that men and women who had once been considered to possess the wrong racial or class credentials gained access to its hierarchy. Probably his most astonishing achievement was his 1958 sweep of Quebec, when he elected twice as many Tories as Liberals. French Canada gave him 62 per cent of its vote – just one percentage point behind true-blue Ontario.

But in the decade that followed, Diefenbaker amply demonstrated that he could neither satisfy nor comprehend the urgent demands of a re-awakened Quebec. He seemed to view the problem of French-English relations, not as a social phenomenon with deep moral significance, but as a partisan issue which he could exploit by appealing to the deep *status quo* feelings of the nation's majority, while obscuring the aspirations of its militant minority. He acted as if he regarded French Canadians, not as one of the nation's two founding peoples, but just as another ethnic group which happened to get here first. It was this misunderstanding which exploded into the battle over the 'deux nations' resolution during the leadership convention, and it was the instinctive response by Quebec's voters that he would never appreciate their longings, which forced him out of power and eventually out of the party leadership.

Although his magic could occasionally penetrate the barriers of language and background, his tragedy was that he could not bridge the gap between words and action. The Diefenbaker of the election platform – soaring bravely in rhetorical flight – became an indecisive and timorous man when confronted by the problems bewildering the nation.

It had been consummate skill in the art of politics that put John Diefenbaker into power from 1957 to 1963. But he treated his office as if he were conducting a daily plebiscite and never realized that a prime minister can't succeed unless he knows when to forget politics and begin to govern. Diefenbaker seemed to forget that his mandate was based on the courage the voters thought they had detected in him to take necessary but unpopular decisions.

During his stewardship, legislation remained more of a posture than a process and few brave new national initiatives were attempted. What really absorbed John Diefenbaker as prime minister was the satisfaction which he felt at being taken seriously for the first time in his long, harsh life.

To live up to his legend, John Diefenbaker had to act – even in office – like a politician who belonged to the era of the barricades. But he found himself operating in the age of the bureaucrats and eventually his terror of the future led him into a repudiation of the present. He projected no sense of the texture of the world that surrounded him and could provide no answers to his doting followers for dealing with the faceless enemies of the digital society of the sixties.

In the end, his government disintegrated, with 17 ministers resigning, retiring, or being defeated during its final 10 months. Added to the curse of indecision about most of the large issues facing Canada in the winter of 1963 was Diefenbaker's congenital inability to carry on the ordinary functions of government administration.

But despite his defeats, the man's strength of will was impossible to exaggerate. At a meeting in Bradford, Ont., during the windup of the 1963 campaign, he clarified, once and for all, where he got the advice he needed to go about his job: 'I ask myself, is a thing right, and if it is right I do it.'

It was this momentous self-confidence that made his speeches such memorably dramatic occasions and that in the end led him to defy the realities and run to succeed himself as a leader. His language was a splendid artifice. His every appearance let loose a hundred verbal balloons, strung together in a wild and violent mosaic.

He would take on a highly moralistic tone, like some gruff sea captain reading from the Good Book during a burial at sea, and the next instant, with an energy born of gloating, dance out his joy at the embarrassment of some political opponent.

But he was at his best when expressing his contempt for all those unnamed dark forces who would thwart his vision, dropping each accusing phrase a tone at a time, as though he was throwing worthless coins into a canyon.

The substance of his discourses seldom added up to any definable position, but on contact he seemed irrefutable and not even the most cynical member of his audience could leave unimpressed and untouched.

In these last sad years, when John Diefenbaker's entire energy was devoted to the shoring up of his own tenure, he seemed to be a man immersed in the flux of nebulous, evil events of his own construction. He began to scrutinize his environment with even more suspicion than usual.

Every visitor to his office, no matter how valid his pedigree of loyalty, was treated and questioned like some hostile witness at a murder trial.

'The Americans told you to ask me that,' he would challenge some baffled professor trying to verify historical detail about his government.

John Diefenbaker must have known that he was beaten and that his brand of politics was dying. But custom and guts can outlast reality. He fought on to the very bitter end, until that final agonizing moment when he returned to Maple Leaf Gardens late on Saturday night to shout: 'Unite, unite; unite,' and then disappeared into history.

The terrible fact about John Diefenbaker's incredible political career is that his great 1957 and 1958 victories condemned him to a permanent sense of anticlimax.

Like most popular heroes, he was frozen in history at the moment of his triumph. The spontaneous affection which erupted across the nation at the time imbued him with the kind of self-esteem that shields an aging man from the terrors of mortality.

Everything that followed his initial victories was only dimly perceived in the inner recesses of his explosive nature. So that when his time for greatness came, he stood in the way of his own vision, and his personal tragedy had to take second place to that of his country.

The essence of that tragedy – and the heart of the Diefenbaker legend – is what might have been. This man had the power in his lap to give his nation, his party and his people genuine greatness. But he gave them only his own legend.

For every Tory who felt as one elderly delegate did on Saturday night when he said in a voice tremulous with tears, 'John, you'll always be my chief,' there were thousands of others who still believed in the legend but could no longer support the man.

[1967]

Bruce Hutchison

Wacky in Wonderland

In the dark and dismal world of politics it is exhilarating to find one perfectly contented man – so exhilarating that this reporter needed a week to emerge from a hypnotic encounter with Premier W. A. C. Bennett, who generously opened his mind and magic casements to the editors of the *Vancouver Sun*.

He inhabits a private cosmos of his own, a kind of fourth dimension, an enchanted fairy castle, a very Eden, where the sun always shines, the flowers bloom perpetually, Adam rejects the forbidden fruit, Eve is chaste, and the serpent unknown. Such, for its maker and genial wizard, is contemporary British Columbia, the best of all provinces in the best of all nations in the best of all possible worlds.

Mr. Bennett's critics may suspect that he has invented his prodigy for political effect but they are quite wrong. With him the thing is unquestionably real, and getting better all the time. A man of puritanical habits, who never touches strong drink, he is innocently intoxicated by his dream – a big dream, brave, radiant, and uniquely British Columbian.

The dreamer is unique, too, strictly *sui generis,* with no parallel in our Western history and no competitor in modern Canada. There can be no competitor because, unlike other politicians, Mr. Bennett does not regard politics as a competition but as an orderly, natural, organic phenomenon like human and vegetable growth, an inevitable progress toward perfection. Life, it's wonderful, once you get the hang of it.

Even his harshest critics are not his enemies, only mistaken men who will repent their mistakes in due time. He has no quarrel with 'my good friends,

235

Pearson and Diefenbaker' and Mr. Gordon is a fine fellow but a little 'fuzzy'. If he must frequently denounce them for ruining the country, there is nothing personal in it. Everyone, including the leader of the provincial opposition, becomes his friend and it is with sincere sympathy, not with any satisfaction, that he sees the New Democratic party destroyed by its internal feuds. The pity of it.

As one who has known six of his predecessors intimately, I am bound to say that he is by far the ablest of the lot, probably the largest public figure ever produced in British Columbia. But he remains a British Columbian, with no place or much interest in national politics, and all the more ardent in his local patriotism because he came here a full-grown man and, with the unprejudiced eyes of a stranger, discovered this province for himself. More clearly than the natives, he sees the glories thereof and improves them.

He also sees the obligations of his discovery. A rich man, Mr. Bennett could easily retire and enjoy his later years in the peace of Okanagan, but for him there can be no leisure until his task is done. That will take at least five years more and perhaps several elections. Everything he has built so far is merely a foundation on which the ultimate wonder will be erected according to plan.

No doubts assail him in the lonely watches of the night. No obstacles frighten him. No barriers can stop him, not even the inherent stupidity of all federal governments. Man's affairs at large may be going to hell rather rapidly in a hack but his exclusive brand of Social Credit will preserve British Columbia safe and immaculate in a naughty world.

After all, what is Social Credit? Not the original theology of Major Douglas, the A plus B Theorem, the Just Price, and the old bag of tricks. Mr. Bennett has long since dismissed that primitive doctrine and completely reinterpreted it to mean simply that the financial credit of democratic government, built up by sound management and thrifty revenue surpluses, must be used as a lever to elevate and wisely guide private enterprise.

Though he has made himself the most successful practising socialist in America, with his state-owned hydro schemes, his railway and his excellent ferry system, Mr. Bennett repudiates socialism, more in sorrow than in anger. When Russian experts came secretly to his office some years ago and asked him how he achieved his many triumphs, he told them, in a friendly way, that communism, like socialism, could not possibly work. Only the genius of the family, the individual citizen, and the free enterpriser would remake Russia in British Columbia's image.

Evidently, though Mr. Bennett is too modest to say so, the Russians have learned their lesson. They are turning to the West's methods, as refined in his laboratory at Victoria.

While he manipulates credit, the premier asks none for himself. He has everything he needs already and is only the people's servant, not their master. They can defeat him at any election and he will go without rancor or regret. In the meantime, however, having read (or perhaps written) Edmund Burke's address to the electors of Bristol, he intends to govern, careless of popularity or votes.

His opponents' worst error is to imagine that all this is a pose, an act put on for the groundlings, a crude electoral stratagem. No, Mr. Bennett means everything he says when he says it. If he changes his mind and policy without notice, as often happens, he believes his second thoughts as sincerely as he believed the first, and the third will be just as valid.

The true explanation of this remarkable personage, I venture to judge, is an inner mechanism hidden from its owner and baffling to the public. He possesses an inner filtering device, a delicate sieve through which he receives only what he wants to know. All the unpleasant things that haunt ordinary men are strained out automatically, life is purified, the sky cloudless and serene at permanent high noon, Okanagan time.

It must be a stern man who can escape the benign infection of his dream. The strongest swimmer soon drowns in the gushing torrent of his words. Or if the conversation becomes awkward for a moment, Mr. Bennett leads the questioner dancing merrily down some side trail and winding, mossy way until he is lost in wonderland and forgets his question.

But Mr. Bennett forgets nothing. His memory, though well filtered, is crammed with facts like the blue books of budgetary figures carried in his brief case, a flawless computer, adding up the data and invariably producing the desired result.

The final result is a man of sixty-eight untroubled years who, in all essentials, remains a boy, with a boy's health, energy, and charm. Yet after an hour or two the charm is rather suffocating. After a week or two you recover from the spell, break through the magic casements for a breath of air, and confront, alas, the actual world where there is no filter. Then the wizard turns out to be only Mr. Bennett, the bustling business man of Kelowna and general manager of his own firm, Happiness Unlimited, with the lowest prices in town.

[1968]

I

Claude Ryan

The Canadian Solution

There are for French Canadians two ways of approaching the Canadian problem.

One consists of identifying French Canada with Quebec and examining all our problems in relation to the interests of Quebec. At the heart of this hypothesis Quebec is first and foremost. It is necessary to pursue it and defend it, putting all other considerations in second place: that is the thesis of 'by itself and for itself' dear to M. Lévesque.

In this perspective the Canadian dimension appears a last resort. It is a rupture of the homogeneous order which would exist if Quebec was alone and completely master of its destiny; it is thus a weight from which it is necessary to strain in order to liberate oneself. Some are still prepared to accept the Canadian reality, provided that this reality does not hinder in any way the progress of Quebec, and that it serves Quebec's interests. Others have already concluded that the Canadian reality is injurious to Quebec, that it is necessary to put an end as soon as possible to an experiment which, in every way, has never been faithfully put to the test.

Between these two opinions there exists a difference of degree, not of nature. The two opinions accept, without discussion, the ideal of the primacy of Quebec. They separate at the chapter on means and strategy. In the long run the two opinions are destined to unite.

The second approach consists in envisaging the French-Canadian problem at the level of the whole country, that is, to begin with the Canadian hypothesis.

At the heart of this hypothesis there is a place for a loyal admission of the

238

difficulties that have sorely tried the French Canadians in Confederation. There is equally room for an explicit recognition of the special position that Quebec – as the principal political expression of the French fact in Canada – ought to occupy in the Canadian body politic.

But the perspective remains Canadian. Canada is accepted not as a last resort from which one would like to be liberated, but as a valuable political reality which one wants to improve. This viewpoint is not that of a supporter of a unitary system, but rather of a federalist. For him the federal régime is the one that best fits our geographic, historic, economic, and political conditions. Without wishing this régime to survive at any price, he rejects the global and defeatist interpretations that some propose about the history of the last century.

This viewpoint also takes account of the evolution which has taken place in English-Canadian opinion in the last quarter-century. Those who adhere to this thesis believe that it is possible and desirable to reform our federation in a manner that will become effective and acceptable to Canadians of both languages. They see that this reform ought to be made up of conversations and faithful agreements between the two groups. They wish to obtain this objective by the road of dialogue rather than by the method of ultimatums. But they recognize at the outset that it is within the Canadian body politic that they look for a solution.

It is impossible, unless one wants to outsmart someone, to pretend to be inspired by both hypotheses. A newspaper should chose one of the two and defend it with courage and clarity. It should do this with the maximum loyalty and frankness. It should give all viewpoints a reasonable opportunity for expression in the news columns. But it would betray its mission if it avoided choice.

We choose the Canadian hypothesis for three principal reasons. The first reason relates to the very tradition of *Le Devoir*. The newspaper, under its first three directors, was a great Canadian newspaper. Henri Bourassa never wanted to limit his horizons to the province of Quebec. He considered that the whole of Canada was his country, that he ought to be at home everywhere in this country. Georges Pelletier also attached a great importance to Canadian realities. He liked to approach the most complex problems, for example those of transport, with an objectivity and a rigour that would have prevented him from closing them within a narrow compass. The third director, Gérard Filion, was of rural origin, but he had learned early at the school of the Catholic Union of Farmers the need for co-operation with the rest of the country. He was often severe toward Ottawa centralizers, but never negative or closed with regard to Canada itself.

The second reason lies in the economic order. It is sufficient to glance at a map of the country in order to establish that Quebec and Canada are tied together in many ways. Quebec's economy presents two important characteristics. It needs external markets for the dispersal of its products. It needs capital from outside for the development of its resources. Why should we say no to Canada today if that must only mean saying yes to others tomorrow? One does not deny his history for the simple pleasure of hypothetically changing partners.

Our most important motives lie in the political order. On the condition that Quebec enjoys all the autonomy which it needs to develop its own life and institutions, we believe that the preservation of the Canadian tie offers precious advantages. The first of these advantages is surely the possibility of maintaining and developing the French way of life in the rest of the country. *Le Devoir* has always maintained an attitude of solidarity with the French minorities in the other parts of the country. Whatever could have been said on this subject for some time, the present direction of *Le Devoir* holds that we must continue to support our compatriots in the other provinces. We refuse to join the prophets of doom who affirm, without ever having worked assiduously with these groups, that the French minorities of the other provinces are doomed to extinction.

The second advantage is less immediate, but no less obvious. Canada offers us the chance of constructing a new type of political society, that is, a society whose political boundaries will be advantageous for the development of different cultures without being rigidly or exclusively conditioned by one culture alone. We are convinced that this type of society can be revealed as more advantageous to the cultivation of fundamental liberties, in the long run, than societies calculated too closely on the single reality of a particular culture. In affirming this conviction we are conscious of enunciating an ideal which is far from having been attained in the Canadian reality. But the difficulties and the checks of the past are not yet decisive enough to justify pure and simple abandonment of the ideal which presided at the birth of Confederation.

A durable political society is built neither on impulses nor on vague desires, but on rational ideas, on a certain conception of man and of life in society, on an objective assessment of reality. Nothing proves that men nourished in different cultures are incapable of co-operating on a certain conception of political life. The entente is surely more difficult when several cultures are called upon to cohabit, but it is not for all that purely and simply impossible.

That being said we insist on adding three qualifications.

We have said advisedly 'the Canadian hypothesis'. We have not spoken of dogma. It is possible that we are mistaken. If that is the case, the facts will indicate it to us in the proper time and place. Placed before the evidence we will not have the pretension of preventing history from fulfilling itself. But while waiting, the logic of events obliges us to fight firmly and frankly for the success of our hypothesis.

In choosing the Canadian hypothesis we are not opting for the status quo. If this hypothesis is to be realized, substantial modifications in the constitution of our country and in the functioning of our political institutions will have to be carried out. It will be necessary to rethink our federalism, to adjust it profoundly. It will be necessary to avoid the errors of the past, to correct the injustices of yesterday, to foresee new methods of work which will realize completely the equality of cultures.

Finally our choice will not prevent us in the least from approaching in Quebec the problems of Quebec. In the order of jurisdiction where it is and must remain (and even in certain areas become) sovereign, Quebec has the right to our first allegiance. It will have it without restriction. In the discusssion of the problems of education, social security, and the development of our resources and of our economy we will not act in the fashion of 'Canadians at large' who would like to solve our problems using norms borrowed from elsewhere rather than by the realistic examination of our situation and our resources. We will think and speak as Québécois without misplaced pride, but without false humility.

These positions seem to us to conform best to the true reality of French Canada.

[1964]

René Lévesque

To Be Masters in Our Own House

What does Quebec want?

It's simply not the right question. The way it's put, it calls for some kind of enumeration: some more of this, and a bit of that, and then a lot of this, too. Etc. Ad nauseam. You answer it, you feel like you're talking about a recipe for political goulash.

While the fact is that from now on Quebec will always want more. Until it gets all. Because the question really is: What does Quebec want *to be*?

The answer: a homeland for a people; *'patrie'*; a nation in the fullest (English) sense of the word.

It's an old dream. A very powerful and no less normal dream, but so long repressed that it's often relegated deep down in the recesses of the French-Canadian mind. Some of us have given up on it. Others are scared of the changes it would require: so they hide it and caress it secretly, when nobody is looking, and since for them it's like an illicit love affair, they'll be the last to admit it.

But they will eventually. For the first time in a couple of hundred years, the dream is now clearly feasible. That was all it needed. As this becomes more evident, the latent majority that was always there will reveal itself and grow and pretty soon fulfil the dream.

In the Quebec election of June 1966, the 'dreamers' got the equivalent of 10 per cent of the votes. Right now it would be at least 15 per cent. A year from now it could be as much as 25 per cent. In the next two to five years, I'm convinced it will become a solid majority.

This is something the younger Québécois can decide without much effort. For him it comes naturally. He has none of the taboos and frustrating memories of his elders. He's been brought up in a world where everyone and everything – from international news to the educational system itself – keep telling him that change is now practically the only stable law. Change holds no fear for him. And when it also promises to supply a purpose worthy of lifelong dedication and enthusiasm, it can look irresistibly attractive.

In the main, older people find it much more difficult. I know. It took me a few years to find my way out of that paralysing web of habits of thought and false teachings of experience in which life tends to imprison us. Throughout Quebec many others are now making or are about to embark on similar agonizing reappraisals. I firmly believe that most of them will arrive at the same conclusion. And I'm not forgetting the many who arrived 'way before I did!

Basically, what we all have to get rid of is that 'fear itself' that Roosevelt once told Americans was the only thing to fear. This French-Canadian fear is mostly rooted in a feeling of political and economic inferiority. It's been fed by many things, from the minority status we 'enjoy' in Canada to our own long neglect of education and the vast areas of perfect incompetence that resulted.

At long last, we are now doing quite a lot about the educational aspect of this morbid breeding-ground of our complexes. It started slowly during and after World War II. In its own groping way, Quebec thus stepped onto the fast track of what's known as 'the acceleration of history'. Like all human societies and more belatedly than most other Western ones, it had to change its pace from a nice slow trot to a furious gallop.

Old values and treasured myths such as the Revenge of the Cradle or the Language as Keeper of the Faith went crumbling down. The incredible range of mobility (travel, jobs, the rush to the cities) started shaking to its very foundations a social order based on long untested assumptions of permanence and protected by thin walls of isolation and ignorance.

This last was the one that really had to go. The speed at which it did became dramatic after Maurice Duplessis died. Ten years ago, something like two-thirds of all adult Québécois had had Grade 6 education or less. Ten years from now, even sooner, a new generation of high-school graduates will be completely in charge – along with the thousands of new 'professionals' who are crowding up from this springboard in numbers that are growing every year. And in fields that used to be other-man's-land: economics, administration, social sciences, teaching (as a male profession), engineering.

That is Quebec's real revolution.

That is what brought about the reawakening of the dream.

Looking back, I personally believe I felt it (a long time before I recognized it, naturally) in the fall of 1962. We, the Liberal government, had just called an election on the nationalization of private power companies. A couple of nights later, a small group of us came up with a campaign slogan: *'Maîtres chez nous'* (Masters in our own home). The moment those three words rang out, the search was over. Even though instinct and common sense cried out that here, potentially, was much more than a call for the take-over of a handful of private utilities.

(Yet I suppose it's very understandable that many political 'pros' refused to see it then, and now would like to wash their hands of almost everything – except maybe their winning – that this call set in motion. After a long enough stay in so-called practical politics, there's a tendency to use words quite loosely, as pure electoral accessories that you can discard as soon as the votes are in, forgetting that words are vehicles for ideas and that ideas remain the most powerful of all explosives. As the late André Maurois once said, there should be an inscription in red on every dictionary: 'Danger'.)

I remember the effect this campaign had on a lot of people. Among the best in the younger generations it was particularly strong, and for most of them lasting enough that later on, when they felt the Liberals were slowing down, they moved out and into the R.I.N. or temporary non-commitment. While for many older people it was like a sudden quickening in a bloodstream gone sluggish. For instance, there was an old gentleman of over 80 who was a prosperous businessman in my riding. Being the type of old-time paterfamilias whose own 50-year-old son was still treated like a clerk, he sent me a kind of royal convocation to an audience, and with a rather suspicious look in his eye he told me: 'I haven't voted Liberal in over 40 years, but *if* you're really serious about being truly nationalistic, this time I may just do it!'

More recently, among the first supporters that appeared from outside our group after we left the Liberals were quite a few white-haired veterans of the Action Libérale Nationale of the thirties and greying ones of the Bloc Populaire of the forties.

They feel that maybe now, at long last, it can be done. Soon they'll know it for a fact. There is enough competence now to tackle the job successfully.

The Quiet Revolution proved it. First and foremost in education. And then by an exciting spill-over into better public administration, electoral reform, modern highways, the new pension plan and other up-to-date ideas about social security, the revelation of economic growth and growing acceptance of the part an efficient state has to play in it. Along with more aggressive and better equipped professional people, labour leaders, entrepreneurs, and intellectuals in the private sector.

All of which gave birth to the Quebec version of a universal happening: the Revolution of Rising Expectations.

Now that we're sure we're really able to do any of *our* jobs as well as anyone else, we'll keep wanting to do more of them ourselves, in our own way and our own language, and so take over Quebec as the homeland that used to be an unattainable dream. That's inevitable. Especially in this urgent age which Robert L. Heilbronner aptly calls the Great Ascent, with all cultural groups of any importance, down to the most hopeless cases, feeling this rage to become national entities and 'to live in the chronicle of recorded events'.

Helping us to appear in this world chronicle, by the way, was the one major result of de Gaulle's 'Québec libre'. A few days ago, I met a student just back from a summer in the backwoods of Peru, where he naturally found Quebec to be as well known as the other face of the moon used to be. Then, after de Gaulle, everybody would be coming up to him and *telling* him all about it! The moment he got back in August, he joined an *indépendantiste* party.

Now you're saying: 'So why not do all of that within the present federal system, with whatever modifications would be mutually acceptable?' Since the Quiet Revolution gave us our first heady dose of collective self-reliance, why not just keep going, and over the next 15 or 50 years muddle through happily to 'a strong Quebec in a new (but structurally unchanged) Canada'?

And that brings up the other alternative: the so-called 'special status'.

Let's take a look at it. We'll soon find that it brings us negatively to the same conclusion the dream commands in a positive way. Instead of walking up to it with our eyes open, it simply means backing up into it blind.

What is a special status? The words could bear any interpretation, making Quebec a province politically somewhat more *différente* than it is already. So a lot of people in federal (and 'federalist') circles are working their heads off trying to keep that content down to a minimum the rest of Canada can accept.

But in actual fact, the *real minimum* on which a consensus has developed among serious and respected proponents of the special status represents an awesome grab-bag of jurisdictions and resources: control over immigration and citizenship, over mass media and manpower policies, over internal economic development and all cultural (and related) external affairs. Plus enough fiscal power to tackle that lot on top of what's already needed for education and research, health and urban affairs among others!

This is what Paul Gérin-Lajoie calmly set down as his and many others' minimum definition of the *statut particulier* at the Liberal convention in Quebec, last October. It brought such an immediate uproar from Ottawa and elsewhere that it was pigeonholed by the party under the leadership of Eric Kierans. Nevertheless it's Paul Gérin-Lajoie who was right.

What he set down is nothing more than the basic institutional equipment any well-defined cultural group requires in order to become and remain the captain of its own modest ship in this stormy world. And that is truly the minimum demanded by Quebec's national-cultural coming of age.

But what it would do to the federal structure is just plain monstrous. In a 'split-level' type of political building it would create something unheard-of: a semi-detached floor! Not even the most imaginative of political architects would agree to work from such a set of Dali-esque blueprints!

And don't forget that as soon as Quebec got some of it, it would bring the cry for more. And more. And all. While the rest of Canada would holler and backlash like mad, wondering ever more loudly about what our politicians and civil servants would do in a federal administration which we'd be making practically non-existent in Quebec.

I*

In the meantime, there is growing mutual distrust and more waste of energy in a country that is dying for sweeping structural changes.

For the constitutional crisis has emphasized at least one thing on which there should be general agreement: our present federal system is one of the most obsolete in the whole civilized world. It's an outdated, creaky, inefficient remnant of a 19th-century colonial experiment in nation building. From incredible Senate to quasi-invisible P.E.I., from overlapping and irresponsibility-breeding establishments to tragi-comically wasteful defence posturing, from the mess in railroads to that in fiscal practices, there's a crying need for a lot of revamping. Apart from U.S. enterprise, it's been said unkindly that Canada is kept going mostly by the Communist world's temporary inability to grow enough wheat!

What is called for above all is a rebuilt central authority, strong and modern. This is the common conclusion that all dedicated federalists come to in their various efforts. Senator Maurice Lamontagne did at a recent 'thinkers' conference'. So does Mr. Kierans in the book he just published. And from their standpoint, they're both absolutely right.

There's only one problem. So does French Quebec urgently feel this very same need for a strong government − of its own! Its own set of free and modern political institutions appears as the only collective tool capable of protecting and developing its vital difference while the whole planet becomes more homogenized in the areas of science and technology and their numberless border-erasing economic applications.

So what we need is not one but *two* strong central governments!

And again the outcome is inevitable. A good drag-down fight between federalists and 'special-status-men' would take us to it in due time, through a few more elections and federal-provincial conferences. The trouble is that enough bad blood could be generated along the way to make the ending arrive unplanned and abrupt, possibly as bitter and damaging as the messiest of divorces.

Now, what is Quebec being offered in exchange for its quite feasible national dream and the political assurance of survival and self-government as a majority in its own homeland?

Simply that after 100 years of frustration and frequent humiliation, French Canadians might eventually be accepted as 'minority but equal' share-owners of the whole of Canada.

It's a nice thought. But it comes a bit late in the day. Let's not go into chapter and verse about those 100 years. Bygones are bygones.

But facts are facts. When a Québécois is told in glowing terms about a future republic (with Mr. Michener promoted to president) and an upcoming national anthem (which, if we're especially nice, could even be 'O Canada' with bicultural verse!), well, if he's past 40 it at least reminds him of long-forgotten childhood fantasies, but if he's younger it just makes him wonder why reasonable people should get so excited over so little.

Even the gentle blackmail about the million or so French Canadians outside Quebec who might find themselves adrift in a cold, cold sea of English unilingualism has lost most of its old sentimental potency. And what's left of it is going about as fast as those minorities are being assimilated, which means real quick. By now, after having been treated for so long just like any other group of newcomers – quite decently as individuals but on a none-of-that-cultural-nonsense basis as a group – a large third or more of them are a lost cause. And the rest are 'passing' just as rapidly as other well-integrated New Canadians, their origin remaining visible only in their names. In New Brunswick, a recent survey showed that behind the brittle façade of élite *survivance,* many ordinary Acadians couldn't care less about such basics as French schooling or TV programs.

I suppose a true feeling for the new country and its great continental sweep could have been nurtured into a strong pan-Canadian identity if the English-speaking majority had wanted it to happen. It didn't. What it actually wanted was something as close to a melting pot and to unitary government as possible.

Let's not kid each other. After that 100 years, Quebec's federal Canadianism is nothing but ashes behind the clichés and the Potemkin-front of the Centennial.

And the homeland is Quebec. As, mind you, it always was. From the very beginning, even when the discoverers and *coureurs de bois* were ranging all over America, home was on the Saint Lawrence. The British conquest made it official. And the last century wiped away what faint illusion might have remained of ever 'belonging' outside Quebec.

One of these days, then, a Quebec majority will decide for its sovereign state. For political independence. That's what I, like many others, have come to believe in. With many others, that's what I'll work for until there are enough of us and it's done.

It *is* separation. But does it have to be the complete break-up, the furious resentment, the maximum mutual damage that a lot of federalists seem to anticipate with a kind of sick delectation when they flatten their lips and hiss: 'Separatist'?

We think not. Or rather we hope not. It's far from certain that we can show enough understanding and enlightened self-interest on both sides – much more than we ever showed before – to go through the inevitable without all the dire prospects coming true.

But if there's a hope, why not work at it?

Very briefly, couldn't it happen like this: While separating politically, why not preserve one very important and mutually profitable association – which is our present common market?

And also maintain our present monetary unity, which would simply require that the central bank become a partnership instead of a wholly owned federal corporation. Just recently, a prominent European public figure was telling us that if the countries in the common-market groupings over there could find an easy way to get rid of their ancient and complicated monetary diversities, they'd jump at the chance. What they're painfully aiming at we have already. Why tear it apart?

This is where some people will cut in with a smirk: 'Ha! so the guy wants to have his cake and eat it too, huh!'

Think again. Total disruption would hurt the rest of Canada, in many ways, much more deeply than Quebec. Even on the monetary question, a friend of mine who disagrees with me completely, the noted financial expert and part-time columnist D. H. Fullerton, estimates that dislocation would cost both of us dearly: our Quebec 'dollar' he stabilizes somewhere around 70 cents, while 'yours' would be no champion either at approximately 80 cents. . . .

As for a common market, obviously Quebec is more a buyer than a seller in our internal exchange, especially in the field of industrial production. So who has more to lose?

But way above and beyond such calculations, how could Canada itself survive as an entity if Quebec's exit from Confederation had to come like an explosion, with years of poisonous fallout in the form of hostility and distrust? How could a 'pakistanized' Canada keep going? It couldn't. It would disintegrate, probably after a lot of slow painful spasms, and the pieces would finally drift into the U.S.

That's the picture Eric Kierans immediately painted as the only possible answer to our proposal when he and I were on TV together a few months ago. Was he right?

I doubt it very much. After all, there should be more to English Canada than just 'holding on to Quebec'. If there definitely isn't, then sooner or later it's cheaper cars and cigarettes for you all, and U.S. citizenship – along with the fading away of a growing (even though 'branch-plant') economy and its managerial society; and the draft, and present and future Vietnams, and a share of the terrific agony the American society is inflicting upon itself.

It's at least worth thinking about before saying: 'To hell with you!'

And what's in it for Quebec?

Mainly a chance to start out with a partner instead of an enemy next door. Also, certainly, a chance, but quite mutually useful, to reduce to a minimum the problems our new state would have to face.

However, this does not at all mean that Quebec could be made to renounce its goal just by loud and repeated Nevers accompanied by the raising of old economic bugaboos. As Mr. Kierans (the same, but in earlier attitudes) once eloquently said in Montreal: 'That is not the question, nor the answer. . . . Let us beware,' he told the English-speaking audience he was then addressing, 'of this economic blackmail we have too often practised against French Canadians.'

Particularly now that every year a greater number of educated Québécois are a bit more resistant to short-term panic than their poor parents were. They know that any honest and competent economic forecast for a whole society has to be at least a medium-term operation if it's to mean anything.

And they already suspect that, seen in that perspective, even a totally separated Quebec would have a good chance to find itself in a much healthier economic situation than it would by remaining in the present federal system.

In conclusion, nothing will stop the dream from being realized, nor the development of that 'exciting discovery' which one of our foremost economic experts, Prof. Jacques Parizeau, described at a Banff conference in October: 'French Canadians in Quebec (can) set themselves concrete objectives, achieve them fully, partially, or even fail to meet them, like any other people. . . . When a society has been for so long in search of fulfilment and has found it within itself, it is very unlikely that it can be distracted from this purpose.'

It won't. So why not start thinking about an acceptable substitute for Confederation? While Quebec decides during the next few years, you have time to see it coming and to get ready. For you the main question will be whether you really want to maintain on this continent a distinctive, non-American, English-speaking society.

If you do, as we wrote in our group 'manifesto' in September, 'there's no reason why we shouldn't, while becoming neighbours politically, find a way to remain associated as partners in a common enterprise . . . made up of all the close ties and complementary relationships we've always lived with in our economic lives. This is one reality that nothing should lead us to destroy, that everything on the contrary tells us we should preserve as a common framework. . . .

'. . . Such an association would not force us to set out onto uncharted waters. Not counting the gigantic model of the European common market, we can find inspiration in countries comparable to ours, such as the Benelux and Scandinavian groups, where co-operation is very close and is proving to be an unprecedented incentive for all the nations involved, but as far as can be seen without preventing any of them from living essentially according to its own tastes and tradition.'

That's how we came to propose: 'a system in which one nation whose country would be Quebec and another which, at last, would be free to reorganize the rest of Canada as it preferred, would agree to associate in their own original adaptation of the common-market formula, thus forming a new ensemble whose name, for example, might very well be the Canadian Union.'

The only basic requirement is that we come to the inevitable constitutional and political parting of the ways with enough mutual good faith, open-mindedness, and imagination.

Which one gentleman from Toronto, Mr. David W., finds unthinkable. 'I do not think you are reckoning with the baser, more vindictive side of the Anglo-Saxon nature,' he writes. 'If Quebec goes out of Confederation you will find to your amazement and dismay that the 14 million non-French will react against Quebec in many nasty ways. The mood will harden across the rest of

Canada and the backlash against your proposed moves will make the white backlash against the Negroes in the States pale into insignificance....'

Brother!

Fortunately another Torontonian, Mr. W. H. G., is much more encouraging: 'When two peoples with different languages and cultures have to live side by side in the same state,' he says, 'it seems that invariably one of them ends up in an inferior position. Real equality between them seems to be impossible. For some time already, we've been attempting uselessly to make the imposssible come true. By trying to maintain Confederation at any price, we risk fashioning a central government without any real power, and even if we should manage to agree on certain things, the final overall result would satisfy no one.'

How much better, he concludes, 'an association that allows both parties to survive in dignity and friendship'!

The many others whose reactions I've been getting generally fall in either of the categories indicated by these two gentlemen.

Do I have to tell you which of them I fervently hope, for all of us, will prevail when the time comes?

[1968]

Fernand Dumont

On Living with Divided Loyalties

The Globe and Mail has informed its readers about the donation I made to the Parti Québécois of a sum equal to the value of the Governor-General's Prize awarded to me lately by the Arts Council of Canada. Your daily has also published around this affair an anonymous article illustrated by a caricature. I am questioned on the 'rectitude of my actions' and on 'a strange use of conscience'. I then claim the right to be listened to.

About the caricature, I will be brief. It has rendered with a perennial fidelity the conventional image of the Quebeckers as seen by too many English-speaking people. We see a can of pea soup right ahead. When, long ago, my father toiled at Welland, he also was called 'pea soup' by his English foremen. I write this not by rancour, but for the sake of memory.

At the moment of the donation, I have published in *Le Devoir* (May 24) an article in which I stated my exact intention. The writer of the article published in your daily asks the question: Is one permitted to act in that manner? In answer, the following remarks will undoubtedly interest some people of Toronto who sent me clippings from *The Globe and Mail* seasoned with insults dictated, of course, by moral preoccupations. Indeed, the problem is a moral one.

The writer of the article states abruptly this problem: If you are a separatist, refuse that kind of a prize. But if you benefit by it, let it clearly be known that you abide by all the Canadian institutions.

I read: 'The Governor-General of Canada in whose person and office is symbolized the confederate nature of this country . . .' For the journalist, a

251

'separatist' is one who intends 'to break up this nation'. Many Canadians of both languages are holding that it is possible to have a confederation without monarchy; others ascertain that there are two nations in Canada. But the author of the article prefers more plain simplifications.

One might say, is not 'separatism' an insuperable limit? I want to remind your readers that the Parti Québécois is not an underground organization, and decidedly not an army of terrorists. It is an official party, according to the most traditional rules of British liberties. Its leader, René Lévesque, is deputy in a legislature of this Confederation. Moreover, those who know a little about Quebec are aware that the term 'separatist' covers many different options. It may designate the most fanatic partisan of absolute independence, and also the citizens, I for one, who demand a radical re-examination of the Confederation Act, and perhaps those who are in favour of a particular status for Quebec.

All these points of view present a complex and irritating classification. But as such, they are the expression of the restlessness and of the problems of a large number of Canadian citizens. Will they have to wait the judgment of history to use fruitfully of all the rights of the state in its actual form?

To stand by the logic of your journalist, I should abstain from directing a scientific review because it receives help from the Arts Council. I would also stop to publish, because I need subsidies from the Council. The CBC being a federal institution, I should stay away from it. And I would have to return to Ottawa my family allowances. But, at the same time, I would refuse to pay my federal income taxes. That kind of reasoning is simple, but impracticable. And morally should not be followed. No Canadian would tolerate that some citizens be banned from the state because of their opinions.

While hoping the fruitfulness of my own political options, I feel myself a free citizen of Canada, respectful of laws and persons. As such, I concern myself with the political arrangement of the arduous relations of our two peoples. Nobody should be considered a traitor if he speaks up his mind out of conspirations and without any bomb in hand.

That is my ordinary behaviour.

But when these day-to-day ethics are to be defined because of an occasion as solemn as the attribution of a prize connected with a political symbol, I then am forced to a double statement. On one part, I am grateful to those who valued one of my books; I admire the efficiency of the Arts Council; I respect the person of the Governor-General; an enduring esteem I have for Secretary of State Gérard Pelletier, for instance. On the other hand, I must let my political options be clearly known. Honest citizens who do not partake in them waited this explanation, I believe.

Being chosen for the prize, I was not previously asked – nor by the Governor-General, neither by the Arts Council or the Secretary of State – if I adhered to the royalty or to the Confederation in its present state. My opinions were already known, and friendly allusions were made to them, at the reception, in Ottawa. This is the proof, I think, of the objectivity of the

Governor, of the Council, and of the Secretary of State. My conscience felt at ease while accepting a literary prize, in these conditions. But the official denomination of the prize urged me to officially denounce something else: that also pertains to conscience.

Anyway, every Canadian may understand that a man of forty, charged with researches and responsibilities, does not take the train for Ottawa in order to play a dubious joke on the Governor-General.

And why spare all this time to give $2,500 to a party? An intellectual and an idealist I am, but I am convinced that certain political parties are financed by more rapid and efficient processes. I rather thought fundamental principles were involved by which should be guided a conscientious citizen.

My approach towards the 'rectitude of my actions' may appear as a too patient one. The anonymous writer of the article invoked Churchill to advocate shortest cuts. But I listened also to the advice of Plato: 'In the search for truth, man must engage himself with his whole spirit and by long ways.'

[1969]

Gad Horowitz

Red Tory

English Canada is not merely a fragment of the American culture. There are significant differences between the English-Canadian and American ways of life. English Canada is being Americanized; the un-American characteristics of Canada are disappearing, but they are not yet gone. They can be retained by an effort of intellect and of will. An intellectual effort is necessary to make us fully conscious of our un-Americanism, and of its value. An effort of will is necessary to do the things required for the preservation of English-Canadian distinctiveness, to pay the price of being Canadian.

What is un-American about English Canada can be summed up in one word: British. The American society was the product of a 'liberal' revolution, and it has remained monolithically 'liberal' until the present day. English Canada's dominant ideology has always been a liberalism quite similar to the American but there has also been a Britishness about English Canada which has expressed itself in two ideologies each of which is 'alien', beyond the pale of legitimacy, in the United States. These two ideologies are 'conservatism' and 'socialism'.

By 'conservatism' I mean not the American conservatism which is nineteenth-century liberalism, but toryism — the British conservatism which has its roots in a pre-capitalist age, the conservatism that stresses prescription, authority, order, hierarchy, in an organic community. By 'socialism' I mean not the American New Dealism which is nineteenth-century liberalism with a pseudo-socialist tinge, but socialism properly so-called — the socialism which stresses the good of the community as against possessive individualism; equality

254

of condition as against more equality of opportunity; the co-operative common-wealth as against the acquisitive society.

English Canada was founded by British Loyalists, rejects of the American revolution. Their purpose was to build in Canada a society which would be not liberal like the American but retain certain important conservative characteristics of British society. Their influence has been crucial and per-vasive. Many students of Canada have noted that English-Canadian society has been powerfully shaped by tory values that are alien to the American mind. The latest of these is Seymour Martin Lipset (*The First New Nation*), who stresses particularly the relative strength of what he calls 'elitism' (the tendency to defer to authority) in Canada.

A few observers, again including Lipset, have noticed that Canada differs from the United States in yet another respect: Our socialism has been much stronger than that of the United States. South of the border, socialism is 'alien'; but in English Canada it has been a legitimate element of the political culture – not un-Canadian, but one of the ways of being Canadian. The presence of a relatively strong, legitimate socialism in Canada has been explained primarily as a result of the waves of British immigration beginning late in the nineteenth century. This explanation is not wrong; it is true that American socialism was borne primarily by Continental European immigrants who sloughed off their socialism in the process of Americanization, while Canadian socialism was borne primarily by British emigrants who did not have to slough off their socialism as part of a 'Canadianization' process, since they came as Britons to British North America. But the explanation is incomplete, because it ignores the oft-ignored relationship between toryism and socialism.

Socialism and liberalism are almost always placed together on the political spectrum, on the left, opposed to toryism, on the right. This is a legitimate approach, but it is one-sided. It stresses certain ideas that socialism and liberalism have in common (especially egalitarianism) when they are contrasted with toryism. But it is also true that socialism and toryism have certain things in common when they are contrasted with liberalism. I refer especially to their common orientation towards the collectivity. Indeed, it can be argued that socialism has *more* in common with toryism than with liberalism, for liberalism is possessive individualism, while socialism and toryism are variants of col-lectivism.

The liberal sees life in society as a competition among individuals; the prize is individual 'achievement' or 'success'; equality is equality of opportunity in the struggle for success. The individual is thought of as self-determining, autonomous, rather than a *member* determined by the class and community of which he is a part. It is *because* the socialist has a conception of society as *more* than an agglomeration of competing individuals – a conception much closer to the tory view of society as an organic entity – that he rejects the liberal idea of equality as inadequate. Socialists disagree with liberals about the essential meaning of equality *because* socialists have a tory conception of society.

In a society which thinks of itself in liberal terms, a society which has not known toryism (a society like the United States) the demand for equality will express itself as left-wing liberalism. It will be pointed out that all are not equal in the competitive struggle. The liberal government will be required to assure greater equality of opportunity, and perhaps a welfare floor so that no one will fall out of the race. In a society which thinks of itself as a community of classes rather than an aggregation of individuals, the demand for equality will take a socialist form: at its most extreme, it is a demand for the *abolition* of classes so that the good of the *community* can truly be realized.

Once we have recognized this, we are in a position to entertain the suggestion that the presence of *both* toryism and socialism in English Canada is no coincidence. The presence of one is related to the presence of the other: where one is found, the other is likely to be found. The relationship can take two forms, positive and negative, both of which exist in Canada:

(1) Since toryism is strongly present in the political culture, at least part of the leftist reaction *against* it will be expressed in its own terms: that is, in terms of *class* interests and the good of the community as an organic entity (socialism) rather than in terms of the individual and his vicissitudes in the competitive struggle (liberalism).

(2) Since the tory and socialist minds have some crucial assumptions and values in common, there is a positive affinity between them. From certain angles they may appear not as enemies, but as two different expressions of the same outlook. This helps to explain the Canadian phenomenon of the *red tory*. At the simplest level, he is a tory who prefers the socialists to the liberals, or a socialist who prefers the tories to the liberals, without really knowing why. At a higher level, he is a conscious ideological tory with some 'odd' socialist notions (R. B. Bennett, Alvin Hamilton) or a conscious ideological socialist with some 'odd' tory notions (Eugene Forsey). At the very highest level, he is a philosopher who combines elements of socialism and of toryism so thoroughly in a single integrated Weltanschauung that it is impossible to say that he is a proponent of either one or the other. Such a red tory is George Grant.

George Grant is a scion of the Loyalists. The nation he laments is the British-Ontarian nation which is now being absorbed into the culture of Michigan and New York. The dying values he mourns are the values of stability, order, tradition. He does not care for the United States because it is liberal. He loves dying Canada because it is conservative. The death of Canada, he says, is the death of conservatism. It is an inevitable death; conservatism, and therefore Canada, are impossible in the modern world.

George Grant is also a socialist, a radical critic of the power elite of corporate capitalism, who would replace this society of competition and inequality with the co-operative commonwealth. He mourns the dying values of tradition and order, but he also mourns the unborn value of equality. The Grant who wrote *Lament for a Nation* is the same Grant who wrote the keynote article ('An Ethic of Community') in *Social Purpose for Canada*. The Grant who dedicated his new book to the Drew-loving columnist Judith Robinson and the Roblinite Conservative Derek Bedson is the same Grant who was an intellectual founding father of the New Democratic Party.

For Grant, socialism is a variant of conservatism. Socialism, like conservatism, uses 'public power to achieve national purposes. The Conservative party . . . after all, created Ontario Hydro, the C.N.R., the Bank of Canada, the C.B.C. . . .' And he reminds us that the tory founders of Ontario Hydro wrapped themselves in the Union Jack to keep the development of electric power out of the hands of grasping private enterprise.

To Grant socialism, like conservatism, is a teleological philosophy: it is based on a doctrine of good, or happiness, a conception of an essential human nature which men are either prevented from realizing, or made to realize, by their social arrangements. Such a conception involves the notion that 'there are ways of life in which men are fulfilled and others in which they are not'. It therefore implies the restraint of certain forms of human freedom, the discipline of certain human passions, which prevent the realization of the good life in the good society. Conservatism is 'essentially the social doctrine that public order and tradition, in contrast to freedom and experiment, were central to the good life'. Socialism is 'the use of the government to restrain greed in the name of social good'. It appeals to the conservative idea of social order against the liberal idea of freedom.

Liberalism, on the other hand, is the doctrine of open-ended progress. It has no conception of an essential human nature which *ought* to be realized; it denies any conception of good which imposes limits on our freedom to make anything we want of our human nature. It does not tolerate the limitation of human action by any idea of good. In the nineteenth century it liberated individuals to exploit one another on the free market without governmental restraint; the passion emancipated was the passion of greed. In the twentieth century, it takes the form of unchecked technological progress, *mastery* of human and non-human nature becomes an end in itself. Liberal ideology is the 'end of ideology' – experimentation in the shaping of society is to be uninhibited by any preconceived notion of good. Good is whatever technological progress happens to produce. Liberal freedom is the 'freedom to change any order that stands in the way of technological advance'. The passion emancipated is the passion to innovate. Automation, for example, is not controlled in order to prevent evil. Nor is it used to create a good society. It is allowed to take its course. The liberal is not willing to stop it, to control it, or to use it for good; he is willing only to make some gestures of alleviation of the suffering it creates, after the fact.

Conservatism in both its pre-capitalist and socialist forms blocks progress with its old-fashioned pre-conceived ideas of good; therefore, says Grant, it is doomed. Nothing can stand in the way of technological advance. Canada is worth preserving because its culture contains illiberal, un-American streams of toryism and socialism. But Canada cannot be preserved because 'end of ideology' technological liberalism, based in the United States, inevitably 'universalizes' and 'homogenizes', eliminates all differences, destroys what it cannot absorb. All 'indigenous' cultures must fall before the all-consuming international liberal (American) culture.

For Grant, the disappearance of English Canada is primarily the result of a change in the economic motivations of our corporate elite and their bureaucratic allies. The Canadian economy once consisted chiefly of the extraction of raw materials for export to Europe together with some secondary industry operating behind high tariff walls. The economic elite of Montreal and Toronto were the pillars of toryism, of nationalism, and of the British connection. The nation was safe because the economic motives of the elite were served by their nationalist-tory-British ideology. Their economic and ideological motives coincided so as to make Canada possible.

Two events occurring more or less simultaneously broke the connection between economic and ideological motivation:

1. Britain ceased to be a world power. She was no longer a powerful economic force pulling trade eastward, nor a powerful cultural and political force providing an 'alternative pull' to that of the United States.

2. The American economy began to expand into Canada. The Canadian capitalists found that they could 'make more money by being the representatives of American capitalism and setting up branch plants'. 'The wealthy rarely maintain their nationalism when it is in conflict with the economic drive of the day.' 'Capitalism is, after all, a way of life based on the principle that the most important activity is profit-making. That activity led the wealthy in the direction of continentalism. They lost nothing essential to the principle of their lives in losing their country. . . . When everything is relative to profit-making, all traditions of virtue are dissolved, including that aspect of virtue known as love of country.'

Once the tie between economics and ideology was broken, the economic elite began to lose its toryism, its Britishness, and its nationalism. 'The wealthy of Canada ceased to be connected with their British past.' The 'older Canadianism disappeared first in Toronto and Montreal, cities that once prided themselves on being most British.' The Canadian economic elite 'developed into a northern extension' of the American, looking 'across the border for its final authority in both politics and culture'. American control need not express itself in the form of direct pressure, for 'the dominant classes of Canada see themselves at one with the continent.' American capital 'incarnates itself as an indigenous ruling class'. Canada becomes an extension of American society, for 'branch plant economies have branch plant cultures.'

These changes coincided with a shift of the economic elite's political weight from the Conservative to the Liberal party. The immediate cause of the shift was R. B. Bennett's red tory programme of social legislation. But the business-Liberal alliance was solidified by the Liberals' readiness to serve as the 'political instrument of the Canadian establishment'. The policy of the alliance was to facilitate the expansion of the American economy into Canada. King and Howe presided over the disappearance of English Canada. The Liberal, the 'anti-national', party 'openly announced that our resources were at the disposal of continental capitalism.'

Some of the old pro-British ruling class maintained the strength of the Conservative party in Ontario for a while, and the old ideology is *still* alive in certain segments of the Conservative party, but it is sputtering to its death. For the Conservative wealthy, like the Liberal wealthy, cannot resist the 'economic drive of the day'. The continentalist elite now expresses itself through *both* the Liberal party and the anti-Diefenbaker wing of the Conservative party. Ontario Conservatism is becoming Americanized.

The Diefenbaker phenomenon was the last gasp of a confused, bewildered Canadian nationalism, rooted in the small towns which are slowest to adjust themselves to a changing society. Diefenbaker's heart was pure, says Grant, his nationalism strong and genuine. His sincerity is proved by his behaviour in the Defence Crisis of 1963, when he sacrificed political advantage to make 'the strongest stand against satellite status that any Canadian government ever attempted', and 'maintained that stand even when the full power of the Canadian ruling class, the American government, and the military was brought to bear against him. . . . It took the full weight of the North American establishment to bring him down.' In manuscript, the subtitle of Grant's book was not 'The Defeat of Canadian Nationalism', but 'In Defence of John Diefenbaker'. Grant is 'saddened by the failure of Diefenbaker', but 'sickened by the shouts of sophisticated derision at his defeat'. Those who mocked him and destroyed him are the establishment, 'the wealthy and the clever' whose real loyalty is to the 'homogenized culture of the American Empire'. They hated him because his conception of Canada as a sovereign state was incompatible with their allegiance to the United States.

Grant's message seems to be that English Canada is dying because the only remaining nationalists – Conservatives of the Diefenbaker stripe – are tied, despite their populism, to a free-enterprise ideology which prevents them from using socialist policies for nationalist reasons.

What then of Canada's social democrats? Why does Grant not look to them for the socialist-nationalist policies which alone can save Canada? Part of Grant's answer is that Canada's socialists are not nationalist enough, that they do not understand the need for a strong link between nationalism and socialism. They are 'good-natured utopians', themselves somewhat affected by the pull of continentalism, too much inclined to play the role of 'left-wing allies of the Liberals'.

But Grant's primary reason for his lack of faith or hope in Canadian socialism is that he lacks faith and hope, period. His determinism is overpowering, his pessimism uncompromising. Not only English Canada, but French Canada (despite the socialist policies of Lévesque and his followers), Britain herself, and *all* un-American cultures the world over must inevitably be absorbed into an American world-culture.

But Grant's pessimism is unreasonable. It is unreasonable because it *identifies* the inevitability of technological progress with the inevitable failure of any attempt to control and use it for human purposes. *Must* Yugoslavia and Sweden and Japan and Australia all end up as replicas of the United States? Surely there are grounds for arguing that they need not. Many cultures are becoming modernized, and in *that* sense Americanized, more like the United States than they were before; but these cultures, because they have histories which differentiate them from the United States, will remain in significant respects un-American. English Canada *may* be such a culture. A conservative should realize that Americanization does not work on a *tabula rasa*. The past cannot be entirely erased. Grant's doctrine of inevitability is unreasonable, finally, because all arguments of inevitability are dubious and ought therefore to be avoided both in prognoses and in programmes of action.

Grant's pessimism and determinism exude death. They ought to be rejected. Once they are rejected, he has a vital lesson to teach.

The existence of Canada was, in the past, guaranteed by the nationalism of our economic elite. They have abandoned nationalism, and are therefore twice cursed: for being an economic elite and for being anti-national. If Canada is to remain in existence, the nation-building role must now be played by forces other than those of entrenched wealth – popular forces with democratic socialist leaders who know where they are going. *English Canada needs a Lévesque.*

Canadian social democrats must become wholehearted nationalists. This involves a recognition that they have – for certain purposes – more in common with uncorrupted conservative nationalism of the Alvin Hamilton type than with Americanized Liberals and Liberalized Conservatives.

Canadian socialism can become the only political force in Canada that combines both nationalisms with a readiness to implement the only type of policy which can save both nations. In English and French Canada as in all small nations, socialism and nationalism require one another.

English Canada is not worth preserving unless it can be different from the United States. Our British past provides the foundations for building on the northern half of this continent a social democratic order (let Canadians call it conservative if they wish) *better* than the liberal society of the United States. A tory past contains the seeds of a socialist future.

[1965]

IX
The Past

John Porter
André Laurendeau
William Kilbourn
William Morton
Melville Watkins

John Porter

Conservatism: The Deep Bond in an Embattled Marriage

French–English dualism in Canadian life has been considered its most important characteristic throughout its history. Lord Durham spoke in his famous report of over one hundred years ago of two nations warring in the bosom of a single state. In 1965, the Royal Commission on Bilingualism and Biculturalism stated that Canada was 'passing through the greatest crisis in its history', a crisis which 'if it should persist and gather momentum could destroy Canada'. The ever-present hostility and jealousy between the two groups, expressed perhaps more by institutional leaders than by large segments of the population, have resulted in great emphasis on the retention of things as they are, and have contributed to the conservatism of Canadian life.

In the twentieth century, with large-scale immigration from continental Europe, the dualism became pluralism, as various groups were encouraged to retain their European identities within a Canadian 'mosaic'. Perhaps because of its place in the British Empire and after 1931 in the British Commonwealth, there never has been in Canada, as in the United States, a strong commitment to the creation of a new nation, a new ethnicity. Nor has there been, in the schools of English Canada at least, the presentation of Canadian history as the unfolding of a great human experiment. Hence, children have not been exposed to strong doses of national sentiment. To be Canadian is not likely to evoke a set of feelings or images about belonging to a particular group with a clear beginning, a set of charter values, a history, and an imagined destiny. Undoubtedly, most Canadians will have some private or ethnic-group view about these things, but it is unlikely that, as a people, they will have an *idée fixe*

263

about their society. There seem to be no overwhelmingly dominant cultural goals such as the pursuit of happiness, progress, equality, or opportunity. There is certainly no rejection of the 'European father' that Geoffrey Gorer saw as a dominant element in American character.

It would be in keeping with the prevailing attitudes about Canadian dualism to treat the French and English groups separately and to show how each – as separate nations, as the French have recently been insisting that they are – have their own peculiar character. Yet, two large groups cannot have lived together in a system of ordered relationships for two hundred years without affecting each other's way of life in some respects. There may be an analogy in this situation to the conflict-habituated marriage, where husband and wife manage to survive an antagonistic union and where the antagonistic relationship in time affects their personalities. Perhaps both groups have a deeply rooted conservatism which has placed them only marginally within the influence of North American values.

One reason why it is difficult to generalize about Canadian national character is Canada's demographic history which, in the absence of comparative studies, appears to be peculiar and inimical to the growth of strong collective sentiments or a common personality system. Where population growth oscillates between very rapid and very slow rates, and sometimes becomes static, where emigration is always high and where immigration depends on the fortunes of the economic cycle, the question arises whether there can be any stable group which holds the collective sentiments of the nation. A strongly held set of beliefs or a basic personality structure would seem to require a relatively stable population or one with relatively stable rates of growth over some considerable time. Shared culture and shared habits are broken up, or never get established, where demographic trends are erratic. There is clearly a difference in this respect between older, established societies in Europe and those which have been created by populating vast vacant regions. Canada and Australia might make an interesting comparison. Both have depended on immigration for economic development at particular times, but it is very unlikely that Australia has been subject to population loss through emigration, as has Canada. European societies, with their long histories and firmly rooted traditions, can experience considerable emigration, and even the frontier surgery of generations of peacemakers, without losing traditional values and behaviour patterns.

Between 1851 and 1951 Canada lost almost as many people through emigration as it gained from immigration. An estimated 7·1 million arrived during this period, and an estimated 6·6 million left. Between 1951 and 1961 (the decennial census years) immigration has been estimated at about 1·5 million and emigration at ·6 million. These numbers may not seem large, but for a country whose population grew from 2·5 million in 1851 to 18 million in 1961, they represent a sizable proportion of the population, particularly when it is considered that in the present century it has been the non-French part of the population which has participated in the migration process. Thus, at any time, many people in Canada have been either newcomers or potential migrants. This demographic condition should be looked at in the light of the doctrine of ethnic pluralism and the toned-down sentiment about a Canadian identity. Under these circumstances neither the newcomers nor their children will be socialized to specifically Canadian values. Nor will there be any particular normative pressures on the potential migrants to stay. If this particular interpretation has any validity, it is difficult to see how a coherent set of traditions, values, and behaviour can emerge.

The absence or weakness of national symbols puzzles many newcomers, particularly those from non-British territories, who want to make a home for themselves and who look for a national symbol system for orientation and a sense of having arrived in a new home.

It is possible that the emigration from Canada reinforces the conservatism of Canadian life. The evidence suggests that it is the younger age groups who move out. The quality that is lost in this way is not known. Are they the most able, the most adaptable, those with the most initiative, those with the most leadership potential, or are they the failures, the weaklings lured by what they feel is an easier life to the south? If they are the former, then the conservative mould of Canadian society becomes more firmly set. In addition to international migration, there has been a high degree of internal migration. Here, too, the older generation stays behind to exercise a conservative influence at the level of regional and community power.

Canadian poets have been found to express a melancholy, a feeling of resignation to misery, isolation, and the feeling that man is, in Robert L. McDougall's words, 'encompassed by forces beyond his ability to control which strike out repeatedly and blindly to destroy him'. Mr. McDougall's assessment of Canadian fiction is similar:

> The representative figure of Canadian fiction is not the innocent Adam, nor yet the Adam of the fortunate fall who is triumphant even in defeat at the hands of the alien tribe – as for example are Melville's Billy Budd or the Joads in Steinbeck's *The Grapes of Wrath*. Nor is he, like Dorothea Brooke in George Eliot's *Middlemarch,* the figure made strong and capable of extended life by voluntary renunciation.
>
> These are positive; our archetype is negative.
>
> In our literature, heroic action remains possible, but becomes so deeply tinged with futility that withdrawal becomes a more characteristic response than commitment. The representative images are those of denial and defeat rather than fulfillment and victory.

Moreover, Canadian literary themes have little social reference. Plots do not deal with the clash of social forces, social progress, social equality, or the achieving of upward social mobility.

It is very tempting to trace these cultural themes of negativism, lack of commitment, withdrawal from social issues, and a feeling of resignation, through the social development of Canada: periods of economic stagnation, the ever-present crisis in English-French relations, religious bickering, and the constant efforts by some to retain a Canada that will not be absorbed by the overwhelming power of its neighbour to the south. The last is frequently expressed as a fear of being 'swallowed up', an image that might be a clue to a collective Canadian anxiety. It is interesting that, in the mid-1960s, at the end of 20 years of enormous economic growth, when Canada achieved a standard of living – at least according to the statistical measures used – second only to the United States, and at a time when Canada was approaching its centenary, there should be an open season, not for rejoicing, but for lamenting the state of national affairs. In *Lament for a Nation* George Grant wrote: 'To lament is to cry out at the death or the dying of something loved. This lament mourns the end of Canada as a sovereign state. . . . We find ourselves like fish left on the shores of a drying lake.' For him, the tragedy is Canada's failure to create a society of tradition and order which would be clearly differentiated from the homogenized industrial culture of the United States. As Robert Blumstock said in his review:

> To Grant, the 'Good Society' is apparently one in which there is a high order of control over action, control in the sense of being determined by a belief in certain immutable truths. . . . His 'Lament' is a decrying of experimentation and flexibility in human affairs.

Despair at the failure of the conservative experiment in North America is an interesting convergence of two elements in the Canadian character, and seems to underlie the lack of social relevance in the Canadian political system. In modern nations, national goals and values are expressed and debated by political parties and political leaders. The political system operates to mobilize the social effort toward the achievement of social goals. The core values of modern nations can be expressed collectively through their politics. But a lack of dynamic polity can be traced to the lack of commitment of the two major political parties which have governed Canada since its beginning in 1867. No one has expressed this lack of commitment more than Mackenzie King, who was the Liberal party, for all intents and purposes, for 30 years. J. W. Pickersgill, himself a Liberal cabinet minister and editor of King's diaries, wrote: 'Mackenzie King genuinely believed and frequently said that the real secret of political leadership was more in what was prevented than what was accomplished.' Ideology did not end in Canada. It simply did not begin.

Tempting as it is to show how literary themes are a reflection of Canada's social and political history, the exercise can be misleading, because Canadian literature can have meaning for only a very small proportion of the population. Canadians are overwhelmingly and enthusiastically consumers of United States culture, both popular and high.

Despite the difficulties presented by the existence of strong ethnic pluralism, migration, cultural contamination from the United States, and the general absence of satisfactory data, there have been many attempts to outline the qualities of the Canadian character. The American sociologist S. M. Lipset has concluded that Canadians are conservative, authoritarian, oriented to tradition, hierarchy, and elitism in the sense of showing deference to those in high status. Canadian values have been shaped by a distinct anti-revolutionary past which contrasts with the strong egalitarianism of the United States, with its emphasis on opportunity and personal achievement as the basis of social rewards.

It would be difficult to disagree with Lipset. The slow manner of democratizing educational systems is one example of how Canada diverges from the egalitarian model. In Canada in 1961 only 6 per cent of the male labour force aged 25 to 34 years had university degrees, compared to 14·7 per cent in the United States. Canada has been far behind other countries in developing tertiary levels of education and removing financial barriers to them.

English and French Canadians are more alike in their conservatism, traditionalism, religiosity, authoritarianism, and elitist values than the spokesmen of either group are prepared to admit. They have been drawn together in a mutual defence of these cultural elements in North America, and some of the more articulate of them look out on a world of social change, including the Americanization of their own society, with much the same ambivalence and fear. Conservatism is, of course, a general quality of all social structure, because behaviour patterns are habitual, but in modern industrial societies there is also, in the interests of adaptability, a readiness for change, a readiness which may be stronger in elites than in the mass of the population. In Canada this conservatism characterizes elites as well as the mass of the population and pervades most of its institutions to a greater degree than in the United States.

In all the present concern for biculturalism we might raise the question if, after all, there is not a single culture in Canada in which the core values are conservative, and on the matter of lesser values the French and the English are subcultural variants. One can only plead again the almost total absence of data with which to provide profiles of major or minor value patterns. It is not yet possible to tell, in the still unfolding North American experiment as a whole, whether the French and the English will together follow the egalitarian model of the United States, or whether their conservatism will prevail.

[1967]

André Laurendeau

"Le Canada tout entier" of Henri Bourassa

Abridged by the editor from "Henri Bourassa" in *Canada's Past and Present: A Dialogue*, Our Living Tradition, fourth series, edited by Robert I. McDougall, University of Toronto Press, 1962.

Bourassa was part and parcel of my childhood: not that I knew him personally at the time, but I had been told his story, and his struggles seemed to me like the struggles of a paladin. He had been knighted by God Almighty to defend French Canadians against the injustices of Great Britain and of the various Canadian governments. Often vanquished, but always proud, always noble, always alert, his feats as a speaker began to look like veritable military campaigns. He had remained for French Canadians – and often in spite of opportunists of his own race, such as Laurier – the living rampart, the spotless and exacting hero fully dedicated to his one task. I often dreamt of this when I was a child.

Later I learned that the man I heard people speak of in these terms, the very man who was a legendary figure in the minds of boys of my age, that man was still alive. He edited a newspaper called *Le Devoir*. In 1925 he re-entered federal politics and was re-elected as the member for Labelle. At that time, like all youths of my age, I was only beginning to awaken to the political issues of the hour. Suddenly we became young men, and neither Bourassa nor many of the nationalists of the heyday of nationalism resembled the mental image we had formed of them.

Amongst these, Bourassa at least differed from the image in one important way. He proclaimed to us a nationalism that was Canadian first and foremost. He seemed to attack French-Canadian nationalism and its new representatives more willingly than he did the traditional British adversary. This became increasingly evident as the years went by. The Great Depression came, and the

French Canadians were compelled to do some thinking. For them, radicalism found expression not in socialism but in a fierce nationalism mixed with strong demands for social and economic reform. And who became one of its most formidable adversaries? None other than Henri Bourassa.

Had we not been told the truth about him? It was said that Bourassa had had a change of heart, and a variety of reasons were given for this: a bad case of scruples, a severe reprimand from the Pope in 1926, political isolation, perhaps just a taste for contradiction. We therefore began to see the life of Bourassa as divided into two parts. There was the life of the fascinating hero who had begun a movement which we were to continue after him; and there was the life of the man who had returned from Rome completely changed, lost to us, who spoke only of religious duty and Canadian patriotism, and who set out boldly to cut down the harvest he had sown.

Such images do not satisfy the mind for long; in the end I found them too simple.

A word about Bourassa's life. He was the son of an artist, Napoléon Bourassa, and of the youngest daughter of Louis-Joseph Papineau – the famous Papineau, the leader of the *patriotes,* the rebel of 1837. He was born in 1868 in the very heart of Montreal. His education was sound enough, though somewhat irregular; he did not even get as far as his bachelor's degree. A sick man at the age of twenty, he moved to Montebello, where his grandfather had been *seigneur,* and there examined its every nook and cranny and became acquainted with its inhabitants. He won their love and respect. At the age of twenty-one he was elected mayor, and he was soon taking an active part in federal politics. In 1896 Laurier asked him to seek election in Labelle. He won the seat, and won it under the most auspicious circumstances: his leader, who had just assumed power, wished to groom him for more important functions.

But Bourassa was no slavish partisan, and as early as 1899 he had parted company with Laurier because of Canadian participation in the Boer War, the beginning of the anti-imperialist campaign he was to follow right up to 1944. He objected to the automatic participation of Canada in imperial wars.

What Bourassa demanded was an authentic autonomy of action for our country, a liberty of choice for Canadians who are, first and foremost, Canadians.

Laurier was wise enough to allow his 'young and adamant friend' to be re-elected by acclamation. In 1904 he founded the 'Ligue nationaliste'. He took part in all the debates in favour of schools for the minorities. Then he turned to provincial politics and launched several campaigns – notably, one against trusts – which were later to mark the beginning of more permanent movements. Provincial politics, however, proved unable to hold him for long. Frequent trips to Europe kept him abreast of international developments and convinced him that the situation was deteriorating. He therefore returned to the federal field.

K

Bourassa now had a powerful weapon for combat: *Le Devoir,* a daily newspaper which he founded in 1910 and around which he gathered a team of brilliant men. He was entering the best years of his life. In January he delivered in Notre Dame Church, during a Eucharistic Congress, a famous speech in which practically every French Canadian of the day could recognize himself. Elsewhere he increased his efforts against imperialism, though this did not hinder him from eulogizing Edward VII as the 'serviteur vigilant et dévoué de ses peuples'. Bourassa opposed Laurier's naval policy, because he saw it as one more gesture that might drag Canada, should conditions prove favourable, into the wars of Great Britain.

In 1910, in the by-election for Drummond-Arthabaska, his candidate defeated Laurier's. Bourassa was unleashed; it was the moment of his greatest power. He was not a cabinet minister, nor a party leader, nor even a member of parliament; yet his influence alone, against Laurier, sufficed during the general elections of 1911 to elect twenty-seven Conservatives or Independents. Defeated in nearly every province, Laurier handed over the government to Borden.

When war broke out, Bourassa had just returned from Europe. He hesitated briefly, and then, much against his better judgment, he accepted the principle of participation – which, however, he wanted to keep moderate. To rabid loyalists, such moderation looked like treason. An Ontario newspaper demanded Bourassa's arrest.

Then came conscription and the Union Cabinet. Laurier, doubtless in order to avoid leaving Quebec to Bourassa, refused to join it – a stand which earned him a complete victory in Quebec but a defeat in all the other provinces. Bourassa fought conscription violently before it was voted on; when it became law, he astonished everyone by his restraint and moderation.

The war over, Bourassa remained a fascinating figure. He played an important role in Ottawa as a member of parliament from 1925 to 1935, where he gave his opinion (and it was an opinion that carried considerable weight) on all major issues. But he was no longer the embodiment of the spirit of his people. It was at this time that he broke with the French-Canadian nationalists and began to denounce 'leurs excès' – and I shall have more to say about this later. Having left *Le Devoir* in 1932, he lived in relative retirement, separated from the nationalists, his natural allies, until he joined them again in 1942, at the age of seventy-four, to fight Mackenzie King over the conscription issue and to support the Bloc Populaire. It was then only that I knew him personally. He died in 1952, more or less forgotten by the younger generation; yet his name remained the object of universal admiration. Michael Oliver, who has studied the work of Bourassa rather closely, considers this aristocrat the precursor, in some respects, of a French-Canadian leftist movement.

When Bourassa proclaims that he is first a Canadian, his Canadianism, it must be noted, does not float between heaven and earth. There were simply for him two ways of living it: one French and one English. 'La patrie' is for him 'le

Canada tout entier'. He believes in the Canadian nation but sees it composed of French Canadians and English Canadians – 'c'est-à-dire de deux éléments séparés [the word is strong] par la langue et la religion, et par les dispositions légales nécessaires à la conservation de leurs traditions.' Canadian patriotism is therefore not a renunciation but an extension of the love one bears one's own. 'Canadian' means, above all else, the acceptance of one group by the other, with the legitimate sacrifices that any marriage must entail.

Bourassa was in fact always guided by the same spirit, whether he spoke in French or in English. Even when his theme led him to use harsh words against English Canadians, the tone was never one of rupture. He denounced racial prejudice wherever he found it – even within his audiences, which he often reprimanded.

When the drama of conscription took place, at the very hour when people from Ontario and certain westerners sought his arrest, was it not moving to hear him say, as though he were unaware of what he saw only too well, as though he were immersed in his idealism and his dream of Canadianism:

> J'appartiens à l'école, moins nombreuse qu'on ne le pense, qui voit plus d'avantages que d'inconvénients dans la co-existence des deux races au Canada. Avec un nombre plus restreint encore, j'estime que le Canada tout entier bénéficiera de cette situation et recevra des deux races le maximum de leur apport au patrimoine politique, intellectuel et moral de la nation, dans l'exacte mesure où chacune d'elles restera le plus complètement elle-même.
>
> [*La Conscription*, 1917, p. 20]

> En dépit des désenchantements du passé et des sombres perspectives d'avenir, il faut penser et agir comme s'il était encore possible de faire une patrie canadienne, de créer un patriotisme national. Quelle que soit la destinée prochaine ou lointaine du Canada et de la province de Québec, tout effort persévérant pour maintenir ou faire revivre les conditions de l'accord de 1865 aura sa pleine valeur.
>
> [*La presse catholique et nationale*, 1921]

Thus Bourassa went so far as to doubt – which is, if I may say so, the method of lucid idealists. To do as if, to act as if despite the pressure of the facts the dream could still come true. It is perhaps the only way to make the dream come true.

He was possessed by a pride that took offence easily. No power, except the Church and his own convictions, ever made him bend. He claimed that people accepted him as he was – and he was a French Canadian, bound to his own.

Bourassa belonged to his environment; he accepted and loved it, even though he judged and whipped it. The pettiness of our politicians has never been scourged so harshly as by him. Our intellectual destitution, the rancidness of our small provincial gatherings, these he soon detected, and obviously they disgusted him. He loved the affairs of French Canada as one loves one's family, though I think he found them rather narrow.

French-Canadian tradition was anti-imperialist, and for this reason Bourassa was to find the bulk of his followers in Quebec. On this point he got along well with French-Canadian nationalists. But the securing of Canadian independence tended to become, from the human standpoint, his primary motive, and this incited him to seek closer ties with English Canadians. He had been quick to understand that we cannot acquire independence if French Canadians and English Canadians spend all their time squabbling: emancipation implied a strong degree of Canadian unity. Here begins, perhaps, his break with French-Canadian nationalists, who are that only or principally that.

When events proved to this high-strung man that French-Canadian minorities could not obtain justice anywhere – whether in Manitoba, Saskatchewan, Alberta, Ontario, or New Brunswick – would there not be a natural temptation to break with the federal régime? Bourassa, however, never seems to have seriously considered this hypothesis. No matter how strongly he asserted his French Canadianism, he had chosen to be Canadian and could not see how it could be otherwise.

But the attitude of French-Canadian nationalism is also quite understandable. A new separatist thrust came in the wake of Bourassa's action, after his battles in favour of minorities – none of which, it must be remembered, had been fully victorious, or at least had not been to that moment. The disciples, consciously or not, took note of these failures, and their drift towards separatism took root in despair. They had in large measure lost faith in the capacity of Confederation to render justice, in its ability to function smoothly, and finally in the very idea of a Canadianism now considered exclusively English-Canadian. They no longer saw how French Canada could live freely in the midst of Canada; and they were at the same time convinced that Canada, a geographical absurdity, and the British Empire, alike divided by internal forces of dissension, could not long survive post-war readjustments. But Bourassa himself always refused to despair.

We seem to be left with a paradox. Here is a man who unceasingly held for 'les siens' an obvious preferential love, yet who was at the same time a founder of Canadian nationalism and who took the French-Canadian nationalist movement as one of his favourite targets.

Bourassa's contradictions come principally from the type of double allegiance that he had accepted from the outset – that is, from the fact that he refused to be only a Canadian, or only a French Canadian. He had decided from the beginning to be both intensely. And so quite often he seems to contradict himself – not in spite of reason, but to a large extent because he is logical.

'The point about Bourassa,' a professor at the University of Toronto has just written to one of my friends, 'is that he does not belong to French Canada alone.' Through his struggles, Bourassa belongs to the whole of Canada. He is a magnificent example of a Canadian: he is the man who rejects all forms of slavery, but who accepts all forms of loyalty. His dedication to Canada was not prefaced by his surrender as a French Canadian. He is a man who sits at the common table but who does not choose to let himself be forgotten. He wants to be welcomed, not exploited, and he wants to be accepted as he is, in the same way that he himself loyally accepts his partner. Such is, I believe, the nationalism of Bourassa which divided his contemporaries but which will contribute to uniting Canadians of today.

[1962]

William Kilbourn

Two Styles of Historian: Donald Creighton and Frank Underhill

'The phrase "literary historian" does not mean someone with a talent for turning an occasional pleasing trope to decorate the collected facts' but rather 'the historian who saw the body of his subject while still it lay scattered in unorganized source materials; who re-created the body by re-animating the form it required.' In these words, from *The American Adam*, R. W. B. Lewis might easily have been describing Donald Creighton. In his first three works, *The Empire of the St. Lawrence, Dominion of the North*, and the Macdonald biography, Creighton's subject forms itself around the central image of the river – the river of Canada – and the hero who grasped its meaning and embarked upon the immense journey to possess and subdue the inland kingdom to which the river was the key:

It was the one great river which led from the eastern shore into the heart of the continent. It possessed a geographical monopoly; and it shouted its uniqueness to adventurers. The river meant mobility and distance; it invited journeyings; it promised immense expanses, unfolding, flowing away into remote and changing horizons. The whole west, with all its riches, was the dominion of the river. To the unfettered and ambitious, it offered a pathway to the central mysteries of the continent . . . from the river there rose, like an exhalation, the dream of western commercial empire. The dream runs like an obsession through the whole of Canadian history; and men followed each other through life, planning and toiling to achieve it. The river was not only a great actuality: it was the central truth of a religion. Men lived by it, at once consoled and inspired by its promises, its whispered suggestions,

274

and its shouted commands; and it was a force in history, not merely because of its accomplishments, but because of its shining, ever-receding possibilities.

Whether the hero's name was Cartier or Mackenzie, Champlain or Simon McTavish, some half-remembered merchant or nameless *coureur de bois*, whether his journey and his mastery were mainly one of stout limb and heart or one of the willing imagination, it mattered little; in the hero's act of penetration and possession of the land of the St. Lawrence there lay the central secret of Canadian history.

The first Canadian statesman to be caught in the Laurentian spell was the great seventeenth-century Intendant of New France, Jean Talon:

> Talon began it. No doubt he had gone out to Canada with his head full of neat, orderly Colbertian assumptions about the future of New France. His first term was almost exemplary. He planned some model villages at Charlesbourg. He built a brewery. He was busy encouraging shipbuilding, hemp production, and manufacture. And yet, almost from the beginning, something began to happen to him. He started writing the oddest letters back to Colbert. He dilated upon the vast extent of the country. He urged the capture of New York. He assured the King that 'nothing can prevent us from carrying the name and arms of his Majesty as far as Florida. . . .' These curious effusions, with their hints of suppressed excitement and their sudden vistas of gigantic empires, surprised and perplexed the minister at home. . . . Colbert made the prudent comment 'Wait' on the margin of one of Talon's most intemperate suggestions. . . . Talon ought to have been impressed by it, but he was scarcely aware of the rebuke. He had suddenly become conscious of the river and of the enormous continent into which it led. He had yielded to that instinct for grandeur, that vertigo of ambition, that was part of the enchantment of the St. Lawrence.

The St. Lawrence had a rival, however, and in the end it did not bring its heroes the possession of the entire continent. 'Something stood between the design and its fulfilment.' 'Two worlds lay over against each other in North America. . . . Of their essence, the St. Lawrence and the seaboard denied each other. Riverways against seaways, rock against farm land, trading posts against ports and towns and cities, *habitants* against farmers and fur traders against frontiersmen – they combined, geography and humanity, in one prime contradiction.' Creighton's first book was the story of the frustration of the original grand design. By his choice of a beginning and end date for his subject (one of the few choices that the historian as artist possesses), Creighton managed to suggest the pattern of tragedy in the story of the empire of the St. Lawrence between the Conquest and the end of the Second British Empire in 1850. His *Dominion of the North* told in longer perspective of the three centuries of rivalry between the rich seaboard colonies, who rebelled and made a nation of the southern temperate zone of the continent, and the proud Judah of the north, which stubbornly held to its original Laurentian and imperial destiny. Creighton's masterpiece, the biography of Sir John A. Macdonald, celebrated the greatest but also the most practical of the Laurentian heroes, the statesman who gave to the northern kingdom the political frame which its nature and economy and history had so long demanded.

Creighton's was a tale of vast dimensions, and he did not shrink from telling it in the grand manner. But rarely after his first book was there the least sign of rhetorical overwriting. He had the natural gifts of the story-teller. He could change the pace and mood of his narrative without losing any of its power. He deliberately prepared his climaxes, and he made it a rule never to cast ahead in analysing the aspects of a given moment in time and so lose both the suspense of the story and the feel of the actual historical moment. He had a poignant sense of the place and an ability to describe in loving sensual detail the homely pastoral landscape of picnic and country fair or the most formal of state occasions. Rarely, but with telling effect, would he break away from the quiet clear development of the details of a political story to illuminate it with some stark dramatic juxtaposition of natural to human catastrophe: 'On a night in early September, 1883, a black and killing frost descended out of a still, autumnal sky on the wheat crop of the north-west . . . before the autumn was out, the depression, like a sinister grey familiar, returned to haunt the Dominion.'

Creighton varied with great care the construction and length of sentences and paragraphs. He was particularly fond of the spare simple sentence at the beginning of a chapter ('In those days they came usually by boat.' 'It was his day if it was anybody's.'), followed by a longer sentence describing, explaining, carrying forward the narrative. These openings always made some precise historical point, but, more important, they were his own unmistakable way of casting a spell, his manner of saying 'Once upon a time.'

Creighton's brief history *The Story of Canada* is a fine example of his narrative style. Cartier's departure from St. Malo, Champlain's first encounter with the Iroquois, the capture of Quebec, the rebellions of Mackenzie and Riel, are all succinctly and dramatically recreated. The book is a gallery of character sketches, a *commedia* of persons captured in the description of a telling gesture or feature. One powerful sentence brings together two of the central actions of modern Canadian history, and evokes the whole struggle of a dominion linking two oceans and encompassing two cultures in its farflung diversity:

> On November 7th [1885], far out in the mountains, at a spot which Stephen determined must be called Craigellachie in memory of his clan's meeting-place and battle slogan, the bearded Donald Smith drove home the last spike in the railway's transcontinental line; and nine days later, on November 16th, while the autumnal sun rose late over plains which were white with hoar frost, the sprung trap in the Regina prison gave and Riel dropped to his extinction.

In spite of his achievement, there is a sense in which Creighton has appeared somewhat isolated from his contemporaries and from the life of contemporary

Canada. Even his narratives tend to grey and sadden a little as they approach the present. On occasions he has wrapped himself in the mantle of Don Quixote to go tilting at Americans, Establishment Liberals, and the Fabians he took for something far worse. In the face of a philistine world of journalist-historians, and the confident, successful, efficient professionals of the learned societies and graduate schools, he has sometimes responded with Eeyore's gloom and baleful eye.

Yet if anyone has reshaped the tradition of Canadian historical writing it has been Donald Creighton. It is difficult to think of a narrative on a nineteenth-century subject by any of his younger contemporaries in the past decade whose style or structure does not owe him some debt. There are times when one could wish it otherwise. One tires of rather patronizing gestures of consideration for the general reader, of earnest and embarrassing attempts at poetic prose, and of clumsy, inappropriate insertions of little Creightonesque tableaux in the midst of dry recitals of facts. None of Creighton's followers, even at their best, quite show his ability to make use of a broad general culture in their writing. But it is a revealing measure of a writer's true stature if the only major fault to be found in him is that he has too many disciples.

In a sense, it is difficult to conceive of a man whose thinking and writing, whose life style and very being, would stand in sharper contrast to Donald Creighton than Canada's other pre-eminent historian of the mid-twentieth century, Frank Underhill. Born in 1889, thirteen years before Creighton, a Clear Grit from that North York farm country beyond the ridges which supplied the Mackenzie rebellion with its best recruits, he has been for almost forty years the chief gadfly of the Family Compact's spiritual descendants and of any and all Canadian Establishments, including that liberal-intellectual one which has embraced but never quite smothered or tamed him with its honours and applause. Where Creighton was a scholar and an artist, the bardic singer celebrating and creating a nation by giving it a past, Underhill was an intellectual, a Socratic teacher, and a Shavian wit. Creighton's chief medium has been the prose narrative of epic dimensions, Underhill's the lecture and the informal essay or review; Underhill has never written a book although his work has been collected in books. Creighton uses several different modes of expression, from that of the ruminative academic to the incantation and the lyric. Underhill's voice never strays far from that of conversation, of clear, simple, brilliant talk.

Creighton's sympathies have been not so much conservative as with the living past itself, and with those great scholars like Harold Innis whom he admired for their refusal to be caught up in intellectual fashions of the day or to turn their history into present politics. Underhill on the other hand attacked the majority of his Canadian academic colleagues 'who lived blameless intellectual lives, cultivated the golden mean and never stuck their necks out'. His historical writing is alive with insights which might never have been gained but for his involvement in the present.

K*

Trained as a classicist at the University of Toronto, a Victorian liberal turned Fabian by three years of pre-war Oxford and the acquaintance of A. D. Lindsay and G. D. H. Cole, Underhill was caught up during the 1920s in the excitement of prairie politics in the halcyon days of the Progressive movement and of his two Canadian heroes, J. S. Woodsworth and John W. Dafoe. In 1933 he became the author of the founding manifesto of Canada's first social democratic party. By the 1950s, while still a sympathetic if pointed critic of the democratic left in Canada, he was 'less interested in the fortunes of political parties as such and more concerned with the climate of opinion . . . which determines to a great extent what parties accomplish or try to accomplish.' He became more and more sceptical of doctrinal political solutions. He wished, a little sadly, that he 'could be as sure about anything as some people I know are about everything.' He compared himself to Huckleberry Finn at the end of his adventures, someone with no political home to go to and needing to light out for the Territory. Certainly much of Underhill's great power as a teacher and a historian came from qualities of candour and humility, gentleness and human sympathy very like those of Huckleberry Finn. But he also had a little of Mark Twain's showman about him. Like George Bernard Shaw he sometimes could be too easily typecast and dismissed as a brilliant clown by the dominions and powers he made fun of. He once compared himself, not altogether inaccurately, to the man who applied to John Morley for a job on the *Pall Mall Gazette* but denied special knowledge of any of a dozen fields Morley named, and when pressed said, 'My specialty is general invective.'

In approaching his central theme, the history of Canadian party politics, Underhill takes the American political tradition for his point of reference. For him, the main agent in the making of Confederation and in Canadian political history since has been a kind of Hamiltonian federalist party. This party has been a coalition of diverse sectional, racial, and religious interests whose chief dynamic has been supplied by the transcontinental drive for power and profit of the big business interests of Toronto and Montreal. For thirty years Macdonald's Conservative party played this role, until it was displaced after 1896 by Laurier's Liberals during the great period of western settlement. A third 'governmental' party forged by Mackenzie King has held power with only two major interruptions from 1921 down to the present day, although in this period the business interests were more divided and more sophisticated than in the era of the Great Barbecue, and the party leadership was no longer so bold and exciting. Underhill recognized a kind of historical necessity in the existence of the first two parties, if the nation was to be built at all. For the last, however, King's party 'of the extreme centre', which effectively dulled the edge of intelligent political debate that made American and British politics so lively, Underhill reserved some of his bitterest attacks. Nevertheless Mackenzie King's very skill in hanging on to power, and his ability to find policies to keep both French and English Canadians together in the same party, in the end won his grudging admiration.

The essential task of Canadian statesmanship is to discover the terms on which as many as possible of the significant interest-groups of our country can be induced to work together in a common policy. . . . Mr. King has been the only political leader of the last generation who has understood [this]. . . . His statesmanship has been a more subtly accurate, a more flexibly adjustable Gallup poll of Canadian public opinion than statisticians will ever be able to devise. He has been the representative Canadian, the typical Canadian, the essential Canadian, the ideal Canadian, the Canadian as he exists in the mind of God.

. . . Mr. King . . . was not the traditional kind of parliamentary leader that you read about in the textbooks. . . . He obviously disliked Parliament. The representative side of democracy he did not find congenial, and he worked out a much more direct but also much more indefinable relationship between himself and the Canadian people. . . . And without any of the apparatus of mass hypnosis and police coercion to which vulgar practitioners of the art like Hitler and Mussolini had to have recourse, he succeeded with hardly a mistake for twenty-five years in giving expression, by way of that curious cloudy rhetoric of his, to what lay in the Canadian sub-conscious mind.

The commonest criticism of Mr. King was that he never gave a definite lead in any direction or committed himself in advance to anything concrete and tangible. . . . But there was one field in which he did . . . – external affairs. And it is in this field that we can now see most clearly that intuitive quality of Mr. King's mind. . . . He grasped what Canadians wanted better than they did themselves, and he was very clear-headed and persistent in moving towards a goal which he saw from the start. . . . He was primarily a North American. He resisted all attempts to make a political or economic or military unit out of the British Commonwealth. . . . Even in the emotional atmosphere of the war he declined all Churchillian invitations into an Imperial War Cabinet. Instead, he was vigorous both in peace and war in strengthening our American ties. . . . He never consulted parliament or people about these steps; he simply kept us informed.

Like King, Underhill was 'primarily a North American'. Yet to develop and maintain the best of the North American democratic tradition in Canada has not been easy; liberalism and the political left have never flourished here. In Underhill's view the oldest and strongest of Canadian traditions from the 'great refusal of 1776' to the Reciprocity issue of 1911 and to the Diefenbaker era, has been 'our determination not to become Americans'. 'We were born saying "No" ' to the Enlightenment and the American Revolution, and for a century and a half we have regularly indulged in outbursts of anti-American feeling and rejected the best that American thought and society has had to offer us. 'But if we allow ourselves to be obsessed by the danger of American cultural annexation, so that the thought preys on us day and night, we shall only become a slightly bigger Ulster. The idea that by taking thought, and with the help of some government subventions, we can become another England – which, one suspects, is Mr. [Vincent] Massey's ultimate idea – is purely fantastic.'   [1965]

William Morton

The Northern Frontier: Key to Canadian History

The northern character springs not only from geographical location, but from ancient origins in the northern and maritime frontier of Europe. That frontier extends from Norway by Scotland and the North Atlantic islands to Greenland and Canada. Within that area from mediaeval to modern times there is discernible a frontier of European culture developing across the northern latitudes in which the forward movement was largely by sea. It was not a Turnerian frontier, but it was a frontier in every sense, and it was this frontier which began the exploitation and settlement of Canada. Many of its characteristics survive in Canada to this day, and presumably will continue to do so indefinitely.

The historical characteristics of this northern and maritime frontier are clear and definite. The most evident was that of coast and river settlement. The largely Precambrian geology of the region afforded few extensive or fertile plains. The shelves in the fjords, the estuaries of seasonal rivers, the terraces around bays, these were the foothold and the baseland the northern frontier afforded to settlement. Even the Laurentian trench in America simply raised the foothold to continental proportions but did not change its character. Moreover, the maritime character of the frontier tended to settlement by the sea, even when extension of the economy inland was possible.

The settlements sometimes consisted of small port towns, but the characteristic mode was the family farmstead. This was the centre of a complex of arable land, pasture, fuel land, and hunting ground much more delicate in its relationships than those of a farmstead in a more favourable climate and a more fertile soil. Land near the stead yielded vegetable and cereal foods, if climate permitted. The outfields and hill pastures gave pasture and hay. The adjoining forests or bogs furnished firewood or peat. The summer was a season of sowing, herding, and gathering in, the winter a season of concentration in house and byre, of relaxation or rationing according to the summer's yield.

The winter was also the season of hunting, whether for food or fur. The northern frontiersman in this lull penetrated the wilderness and used it to supplement the returns of the farmstead. The dependence of any one farmstead or settlement on the hunt varied from place to place, but hunting as a seasonal occupation was always one characteristic of the northern frontier.

Fishing was equally a supplementary occupation to a degree also varying with locality. It too furnished an addition to the diet, and even forage for the cattle. The run of the fish in the rivers was seasonal, and curing by smoking or drying made fish, for example the eel fishery of the St. Lawrence, an indispensable part of the diet of the northerner. The sea fisheries were summer fisheries, but tended to equal cattle raising in importance, to take the men away for the season and thus to demand co-operative effort and specialization. They might also yield a staple for trade.

The fisheries, it may be supposed, were the origin of the seafaring that made possible both the migration of the frontier across the North Atlantic and also the amount of trading which took place between it and the central lands of the European metropolis. Certain it is that the northern frontier was much more a maritime than a land frontier, a character which to a curious degree Canada retains even yet, and which will increase again as arctic navigation develops. The pioneers of that frontier were not long hunters or the *voortrekkers*, but fishermen seeking new fishing grounds, seamen-farmers in quest of new island pastures, Viking voyagers who sought in new lands whatever fell to them of plunder, trade, or homestead.

The northern and maritime frontier had its own northern economy with characteristics equally explicit. It was an extensive and a gathering economy, dependent on new lands, new seaways, and the transport the seas and rivers afforded. It required a base of arable soil and habitable climate for the farmstead settlements. The farmstead was a highly self-subsistent unit, but it was the base of an economy which as a whole was an exchange economy to a high degree. The surplus staples of fish, fur, and timber, with exotics like arctic ivory and oil, falcons, and polar bears, earned the funds with which to buy the metals, the cereals, the church goods, and the luxuries the northern settlements needed or desired. Some of the traffic was interregional; it was, for example, its timber that made Vinland of primary interest to the Greenlanders.

That the Canadian economy historically has been an economy of this kind requires no demonstration. The great staple trades have been extensive, in-gathering trades. The population which carried them on lived in and worked from relatively narrow bases of good land in the sea inlets and river valleys; most of Canada is simply a hinterland extensively exploited from the soil base of the St. Lawrence and Saskatchewan valleys, and from the delta of the Fraser. The Canadian economy has also largely bought its external supplies by the sale of surplus staples.

The first discovery and early exploration of the lands which were finally to be united in Canada were the outcome of the advance westward of the northern and maritime frontier of Europe and the extension of the northern economy to America. These discoveries and the first occupation of Canadian shores were made by way of the northern approach. Somehow, by methods yet only guessed at, the Viking frontiersmen, the Bristol traders, and Norman fishermen made their way across the North Atlantic. Their sea skill and navigational science were so far developed that they could use the brief and uncertain easterlies of late spring and early summer which blow as the belt of the westerlies shifts north with summer to make their way across by a northern route. They did not, like the Spaniards and the Elizabethan English, use the long but certain southern route of the trade winds. The discovery and occupation of Canada was separate and distinct from the discovery and occupation of the Americas.

Nor was it the result of high-pitched, scientific exploration aimed at the trade of Asia. It was the outcome of the piecemeal ventures of Norse seamen-farmers probing the northern seas for new harbours and fisheries, new hay meadows and timber stands. The process is scantily documented. Government archives record it scarcely at all; it can now be understood and comprehended only by an understanding of the character of the northern frontier and economy, an understanding which is as bold an extension of the hints of the sagas as were the original voyages themselves.

The evidence, however, is slowly accumulating to suggest that between the last connections with Greenland and the voyages of the Bristol seamen there was no break in sea knowledge or experience. The Bristol men, with the knowledge of the Azoreans and, presumably, of the Normans and Bretons, were taking over the western half of the old Norse sea empire, and were being caught in the westward tug of the northern frontier. It is scarcely to be doubted that their own efforts would have discovered 'the Newfoundland fisheries if John Cabot and Henry VII had not imposed on their limited and practical efforts the scientific concepts of the Italian navigators and the first imperial impulse of Tudor England. In any event, the outcome was the same. Asia was not discovered, nor was the English empire founded in the fifteenth century, but the Newfoundland fishery of the English west country, and of Normandy and Brittany, was in being by the opening of the sixteenth.

This, then, is the first orientation of Canadian historiography. Canadian history is not a parody of American, as Canada is not a second-rate United States, still less a United States that failed. Canadian history is rather an important chapter in a distinct and even an unique human endeavour, the civilization of the northern and arctic lands. From its deepest origins and remotest beginnings, Canadian history has been separate and distinct in America. The existence of large areas of common experience and territorial overlap no one would deny. History is neither neat nor categorical; it defines by what is central, not by what is peripheral. And because of this separate origin in the northern frontier, economy, and approach, Canadian life to this day is marked by a northern quality, the strong seasonal rhythm which still governs even academic sessions; the wilderness venture now sublimated for most of us to the summer holiday or the autumn shoot; the greatest of joys, the return from the lonely savagery of the wilderness to the peace of the home; the puritanical restraint which masks the psychological tensions set up by the contrast of wilderness roughness and home discipline. The line which marks off the frontier from the farmstead, the wilderness from the baseland, the hinterland from the metropolis, runs through every Canadian psyche.

The northern economy was self-subsistent only at the base. Even there it was not necessarily so, as the extinction of the Greenland colonies grimly demonstrated, and as the plight of the prairie provinces in the 1930s re-emphasized. As a whole, however, the northern economy was a highly dependent one. It was a hinterland economy dependent on the sale of a few basic staples and a few exotics in a metropolitan market.

That is, the whole culture of the northern and maritime frontier, to succeed as well as survive, required from outside a high religion, a great literature, and the best available science and technology to overcome its inherent limitations. These very limitations of climate and of material and human resources made the frontier dependent on a metropolitan culture for those essentials. The alternatives were extinction or complete adaptation to the lowest level of survival in northern conditions. Was not the basic difference between the north European and the Eskimo that the former had a central and metropolitan economy and culture on which to draw, while the latter had none until very recent times and lived in a wholly and wonderfully self-subsistent culture?

The northern economy, then, was a dependent one, both for the markets which absorbed its staples and exotics, and for the supply of the needs of mind and body which raised life on the northern frontier above the level of subsistence and enabled it to produce in Iceland the literature of the sagas and in modern Canada the political fabric which unites the technology of a highly civilized and industrialized baseland with the exploitation of the resources of a harsh and enormous hinterland.

British America had the same northern character as French America, a base for the fisheries and the fur trade, for trade by the St. Lawrence with the continental interior, and for naval power and Northwest exploration. How true this was is apparent if a glance is taken at what Imperial policy actually did in British North America between 1783 and 1871. It not only paid much of the cost of government and defence; it preserved the territorial claims to which the Dominion was to be heir. From 1818 to 1854 it employed Franklin and his fellow explorers in the same scientific exploration that under Cook's genius had led to the opening of the Pacific and the colonization of Australia and New Zealand. At the same time it halted Russia in Alaska by diplomacy, and forestalled it in the arctic archipelago by the great feats of naval exploration of Ross, Parry, and M'Clintock. By so doing, it laid the groundwork for the Canadian occupation and development of the Arctic. This Imperial policy was not only a major element in Confederation, in ensuring its achievement, but also in delivering to it, as to a new metropolitan base, the whole of north-western and arctic hinterland. By this stroke, the northern and maritime frontier of the empire of the North Atlantic became a northern and a continental one in the Dominion of Canada.

[1961]

Melville Watkins

Technology in Our Past and Present

Throughout its history, Canada has been a marginal area relative to centres of population, purchasing power, military power, and technological innovation. Technology has been a force emanating abroad, and change, for Canadians, a mostly passive .adaptation to external opportunities and pressures. With a majority ethic that reflects liberal-bourgeois origins, the primary goal has been national economic development. The need to provide security for foreign capital – which increases the rate of economic growth both through increasing the supply of savings and by being the carrier of the new technology – underlay the emergence of the nation and has worked since to constrain Canadian nationalism from 'excesses' on the left. Historically, the Act of Union of 1840 and Confederation were the political preconditions for continuing access on reasonable terms to the London capital market; in recent years, even the mild restraints on foreign owners such as those proposed by Walter Gordon are labelled left-wing by Bay Street. The ease of emigration has reinforced tendencies to maintain in Canada a reasonable approximation of the American way of life. The feasibility of medicare, for example, hinges on devising arrangements that are sufficiently satisfactory to the doctors as to discourage their emigration to the United States. At the same time, proximity to the world's greatest liberal democracy has complicated the satisfaction that might otherwise have accrued from flag-waving, and has compelled the steady cultivation of a European link as a counterweight to the American fact but at the price of inhibiting Canadian autonomy. Spatial vastness and the French fact have facilitated regionalism

285

and provincialism, just as they have inhibited nationalism even of the liberal variety.

The national history of Canada can be written around the theme of changing technologies, from the river economy of fur to the national economy of wheat to the regional economies of electricity. Except for short periods when fur and wheat were at their peaks, regionalism has been the rule rather than the exception of the Canadian experience, and Canadian nationalism has been largely a conscious strategy of pasting over the cracks. The present boundaries of Canada were defined by the fur trade in the process of retreating in the face of settlement. Areas held by the fur traders tended to be those with limited alternative opportunities for attracting and holding settlers; hence a polity resulting from the exploitation of fur necessarily rested on weak foundations. The new transport technologies of canals and railways created economic and political possibilities that far surpassed those flowing from the canoe. The Act of Union was necessary to build the canals; Confederation and the National Policy were necessary to build all-Canadian railways. The supply of timber to the British Navy was a keystone of Canada's permanent economic development, while the British Navy provided the military power necessary to hold a St. Lawrence polity distinct from the United States.

The persistent difficulties of Canadian book publishers are striking evidence of the limitation of Canada as a nation-state in the Gutenberg environment. The absence of both a single and a unique language has been crippling. The newspaper gave a fresh impetus to urbanization – and hence to new metropolitan centres as foci independent of established centres – but no metropolitan paper in Canada has been able to attain national stature analagous to that of the London *Times* in Britain, or even of the *New York Times* in the United States. In every dimension electricity appears to have weakened an already weak national polity and economy. Hydro-electricity has become the essential ingredient of a host of new staples which find their markets in the United States and fail to utilize the patiently assembled transcontinental transportation system extending from the St. Lawrence. Public ownership, as an expression of the collective will, has had more room to flower at the provincial and metropolitan levels than at the national level. Radio and television have been used, or misused, in a largely futile attempt to foster nationalism, with a consequent failure to exploit adequately the potential of public ownership of the media to offset commercialism and provide free education. The increasing complexity of technology and of life in general has meant an increased insistence on education, or on human capital, as a critical input for economic growth. The limitations of Canada as a nation-state in the age of print are reflected in provincial responsibility for formal education with a consequent absence of national standards and national curricula. The teaching of national history creates national myths which facilitate nationalism – but there are ten versions of Canadian history taught in the schools. As learning becomes continuous in the age of automation, an insistence on national content is likely to be seen as irrelevant to the main challenge of coping with new technologies, community life, and global politics.

The National Policy of the nineteenth century was the ideological content of the new technology of the railway wedded to the old river economy of the St. Lawrence. As a manifestation of nationalism and as an instrument of nation-building, the National Policy was more the commercial imperialism of the St. Lawrence merchants than a broadly based mass movement. National politics were dominated by acrimonious debates about railway subsidies and tariffs. Foreign policy was rigidly determined by the conscious desire to maximize the national *economic* welfare. In a recent study of the major disputes that characterized Canadian-American relations in the years 1883-1900, it becomes painfully obvious that the common element in Canadian policies – from fishing rights in the North Atlantic to the Alaska boundary settlement – was the exclusive concern with national economic benefits. George Hees was in the historic Canadian tradition when, during the 1965 federal election campaign, he drew the attention of his tobacco-growing constituents to the potential gain which the illegal declaration of independence by Rhodesia would bring to them; even racism breeds profits somewhere. Canadian nationalists still take pride in the extent to which national policy lowers individual income while raising national income. To demonstrate, as Professor Dales has done, that it is theoretically possible for the tariff to do this may only strengthen the hand of the economic nationalist. It is not surprising, however, that some find little emotional satisfaction in such a coarsely materialistic conception of what it means to be a Canadian. V. C. Fowke has shown that the old National Policy – high tariffs, railway building, and promotion of mass immigra-tion – was obsolete by 1930; no new national policy has emerged to replace it in spite of frequent appeals by Canadian historians. One can sympathize with Fowke's attempt to find an emerging national policy based on the welfare state, but one is compelled to recognize that as welfare has grown in importance, federal powers have been eroded relative to provincial and municipal powers.

The spread of the railway permitted the U.S. corporation to swell to national proportions. A similar development in Canada was checked by the tendency of American companies to ignore the Canadian-American boundary and to refuse to regard investment in Canada as foreign. As early as the 1850s, U.S. entrepreneurs were investing directly in Canadian lumber mills. The process of foreign control of export-oriented industries based on superior access to technology and markets became cumulative. The imposition of the tariff and the increasing exposure of Canadians to American advertising hastened the spread of American direct investment in Canadian subsidiaries and branches producing for the Canadian market. Wheat as a staple encouraged immigration and by increasing the size of the national market facilitated industrialization based on mass-consumed, mass-produced commodities in which American technology was dominant. A functioning transcontinental economy was revived around wheat in the decade prior to World War I, with considerably more substance than its predecessor based on fur. But within the wheat boom were to be found the nationally corrosive influences of electricity and of the increasing orientation of the Canadian economy, on the import side, to the United States rather than the United Kingdom.

The weakening of the national economy has been paralleled by the increasing strength of both regionalism and continentalism. If the former was highlighted by the election returns of November 8, 1965 (the Liberal power failure), the latter was vividly exposed by the (literal) power failure of November 9. In his *Lament for a Nation*, George Grant argues that because continentalism is inevitable the Canadian nation-state is an impossibility. But Grant reaches his conclusion by dubious means: he assumes that the new technology is simply more of the old centralization and homogenization and that there was in the past a golden age of Canadian nationalism, the disappearance of which is now worth lamenting. Nor is it sufficient to cite, as Grant and others do, the increasing economic interdependence of Canada and the United States, in terms of trade and investment, as convincing evidence of lessening Canadian autonomy. In economic policy, to learn the lesson of Keynes is to appreciate that monetary and fiscal policies, rather than continental automotive industry agreements, are the means preferred by economists to achieve the legitimate goal of national full employment. In foreign policy, a meaningful Canadian approach is denied, in some part at least, by the Ottawa Establishment's preference for secret diplomacy rather than frank and candid public discussion, and for national economic interest rather than global issues as the primary content of Canadian-American relations. It is arguable that the war in Vietnam is as relevant to election campaigns and to Canadian-American relations as where the Chevrolets are produced. Grant's despair – or, more accurately, his whimsical regret – has the curious quality of denying the relevance of the supranational protest and dissent which is now so clearly a part of the electric environment.

In the twentieth century, American periodicals (such as *Time* and *Life*), Hollywood, and radio and TV piping American programmes into Canadian homes, have created mass taste on a continental basis. The Canadian response has been to force the burden of nationalism on to the new media. The CBC is hailed by the Committee on Broadcasting as 'the most important single instrument available for the development and maintenance of the unity of Canada'; it is hardly surprising that the Committee then finds the CBC wanting. To charge that the CBC 'must awaken Canadians to Canadian realities' invites the countercharge that Canadians should simply be awakened. The banality of Canadian content rules is adequately exposed, albeit inadvertently, by the Committee's remark that 'Religious and educational programs made outside Canada have been a problem.' The inherent difficulty involved in effectively wedding conventional nationalism, which has emerged around the printed word, with broadcasting, lends a quality of the absurd to the reports of Commissions and Committees. New nations have the advantage of being able to use the new media, particularly radio, to create nationalism without competition from the historical residue of print.

Canada was only the first to receive the smothering embrace of enveloping U.S. technology as the United States moved to its present position of forming a virtually world-wide environment. American direct investment grew rapidly, for direct investment was *the* efficient medium of communication for the massive information movements required by modern industrial techniques and modern advertising. American television programmes while blanketing the world also awaken it; they may yet turn out to be the most effective technique imaginable for creating anti-Americanism. Canadian nationalism of the type symbolized by Mr. Diefenbaker is, at least in part, a technological backlash analagous to Goldwaterism within the United States. Conversely, nationalism of the type espoused by M. Lévesque reflects, at least in part, the felt need for a collective existence that transcends both individualism and conventional nationalism.

Western man is becoming increasingly involved with collectivities other than the nation. Note such instances as: the revival of the city state as metropolitan area, with urban planning much more acceptable than national economic planning; the centralization of corporate decision-making, with corporate planning the vogue among those who oppose national planning; the evolution of the national corporation into the multi-nation corporation, with a world-wide corporate image rather than a national image, and staffed by men of global perspective who allocate resources without respect for national boundaries but who care about local respect and participation; the expansion, albeit slowly, of international agencies and the growing number of supranational civil servants; the evolution of the university as ivory tower into the multiversity as environment, with a staff of modern nomads and a student body that prefers teach-ins to textbooks; the new interest in church union that may heal the schisms that have rent the Catholic church and create a new theology that makes irrelevant the issues on which sects have flourished historically; the return of family life as evidenced by TV-togetherness and the baby boom. To list these diverse collectivities is to begin to map the social web that will be essential for existence in a functioning 'global village' of all mankind.

The most deliberate manner in which to discuss the proper role of the nation-state is by the use of a functional approach, that is, by posing the question: what is the role of the nation-state relative to those of other collectivities such as intra-national regions, extra-national regional blocs, and supra-national authorities? There would be widespread agreement that present military technology already compels supra-national authority. Similarly, the rising revolution of expectations within the poor countries compels a concern with *world* economic welfare and *world* economic growth. Within the nation-state, however, decentralization is feasible. Particularly for Canada, where national goals have been primarily economic, there is no reason to assume that decentralized decision-making must be inferior to centralized decision-making. The provinces already play leading roles in the fields of transportation, education, and welfare, and there is considerable scope for the further decentralization of monetary and fiscal policy. This is not to argue that the nation-state is now obsolete, but rather to suggest that it will survive by recognizing its limitations. Post-print nationalism must grow out of a genuine national society which can support a national government able to perceive and achieve national goals that transcend economic liberalism. There is no task today more urgent than that of recognizing and effecting social goals and aspirations which transcend individualism while avoiding the dead-rot of centralism and bureaucracy.

This is to suggest that, putting conventional political ideology aside, the greatest potential for Canada as a national society may lie in a substantial rejection of the market economy as the cornerstone of the market society and the market mentality. Canadian historiography notwithstanding, national policy has been little more than marginal tinkering with the price system via the tariff and the shoring up of private enterprises until they can stand on their own feet or after they are reeling bankrupt. The history of Canadian railways adequately demonstrates the point. The greater reliance in Canada than in the United States on public ownership and the lesser fanaticism evident in discussion of the virtues of free enterprise are features by which the Canadian way of life can already be reliably differentiated from the American. To downgrade the market might ultimately permit Canadians to rise above that vulgar materialism which has masqueraded as nationalism. The boredom of the young with mere affluence is a heartening sign. The major burden of the tariff is not the extent to which it has lowered the standard of living – real though that is – but rather the extent to which, by monopolizing politics, it has narrowed vision and lowered the quality of national life. To reject the market would significantly differentiate Canada from the United States, thereby lessening the invidious comparisons that have eaten at the soul of Canadian nationalism. It is also possibly the only national policy that can hope to maintain any national commitment within Quebec. Its potential might be thought to be severely constrained by the possibility of a considerable exodus to the United States, though, in the present state of the world's population, emigration could be easily offset by immigration. It has working for it the increasingly unattractive character of American foreign policy.

Advocating the rejection of the market, however, should not be interpreted as simply implying the acceptance of the traditional shibboleths of the Canadian left. Tariffs and the harassment of foreign owners are not endorsed, for their main effect is to protect the Canadian commercial establishment and impede the inflow of the newest technology. A tariff designed to breed infant industries now tends more often to shelter the senile. By encouraging American companies to establish plants in Canada, a tariff deemed necessary to ensure Canadian survival has increased the threat to survival. By encouraging in Canada a 'miniature replica' of the American manufacturing system, the tariff has nurtured an inefficient industrial structure that needs continuing tariff protection. The history of the Canadian tariff needs to be written around the theme of self-fulfilled prophecies. Adverse effects alleged to result from foreign ownership are more obviously attributable to the Canadian tariff and the remedy is tariff reduction. In so far as monopoly power inheres in direct investment – since otherwise the foreigner would not have an advantage over domestic firms – there is a case for some control of foreign investment on economic grounds alone, since otherwise the economic gains for Canadians will not be so large as they might be. But to place significant impediments on foreign ownership and do nothing else risks turning Canada into a technological backwater. More consideration needs to be given to the feasibility of patent and licensing arrangements as alternatives to foreign ownership and, in particular, to the potential for a much more active role for government in encouraging scientific research. The backwardness of Canadian entrepreneurship, on which the foreigners' advantage rests at least in part, could be alleviated by educating top management, increasing social mobility, and increasing the scope for public rather than private entrepreneurship.

There is much to be said, particularly in marginal areas, for accepting the new technology and devoting political energies to its humanization. The electric technology creates a vast potential for improving the environment – for collective action to programme a more meaningful existence. Urban and regional planning is the most obvious case in point. At the national level the greatest potential for Canada almost surely lies in a radical reformation of foreign policy. In this area, Canadian policy has long been guided by the goal of maximizing national economic welfare and, since a foreign policy independent of Britain has been tolerated, by the technique of publicly supporting the United States with any criticisms whispered privately. Secret diplomacy has had its day, and the potential area for disagreement with U.S. foreign policy steadily widens. The crassness and the simplicity of Canadian foreign policy has masked its ultimate innocence and irrelevance. The terror and the chaos loose in the world are too rarely glimpsed and a genuine involvement in the fate of mankind thereby evaded.

But even radical suggestions, so long as they are clothed in the garb of nationalism, are ultimately transcended by the radical message of the new and emerging technologies. As we move into outer space, it is time that we make this planet habitable. What is required is for us to take seriously the idea of mankind as a concept transcending nationalism in any form. Political action is too easily confused with government policy and too rarely understood as the goal-implementation of any collectivity; hence non-national groupings espousing global goals cannot be dismissed as naïve if they work outside the formal political structure, for the latter might be regarded as the residue of the old technology. Policy is too easily regarded as the content of government activity and too rarely linked to the collective aspirations of man which transcend momentary institutional arrangements. It would be criminal to stand idly by as spectators applauding the decline of the nation-state. But it would be equally derelict to imagine that nationalism can be an adequate answer to our present discontents. The compelling need for the future is not for national societies in a world community — desirable though such a social system would be today — but rather for a world society fit for a global village.

> To feel one's attachment to a certain region, one's love for a certain group of men, to know that there is always a spot where one's heart will feel at peace — these are many certainties for a single human life. And yet this is not enough. (Albert Camus, 'Summer in Algiers')

[1966]

X
Place des
Arts

Wyndham Lewis
Northrop Frye
Milton Wilson
Jean Ethier-Blais
Morley Callaghan
Elizabeth Kilbourn
Richard Kostelanetz
Neil Compton
Edgar Kaufmann, Jr.
Robert Fulford

Wyndham Lewis

Leviathan and the Canadian Ahab

The Canadian consciousness must always, to a peculiar degree, be implicated with nature, seeing that Canada is first and foremost a raw-material nation, and, still more important, is everywhere on the frontiers of the wilderness.

The development of the cultural life of Canada will necessarily be conditioned – or so it seems to me – by these facts, however present-day anti-regionalism there may seek to ignore them. On the other hand, its situation on the North American continent also deeply involves it in the Machine Age. The neighbourhood of Canada and Detroit is a formidable fact. The culture of this northernmost of the nations of the western hemisphere might develop, consequently, a dual personality. The pull of nature, however, will probably exceed that of the attraction exercised by the blast furnace and power house. Further, the Anglo-Saxon genius has always displayed great affinity with primitive nature. The French Canadian would, after his Latin fashion, continue to take more interest in man than in primitive nature. The latter is really, in practice if not in theory, and in spite of Rousseau and his school, almost an English monopoly.

An Ossianic pantheism pervades the literature and the life of the Briton: a passionate inclination for the virginity of nature and for the most unruly moods of the elements. Evidences of this can be traced as much in the fondness of Shakespeare for thunder and lightning as in the appetite of the twentieth-century boy scout for getting lost on quite wild little mountains and practising woodcraft in the home-spinney.

These are the things, however, that have spelled Empire: that 'violent trading' of the English, as a Frenchman has called it, which eventuated in the North American continent speaking English and which resulted in Hudson Bay, Ellesmere Island, Prince Patrick Island, and other cozy little spots bearing Anglo-Saxon names, rather than the Spanish, French, German, Italian, or Dutch. Such reflections are appropriate in approaching the question of what kind of culture may be produced by the population settled in such close neighbourhood to so overpowering and top-heavy a mass of primitiveness as is to be found in Canada north of the narrow settled belt – from the Bush up to the muskeg and beyond to the icepack.

The question in fact is whether all this unassimilable mass of 'nature' will in the end be left alone (just as we seldom turn our eyes to interstellar space and have long ago lost interest in the moon, except for crooning purposes): or whether this proximity of the wilds will continue to influence the descendants of the contemporary Canadian. Surely the latter will be the case – just as certainly as a people who inhabit a seacoast are conditioned by the neighbouring ocean and its rude habits, the works of their bards being full of splashing and tossing, of shipwreck and of ships inopportunely becalmed.

Now it seems to me that for a person with these tastes and these traditions, Canada, artistically, offers extraordinary opportunities, and that those on the whole have been surprisingly neglected. One would have expected, for instance, Canada to have produced one outstanding poet, inspired by the scene and by the history that is there. This has not occurred.

But pictorially, in a sense, it has. In 1920 a movement announced itself in Upper Canada under the name of the Group of Seven. This painting is, in fact, the blazing of a trail and a rough charting – a sometimes crude advertisement of a rich aesthetic vein – rather than a finished achievement of authentic beauty.

The key man in this Canadian regionalist school is Alec Jackson, because without him it is doubtful whether the school would ever have existed. Tom Thomson, generally regarded as the star member of the school, died in mysterious circumstances up in one of his Northland lakes, in 1917. He was a commercial designer – as all of them were at one time or another, except Harris. In 1913-14, Thomson, then a weekend artist of no particular distinction, became acquainted with Jackson, not long returned from Paris, and a spark was struck. They shared a studio, and by the end of 1914 this contact had transformed Thomson into a remarkable colourist, equipped to get on to his canvas some of the cold vivacious beauty of the spring woods in the Algonquin country. For the rest, his ten years of commercial designing at Grip Limited supplied the formal accessories and the organizing habit.

It would be idle to pretend that the oils, large and very small (mostly the latter), produced by Thomson during a mere three years – 1914 to 1917 – which is all that is of interest, would set the Thames or the Seine on fire, because they would not. Most gallantly this little group (for the rigours of the social climate were so formidable that only the toughest could survive) pioneered. When the hostility of the press and the public held them up, they retreated into commercial design, but always to emerge again as – for the time and the place – militant and iconoclastic. Their work was rude: they chopped out their paintings as if they were chopping wood. They adopted often the brutal methods of the billboard artist to put their country across big and harsh and plain: with all its emptiness and savagery – its trees that crawl along the surface of the frozen earth because they cannot stand erect in the Arctic wind; its shack-hamlets submerged in snow; its Northern Lights, and all the other things you do not meet with anywhere else. Sometimes they painted a beautiful or an original picture. Most of the time they were blazing the way for others, opening up the Canadian scene – for I am sure Jackson did not expect his school to end with the 'Seven'.

The members of this school are dispersed, have 'gone west', have disappeared or died. Only Jackson is left. He had much to do with starting it all: now he stands there alone in Toronto before his easel, in the Studio-building in the Ravine, painting doggedly, the 'grand old man' of Canadian painting.

Canada will always be so infinitely bigger physically than the small nation that lives in it, even if its population is doubled, that this monstrous, empty habitat must continue to dominate this nation psychologically, and so culturally, as I started by saying. The Northland, as they call it, 'the forty miles of white water', the 'beaver ponds', the virgin beauty of Mississauga, these are what cause us to give Thomson a hearing for his crude song. It is not generally realized how, at a relatively short distance north of the cities strung out across Canada in a wavering line, the Bush, the wilderness, begins, with its multitudes of lakes and streams. But Jackson went much farther afield even than Thomson: to Great Bear Lake and to the Polar Sea, and brought back grisly records of what he had seen.

With Alec Jackson I will bring this article to a close, for he interests me the most. He is himself like a bit of nature and the rock is always more important than the man. And with Jackson let me associate Gagnon, as the French and English are conjoined in their native Quebec.

French Canada had in Clarence Gagnon, who died in 1942, a sort of national painter. These two artists are very different, though superficially their canvases have a kind of family look. Both come from the province of Quebec; in the pictures of both there is a lot of snow. There the similarity ends. Whereas Gagnon painted very attractively (mostly in his studio in Paris) an exotic world of brightly clad peasant-puppets, in their snow-bound hamlets, Jackson paints the same little Quebec hamlet for preference deserted, battened down, all but submerged in the white pest of the Canadian winter. Gagnon's is an innocuous snow, almost as if it were a stylistic device of nature (a very good-natured nature!). But Jackson's is like a white lava to smother and blot out. It is not even white! Often it is a depressing spectral grey, or acidly greenish; not at all like the sparkling blue-and-white of the icing merchants (among whom it would be unfair to count Gagnon).

The village is not where Jackson is most at home. He has painted some excellent villages: but where there are few signs of man is where he really likes to be, where there is just Jackson and Nature. 'Nature' for Jackson does not mean what it did for Turner, a colossal and sumptuous pipe-dream akin to the Kubla Khan of Coleridge, nor what it was to Van Gogh, a barbaric tapestry at the heart of which was man and his suffering – his human rhythms branching out, the tormented nervous system of nature responding to man's emotions. In Jackson's case it is Nature-the-Enemy as known to the explorer.

Yes, it is an affair of Jackson-against-nature and vice-versa. Jackson being what is called a 'fighter' likes this situation. His painting expeditions are as it were *campaigning seasons,* rather than the breathless rendezvous of a 'nature lover' with the object of his cult. It is impossible to associate the notion of pleasure with these grim excursions, or at least nothing sensuous. If anything there is too little that is sensuous; he handles nature roughly. Few have tried to paint the snow. These snowscapes of his fill one with the fascinating ennui of the chapters of the log of a polar explorer: one of those grand monotonous books where one wonders how many more hundreds of pages must be traversed or trudged through (on seal-meat and pemmican) before one reaches that extraordinarily overrated abstraction, the Pole.

There is gaiety somewhere in Jackson, but it is rationed. His vision is as austere as his subject-matter, which is precisely the hard puritanic land in which he has lived: with no frills, with all its dismal solitary grandeur and bleak beauty, its bad side deliberately selected rather than its chilly relentings. This is a matter of temperament: Jackson is no man to go gathering nuts in May. He has no wish to be seduced every spring when the sap rises – neither he nor nature are often shown in these compromising moods. There is something of Ahab in him; the long white contours of the Laurentian Mountains in mid-winter are his elusive leviathan.

[1946]

Northrop Frye

Ned Pratt

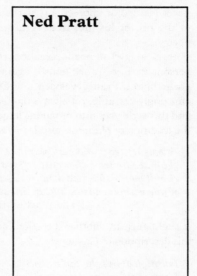

The work of E. J. Pratt has genuine simplicity, but, as William Blake wrote, there is a wide gulf between the simple and the insipid. Simplicity is difficult, not easy; it destroys laziness and prejudice, it does not confirm them.

Pratt's life has been outwardly quiet, but he has been one of those creators Henry James spoke of, who do not need to search for experience because they are the kind of people on whom nothing is lost. Born in Newfoundland in 1883, his first impressions were of Newfoundland fishing villages, where, in the words of one of their folk songs, 'fish is low and flour is high', and where men fought for their food at the risk of their lives. More than once his father, who was a clergyman, had to inform a fisherman's wife that her husband would not return from the sea. Newfoundland was followed by Victoria College, where he was graduated in 1911, and by graduate work in theology and psychology. In Methodism at that time the battle of 'higher criticism' had been won, Biblical archaeology was opening up, there was general enthusiasm for such new world-pictures as 'evolution', *Angst* and *Existenz* were unheard of, and there was no difficulty – certainly the poet has never found any – in being Christian and liberal at the same time.

Finally he became a teacher of English literature at Victoria College, and remained there until his retirement as Professor Emeritus in 1953. Each of these strata of experience can be easily traced in his work. As a student of literature he struck his roots directly into Shakespeare and the major Romantics – poets great enough to allow him to find his own mode of poetic speech for himself. He has never followed or started any particular 'trend' in poetry, never learned or imposed any particular mannerisms of expression. The record of the rest of his life, from *Newfoundland Verse* in 1923 onwards, is in his poetry.

It is a law of poetic creation that the poet who is willing to lose his personality in his work finds it again. Out of his self-effacing concern with the poetic object, Pratt developed a flexible, unpretentious speaking style which is amazingly versatile, yet always unmistakably his. A slight turn in one direction, and this style goes into broad burlesque, with comic rhymes and anticlimaxes in the tradition of *Hudibras* and *Don Juan*:

> *A walrus' heart and pancreas,*
> *A blind Auk from the coast of Java,*
> *A bull moose that had died from gas*
> *While eating toadstools near Ungava.*
> ['The Witches' Brew']

A slight turn in another direction, and it becomes delicate and fanciful, as in this description of Cassiopeia:

> *For high above the table head*
> *Shall sway a candelabrum where,*
> *According to the legend, dwelt a*
> *Lady seated in a chair*
> *With Alpha, Beta, Gamma, Delta,*
> *Busy braiding up her hair.*
> ['The Depression Ends']

It can dramatize a poker game or a whale hunt, summarize history or expound science, swivel easily from the colloquial to the eloquent. In a tragic context, the same style can achieve the peculiar virtue of narrative, of being able to communicate the most deeply impressive moments in a bald, flat statement, as in the account of Lalemant's martyrdom in *Brébeuf*:

> *Lalemant died in the morning at nine, in the flame*
> *Of the pitch-belts.*

'Ther is namore to seye,' as Chaucer, who ought to have known something about narrative, so often remarks.

Pratt's moral standards have few surprises: he is much more of a spokesman than a critic of public opinion and generally accepted social reactions. The reason – or one reason – is that he is almost always dealing with a society in a state of emergency: a Newfoundland fishing village depending on the next catch; a nation at war anxiously scanning the headlines; a band of missionaries surrounded by hostile Indians; sailors or railway workers trying to finish a dangerous quest on schedule. Such societies are engaged, and those who go out to meet the engagement are quite obviously heroes: there is no time to analyse motives or question values.

The conception of heroism in Pratt is of the kind that belongs to our age, and to an industrial democracy. It is the whole group engaged in the quest that is the hero. When Pratt names an individual hero, like Brébeuf, he thinks of the heroism as like that of a soldier who has received a medal for valour – as representative rather than isolated. The cowards and slackers who desert the quest are usually ignored. In the story of the *Titanic* there are many obvious things to consider: the 'hap' or mysterious fate that attracted Hardy, the outrage at the incompetence of those in charge that brought some blistering essays from Conrad, the vainglorious confidence that the ship was unsinkable which seems, in retrospect, to have almost deliberately aimed at the iceberg. But Pratt pays little attention to any of this. His chief interest is in the society of the first-class lounge, with the luxurious food, the music, the gossip, and the brilliantly described poker game. It is a brittle society, without much human point to it – until disaster strikes. Then it becomes the beleaguered group that the poet so well understands, and its genuine humanity suddenly becomes the focus of the poem, and the key to its meaning.

Pratt's religious views are never obtrusive, but they organize all his poetry. Considering that he has a degree in theology, it is not surprising that they should be consciously held – he can hardly have acquired his Christian archetypes in the way that a sleeping camper acquires mosquito bites, involuntarily and in the dark. They come out most clearly in two extraordinary poems, 'The Truant' and 'The Depression Ends'. 'The Truant' presents us with the figure of a 'Great Panjandrum', a prince of the power of the air, who talks as though he were God, who obviously thinks he is God, but who is no more God than Blake's Urizen, Shelley's Jupiter, Byron's Arimanes, or Hardy's President of the Immortals. He is the mechanical power of the universe: he controls the stars, the movement of matter, the automatic instincts of living things, even reason and consciousness. It infuriates him that something in the human soul should elude him, and as he screams at man in the 'shrillest tenor' which is the voice of tyranny, he gradually takes on the outlines of Satan the accuser. What he has to accuse man of is his mortality. As far as we can see, everything man does, however heroic, vanishes and leaves not a rack behind. The Panjandrum should know, for he was in the 'grey shape with the paleolithic face' that sank the *Titanic,* in the mechanical mantrap sprung at Dunkirk, even in the 'leopards full of okra pods' in *The Great Feud.* He was certainly in the Iroquois torturing Brébeuf, knowing that they could kill anything that could die, driven by a demonic curiosity to find somewhere in Brébeuf's body the source of his strength, the origin of the word of command that had driven him into the wilderness. Brébeuf represented a more advanced civilization than the Iroquois, but that was not why he was there: his origin was not in France

> *But in the sound of invisible trumpets blowing*
> *Around two slabs of board, right-angled, hammered*
> *By Roman nails and hung on a Jewish hill.*

L

Similarly the 'genus homo' in 'The Truant' taunts the Panjandrum with his lack of real intelligence, but the real source of his strength is his knowledge that for him there can be no God who has not also been a human being, suffered with the beleaguered society which is Pratt's hero, yielded to the power of death, and yet conquered it too. His language towards the Panjandrum is humorous, erudite, arrogant, but behind all his brilliance is his awareness of 'A dying thirst within a Galilean valley'.

'The Depression Ends' is the poem that most vividly summons up, for those who know him, the personality of Ned Pratt: his kindness and his genius for friendship, his epic generosity and hospitality. No one who has ever encountered his limitless good will can doubt that he would, if he could, give an 'apocalyptic dinner'. But as the poem goes on, the significance of this adjective begins to sink in. This is no stag party: this is Pratt's beleaguered society on the march. All the oppressed and hungry and neglected in human history, all the lame and halt and blind, all the slaves and the poor, all the invisible proletariat who are the people of God, are shuffling raggedly and dazedly into a splendid feasting-hall. The hall turns out to be the starry heavens, their original birthright and their dwelling-place, as the emptiness of outer space and the empty inner spaces of hungry stomachs are simultaneously filled. At one pole of human life is a cross, at the other is a last supper; and these two poles give position and meaning to everything that occurs between them.

The prevailing idiom in Canadian poetry when Pratt began to write was that of the romantic lyric as practised by Carman, Roberts, D. C. Scott, and Marjorie Pickthall. It was an idiom that was most successful in evocative nostalgia, as in Carman's 'Low Tide on Grand Pré', in fairylike fantasy, as in Scott's 'Piper of Arll', in wistful charm, as in Marjorie Pickthall's 'Little Sister of the Prophet'. The noises that exploded in *Newfoundland Verse*, the pounding of surf, the screaming of wind, the crash of ships on rocks, rudely shattered these moods. Yet if we look back to earlier Canadian poetry, we can see that the effort to convey something of the size and variety of the country through narrative, often realistic narrative, was much more deeply rooted in Canadian literature. There are no Canadian lyrics of any account before about 1880, but there are several quite striking nineteenth-century experiments in narrative, which in their various moods and themes – bleakness in Heavysege, fantasy in Duvar, mythopoeia in Isabella Crawford – not only anticipate Pratt but indicate how sure Pratt's technical instincts were.

It is because his imagination has been so concrete, so devoted to realizing the Canadian environment directly in front of him, that Pratt's career has been so odd a mixture of the popular and the unfashionable. When everybody was writing subtle and complex lyrics, Pratt developed a technique of straight-forward narrative; when everybody was experimenting with free verse, Pratt was finding new possibilities in blank verse and octosyllabic couplets. He had the typical mark of originality: the power to make something poetic out of what everybody had just decided could no longer be poetic material. He worked unperturbed while the bright young men of the twenties, the scolding young men of the thirties, the funky young men of the forties, and the angry young men of the fifties, were, like Leacock's famous hero, riding off rapidly in all directions. Meanwhile he was reaching an increasingly large public in Canada, and by 1940, when *Brébeuf* appeared, he was established in Canada as one of the few good popular poets of the twentieth century. He has never been afraid to be topical, is in fact rather impatient with poets of 'still life', and he has accepted both the responsibilities and the risks that go with being a kind of unofficial laureate.

Many popular poets are either deliberately bad poets, or, if good ones like Burns or Kipling, are admired for bad reasons, as anti-intellectual rallying-points. Pratt has never been what we ordinarily think of as an 'intellectual'. He is not a poet of verbal jig-saw puzzles, of ambiguities or dense textures or erudite allusions, nor has he ever built himself a religio-political Eiffel Tower from which to look down on the human situation. His moral and social values are where those of most sensible people are, and where the heart usually is in the body, a little left of centre. But he has never been anti-intellectual either, a feat which requires a good deal of integrity in this age. He is a scholar and university teacher, with graduate degrees in several disciplines, who works with the whole weight of poetic tradition behind him, and has never talked as though he undervalued culture or intelligence. Yet he has been able to introduce poetry to thousands of readers, including high-school children, with little if any previous experience of it. Meanwhile the cycle of fashion has come full circle, and Pratt looks much more modern and contemporary, if that is a virtue, in 1958 than he did in 1938.

His work now, of course, has a stature and an authority that reaches beyond Canada. But he will always have a special place in the affections of Canadian readers (I am speaking by synecdoche of English Canada). His work began with Newfoundland, and his latest major narrative ends in British Columbia. On his seventy-fifth birthday the CBC recorded tributes to him from all over Canada, some of the most eloquent being from the province of the ice-floes and from the province of the last spike. It was a sign that the work he had helped to do had been, not of course done, but well begun. In defiance of every geographical and economical law, Canada has made itself not simply a nation but an environment. It is only now emerging from its beginning as a shambling, awkward, absurd country, groping and thrusting its way through incredible distances into the west and north, plundered by profiteers, interrupted by European wars, divided by language, and bedevilled by climate, yet slowly and inexorably bringing a culture to life. And as long as that culture can remember its origin, there will be a central place in its memory for the poet in whom it found its tongue.

[1958]

Milton Wilson

The Importance of Being Colonial

Very few postwar British or American poets are likely to try to compete with 'The Marriage of Heaven and Hell' or the 'Ode to the West Wind' in the strident way Irving Layton does. What makes it possible to try without feeling superfluous? Or, to rephrase the question for an unsympathetic reader, why drag out these embarrassing Romantic clichés? How can any poet be so dated with so much conviction?

We have often been told of our necessary dullness because we had no Revolutionary War, no French Revolution, no War Between the States. In poetry likewise we had no Renaissance, no Neo-classicism, no Romanticism. But one of the advantages of a poetry less than a hundred years old is that all the things that couldn't happen when they should have happened keep happening all the time. In Canada nothing is more tedious than literary quarrels in which the opponents try to date one another – the sort of quarrel which you win by pretending to react against your opponent's reaction. Here our critics, fed on historical surveys of English literature, go easily astray. A reviewer has remarked of Phyllis Webb that she falls back 'on poses fashionable in Bloomsbury in the 1920s and still considered *avante-garde* in Montreal'. Whatever one thinks of Miss Webb's poetry, such a remark seems irrelevant – almost un-Canadian. Having begun a millennium too late, there is not much point being correctly fashionable. The Canadian poet can be *avant-garde* with whatever material he chooses. Our tradition in time tapers even less than our background in space. This may explain why our poets find it easy to be mythological without being condescending or coy.

I even wonder whether colonialism may not be, in theory at least, the most desirable poetic state. It gives you a catholic sense of all the things poetry can do without embarrassing you by telling you what at this particular moment it can't. Dudek's *Europe* is the sort of poem that a nineteenth-century American might have written but never did; no contemporary American would think of trying anything like it. The Canadian poet has all the models in the language (not to mention other languages) at his disposal, but lacks the deadening awareness that he is competing with them. This heightened availability of poetic resources makes credible a work like Reaney's *A Suit of Nettles*, with its extraordinary sensitivity to shades and sorts of poetic idiom and its willingness to experiment in such a comprehensive way, or like *The Boatman*, with its exhaustive, interknit survey of a poetic world. The pull of the native tradition is toward the inclusive, the self-sustaining, even the encyclopedic.

I find it difficult to imagine much of this being written in Great Britain or the United States. It is certainly no guarantee of excellence, but the past fifteen years already seem to me the most distinctive period in the history of our poetry.

[1962]

Jean Ethier-Blais

Paul-Emile Borduas

I should like to draw a portrait of Borduas at three crucial moments of his life: first, Borduas on the eve of his departure from Canada for Paris; second, Borduas in Montreal some eighteen years later, around 1945, at the height of his success as an innovator in painting and a social reformer; and finally, Borduas in Paris, a few years before he died.

Who was this young man leaving for Paris in 1928? His contemporaries described him as a frail and innocent-looking young man, with one conspicuous feature: dark and profound eyes, which gazed upon the world apparently always in surprise. These are key words; Borduas, at the time he left for Paris, was profoundly immature. He had not yet decided what he was or what was to become of him. He was truly the young provincial, carried away by events and by the fact that his natural gifts were strong enough and his personality weak enough for him to be at the same time both protected and encouraged by his environment. Indeed, Canadian students in these years, in Paris, remember Borduas quite well, but not, as one might today imagine, as a forceful painter and thinker, rather as one who was polite and withdrawn, as a man who shared in the general laughter of students without seeming to have understood the significance of the joke. I was told by one of them that Borduas was not quite a figure of fun for the sole reason that he looked too angelic. He had no self-assurance. But he worked hard, and let us not forget that on the eve of his departure for Paris, as well as during his first stay there, Borduas was steeped in a religious and mystical atmosphere. His future had been thought out for him; he was meant to become Quebec's foremost religious painter. He had the looks for the job.

306

By 1946, the year of the first Automatist Exhibition, a man totally different from the one his elders and protectors expected has developed. The angel has flown away (where to, no one knows) and has been replaced by a man of considerable energy. I met Borduas in 1947, at one of his exhibitions. He was standing in the centre of a white room, the walls of which were covered with his paintings. Abstract, of course. Borduas was talking to elderly people who were listening with great attention and respect. I had been brought to this exhibition by one of his friends, a poet and a Jesuit, François Hertel, who introduced me to Borduas as 'a famous young writer and disciple of Claudel'. Hertel knew what he was doing, for Borduas, in spite of his simplicity of manners, had a weakness for celebrities, however young.

Borduas explained his painting at great length to me, but I have entirely forgotten what he said. I remember only the man. He had indeed extraordinary eyes, though certainly not the piercing, penetrating eyes one usually associates with a painter. No, Borduas's eyes were of a mellow and questioning kind, dark brown and deeply inserted in the orbits. They were tender, in fact, and although I have never seen a doe I cannot imagine one without associating it with Borduas. When speaking with someone, Borduas bent his head and faced him from underneath, with melancholy. He was a small man, all bones, badly built, as a matter of fact, with short legs and arms, and a big head. One could see at first glance that he was suffering from a strong physical inferiority complex. He tried to make up for his lack of a domineering physique by a constant agitation, by making movements in every direction, to the point that, when he explained the meaning of one of his paintings, he sometimes looked like an aviator describing, arms extended, one of his most perilous exploits. In 1947, Paul-Emile Borduas was no longer the young student who did not quite understand the jokes; he was regarded as a master by a whole generation of painters, and as a dangerous anarchist by those art functionaries who were entrenched in administration and religion. He was preaching revolt against the conformist atmosphere of French Canada. He had youth on his side, and his painting was already acclaimed as opening what is usually called 'new vistas'. Surrounded by his disciples, he reclined on couches and explained his doctrines. His photograph was taken, and pictures of him were already considered as documents. He was a celebrity. He enjoyed being one and thoroughly played the part....

Borduas lived in Paris towards the end of his life.... His *atelier* was on the first floor and had once been a shop. It was large and comfortable, extremely well-lit and filled with the master's works.... He usually sat on a huge divan, legs and arms crossed, head bent to one side, smilingly looking at his guest, with his patient eyes timidly but unwaveringly probing. He laughed frequently and drank quite an extraordinary number of little glasses of cognac, smoking, crossing or uncrossing his arms and legs, smiling as he explained at length some obscure point of painting or of philosophy. Yet in spite of Borduas's laughter, of his apparent creative facility, there was a cadaverous atmosphere in his *atelier.* One could, as it were, smell death. Borduas's face was wrinkled beyond imagination; magnetism alone seemed to hold his bones together; he literally floated in his clothes. He was a dying and unhappy man; he had just started his career anew and was apparently unsuccessful, at least in Paris. Furthermore, he knew that the mode of painting he was experimenting with was a thing of the moment. Where would it lead him? He had discovered, during his first year in Paris, the pleasures of fast driving. He drove exceedingly fast, and his driving habits were, to say the least, poetic. Borduas was in fact entering a period of transition, intellectually and morally, a period of deep self-searching. He was like a man waiting for a job to begin, for the signal to be given to start work. This sense of an uncertainty about the future was strongly felt by Borduas's friends at that time. In fact, there was no uncertainty. Borduas died, and that put a stop to all possibilities....

Borduas had begun, some time around 1944-5, to think in revolutionary terms: revolution in painting, revolution inside the French-Canadian historical and sociological context. It all coincided in time: automatism and social revolution. When one considers, therefore, the artistic value of automatism, one should not divorce it from the sociological analysis of French Canada which accompanied its development.

What is automatism? It is an artistic doctrine, the gist of which is that the artist must become the creative instrument of his own personality. Borduas expressed this thought beautifully. In *Refus global*, he wrote: 'Gradually the calculated act must give way to the act of faith.' We must, from the very start, eliminate the notion that automatism implies a complete abandonment by the artist of his inner judgment, of his powers of reason. This would be too simple. One does not, and could not, become an automatist at will; the goal is achieved only as a result of a painful and long process of acceptance and rejection. Borduas starts from the principle that it is only at the end of a slow process of decantation, of intellectual and spiritual asceticism, that subconscious forces can, and will, be released. He compares man's subconscious life to 'tumultuous rivers', and adds: 'The scientific method has made it possible to bridle our tumultuous rivers inside a strait-jacket.' To become an automatist is precisely to reject this scientific method, which has kept the artistic development of mankind in check. Borduas interprets history as a constant refusal by the leading spirits of humanity to accept the reality of the subconscious mind, a reality which he sees embodied in the eternal themes of magic, the objective mysteries, love and change. To this global refusal by past generations to accept intellectual, psychological, and moral transformation, the automatists oppose complete acceptance. As Borduas put it, 'It is with joy that we take the entire responsibility of tomorrow.' And it is at this point in the development of his artistic theory that Borduas enters into direct conflict with political and religious authority; for he adds: 'Salvation can come only after the greatest excesses in the exploitation [of the soul, of the intellect] have been reached. The present authorities have reached these excesses; they *are* these excesses.'

It is not in the least surprising that the 'present authorities' should have reacted to this pronouncement with pained surprise, a surprise which quickly turned into a sort of sour violence. They were even more shocked when they realized what Borduas's philosophy of French-Canadian history really was. We all know the motto of the province of Quebec is *I remember*. It is both an appeal to the past to stay with us and a refusal of the future. Borduas decided to change all that. 'The past,' he said, 'must be accepted with birth. It should never be considered as a sacred value. We owe the past nothing.' Within the leading intellectual circles of Montreal, in 1948, this premise was anathema. As a matter of fact, it might still be. This much, coming from a teacher who was really a provincial civil servant, was bad enough. But worse was to follow. Borduas divided French-Canadian history into three stages which he saw as being dominated, first by *fear*, then by *anguish*, and, finally, by *nausea*. The French Canadians, he noted, were as early as 1760 a colony 'precipitated inside the smooth walls of fear'. He visualized the history of the French-Canadian people as a huge conspiracy of the clerical and professional ruling classes designed to keep the people in a state of fear and ignorance. The aim of this conspiracy was, of course, to permit the ruling classes to play, in peace, their role as intermediaries between the English governing class and the ignorant mass of French Canadians. In a spiritual sense, Borduas considered the evolution of the French-Canadian ruling classes as premeditated treason. It follows that the historical plight of the French-Canadian people saddened him. He ascribed it to its generosity of spirit; but, he adds, 'fatality is stronger than generosity', and by this he meant that history was moving forward and that the old order was on its way out. What I consider to be of importance in Borduas's attitude is, first, that his global analysis of the evolution of French-Canadian society – or rather its lack of evolution – should have proceeded from an artistic source. It gives it historical strength, it gives detachment to his thinking. But more important still is the fact that, for the first time, a creative group accused the French-Canadian Church, as a social force, of having hindered the natural development of the population. Borduas considered that he and his disciples had entered into the age of nausea. They had to speak out against exploitation and narrowness of mind.

They did speak out, in the form of a mimeographed pamphlet which appeared in 1948 under the title of *Refus global*: a complete and utter rejection. The title was a play on words, for not only did Borduas and his friends reject everything which present-day French Canada stood for, but they also accused the intelligentsia of 1948 of having utterly rejected their civilizing mission. Reaction was swift. Borduas published *Refus global* in May of 1948, and he was expelled from the Ecole du Meuble in September. He had become a martyr to the sacred cause of liberty. He was not unhappy; his paintings sold, and he could live, although poorly. He could paint, and he could express his ideas. He advanced amongst his chosen disciples within a cloud of sufferings and righteousness. But he experienced the fate of most prophets, and his disciples, during the next five years, went their own way. The most famous of these separations is, of course, that of Riopelle, who broke away from Borduas on technical grounds, but presumably also because Borduas admitted less and less of discussion inside his group and seemed more and more to think that his intuition was law.

In 1953, Borduas, who felt isolated, left Canada for the second time and spent the summer in Provincetown, where he painted forty canvases in a state which he later described as approaching ecstasy. He continued to let himself be guided by inner development, abandoning himself entirely to psychological painting. In September, he moved to New York, where he stayed until 1955. One must not belittle the influence exercised on Borduas by modern American painting. It was in New York that Borduas discovered that painting was not only, as he had believed since the beginning of the forties, a question of expressing oneself through form, but that there existed certain problems in the art of painting which had nothing to do with the sole release of one's emotions. One of these problems, for example, was the quest for space. Painting could become the expression of dimensional qualities. The aim of Borduas in New York was to blend emotion with space, to translate his inner development in terms not only of lines and colours but of physical depth as well. His painting became less and less profuse. His colouring, which had been at the same time both rich and dense, became sparse, and the few colours used were basic. Even more revealing, masses began to appear in Borduas's works. Until New York, there had been something fluttery about Borduas's manner of painting: light strokes in great quantities, colours mixed and interpenetrating, waves of multi-coloured strokes succeeding one another. For the eye it was often an enchanting spectacle, but, examined within the frontiers of Borduas's development, this method was bound to disappear in the same proportion that Borduas's character affirmed itself. This happened in New York. Borduas's painting became clearer and geometrical. Those heavy blocks of white, brown, and black paint which have become so familiar began to appear on the canvas. Not yet the utter simplicity of line which was to be found later, not yet the apparent drabness of colouring. But the heavy affirmative blocks are there. They signify that Borduas has reached pictorial maturity.

He had also reached maturity as a man, and the time had come for him to return to Europe, to be confronted again with his past, to face as an adult non-figurative painter, as a non-believer, the youth who had studied in the conformist and religious atmosphere of Paris from 1928 to 1930. In 1955, Borduas came back to Paris and settled down in the *atelier* in the rue Rousselet where he was to die in 1960....

Borduas was a typical French Canadian; his religion was built on terror. He left this world sure of the fact that he did not believe in Christ, or in Catholicism. But his whole social thinking is Catholic-inspired. It is a blasphemous kind of Catholicism, but it is Catholicism none the less. He believed in liberty, the liberty to believe or to disbelieve. And this is what he offered his disciples — the liberty to be free, but nothing else. He offered them the choice of plunging into the abysses of their own personalities; and, as soon as they became afraid of what they found inside themselves, he talked about the supremacy of psycho-analysis. It was truly a replacing of one religion by another. It is not surprising, therefore, that Borduas found himself, in Paris, rather isolated. His work symbolizes this solitude, about which he so often complained. Far away from Canada, he visualised his country as a land of great intellectual and moral possibilities. One cannot help but think that his last paintings, all white, are to be closely associated with our own snow symbolism. These vast expanses of white colouring contain all the sadness of exile as well as all the freshness of the native winter. Borduas has gone back over the past and has sought to blend with his origins. Just as Cézanne painted and repainted his mountains in Provence, so Borduas re-creates this abstract geography. Abstractness forbids him from giving density to the contours of this landscape; but he will at least re-create it symbolically. Borduas's last paintings are the Canadian landscape seen from the inside, this whiteness representing at the same time the physical presence of Canada, its psychological nudity, and its void. . . .

Borduas's influence has been preponderant and pervasive. I doubt very much if there is one Canadian painter of note who has not been influenced by Borduas's style, by his example as a man. He is the Canadian artist who best represents the qualities and defects of our society. One does not know what the future of abstract painting will be; Borduas, for personal and necessary reasons, chose to link his destiny as a painter with the development in time of abstract painting. In that sense, he might disappear as a painter. He will not disappear as a man, the first one in French Canada who has had the deep-felt courage to go to the very end of his thought, to accept the solitude inherent in revolt, to choose despair where success could have been easy, to choose beauty where humdrum painting could have been socially rewarding, to choose inner and truthful development where ambition could have reaped the most honourable rewards our society can give.

[1964]

Morley Callaghan

How Can a Writer Live in Toronto?

People sometimes ask me a strange question. They say, 'Why do you live in Toronto?' This question comes not only from those I have met casually for the first time, but often from people who have lived most of their lives in Toronto, and it always leaves me with an apologetic air and an evasive answer never quite expressed. I know what they mean. They mean that I don't own a bank, an industrial plant, or an advertising agency that links me to this one spot on the earth; being a writer I could just as easily live in Montreal, Mexico City, or among the palms and temples of the south. To make it worse, even my wife the other day asked me in a puzzled tone why we had gone on living in Toronto.

To the professor from St. Louis who asked me why I lived in Toronto, I tried saying casually, 'Why, I was born in Toronto.' For a moment he was silent and I thought I might have found the right easy answer. 'How odd,' he said finally. 'You're the only writer I know who lives in the place where he was born.'

Others have suggested that possibly I like being surrounded by a group of friends, 'makers of Canadian literature', in this new Athens of the north, but then I have to explain shyly that I don't seem to have many literary friends and that the great new cultural wave seemed to have missed my street, as the tornado that struck Windsor last summer missed many of the streets of that town. Is my publisher in Toronto? No. When I write fiction stories do they appear in the Toronto magazines? No, the American magazines. Is my business, such as it is, conducted in Toronto? No, my agent is in New York. Is there anything on earth that I do in Toronto, as a writer, that I couldn't do just as well, if not better, somewhere else? And the answer is 'No.'

312

Even the fact that my children go to school in Toronto never seems to be sufficient justification for living here to those who would lead me beyond the horizon. So I have stretched myself out on a couch, pretending that a psycho-analyst is just behind me, leading me on, and I have torn into my dreams and broken thoughts, trying to reveal to myself the cause of my Toronto bondage. And I find myself defending Toronto, laughing at it and being cynical about those other cities recommended to me.

New York is always there in my mind as the right city, but I have lived in New York and I don't know many writers who go on living there year after year without getting a little sour or brittle or tired. Of course, that's true of New York, but isn't it also true that I have been sour and tired in Toronto? Oh, it is indeed. And there are places to pass the time in New York, comfortable places with pretty faces, and in that city you want more and more of the life around you – you want to possess it and it gets that it eats you up, and when enough of you has been eaten away, you get tired and alcoholic.

A friend of mine in Montreal, Frank Scott, the professor-poet, is always saying that Montreal is the right place, for that lovely city seethes with ideas and has an intellectual life that is foreign to Toronto. But I think he has it all wrong. The English-speaking people of Montreal are pretty much like the people of Toronto; in fact, walking along the Montreal streets I'm always meeting somebody who used to live in Toronto, and they all swear they are much happier than they were in the Ontario Athens; but they look just the same to me and they talk just the same and they have the same ideas and the intellectual structure of their lives was clearly shaped in Toronto and they can't get away from it. This I perceive with a certain feeling of glee. These Ontarians have run four hundred miles trying to catch falling stars, and they have dug themselves into Montreal and have quaffed wine and heard moon songs and made themselves comfortable in ways in which the time passes easily. But they don't fool me – Toronto is in the mind. The notion that Montreal has a dazzling intellectual life like that of Paris, which makes the intellectual life of Toronto seem pathetically provincial, is a myth. Montreal has charm and fine restaurants and happy bistros, and there one can forget easily that Toronto is deep in the mind; one can laugh and struggle to maintain the illusion, but the truth is that the English-speaking people of Montreal and Toronto think the same thoughts. This they refuse to believe. It may be, of course, that I have gone a bit crazy and think of myself as a leader in the underground resistance movement, and whisper to myself the story of those glorious days in France during the German occupation when French writers of the resistance went right on creating and publishing their writing under the noses of the watchful conquerors. Their resistance gave them a creative strength and their attic rooms and their cellars were their temples of art, and they felt a certain contempt for those writers who had run from the conquerors and were living in comfort abroad.

The people of Toronto are a quiet, pleasant people who like to lead an orderly life. They are reasonably polite. They don't like the social life of the cafés, and the crowded boulevards have no charm for them, but they like an indoor life, and their living rooms and drawing rooms take the place of the cafés and the bistros. I should say rather that this was the Toronto of twenty-five years ago when the polite cultural life represented a vast imitation British Dullness. This dullness is still all-pervading among the nicer people, but in the meantime, under their noses, the life around them has changed. Toronto in the last ten years has become a big, hard, rough, sprawling North American city with a Bay Street that is one of the biggest gambling markets in North America. The town crawls with taverns, the streets are filled with strange accents. It is the centre for whatever there is of the publishing, painting, writing, music, and theatre life of English-speaking Canada. It has become a hard-driving city, a great place for a hard guy after a fast buck. And it has the biggest university in Canada and probably more intellectual apathy than any other city of its size.

I come now to my acceptance of the reality of my life in Toronto. I walk around the streets, I go from house to house, nursing my necessary illusion that the orderly life of the place and the simple friendliness of the people is a discipline for me. I deceive myself into thinking that I live a monastic life, but that like a monk in his cell in the long night, my imagination may be stretched and strained and fired and make for me the stuff of exalted dreams. The hard routine of a strict monastic rule may be very good for the soul. The orderly, unexciting, strict Toronto life, I go on telling myself year after year, cannot distract me, cannot give the illusion of gay living, and if the flesh groans the spirit may grow stronger.

There is one other aspect of the matter. I have tried wandering into other cities, and pressing on to distant shores, and have found after a few weeks in a strange place, the urge to move on grows strong, the old weariness gripping me, makes me believe that each new place will be charming because it is new. Well, a writer can stand only so much of this restless boredom; he will go on and on, once he starts wandering, seeking the unexpected scene, the new lovely face, with the charm of novelty always pulling him on and finally wearying him to death. If you stay in Toronto, the longing remains deep in the soul, and since it can't be satisfied you can't be wearied, and your mind and your imagination, should become like a caged tiger. O Toronto! O my tiger city!

[1954]

Elizabeth Kilbourn

Harold Town Talks

I have done very little travelling, but it impresses me that I have nowhere to go, no reason for going.

I find great beauty in the city and I've found enough to keep me busy thinking and feeling just walking up one street, from Rathnelly to the Severn Street studio. There's enough there to last me a lifetime. And I found in the two years that I did that, even pursuing the same street day after day, that I could still find something new. And this was kind of a dull street – just Roxborough – not an exquisite one.

There was a time, I guess it was in 1952, when I was doing a lot of paintings that had to do with neon signs. And certainly the neon wasn't pretty but it fascinated me for two or three years. I suddenly realized, walking up that hideous bit of Bay Street from Wellesley Street to Bloor which has mostly showrooms for cars and automobile parts – I suddenly realized these signs were beautiful, all those gorgeous blues, and I realized that if an Egyptian from the time of one of the great Pharaohs were to walk down the street he would have found them a mystery, an overwhelming mystery. There's everything here.

When I was young, I think I was a bit of an embarrassment to my father because I was so emotional. I used to leap up and down and tremble, and that sort of thing. I loved colour. It was part of my nature. Not much I could do about it. I started drawing very young, if that means anything. Like Louis Armstrong says, you either got it or you ain't.

I sold my first paintings when I was thirty. I sold no fine art until then, and then it was sold for appallingly little. In 1953 I would have been twenty-nine I guess – I sold the odd print for $15 or $20 and I was reluctant to do this because I wasn't certain whether these things had fifteen dollars' value. I had a real diffidence about prices. I had to earn my living entirely by commercial art.

I tramped around this city for a long time, earning my dough the hard way, not being a beatnik or a guy who says to hell with society. I've never stolen and I've never cheated and I haven't lied much. I did a job that society wanted, because I thought, what the hell, this is the only way in the long run. There's one thing about hack work, you develop the necessary muscles for doing the simple road work in your trade, so when somebody says to me, we want an illustration by next Wednesday, the illustration is there. I don't think this is important in the long run, but I could have easily lived off women or drunk or done all the things artists are supposed to do, just live very casually. I did it the formal way, did hack work and I don't regret it. Sometimes I resent the waste of time because I think it's best when you don't do anything but pure work.

So often if you're rejected by society as a creative person you sort of live by your wits only. I suspect that you spend so much time living by your wits that in the end you're not doing any more creative work anyway. At least I was painting all the time.

And I'm not, and I can't say this strongly enough, I'm not very impressed that I'm a painter *per se*. It just happens to be the way I'm made. I could also have been a plumber or something. I don't think artists should feel they're different. I think this is soul-destroying. I have as much admiration for a first-rate plumber as I could have for myself. It's a job. I'm stuck with it and it's my problem. I'm still amazed and always will be amazed that anyone buys anything. To me it's a kind of miracle that anyone should be interested in something that I have to do. Just like an African chief. Everyone runs around collecting his spit. Sometimes it seems sort of ridiculous. I try to keep a reasonable approach to myself. Naturally there are moments when I see a picture that really goes and I'm ecstatic. But generally I try to be aware of the fact that this is a compulsion with me and I'm not such an extraordinary being because of it. I think artists can very easily start listening to their own voices and watching their own hands. I think a certain amount of difficulty is necessary for an artist. So he keeps reassessing himself.

I've said about myself that I'm arrogant but that I have no conceit. I don't think it's remarkable for me to be a painter. But in my job I have utter and absolute confidence in myself. And in the rightness of what I'm doing. I question it, but I question it on my terms. I can't express how important this is, to put yourself in the right relationship to space and everything around you. Every time I look at the hill across the way, I realize that everything I've done is insignificant. Things are so beautiful.

In some ways I think my art is totemic. I become fixated with some form I see around me, or something I imagine, you know, the way Currelly of the Royal

Ontario Museum fascinated me. I have a tendency quite openly to pay homage to whatever fixates me, for instance in my homage to Currelly. The fascination became totemic in the way that I thought of him with his totem poles and things all sort of mixed up. I suppose it's all sort of surreal.

The museum has played an immense role in my creative life because even though I don't go there much now I used to go there a lot when I was younger. I had no idea how good it was till I got to New York and had seen some other museums. To me the museum is like a miracle, like one of those Chinese boxes that open up, filled with miracles. Currelly created a toy for the whole city.

There's so much greatness in the early periods – the Museum has a really great Chinese collection, in the primitive periods and Babylon, I sometimes feel the eulogization of Michelangelo and the High Renaissance period excessive to the point of making me rather sick. I think some of the Assyrian things from the time of Hammurabi – those lion hunts, they're gorgeous sculpture.

The series of collages, the Walls for Hammurabi – for instance, the one the National Gallery has, Square in Nineveh – come from two things. They come from an historical interest in the Museum's collection and they come from the walls that I knew so well in schoolyards as a child and as much as anything from the simple fact that despite games and romping, my memory of schoolyards is concerned with talk more than anything else. It seems there were days when it was either so hot or so cold or the football was missing and so we stood and talked, and we talked about Joe Louis or whatever it was fixated young boys at the time, and our toes would be going back and forth in the snow making patterns or slowly picking paint off the fence, or more often leaning against the wall of the schoolyard, digging out the mortar between the bricks and maybe writing our initials over and over again with the end of a pencil or a penknife. That's where those walls come from – that and the desire to preserve bits of material that interests me.

I don't deny any school of painting. Everything's fine with me. There is a lot of painting I don't like but all of it has something to give you. I think everything's game. We're in the world, why deny the thing? It's important for a painter to love, not reject. I love everything, even the bad, even the hideous signboards, they can be delicious. Some bad paintings I find very exciting, they do things that are so wrong they come close to being right. They are closer to being creative in their ineptitude than a lot of what I call factory-produced painting.

The greater danger I think in painting is arriving at your style too early. I think every so often you should throw out all your brushes – every one, even the ones you love – and get some other kind of brush, just to see what will happen.

Making prints is discipline. I've always done things that I thought were good for me and not necessarily enjoyable. The same with doing collages – I thought this would be very good discipline. I don't think that it's too right to lock yourself in a studio and throw juice on a painting day after day. I think you're

M

likely to be seduced by the sensuality of the process. I think this is an intrinsic danger in Riopelle.

I try to achieve the most extraordinary colours. I work at it. Nothing comes easy, no matter how much facility you've got. Even facility implied difficulty. Just because my hand works nicely doesn't mean to say it doesn't try to work a little more profoundly.

An artist has to force himself to see things. I think painters are as liable to visual indifference as anyone else. There are times when I'm not feeling so well, and I force myself to look and I come alive again. Just because a person is basically creative doesn't mean that he will achieve any immaculate state of creativity. I think you've got to stay in training the way a football player does.

I always keep coming back to sports when I talk about art because art is a pretty physical thing. If you feel good, if you feel your left hand's working beautifully and that's the day you could knock out the champion, it's a great help. It's not to say that you're going to make a great painting – but it's a big help.

It's possible to be very wild in painting, and very automatic and then seriously consider it later and still have it an integral thing. I just don't believe in any rules. Some pictures just go in a lump, and some linger.

I would say that I was an anti-romantic, though it is not to deny that there are romantic elements in some of my paintings. But I would say I was a classical painter because I put form above everything. And to me the perfect exhibition is one with as many utterly different paintings as possible. This has been a sort of goal of my creative work up till now – to make every picture different. Of course it's much easier for a dealer to have fifty pictures with one theme, like a circle or something, and fifty pictures with another, and you achieve a trade mark and you can say this is the Bloor-and-Bay period and this is the Wellesley-Harbord period. To me it's a gimmick, it's the package deal.

It's all so personal, the problem of painting, the problem of creation, that being part of one gang at a certain time doesn't in any way obliterate you or your future. But all painters arrive at a point where they're in trouble when they're categorized too early. Nothing is so true as the fact that society will take you up very quickly and they'll burn you down just as quickly.

It's like a ball game now. You get batting averages. There are already too many people living on the fact of just watching what artists are doing. There are so many artist watchers, and soon they'll have books published on how to watch an artist – 'this is an obvious red-billed twirper, action and tachist variety, found usually in New York'. It's a bad thing.

I've always wanted to do big canvases but I've never been able to afford them. I've worked in real squalor until recently, genuine squalor, and I never realized it until now. I think there's a tendency to paint large paintings now, not because as some critics have suggested the content is smaller and they're being blown up to impress people.

I think it's a desire of painters to go back to the kind of monumentality which epitomized the Renaissance, the great period in Egypt, in Babylon, even England – they used to paint portraits twelve feet high. And I think it's an attempt to bring grandeur back into a mechanical society. In the face of constant destruction, of obliteration, of the general stupidity of the international situation, artists are trying to express a largeness, a spiritual largeness – that this is creativity and to hell with your bombs.

[1960]

Richard Kostelanetz

The Glenn Gould Variations

'Okay, I'd like to help you,' Glenn Gould told me over the telephone, 'but I have two stipulations. You shan't interview any of my family or friends. They won't honour your request. Second, that we do as much of this as possible over the phone.' That was the beginning of a friendship that promises to be, telephonically, mine for years to come. Though an impatient man, Gould is remarkably generous about time spent on the phone, even returning as soon as possible the calls his answering service collects; but he is reluctant to make face-to-face contact. We have spoken at all times of the day and night, between distances as various as a few miles across New York City to New York– Toronto (his home), from a few minutes to over two hours. 'Let's talk again soon. All the best.'

Gould takes the cue of Marshall McLuhan, a local acquaintance, and makes the telephone an extension of himself; and he not only does as much business as possible by phone but he would sooner telephone his family and friends – extend himself literally into their ears – than visit them or even have them visit him. His parents, who live some hundred miles away, receive his calls often; but he sees them only a few times a year, mostly for brief vacations. He has a secretary whom he meets once a year for a ritual drink; but in the evening he dictates letters and essays to her over the phone, and the following afternoon she sends the carbons to him by taxicab. A telephone conversation before bedtime in tandem with Nembutal helps him get to sleep. Gould lives alone, spends most of his day at home, sees few people; nevertheless, he is constantly in touch with everyone important to him, at once, with minimum fuss.

320

His exploitation of the telephone is only one facet of a technologically sophisticated existence, for Gould takes McLuhan's ideas about the electronic media more seriously than McLuhan takes himself. Some years ago, Gould deduced that not only was concert-giving a real pain but the performances he offered were not as perfect as those available on record. 'One was forced to compete with oneself,' he remembers. 'Because I couldn't do as well, those futile concerts reduced my inclination to practise to nil.' So, in 1964, he confirmed a decision made four years earlier and completely gave up the old-fashioned custom of concert-giving in order to channel his performing primarily into the new technologies of recording machines, radio transmission, and television. He frankly sees no justification for playing compromised performances before mere thousands of people when records extend his best rendition into millions of living rooms. Moreover, the act of putting a certain piece on record 'frees you to go on to something else', particularly pieces unfamiliar to the conservative concert-hall audience. Beyond that, the benefits for Gould are as much psychological as esthetic; for where he was once a notorious hypochondriac, now, he says, 'Since I stopped giving concerts, I've scarcely had so much as a sniffle. Most of my earlier illnesses were psychosomatic – a sheer protest against my regimen. These past four years have been the best of my life.'

Gould used to give live lecture-demonstrations; but once the Canadian and British Broadcasting Corporations both let him do the same on television – extend his pedagogy across two countries – he has reduced his appearances before live audiences to a bare minimum, regarding the few that he now gives each year as an excuse to travel to places he has not visited before and to keep the habit of facing live audiences, 'just in case'. Whereas he once taught classes at the University of Toronto, more recently he has been expressing his 'irrepressible hamminess' over the weekly, hour-long Canadian radio program *The Art of Glenn Gould,* on which he is liable to give a lecture, let the producer play his records, or even dramatize a parody he wrote of a music critics' conference, where he mimicked many of the voices, sometimes doing two at once. (He rehearsed this one for me over the long-distance phone.)

If his output is, by his design, as electronic as possible, so is his intake; for he simply connects himself into a variety of inputs and they feed into him. 'I'm not interested in gadgets per se, but in what they can do for me.' Gould watches a lot of televison, exploits his hi-fi set, reads several newspapers (products of *wire* services), carries a radio with him all the time, and at home sometimes listens to both the AM and FM simultaneously. 'Quite mysteriously, I discovered that I could better learn Schoenberg's difficult piano score, *Opus 23,* if I listened to them both at once, the FM to hear music and the AM to hear the news. I want to stay in touch.' Gould can learn a Beethoven score while carrying on a conversation; and he often reads one of the many magazines to which he subscribes while listening attentively to someone on the telephone. Afterward, he will remember details from both inputs for Gould appears to be, as

McLuhan puts it, omniattentive. He is able to produce so much, I suspect, precisely because his intake is so high; and as a result, he functions like a revved-up machine, continually digesting all experience around him and transforming it into several kinds of manufacture. Indeed, his predominant interest is neither music nor writing but that machine, which is, after all, his primary instrument and, perhaps, his most extraordinary work of art. Its operation seems to provide his greatest visceral pleasure; and upon it he lavishes especially tender care and scrupulous attention.

Whenever he plays, he hums and chants, sometimes quite audibly; and although the engineers put a wall of baffle around his chair, the superfluous sound still creeps onto the final product. 'It's a terrible distraction that I don't like either. I wish I could get rid of it,' he says, 'and I would if I could, believe me; but I can't.' This is perhaps his sole confession of inexcusable weakness. Piano or not, his performances of Beethoven generally strike critics as less distinguished and even less inventive than his Bach, while some Schoenbergians regard his recordings of the master as distinctly sloppy and perversely romantic.

The hum is another symptom of his intense involvement with performing; for at the instrument, Gould is a coiled dynamo of energy. Nearly every part of his body moves as he plays – his large head sways from side to side, and as his right foot operates the piano's pedals, his left shifts to preserve his balance. Only his broad hips are stable and relaxed. His fingers, neither long nor stubby, are well-muscled; and his famous trills are as spectacular to see as they are to hear – his fingernails literally flutter over the keys. Although he sits considerably lower than most pianists – only fourteen, rather than the usual twenty, inches off the floor – he seems to bear down on the piano; and everything he plays conveys a sense of highly tempered but incipiently overwhelming energy. At baroque counterpoint technique – the ability to articulate two or more melodies at once without subordinating one to the other – Gould is a master; and he also exhibits particular genius for phrasing – for articulating both the precise notes and the subliminal character of every passage of notes (rather than building a climax) – and for discovering a tempo so unusual and yet effective that it offends before it convinces. As a result, even in Bach's superficially repetitious *Well-Tempered Clavier*, Gould amazingly manages to bestow on each prelude and fugue an individual identity. Achieving such precise musical articulation involves incredibly exacting rapport between the head and the hand – between the sounds the mind wants to hear and those the fingers can produce; and it is precisely by playing from the fingers that he adapts harpsichord technique to the piano.

A perfectionist by personal taste, he rejects a section merely because an eighth note has slipped from a line; and he often instructs the tape editor that a few bars from the third take of a certain section should be spliced into an entire section of the second take, which should in turn be integrated in place of similar material in the original. Sometimes Gould will record several distinctly different interpretations of the same score and then pick judiciously among the available results, even splicing two originally contrary renditions into his final integral version. In the end, therefore, the record of a Gould performance that we hear is really a carefully patched collection of segments. Some performers and critics think that fiddling with bits and pieces represents a kind of artistic 'cheating', particularly when incisive editing produces the kind of inspired performance unlikely, if not impossible, in a sustained recital; but more concerned with ends (the record) than means (how he made it), Gould believes that the performer is obliged not only to play as well as possible but also to edit his rendition exactly to his conception of excellence. 'A performer should treat tape as a film director treates his rushes.'

His attitude to recordings is an intrinsic dimension of his enormous technological bias and sophistication; and as a writer he is, appropriately, best known as the philosopher of the recording. Indeed, his essays on the prospects and influence of recordings comprise as thorough and imaginative an exploration of this issue as has ever been done. Here Gould flatly suggests, 'the habit of concert-going and concert-giving, both as a social institution and as chief symbol of musical mercantilism, will be . . . dormant in the twenty-first century.' More specifically, Gould argues that the development of recordings, a product of electronic technology, has thoroughly changed the musical situation in various ways. Our generation values a sound that is possessed of a great degree of 'clarity, immediacy, and indeed almost tactile proximity', a sound that was neither available to nor wanted by the musical profession or public two generations ago. For instance, where orchestras once attempted to create a sound splendid enough to fill a concert hall, now the desired sound, even in a concert, is more appropriate to the scale of a living room. Indeed, in his own record-listening, Gould is particularly sensitive to the effects produced by various strategies of microphone placement. Second, records make continuously available to the musical audience certain kinds of esoteric music, particularly preclassic and highly contemporary, that would otherwise be heard only on rare occasions, if at all. Third, records do for music what the art book did for art; for where the latter is, in André Malraux's famous phrase, a museum without walls, so recordings create in every man's library both a concert without halls and a musical museum whose curator is the record owner; therefore, all known musical styles – indeed, all kinds of music – are, thanks to records, available to the record owner at once. (This may explain why Gould's own taste embraces such contrary enthusiasms as Strauss and Schoenberg.) Fourth, the performer shares responsibility for the final product with the record's producer and his editors and technicians. Fifth, all the available recordings of a particular piece create a living 'tradition' that forces the work's next performer to offer something distinctly original. 'If there is any excuse to make a recording,' Gould has said elsewhere, 'it is to do it differently – as it has never been done before. If one can't quite do that, abandon the project and move on to something else.'

Finally, 'Within the last few decades . . . music has ceased to be an occasion, requiring an excuse and a tuxedo and accorded, when encountered, an almost religious devotion; music has become a pervasive influence in our lives, and as our dependence upon it has increased, our reverence for it has in a certain sense declined.'

In background, the cosmopolite is indubitably a provincial; yet this isolation from cultural fashion probably endowed him with that eccentric individualism that, once the world accepted it, made him extremely cosmopolitan. He was born in Toronto, Ontario, in 1932, of prosperous Presbyterian parents; and though he is no longer a churchgoer, Protestant ideas still haunt his consciousness. His entire education took place in his home town, much of it literally at home. His first piano teacher was, prosaically enough, his mother; and thanks to tutoring, he combined his musical education with sporadic attendance at the public schools. He entered Toronto's Royal Conservatory of Music at nine, precociously graduating at twelve, but continued to study there until his late teens. To this day his accent retains that Toronto mixture of elegant diction and anglicisms overlaid with Midwestern intonations. An autodidact by inclination and a shaper of his own destiny by insistence, Gould as a teenager discovered Schoenberg and other contempory composers, even though his teachers had not championed them; and he now considers twelve-tone technique 'the only really valid linguistic innovation in the twentieth century'. Around this time, he also worked out wholly on his own that stunningly original interpretation of Bach's *Goldberg Variations* in which he successfully appropriated a harpsichord piece for the piano. Yet he was not a child prodigy in the conventional Menuhin sense; and when he first attracted public notice, at the age of twelve, his instrument of virtuosity was not the piano but the organ. 'That was the only period of my life when I enjoyed giving concerts,' Gould now judges. 'Performing before an audience gave me a glorious sense of power at fifteen.'

When he has a lot of work to do, he drives up into Northern Ontario, where he will check into a motel or one of the older hotels in the area and work there. His favourite method for 'cooling off' his machinery is driving alone through the lumber towns along the Lake Superior shore while listening to rock music on the radio. He prefers northern climates to tepid ones – London being the only city that might woo him away from Toronto; and in general, he would like to spend more time in the country. 'I've got to have hills, water, and leaden sky,' he says. 'My ability to work varies inversely with the niceness of the weather.' His most enjoyable recent visits were spent in Canada's northernmost territories, and in 1967 he produced a radio show about this region – his first extended venture into non-musical reportage. Indeed, 'The Idea of North', in which he superimposed contrapuntally various conversations and phrases into an essay on the effects of isolation, was so well received that the CBC gave Gould a five-year contract solely to produce radio specials. 'It's now my favourite medium.'

In the past few years he has literally redesigned his style of life, just as he transformed his piano exactly to the specifications he wanted – rearranged his environment and ultimately himself as his own most thoughtfully created and favourite work of art.

The paradox is that Gould is a reclusively private person who lives, via the media, an extremely public life, in constant 'touch' with the world community; for not only do his records become the intimate possessions of millions of people but the world's activities are also immediately present to him. This explains why Gould feels himself related more to the mass than the elite; for where a truly private person loves and is loved by some*one*, Gould loves everyone and everyone in turn loves him. He writes for a public of readers, broadcasts for a mass of listeners; and even over such a functionally private medium as the telephone, he is performing – behaving as he would in public. He simply knows and has known no other way. Indicatively, the 'individuals' that appear in his parodies and satires are invariably drawn upon either public figures or media stereotypes. Gould has, by a series of choices, set up a certain mode of life; and although he is as much the victim as the beneficiary of his system, he knows he could, by other choices, reprogram his circuits to achieve an entirely different style.

[1967]

Neil Compton

Cancult and the CBC

Montreal is the best place in the world in which to watch television. With the aid of a community cable or rooftop antennae, Montrealers can tune in the programs not only of three Canadian networks (two English and one French), but also of three American ones from stations in northern New England. The two English-Canadian networks frequently feature programs from the BBC or ITV in Britain; less frequently, the French network uses material produced in France.

The viewer's choice extends from the usual quizzes, panel games, and situation comedies to bold experiments in documentary and drama. There are productions of Molière, Sheridan, and Shakespeare – and of Albee, Pinter, and Beckett. (Nothing lights up network switchboards with indignant calls like a good sordid modern play.) On the late show recently there have been opportunities to see such films as *Rashomon* and *L'Avventura*, all uninterrupted and unabridged.

However, the cacophonous and kaleidoscopic airwaves of Montreal are more than a viewer's paradise: they are also an epitome of the conflicts and confusions of the country as a whole. On the one hand, Canada largely owes its existence as a sovereign state to the triumph of communications policy over geography, economics, and cultural diversity. Yet the very electronic media which make Canada possible are presently adding to the strains and tensions which endanger the confederation.

Canada, of course, is a geographical absurdity – 80 per cent of the population lives in a three-thousand-mile strip along the American border. The strip is not even continuous but cut by formidable natural barriers. Far more Canadians have visited the United States than have visited any province other than the one in which they live. Surveys have shown that Canadians in the various regions often share more attitudes with their immediate neighbours to the south than they do with their fellow countrymen in other regions.

National unity under such circumstances can be achieved only at a price. The railways, telegraphs, highways, airways, and waterways that keep traffic and information moving from east to west have been expensive to build and maintain; often they duplicate services that might have been more cheaply and conveniently available in the United States.

The combination of immense capital costs and comparatively low returns has meant that government rather than private initiative dominates the communications field.

At this moment, cultural diversity is probably a greater problem to Canada than either geography or economics. If we apply to the Canadian population Karl Deutsch's definition of a 'people', which stresses 'complementary habits and facilities of communication' (including shared language, memories, customs, preferences, libraries, statues, signposts, and the like) we find English and French Canadians lacking in many of the necessary common characteristics. The difference is more than a matter of mere language: as Deutsch says, the Swiss, with their four languages, are one people. The Canadians, with two, are not. Not quite, and not yet.

The Canadian Broadcasting Corporation conceives its mandate from Parliament to involve four objectives:

1.   To be a complete service, covering . . . the whole range of programming.
2.   To link all parts of the country . . . through the inclusion of . . . national and common interests in its program services; [and to bring] the national program service to as many Canadians as finances allow.
3.   To be predominantly Canadian in content and character . . . contributing to the development and preservation of national unity.
4.   To serve equitably the two main language groups and cultures, and the special needs of Canada's various geographical regions.

Three of the four aims are explicitly concerned with creating a sense of Canadian identity, and the fourth (the provision of a complete service) is really a means to achieve the others. Evidently the CBC considers itself an instrument for the forging and maintenance of a distinctive bilingual Canadian nationalism. So far as I know, no other broadcasting system in the Western world conceives of its function in quite these terms. The American networks certainly do not have any comparable ambition, and the various European agencies are the expressions of long-established national cultures. The closest parallel of which I am aware is the Australian Broadcasting Corporation, but the ABC has neither to cope with two languages nor to compete with the combined blandishments of three wealthy American networks. (It is also supported entirely by public funds.) The CBC's operations are carried out on behalf of a total audience not much larger than that of the New York viewing area, scattered over a territory one-fifth larger than the continental U.S.A., and in the face of strong competition for audiences and sponsors from private commercial stations on both sides of the border whose total annual income far exceeds that of the CBC.

Can a medium of mass communication in a free society really accomplish such a purpose? There have been many attacks on the CBC for its allegedly impractical, utopian, and paternalistic policy. Critics usually claim to speak on behalf of the great majority of Canadians (though cynics might suspect them of representing more limited interests). However, the evidence is overwhelming that Canadians in general approve of the Corporation's objectives. In 1963, the CBC commissioned an elaborate survey of 'what the Canadian public thinks of the CBC'. It showed that well over 90 per cent of the population approved even the most high-minded statements of CBC purpose, and that slightly smaller majorities thought the Corporation fulfilled these aims well or very well (the one exception being 'helping French and English Canadians to understand and learn about each other'; only 57 per cent thought the CBC did well here).

However, even the most starry-eyed CBC executive knows that program policy cannot be based on the expectations aroused by such a survey. The commercial rating systems may be very crude indicators of the real involvement between viewers and their TV sets, but they are accurate enough to indicate a depressing contrast between what viewers say and what they do. Most of us, whatever may be our theories about the immense potentialities of broadcasting, turn to televison (as others turn to detective stories or science fiction) primarily for relaxation and amusement. Any realistic daily program schedule must contain a very high proportion of light entertainment, and this necessity involves the CBC in some extraordinary compromises with its own principles.

The bitter fact is that most Canadians have formed their taste in entertainment from the most popular American network shows. Almost the only Canadian productions which attract an equal or greater audience are televised games of the National Hockey League. In order to hold on to its audience and prevent them from switching to rival channels, the CBC must devote most of its time during prime viewing hours to American programs.

The only adequate answer to the challenge of American influence would be the development of a genuine indigenous Canadian popular art. There is, for instance, no successful Canadian equivalent to such classic American TV genres as the western or the family situation comedy. Whatever may be their artistic limitations, such dramatic stereotypes enshrine profound (if sometimes inaccurate) popular intuitions about American life. For better or for worse, Canada seems to be a land without comparable myths of its own.

The CBC English network has done its best to supply the lack, but with indifferent success.

On the French TV network, though, things are so very different that when Montrealers switch from Channel 6 to Channel 2, they seem to be transported to a different city. Radio Canada has all the energy, imaginative vitality, and rapport with its audience that English-speaking producers long for. The French-Canadian community might have been specially designed to support a popular television service: it is homogeneous, large enough to provide a variety of audiences but not so large as to be formless, and it is protected from undue outside influence by the language barrier. Since the French TV network began operation, French Canada has ceased to be frightened by the bogy of assimilation – which kept her for generations in a state of defensive isolation from the world – and has begun to take an ebullient and aggressive delight in her own unique identity. It is impossible to doubt that television has played a vital part in stimulating this renaissance.

Thus the CBC's attempt to serve Canada's two cultures equitably succeeds, in so far as it does, at the expense of national unity. The more effectively it serves either community, the more it will reinforce those characteristics which set them apart from one another. Naturally, the Corporation is aware of this problem and has tried to solve it. There have been a number of rather self-conscious and embarrassed bilingual variety shows which served to dramatize rather than bridge the gulf. Dozens of programs on all four networks have undertaken the task of explaining the French and the English to one another. It is doubtful whether these have been very successful in influencing the mass of the population. There are, after all, many pitfalls in the way of mass communication. Even apart from the general tendency of the media to focus on and dramatize the conflict and violence in any situation, one is reminded of the experiment recently carried out by the BBC: a radio program of advice on travelling in France ended by discouraging more potential tourists than it encouraged because more listeners were frightened by the prospect of problems they had not expected (language, currency, etc.) than were reassured by the helpful hints. The Canadian confederation has rested for years on certain convenient mutual misunderstandings between English and French Canadians. Now that the new media are ensuring that they understand one another only too well, discord rather than harmony is the initial consequence.

For all this, however, the CBC is one of the great forces for reason and civilization in Canada. Once we grant the fact that a native popular culture does not and probably cannot exist in English Canada, we are free to recognize that CBC program policy has been about as liberal and imaginative as one could reasonably expect of a great public communications system.

The new media have often been accused of battening parasitically upon the creative energy of real art, vulgarizing its themes, and seducing its practitioners with fame and money. This may be so in societies with a deeply rooted traditional culture, but it has not been so in Canada. With its small, dispersed population and puritan, philistine outlook, English Canada in particular had virtually no serious professional tradition of music or theatre at the time that the CBC was established. Now, half a dozen cities have cadres of actors, musicians, and dancers who are able to earn a tolerable living by combining live performance with appearances on radio or TV. The Corporation's budget for serious programming in the field of the arts may be small in relation to the whole, but it is enough to insure that composers, playwrights – even poets – can hope for at least occasional commissions which involve few or no concessions to popular taste, and sometimes not even to the medium.

It is usually on radio that such minority intellectual and artistic interests are now catered to. Almost deserted by commercial sponsors and banished from the living room by the family TV, CBC network radio has become a kind of middle-brow Canadian magazine or newspaper – the electronic equivalent of *Maclean's* or *The Globe and Mail*. As one might deduce from its middle-class ambience, it is probably the most eloquent and influential instrument of enlightened nationalism in Canada.

Canada's marginal culture – occupying a middle ground between British and American, English and French, civilization and wilderness – appears to favour the interpretative and critical, rather than the fiercely creative, intelligence. Life in Canada inculcates a respect for the brutal, objective thusness of nature and an awareness (sometimes a wry one) of the validity of opposition to it. Canadians tend to become singers, pianists, actors, critics, and diplomats rather than composers, dramatists, poets, or political geniuses.

This is the ideal temperament for documentary, and the greatest triumphs of Canadian broadcasting, as of Canadian cinema, have been in this field. The CBC's audience has become accustomed to workmanlike documentary programs as part of the regular weekly diet on both radio and television and occasionally these sober factual productions come close to the heights of poetic truth.

Recently, the documentary spirit has been tending toward irony, another mode encouraged by Canada's comparatively helpless proximity to stronger or wealthier neighbours. The basic technique is simple – to juxtapose pictures and commentary (often by the subject himself) in order to achieve almost Swiftian satiric intensities.

Irony and parody are also the mode of the TV comedians Wayne and Shuster. Their relentless spoofing of every sacred or profane cow – from biculturalism and the Stratford Festival to cool jazz and teen-age fashions – is more obvious and less sophisticated than the documentary tradition I have described, but it probably comes closer to the expression of a native popular art than anything else on the CBC English network. The conclusion seems to be that though Canadians may lack a strong sense of their own identity, they do not allow this to inhibit them in deflating fraud or pomposity, whether it be native or foreign. In developing this genre, the CBC may, like Holden Caulfield, have found its own unique way of confronting the modern world.

[1964]

Edgar Kaufmann, Jr.

Canada's New Turn in Architecture

Something powerful and new is stirring in Canada, something bound to affect architecture everywhere before long. Architects, patrons of architecture, and students of it ought to see this for themselves. See, and sense; because if I am right this is no mere elegant fashion or suitably certified style, it is a new turn in how to think about buildings as human implements and poetic human expressions. The new direction shows clearly in Canada despite plenty of shallow, up-to-date architecture at Expo 67 and in the cities of Toronto and Montreal. The fair at Montreal ended stories about the end of world's fairs, principally because it partook of bigger and more durable ideas that are finding expression in architecture in Canada.

One big idea is that the unit of architecture is no longer an individual building, but a whole milieu. Thus architecture without the disciplines of planning is scarcely conceivable. Sometimes an interrelated group of buildings is roofed together (as at the Scarborough College campus outside Toronto), sometimes towers and blocks rise independently from a platform which in fact unites them in an elaborate catacombery of shops, subways, and sunken areas (as in Montreal's spectacularly successful Place Ville Marie fed by the brand-new Métro that rolls on rubber tires). One element dominates these new complexes – the street, whether motorized as a subway, an escalator, an elevator bank, or separated as a pedestrian mall with vistas and planting, or lined with services for food, shopping, and entertainment as in the classic arcade. There is always the path along which accumulate bigger or smaller volumes of space devoted to more sedentary occupations. And the path predominates as a whole.

331

Even when the interconnections lie mostly concealed below ground this unity is expressed by a plaza, crossed by random paths according to the memorable image of Giacometti's sculpture. Here architecture has a new theme: the path. Pediment, portal, porch seem too static for our age; at best a cantilevered canopy over the path may indicate a change of direction or a change of pace.

Expo 67 created a passacaglia of pathways which made it one of the easiest expositions to negotiate despite its thousand acres. Segregated pedestrian streets predominated, fed by four motorized and separate systems on land and water that met more needs than any one visitor was likely to feel. And many of the larger exhibition buildings had their own powered systems for raising and lowering visitors through their spaces. But it was the coordinated networks of passage through the whole grounds that held Expo together as an experience; assisted, to be sure, by the site on points and islands amid the St. Lawrence River, whose busy traffic and huge port facilities merged into the distant rises of Montreal City as a backdrop. Divided into four areas of activity, with waterways and parklands interspersed, Expo 67 was conceived as a whole in the spirit of architecture today.

A second big idea is that style arises from problem solving, and varies with the occasion. This is quite different from the ordinary concept of style as the expression of an age (modern, medieval, or Ming) or of a race (Maori, Maharashtra, or Mixtec); and equally different from the artist's favourite concept of style as a personal expression: 'Style is the man.' The new feeling for style arises from an insight that artists borrowed from scientists and logicians, and that John Andrews, the architect of the Scarborough campus, phrased thus, 'Being free to formulate a question is the first step in solving it.' It will not do to present a problem to an architect today; he wants to be in on exploring exactly what the problem is. And it will not do to approach a client with a style ready-made, a yardage of effects and details that can be cut to fit the case; what is apt is an open mind and an open eye, ready to seize the characteristic tone and language of the occasion. For this approach architects have had to assemble a new kit of tools; where once T-squares, modules, and aesthetic theories were enough one now finds computer engineering, use vectors, climate and soil analyses (often through new films and aerial photography), and of course traffic networks.

If one adds together these two ideas, that architecture is milieu and that style is of the occasion, clearly enough something is going to happen to the old dichotomy of architecture opposed to nature or architecture as an outgrowth of nature. In fact the problem disappears; the new architecture tends to fit site to use and adapt use to site without worrying.

In the city of Toronto, these new approaches to architecture are convincingly united at the Scarborough campus. Interrelated practical problems and a unified architectural high command, focused on buildings meant to last as well as to grow, naturally yield results more powerful than the ephemera of a fair. Scarborough College has made architectural history.   [1967]

Robert Fulford

Expo and the Art of the Environment: A Hope for the Future

The most curious fact about Expo was that many people who found difficulty getting in to see the pavilions and the films – people, in fact, who hardly got to see *anything* – still came away happy. They were pleased just to be there. Wandering around, digging the scene, riding the minirails, was for some the greatest of Expo pleasures.

But behind the sense of joy one felt on the site – and saw reflected in the eyes and the attitudes of so many others – there was a more specific cause: Expo itself, exclusive of its contents, was carefully designed as a 'happening' that would be exciting and stimulating. And this fact may very well tell us something important about the future of our cities.

The city is, according to received wisdom, man's greatest work of art – indeed, his *only* collective work of art. Curiously, however, and despite our vast experience, we still don't know much about building cities. There are great city-places in the world – say, for instance, St. Mark's Square, in Venice – but we can't say precisely how they happened or how, in our own terms, we can equal them. We are all of us city-planners in one way or another: when you vote for a city councillor, or decide where to buy a suit, or choose to live in this district rather than that one, you are making decisions that affect the shape of your city and your children's city. In this sense, every city is the result of several million individual decisions. But making these decisions on a rational basis, so that we can create environments that will be good to live in, remains beyond us. The computer that can put together thousands of details in order to send a couple of men into orbit around the earth still doesn't know how to orchestrate the avarice of the real-estate developer, the talent of the architect, the promises of the politician, and the needs of the citizen. Expo naturally didn't solve any of these problems, but it pointed us towards some partial solutions.

At Expo the space belonged to the people. You could hurry, or stroll, or stand still. You could eat your lunch in a space that was clean and quiet but still not far from the action. You could just sit down and look at the other people – who were, as it happened, one of the great unexpected sights of the fair. Expo was a place for human beings to be themselves; not a place essentially for cars, or essentially for money-making, or essentially for efficiency.

There was an openness and generosity about its design that made it a very special sort of city space. It became, as Jeremy Baker noted in the Montreal *Star,* the real though temporary city centre of Montreal. 'We are going to experience strong withdrawal symptoms when the fair ends,' he wrote. For the fact is that, during six months, one North American city, only one, had a single large place designed for nothing less than the glorious purpose of making people happy to be there.

Consider Expo as a city centre. First, cars were all but banished; pedestrians thus had the right of way and most of the space. Immediately this meant the noise level was far lower than otherwise, that the air was clean, that the streets were safe.

Second, the main transport system – the Expo Express – was free of charge, unlike the transport systems in all other city centres. And, come to think of it, why shouldn't downtown transport be free? We all have to pay for it anyway, and making it free would encourage people to abandon their cars at the edge of downtown.

Third, the other form of transport, the minirail, was exciting – and why shouldn't we have this, too, in our city centres, outdoor transport placed above the heads of pedestrians so that neither walker nor rider interferes with the other? (Furthermore, the minirail was *fun* – and there's no reason why this, too, can't be borne in mind by future transport planners in the cities.)

Fourth, Expo was clean – far cleaner than any North American city centre – simply because the people running it determined that it had to be. There is no reason why ordinary cities can't be equally vigilant.

Fifth, Expo had, despite one of the wildest collections of architectural shapes in history, a sense of visual unity. This, too, was the result of careful planning; and this, too, can be applied to the new cities we are building and the old ones we are re-building.

'The fact is that the streets, the city milieu, have now taken on a new importance in our society. Whether the individual buildings are good matters less than the *situation.*' This is Arthur Erickson talking. Erickson has designed some of the most beautiful architectural shapes in Canada – Simon Fraser

University, spectacularly located on a mountaintop, is the most famous – but he believes we will come to place more and more emphasis not on individual buildings but on city spaces. 'At Expo what mattered was that the environmental aspects of it – the landscape, the street furniture, the graphics, the transport – all worked together. The real effects of this we won't be aware of for some years.'

Another architect, Raymond Affleck – whose magnificently named firm, Affleck, Desbarats, Dimakopoulos, Lebensold, and Sise, designed two major theme complexes – has already begun to notice the difference. 'Now every facet of the community is affected. We have clients who come to us and refer specifically to Expo standards when they tell us what they want.'

Affleck described the revelation of arriving at Expo the first day the crowds were there. 'We had our nose to the grindstone for four years, and then the first day was the experience of our lives. Here they were, all these people, this was the *real* "Happening", not the buildings or anything else non-human. In many ways Expo is the prototype of the leisure city in the era that is quickly enveloping us, and this is the message people are getting out of it. It's a place to be, an urban scene where people behave in a wonderful way to each other. This quality of human behaviour has been the important thing. That trip on the minirail – now *that's* what urban architecture is all about: moving around, that sense of movement and surprise. That's what we should have in our cities.'

'The Expo corporation and the work it produced,' Affleck went on, 'could be a model for the solution of the whole problem of urban renewal. Three levels of government worked together with architects, engineers, and businessmen, and what they produced was not only a physical miracle of construction but also the most sophisticated kind of work.'

It could be argued, of course, that this was only a special occasion, in a special country, at a special time. As Affleck said, 'Canadians felt that this was their total Canadian thing. The challenge was so sharp. It was like a wartime thing. It *had* to be a success.'

If all this could be accomplished for a big party like Expo, why couldn't similar miracles be worked for the *really* important places, the places where people live and work, in Canada and other countries?

In Canada itself Expo had one very special effect: it brought into play, in a city-like situation, the talents of a whole class of people we hardly knew existed before. Jean Boucher, the director of the Canada Council, made the point shortly before Expo ended: 'Most of what man has done in this country has been ugly – but there is a sort of visual revelation dawning on us now. What people will retain of Expo is an artistic visual experience.

'For the first time, the country put to use an unbelievable number of artists and designers. I think that the country will have to go on using these people. They are here, and they have demonstrated they can make things that are beautiful and effective as well. From now on it will be more and more difficult to build things which will not be aesthetically designed.'

The chief of Expo's design division, Norman Hay, is now busy on a vast, intricate network of man-made islands to be created by the province of Ontario along the Canadian National Exhibition's waterfront.

Ron Haggart wrote in his Toronto *Star* column: 'After we have all seen Expo, how can any of us, ever again, be content with the cities in which we live?' How indeed? Four months after Expo opened, Montreal announced a new preliminary plan for the city and the planners' research superintendent defined it in terms every Montrealer could by then comprehend: 'What we really want to do,' he said, 'is to generate the same sort of feeling that we've seen at Expo — fun and pride.'

Montreal's plan is intended to take some account of the awesome future of metropolitan construction in North America and Europe. We are, whether we like it or not, now embarking on a period of city-building that will dwarf anything in the history of the world. North America will have to build as much living and working space in the next few decades as in the last two centuries. Right now we don't know how to do it. Possibly Expo has helped us to learn.

It was a great place to visit; maybe, in a sense, we'll find ourselves eventually living there as well.

[1968]

Acknowledgements

For permission to reprint copyright material the editor and the publisher offer grateful thanks to the following publishers, authors, and agents:

Annals of the American Academy of Political and Social Sciences for "Conservatism: The Deep Bond in an Embattled Marriage" from "Postscripts: Canadian National Character" by John Porter in the March 1967 issue.

Georges Borchardt, Inc., for "Europe's Last Chance" from *Canada, Europe's Last Chance* by Claude Julien, Macmillan of Canada (1968).

Charles Bruce for "Atlantic Cadence" in *Century 1867–1967*, Southam Press (1967).

Morley Callaghan for "How Can a Writer Live in Toronto?" from "Why Toronto?" in *Our Sense of Identity*, edited by Malcolm Ross, Ryerson Press (1954).

Canadian Forum for "The First International Nation" by Barbara Ward in the October 1968 issue; for "A Hard Lesson for Africa" from "Yugoslavia of the West" by Ali Mazrui in the October 1968 issue; for "The Female Style in Politics" from "Of Marsh and Men" by Adrienne Clarkson in the March 1969 issue; and for "Declaration of Independence" by Leonard Beaton in the April 1968 issue.

The Canadian Institute of International Affairs for "Unlovely Canadianism" from "Problems of Canadian Nationality" by Harry G. Johnson in *International Journal* 16, no. 3 (Summer 1961).

The Canadian Institute of Public Affairs for "Letting People Be Different" from "Canadian Issues as Seen from Outside" by Richard Crossman in *Order and Good Government*, edited by Gordon Hawkins, 33rd Couchiching Conference, C.I.P.A. (1964); and for "On Becoming Canadian" by John Hirsch from *Concepts of Federalism*, edited by Gordon Hawkins, 34th Couchiching Conference, C.I.P.A. (1965).

Edmund Carpenter for "The Eskimo and His Art" abridged from his article "Arctic Art".

Hayden Carruth for "In Haste, with Love, to Canada", copyright © 1970 by Hayden Carruth.

Commentary and Neil Compton for "Cancult and the CBC" from "Television and Canadian Culture" by Neil Compton in *Commentary* (November 1964), copyright © 1965 by the American Jewish Committee.

André Deutsch Limited, International Famous Agency, Inc., and the Canadian publishers, McClelland and Stewart Limited, Toronto, for " 'The Jewish beavers of this land . . .' " from *Son of a Smaller Hero*, copyright © 1955 Mordecai Richler (published in the United States by Paperback Library).

Kildare Dobbs for "Canadian Heroes?" from *Saturday Night*, February 1968.

Fernand Dumont for "On Living with Divided Loyalties" from a letter to the editor of the Toronto *Globe and Mail*, June 7, 1969.

James Eayrs for "Canada's Black Fact: From Pullmans to Reservations to Igloos" from the Toronto *Daily Star*, February 28, 1969; for "The Scrutable Canadian: Lester Pearson" from the Montreal *Star*, January 10, 1968; and for "The Undefended Border" from "In Defence of a Border" in *Canadian Forum*, June 1967.

Editions HMH for "Return to Winter" from *Mon Babel* by Pierre Trottier (1963).

Douglas Fisher for "Ontario's Ancient North".

George Grant for "To Be a Citizen in North America", abridged from a speech given at the first teach-in at the University of Toronto in 1965.

Roderick Haig-Brown for "British Columbia: Loggers and Lotus Eaters" from "B.C.: The Profligate Province" in *Century 1867–1967*, Southam Press (1967).

Anne Hébert for "Quebec: The Original Heart" from "Quebec: The Proud Province" in *Century 1867–1967*, Southam Press (1967).

Gad Horowitz for "Red Tory" from "Tories, Socialists and the Demise of Canada" in *Canadian Dimension*, May 1965.

M.G. Hurtig Ltd. for "Boil Me No Melting Pots" by Larry Zolf from *The New Romans*, edited by Al Purdy (1969).

Sybil Hutchinson for "Local Grains of Sand" by James Reaney from *Edge*, Autumn 1964.

Bruce Hutchison for "Wacky in Wonderland" from "Magic in Bennett-land" in the *Vancouver Sun*, 1968.

Naim Kattan for "Montreal Comes of Age" from the *Tamarack Review*, Spring 1968.

Edgar Kaufmann, Jr., for "Canada's New Turn in Architecture", copyright © 1967 by *Harper's Magazine*, May 1967.

William Kilbourn for "Tory Ontario" from "Southern Ontario: The Loyalist Heritage Clings" in *Century 1867–1967*, Southam Press (1967).

Richard Kostelanetz for "The Glenn Gould Variations" from *Master Minds*, copyright © 1967, 1969 by Richard Kostelanetz, and published by Macmillan, New York (1969).

Douglas LePan for "In Frock Coat and Moccasins" from "The Dilemma of the Canadian Author" in *Atlantic Monthly*, November 1964.

Mrs. Wyndham Lewis for "Leviathan and the Canadian Ahab" by Wyndham Lewis in *The Listener*, August 29, 1946.

J.B. Lippincott Company and Harold Matson Company, Inc., for "Letter to a Brother" from "To Stuart Lowry" in *Selected Letters of Malcolm Lowry*, copyright © 1965 by Margerie Bonner Lowry.

Jack Ludwig for "Canada: Kept Woman or Free?" copyright © 1970 by Jack Ludwig, first published in the Toronto *Globe and Mail*, May 9, 1969.

The Macmillan Company of Canada Limited for "Ned Pratt" by Northrop Frye from the Introduction to *The Collected Poems of E. J. Pratt*, second edition, edited by Northrop Frye (1958); and for "Canada and French-Canadian Nationalism" from "The New Treason of the Intellectuals" in *Federalism and the French Canadians* by Pierre Elliott Trudeau (1968).

McClelland and Stewart Limited, Toronto, the Canadian Publishers, for "Expo and the Art of the Environment: A Hope for the Future" from *This Was Expo* by Robert Fulford (1968); and for "The Importance of Being Colonial" from "Other Canadians and After" by Milton Wilson in *Masks of Poetry*, edited by A. J. M. Smith (1962).

McClelland and Stewart Limited, Toronto, the Canadian Publishers, and Collins-Knowlton-Wing, Inc., for "The Religion of Work and the Dirtiest Job in the World" from *The Smug Minority* by Pierre Berton (1967).

McGraw-Hill Company of Canada Limited for "Technology in Our Past and Present" from "Technology and Nationalism" by Melville Watkins, and for "Nationalism in Canadian Literature" by Frank Watt, both in *Nationalism in Canada*, edited by Peter Russell, copyright © 1966, McGraw-Hill Company of Canada Limited.

W. O. Mitchell for "A Boy's Prairie" from *Who Has Seen the Wind*, Macmillan of Canada (1947). Farley Mowat for "Newfoundland: 'T'ree Hunnert Year Gone By'" from *Century 1867–1967*, Southam Press (1967).

Farley Mowat and the Canadian Publishers, McClelland and Stewart Limited, Toronto, for "The Canadian Arctic" from *Canada North* by Farley Mowat (1967).

The *New Statesman* for "How To Live on the Margin" from "On the Margin" by Ronald Bryden in the January 29, 1965, issue.

The *New Yorker Magazine* for the excerpts from "The Mohawks in High Steel" by Joseph Mitchell, reprinted from the *New Yorker*, September 17, 1949, copyright © 1949, The New Yorker Magazine, Inc.

Christina Newman for "Ottawa Man" from "How To Spot the Ottawa Man: A Concise Guide" in *Maclean's*, October 6, 1962; and for "Ottawa Farewell" from "Ottawa Letter" in *Saturday Night*, March 1969.

Peter Newman for "The Diefenbaker Legend Will Live On" from the Toronto *Daily Star*, September 12, 1967.

Harold Ober and Associates Incorporated and the *New York Times* for "The Man in the Mask: Pierre Trudeau" by Marshall McLuhan in the *New York Times Book Review*, November 17, 1968, copyright © 1968 by The New York Times Company.

Don Owen for "Leonard Cohen: The Poet as Hero" from "Leonard Cohen: The Poet as Hero, 3. Cohen Remembered" in *Saturday Night*, June 1969.

The Oxford University Press, Toronto, for "Running to Paradise" from *Running to Paradise* by Kildare Dobbs (1962).

The Regents of the University of Wisconsin for "The Northern Frontier: Key to Canadian History" from *The Canadian Identity* by W. L. Morton, University of Wisconsin Press (1961).

Claude Ryan for "The Canadian Solution" from "The Position of *Le Devoir* in the Present Canadian Crisis" in *Le Devoir*, September 18–19, 1964.

The Ryerson Press, Toronto, for "Coming of Age in Quebec", "Religion in French Canada", and "The Strong Women of Quebec" reprinted from *Convergence* by Jean Le Moyne (1966).

Gordon Sheppard for "Violence and the French-Canadian Male" from "A dilemma with no exit?" in the Toronto *Telegram*, April 26, 1969.

The Toronto *Daily Star* for "Moral Imagination: Canadian Thing" from "Where the Promise Comes From" by Hugh Hood in the December 9, 1967, issue, and for "To Be Masters in Our Own House" from "Why I believe a free Quebec is the best thing for you too" by René Lévesque in the January 20, 1968, issue.

The University of Toronto Press for "Paul-Emile Borduas" abridged from the article by Jean Ethier-Blais in *Canada's Past and Present: A Dialogue*, Our Living Tradition, fifth series, edited by Robert L. McDougall, copyright Canada 1964 by University of Toronto Press (in association with Carleton University); for "Two Styles of Historian: Donald Creighton and Frank Underhill" from "The Writing of Canadian History" by William Kilbourn in *Literary History of*

Canada, edited by Carl F. Klinck,©University of Toronto Press 1965; for " 'Le Canada tout entier' of Henri Bourassa" abridged from "Henri Bourassa" by André Laurendeau in *Canada's Past and Present: A Dialogue*, Our Living Tradition, fourth series, edited by Robert L. McDougall, copyright Canada 1962 by University of Toronto Press (in association with Carleton University); and for "After 300 Years, Our Neurosis Is Relevant" from the contribution of Hugh MacLennan to *The Price of Being Canadian*, edited by D.B.L. Hamlin, 7th Winter Conference, Canadian Institute of Public Affairs, copyright Canada 1961 by University of Toronto Press.

Waterloo Lutheran University for "Harold Town Talks" by Elizabeth Kilbourn in the *Waterloo Review* no. 5 (Summer 1960).

Edmund Wilson for "A Turgenev? In Toronto?" published as "Morley Callaghan of Toronto" in *O Canada: An American's Notes on Canadian Culture*, copyright © 1964, 1965 by Edmund Wilson and published by Farrar, Straus and Giroux, Inc.

George Woodcock for "Encounter with an Archangel" from the *Tamarack Review*, Winter 1963.

The editor's introduction contains material that appeared in different form in *The Making of the Nation* by William Kilbourn, The Canadian Centennial Library, McClelland and Stewart (1967).

Every reasonable effort has been made to trace ownership of copyright material. Information will be welcomed which will enable the publisher to rectify any reference in future printings.

 The editor wishes to express his gratitude to the Centennial Commission for a grant toward the preparation of the manuscript.

1867 | 1967

Biographical
Notes

LEONARD BEATON, educated at McGill University and Cambridge, has been with the Montreal *Gazette*, Reuters, *The Guardian*, and *The Times* of London. He is a former director of the Institute of Strategic Studies and has written *The Spread of Nuclear Weapons, Must the Bomb Spread,* and *The Struggle for Peace.*

PIERRE BERTON is a television and radio personality, journalist, and the author of many books, including *The Mysterious North, Klondike,* and *The Smug Minority.* He was writer and narrator for the NFB film *City of Gold.*

CHARLES BRUCE, a retired news agency executive, was born and educated in Nova Scotia. A poet and novelist, his works include *The Mulgrave Road, The Channel Shore, The Township of Time,* and *News and the Southams.*

RONALD BRYDEN was born in the West Indies and educated in Canada. For some years a book reviewer for the *Spectator* in England, he has been drama critic for the *New Statesman* and *The Observer* since 1963, and is the author of *The Unfinished Hero.*

MORLEY CALLAGHAN is a novelist and short-story writer. His numerous books include *The Loved and the Lost, The Many Colored Coat, A Passion in Rome,* and *That Summer in Paris.*

EDMUND CARPENTER is in the Department of Anthropology at San Fernando State College in California. He taught for many years at the University of Toronto and was co-editor with Marshall McLuhan of the review *Explorations.* He was a co-author with Frederick Varley and Robert Flaherty of *Eskimo,* and has published many articles on Eskimo culture.

HAYDEN CARRUTH, a free-lance writer and editor, has published six volumes of poetry, a novel, and a book of criticism. Two collections of his poetry and two anthologies he has edited will soon be published. His latest work is *Nothing for Tigers.*

ADRIENNE CLARKSON, the hostess of *Take Thirty* on CBC-TV, taught English at the University of Toronto and is the author of *A Lover More Condoling.*

NEIL COMPTON is head of the English Department at Sir George Williams University and has been

341

on the Humanities Research Council of Canada. He is a regular contributor to the New York magazine *Commentary*.

RICHARD CROSSMAN is Lord President of the Council in the British Labour government. He has written *The Charm of Politics, A Nation Reborn,* and *Planning for Freedom.*

KILDARE DOBBS is an associate editor of *Saturday Night,* a free-lance writer, and author of *Running to Paradise* and *Reading the Time.*

FERNAND DUMONT is a professor of sociology at Laval University. He is the author of *Le Lieu de l'homme* and co-editor of several other books, including *Littérature et société canadiennes-françaises* with Jean-Charles Falardeau.

JAMES EAYRS is Professor of International Relations at the University of Toronto, co-editor of the *International Journal,* and a columnist for the Toronto *Star.* His books include *In Defence of Canada, Northern Approaches,* and *Minutes of the Sixties.*

JEAN ETHIER-BLAIS is an associate professor of French at McGill University and a literary critic for *Le Devoir.*

DOUGLAS FISHER is a political columnist for the Toronto *Telegram.* He was formerly a Member of Parliament and Deputy House Leader for the N.D.P.

NORTHROP FRYE is a scholar and teacher, now University Professor at the University of Toronto. He contributes frequently to learned journals and has published several books, notably *Fearful Symmetry* and *Anatomy of Criticism.*

ROBERT FULFORD is editor of *Saturday Night,* host of *This Is Robert Fulford* on CBC radio, and a book critic. He is the author of *Crisis at the Victory Burlesk* and *This Was Expo.*

GEORGE GRANT is in the Department of Religion, McMaster University, and the author of *Lament for a Nation.* He delivered the 1969 Massey Lectures on CBC radio.

RODERICK HAIG-BROWN is a novelist, essayist, and writer of nature books and juveniles who lives in British Columbia. His books include *The Farthest Shore, The Living Land,* and *Captain of the Discovery.*

ANNE HÉBERT is a French-Canadian poet, novelist, and short-story writer. She has published *Le Torrent* and *Les Chambres de bois,* among other books.

JOHN HIRSCH, former director of the Manitoba Theatre Centre, has directed plays at the Stratford Festival (Ontario) and at the Lincoln Center, New York.

HUGH HOOD is in the Department of English, University of Montreal. His publications include *Flying a Red Kite, White Figure, White Ground, Around the Mountain, The Camera Always Lies,* and *Strength Down Centre: The Jean Beliveau Story.*

GAD HOROWITZ is in the Department of Political Economy, University of Toronto, and is a frequent contributor to various journals. He is the author of *Canadian Labour in Politics.*

BRUCE HUTCHISON, editorial director of the Vancouver *Sun,* is a political journalist, author, and short-story writer. His many books include *The Unknown Country* and *Mr. Prime Minister.*

HARRY JOHNSON is a professor of economics at the London School of Economics and the University of Chicago. He was on the research staff of the Royal Commission on Banking and Finance in 1962. His publications include *The Canadian Quandary, International Trade and Economic Growth,* and *Money.*

CLAUDE JULIEN, foreign affairs editor of the Paris newspaper *Le Monde,* and a frequent visitor to North America, is the author of *Canada: Europe's Last Chance.*

NAIM KATTAN is an officer of the Canada Council and a frequent contributor of articles in French and in English to various journals and magazines.

EDGAR KAUFMANN, Jr., Adjunct Professor of Architectural History at Columbia University and a director of the Society of Architectural Historians and of the International Council of Societies of Industrial Design, was responsible for five publications about Frank Lloyd Wright. His latest book is *Design in the Modern World.*

ELIZABETH KILBOURN teaches humanities at York University. An art critic and broadcaster, she is the author of *Great Canadian Painting.*

WILLIAM KILBOURN is a professor of history at York University, a Toronto alderman, and an author (*The Firebrand, The Elements Combined, The Making of the Nation, Religion in Canada, Pipeline*).

RICHARD KOSTELANETZ is an American critic, the author of *Master Minds,* and *The Theatre of Mixed Means,* co-author and editor of *The New American Arts,* and editor of several anthologies. His pattern poetry has been published in various magazines and anthologies.

ANDRÉ LAURENDEAU was editor-in-chief of *Le Devoir* and served as co-chairman of the Royal Commission on Bilingualism and Biculturalism. He wrote *Voyages au pays de l'enfance* and *La Crise de la conscription.* He died in 1968.

JEAN LE MOYNE is with the National Film Board. He was co-founder of the review *La Nouvelle Relève,* literary director of *Le Canada,* and editor-in-chief of *La Revue Moderne.* He is the author of *Convergence: Essays from Quebec.*

DOUGLAS LEPAN is principal of University College, University of Toronto, and a novelist and poet. He has written *The Net and the Sword* and *The Deserter.*

RENÉ LÉVESQUE is the leader of the Parti Québécois and a member of the Quebec Legislative Assembly. He is the author of *An Option for Quebec.*

WYNDHAM LEWIS was a British painter and writer who lived in Toronto for a time. His numerous books include *Apes of God, Demon of Progress in the Arts,* and *Human Age;* his novel, *Self-Condemned,* is set in Canada.

MALCOLM LOWRY, a British writer, lived in British Columbia from 1939 to 1954. During this period he wrote *Hear Us O Lord from Heaven Thy Dwelling Place* and *Under the Volcano.*

JACK LUDWIG is a Canadian who teaches English at New York State University at Long Island. He has published short stories in various Canadian and American journals and two novels, *Confusions* and *Above Ground.*

HUGH MACLENNAN is in the Department of English, McGill University, and is a novelist and essayist. His works include *Two Solitudes, The Watch that Ends the Night, Cross Country, Thirty and Three.* His latest work is a novel, *The Return of the Sphinx.*

MARSHALL MCLUHAN is director of the Centre for Culture and Technology and is in the Department of English, University of Toronto. He is the author of *The Mechanical Bride, The Gutenberg Galaxy, Understanding Media,* and *The Medium Is the Massage.*

ALI MAZRUI is the Dean of Social Sciences at Makerere University College in Kampala, Uganda.

JOSEPH MITCHELL has been on the staff of the *New Yorker* since 1938. He is the author of *McSorley's Wonderful Saloon, Old Mr. Flood, The Bottom of the Harbor,* and *Joe Gould's Secret.*

W. O. MITCHELL is Writer-in-Residence at the University of Calgary. His books include *Who Has Seen the Wind, Jake and the Kid,* and *The Kite.*

WILLIAM MORTON is in the Department of History, Trent University, and is president of The Champlain Society. He is the author of *The Progressive Party in Canada, The Canadian Identity,* and *Manitoba: The Birth of a Province.*

FARLEY MOWAT is the author of *People of the Deer, Ordeal by Ice, Lost in the Barrens,* and *Never Cry Wolf.* His latest book is *The Boat Who Wouldn't Float.*

CHRISTINA NEWMAN is a magazine writer and has worked for *Maclean's* and *Chatelaine,* and was the Ottawa editor for *Saturday Night.* She is now working on a book with her husband, Peter Newman.

PETER NEWMAN, now editor-in-chief of the Toronto *Daily Star,* was its Ottawa editor for many years. He has also been with the *Financial Post* and *Maclean's.* He is the author of *Renegade in Power* and *The Distemper of Our Times.*

DON OWEN is a film director and was formerly with the National Film Board. He directed, among other films, *Nobody Waved Good-bye* and *The Ernie Game.*

JOHN PORTER is in the Department of Sociology, Carleton University; he is a member of the Social Science Research Council and is on the editorial board of the *Canadian Review of Sociology and Anthropology*. He is the author of *The Vertical Mosaic* and co-editor of *Canadian Society*.

JAMES REANEY is in the Department of English, University of Western Ontario; he is founder of the literary magazine *Alphabet*, and a poet and dramatist. His works include *The Red Heart*, *A Suit of Nettles*, *Twelve Letters to a Little Town*, and *The Killdeer and Other Plays*. His latest work is *Colours in the Dark*.

MORDECAI RICHLER, a Canadian writer living in England, is a regular columnist for *Saturday Night*, and the author of *The Apprenticeship of Duddy Kravitz*, *Son of a Smaller Hero*, *Cocksure*, *Hunting Tigers under Glass*, and *The Street*.

CLAUDE RYAN is the editor and director of *Le Devoir* and a frequent commentator on Quebec politics for the CBC.

GORDON SHEPPARD is a film-maker and a free-lance radio and television commentator and book reviewer who lives in Montreal.

PIERRE TRUDEAU is prime minister of Canada. Before his election he was a frequent contributor of articles to various journals and a co-founder of the review *Cité Libre*. He is the co-author of *Two Innocents in Red China* and the author of *The Future of Canadian Federalism* and *Federalism and the French Canadians*.

BARBARA WARD (Lady Robert Jackson) is on the editorial board of *The Economist*. Her many books include *Five Ideas that Change the World*, *India and the West*, and *The Rich Nations and the Poor Nations*.

MELVILLE WATKINS is in the Department of Political Economy, University of Toronto, and a national vice-president of the N.D.P. He was the chairman of the task force set up by the Pearson government to investigate American control of Canadian industry.

EDMUND WILSON is an American critic and writer. His numerous works include *I Thought of Daisy*, *Memoirs of Hecate County*, and *O Canada: An American's Notes on Canadian Culture*.

MILTON WILSON is in the Department of English, University of Toronto. He is the compiler of *Recent Canadian Verse* and editor of *Poetry of Mid-Century: 1940–1960*.

GEORGE WOODCOCK is in the English Department, University of British Columbia. He is the editor of *Canadian Literature*, a critic, and a writer. His works include *The Crystal Spirit: A Study of George Orwell*, *Anarchism: A History of Libertarian Ideas and Movements*, and *Asia, Gods and Cities*.

LARRY ZOLF is a producer with *Weekend* on CBC-TV. He is a trained historian and was an archivist with the Ontario government. He is a film critic for *Maclean's*, has written for *Saturday Night*, and has contributed to an anthology, *The New Romans*.

Index of authors